The Theory
and
Practice
of
Psychotherapy
with
Specific Disorders

Edited by

MAX HAMMER, Ph.D.

Professor of Psychology
University of Maine
Orono, Maine

CHARLES C THOMAS • PUBLISHER

Springfield • Illinois • U.S.A.

Published and Distributed Throughout the World by

CHARLES C THOMAS • PUBLISHER

BANNERSTONE HOUSE

301-327 East Lawrence Avenue, Springfield, Illinois, U.S.A.

© 1972, by CHARLES C THOMAS • PUBLISHER

ISBN 0-398-02539-8

Library of Congress Catalog Card Number: 72-75918

With THOMAS BOOKS *careful attention is given to all details of manufacturing and design. It is the Publisher's desire to present books that are satisfactory as to their physical qualities and artistic possibilities and appropriate for their particular use. THOMAS BOOKS will be true to those laws of quality that assure a good name and good will.*

Printed in the United States of America

JJ-23

Contributors

GERARD CHRZANOWSKI, M.D., *Associate Professor of Clinical Psychiatry, New York Medical College; Training Analyst, William Alanson White Institute; Medical Director, Bleuler Clinic, New York, New York.*

GEORGE C. CURTIS, M.D., *Acting Director, Department of Clinical Sciences, Eastern Pennsylvania Psychiatric Institute; Associate Professor of Psychiatry, University of Pennsylvania, Philadelphia, Pennsylvania.*

JARL E. DYRUD, M.D., *Director of Clinical Services, Department of Psychiatry, University of Chicago, Chicago, Illinois.*

EUGENE T. GENDLIN, Ph.D., *Associate Professor of Psychology, Department of Psychology, University of Chicago, Chicago, Illinois.*

MAX HAMMER, Ph.D., *Professor of Psychology, Department of Psychology, University of Maine, Orono, Maine.*

LEON SALZMAN, M.D., *Professor of Psychiatry and Director of Psychoanalytic Medicine, Tulane University School of Medicine, New Orleans, Louisiana.*

IRVINE SCHIFFER, M.D., *Associate Professor of Psychiatry and Research Professor, Department of Political Economy, University of Toronto, Toronto, Canada.*

LEONARD J. SCHWARTZ, Ph.D., *and* ROSLYN SCHWARTZ, Ph.D., *Brightwaters, New York.*

ROSE SPIEGEL, M.D., *Training Analyst, William Alanson White Institute; Associate Psychiatrist, New York State Psychiatric Institute, New York, New York.*

BENJAMIN B. WOLMAN, Ph.D., *Professor of Psychology, Doctoral Program in Clinical Psychology, Long Island University, Long Island, New York.*

Dedicated to Clara,
Bradley and David

Preface

THIS IS NOT just another psychotherapy book. Most psychotherapy books on the market do not present anything really new in regard to the theory or practice of psychotherapy, and the format is basically the same in all of these books. This book is unique in several basic ways. It presents a theoretical discussion of the essence of the psychotherapeutic process which goes beyond just the remediation of pathological symptoms and also acquaints the reader with the essence of the growth process which enables one to continue one's personal growth beyond the removal of pathological symptoms to personal maturity, fulfillment and self-realization.

This book is also unique in that its format approaches the understanding of the therapeutic process through the understanding of the treatment of patients with specific psychopathologies discussed by consistently successful professional psychotherapists. When I was a graduate student in training to become a psychotherapist and even later, in the early years of my professional experience, I wished desperately that I could find a book in the area of psychotherapy, authored by outstanding psychotherapists, which discussed in some depth the treatment of persons with specific pathological disorders, so that I might gain a wider perspective and a more profound understanding of the nature of these pathological disorders and the means by which the patient could be helped to resolve and transcend them. I could never find any such book on the market. Recently some of my graduate students in psychotherapy and also some of my professional therapist colleagues have expressed the same kind of concern and interest to me and so, with their encouragement, I have decided to take it upon myself to try to fill this gross deficiency.

This book is unique as well in that in addition to the various major neurotic and psychotic disorders it also covers areas rarely, if ever, found discussed in other psychotherapy books, such as psychodynamics and psychotherapy of suicidal patients, psychotherapy of patients with psychosomatic disorders, psychotherapy of patients with acting-out disorders, psychotherapy of patients with sexual disorders, psychotherapy with the aged and an entire chapter devoted to establishing some basic criteria for an effective therapeutic process.

Essentially this book is designed to serve as a source book or reference book for professional psychotherapists and students studying to be psychotherapists in such fields as psychology, psychiatry and social work, and it could also be useful as a textbook for advanced courses in psychotherapy and as a supplementary text for basic courses in psychotherapy. Each of the contributors has deliberately taken the pains to try to communicate in a way which will be intelligible to the student as well as offer material which will be new, informative and challenging to the more sophisticated clinician. This book goes beyond being what may be called a how-to-do-it type primer. It is not intended to be a structured "cookbook" or set of formulas blueprinting the course of psychotherapy.

In essence, the book was created to provide the reader with exposure to the newest, most creative and most effective approaches available today, in regard to the treatment of the most basic psychopathological disorders that a psychotherapist is likely to encounter, written by some of the most outstanding therapeutic practitioners in the field of psychotherapy. The term "approach" is meant to convey a meaning of being more than just a system or school of psychotherapy but rather it is really the sum and integration of the therapist's understanding of the essence of psychotherapeutic practice, the essence of the nature of the disorder under consideration and what he has learned over long years of experience working with patients of the particular type that he is discussing, as well as what he is as a person.

Each contributor to this book is a renowned authority in the area of the treatment of the particular disorder about which he is writing, and he shares with the reader his understanding of the basic nature of the disorder along with the therapeutic considerations and insights that he has found to be most valuable in dealing effectively and successfully with persons with this particular kind of pathology. Case illustrations are appropriately supplied in order to help clarify for the reader how this contributing therapist deals with the particular kinds of patients under discussion. However, the suggestions made by each contributor should in no way be interpreted as the *only* way such problems can be approached and resolved. Rather, it only represents the way that one outstanding clinician tends to deal with the special problems involved in the treatment of persons with the particular disorder under discussion, and it is meant to serve only as a helpful guide for the reader.

As the reader may have already gathered, the emphasis in this book is primarily focused on the professional and practical aspects rather than on the academic aspects of psychotherapy. It is meant to fill a void and be consistent with a growing trend today in which professional clinicians and students studying to be psychotherapists want material to study which will provide them with the necessary skills most relevant to exactly what they will be doing in their professional career rather than the strongly academic emphasis to which they have been exposed at most educational institutions.

Even though a wide variety of theoretical and practical approaches are presented and described, this book is not intended to be a book on comparative systems or schools of psychotherapy; and even though relevant research findings are included in many of the chapters, this book is not primarily designed to be a compilation of research statistics in the area of psychotherapy. There are already numerous such books on the market. Rather it is a book that recognizes that psychotherapy is not something that can be learned by being exposed only to theories, techniques or research findings. Psychotherapy is not just *a doing*, as such, and therefore there is no formula that has to be mastered. Rather it involves a sensitive being-with and understanding of patients from which then flows the therapist's appropriate responses. One has to hear before one can act appropriately and meaningfully. Thus, the best way for one to really come to learn anything significant about effective psychotherapy is to have those clinicians who are truly masters of the art and science of psychotherapy share with others their sensitive and profound understanding of the nature of psychotherapy with patients with particular pathological syndromes.

The contributors to this volume are persons who have not only mastered the essence of the therapeutic process and the essence of the pathological disturbance which they are discussing, but they are also, themselves, the highly creative, freely spontaneous and fully mature persons that one would like his patients to be. This combination of attributes well qualifies these contributors to be referred to as masters of psychotherapy. It is the basic underlying assumption of this book that exposure to this kind of psychotherapist, more than any other single factor of training, contributes to the development of the kind of sensitivity in the reader which enables him to be better able to hear and understand his patients and therefore to be a more effective psychotherapist. It is for this reason that this book takes the form that it does.

Although the chapters are arranged in terms of specific pathological diagnostic syndromes, this is not to suggest that it is the symptoms or diagnostic category, as such, which is the object of treatment rather than the *person* who is manifesting the particular syndrome of symptoms which happens to be categorizable into a diagnostic label. The chapters were arranged in this fashion because it was felt that it would be easier to more clearly illustrate similarities and differences in regard to therapeutic practice and philosophy, related to specific kinds of conflicts and problems that some patients typically manifest, and thereby facilitate and maximize learning by the reader. The fact that some overlap in discussion must of necessity accrue as a function of this kind of arrangement is not considered, by this editor, to be a drawback but rather an advantage because the overlap tends, for the most part, to be more complementary than redundant in the material that it covers which should only serve to elucidate even more some of the not too well known therapeutic approaches.

In essence, this is a book whose *primary* focus concerns itself with *psycho*therapy—that is, with the establishment of a psychic integration in the patient rather than other, nonpsychotherapy forms of treatment which are currently very much in vogue such as behavior modification. Although it is not the primary focus of this book, in several chapters the reader will find discussions which illustrate the use of behavior modification techniques with appropriate aspects of a particular emotional or behavioral disorder. For the reader who is new to this approach to treatment, behavior modification techniques deal almost exclusively with the patient's behavior or symptoms to the exclusion of intrapsychic factors, in an attempt to modify his maladaptive behaviors so as to help him adjust better to his environment and thereby obtain the rewards which such an adjustment can bring. In essence, the patient is encouraged to exchange his socially maladaptive behavior for more adaptive behaviors through the use of conditioning procedures which offer appropriate kinds of rewards for the acceptable behaviors sought and punishments for the unacceptable behaviors which the therapist wants to extinguish.

Psychotherapy, on the other hand, concerns itself more with psychic integration and psychological health than with behavioral adjustment and therefore focuses upon the patient achieving a deep level of self-understanding and then permitting that understanding and sense of integration to determine the patient's specific relevant behaviors. Behavior then in psychotherapy is not singled out and considered apart from the rest of the person but is considered to be an inextricable part of an integrated and congruent whole which is comprised also of one's self-concept, attitudes, values, feelings and the like. Psychotherapy is particularly distinguished from other forms of treatment by the fact that in addition to learning about himself, the patient learns something basic about the psychologically healthy process of being nondefensive and open to the truth of himself so that in the future he can come to resolve his own conflicts and problems without having to keep coming back to a therapist for "patchwork."

However, this book does not intend to suggest that the psychotherapeutic approach is the preferred mode of treatment in all instances to the behavior modification approach but rather tries to illustrate under what circumstances each might be most appropriate and parsimonious to produce effective therapeutic change. So the real issue is not *whether* to use psychotherapy or behavior modification but rather *when* to use psychotherapy or behavior modification. For the most part behavior modification techniques have usually been restricted to and found to be most effective when used in the treatment of those learned maladaptive behaviors which do not emanate from a severely emotionally disturbed person and also with learned or conditioned fears in which the conditioned stimulus or basic cause of the fear is readily identifiable. Thus, for example, if a child accidentally gets locked in a dark closet, it may be possible to help him extinguish his ensuing fear of the dark and of small, enclosed places through the use of behavior modification techniques because the cause of his fear is easily identifiable. However, it would be much more difficult, for example, to identify the conditioned stimulus or cause of an arm "paralysis" in a patient with an hysterical conversion reaction, and therefore it would be extremely difficult to treat such a patient with behavior modification techniques. Thus, the relatively limited use of behavior modification practices accounts for its relatively limited representation in this book.

This book offers the reader many unorthodox as well as the more orthodox approaches to psychotherapy, but this is not to suggest that because an approach is unorthodox that it is therefore some kind of a gimmick. An approach ceases to be therapeutic and becomes a gimmick, not when it is just highly unusual or contrary to accepted theory but rather when it is used to deny and substitute for the therapist's inability to really hear and understand what the patient is saying and what the essential problem really is. It is at this point that the therapist may resort to some kind of gimmick in order to try to produce some predetermined therapeutic effect without the necessity of having to first understand the patient. However, an approach is not a gimmick, no matter how unorthodox it may be, if it arises directly out of being a result of understanding what is necessary and appropriate for helping the patient at the moment to resolve a conflict or problem.

Thus, for example, some therapists may devise a gimmick for dealing with silences during the therapy session and they will apply this technique to all patients in all circumstances when there is an extended silence, but this will very seldom prove to be therapeutic. But if the therapist hears and understands what the silence really means to the patient then he knows how to react. Thus, for example, if he feels that the patient is silent because he is trying to make contact with, and clarify for himself, some inner feeling, then he may just continue to permit the patient to remain silent and by so doing communicate his encouragement to the patient for him to continue the inner struggle. But if, in the patient's silence, the therapist hears that the patient is using the silence as a means of defying or defeating the therapist then he may act and confront the patient with the truth of what he feels in order to have him explore why it exists or else the therapist might explore himself in order to identify what it is that he may have done which could be fostering a combative or competitive relationship with the patient.

Some readers may perhaps feel that the many varied approaches presented in this book will only confuse the reader and make him more uncertain about the direction or model that he should follow. However, the reader should recognize that because the approaches are varied it does not mean that they are discrepant. The patient is multifaceted and therefore the therapist can make contact with him through a variety of means, such as through the patient's feelings, thoughts, symbolic communications or behavior. Regardless of the means by which the therapist makes contact with the patient, the important thing in psychotherapy is to ultimately produce an intrapsychic integration which eventuates in a greater degree of integration and harmony between these various facets. As a result there is no longer a sense of discordance or contradiction between the patient's thoughts, feelings, values, behavior and the like.

This book makes no attempt to sell the reader on any particular approach as being best. The view held by most sophisticated therapists is that there really is no one best approach that is suitable and effective for the treatment of all kinds of patients. This book only attempts to offer the reader an honest and accurate representation of the various approaches which exist in the field of psychotherapy today and to help him to understand that in many instances several different approaches may all be equally valid and effective if it results in producing in the patient a true sense of integration and liberation from his conflicts.

Although the first chapter of this book is addressed to students, it is intended as well to convey a basic message to professional psychotherapists at all levels of experience. The author presents a new interpretation and understanding of the essential nature of the psychotherapeutic process and singles out the importance of the person of the therapist as the essential factor in achieving meaningful therapeutic results. A workable definition of psychological health and psychopathology is offered and related to the essence of the therapeutic process. Included in this chapter is a particularly unique discussion rarely found in the therapy literature dealing with the basic motivations for wanting to become a psychotherapist and is meant to serve as an aid to the student and practicing psychotherapist in alerting him about some of the personality needs that are likely to serve as obstacles and pitfalls to conducting psychotherapy successfully. In general, this chapter provides the reader with a frame of reference by which the other chapters in this book can be more meaningfully and critically evaluated and appreciated.

Although the editor recognizes that there is no absolute distinction and separation between anxiety, phobia and obsessive-compulsive neurosis, they are presented in this book in three different chapters in order to provide the reader with an opportunity to achieve a more precise understanding of the nature of these disorders and the treatment of persons with these disorders as well as providing an opportunity for contrasting these approaches with some of the newer and also the more classical approaches to the treatment of persons with these disorders.

The author of Chapter 2 insists that not all forms of psychopathology require intensive and complex procedures when simpler ones can work in appropriate circumstances. He presents his case for the utilization of behavior modification approaches for the treatment of some persons with anxiety reactions. His approach is based primarily upon the formulations of the behaviorist, B. F. Skinner, but in contrast to some behavior therapists the author suggests that he finds no incompatibility with the psychoanalytic approach but rather sees these two approaches as being complementary to each other rather than dichotomous opposites. Again, in contrast to more strict behavior therapists, the author discusses the importance of the relationship between the therapist and the patient as being an essential aspect of effective psychotherapy.

The author of Chapter 3 incorporates the theoretical formulations of H. S. Sullivan along with his own unique theoretical contributions in discussing the treatment of patients with phobias. It is his contention that in most cases involving phobias, unconscious symbolic messages are involved and are therefore not easily amenable to behavior modification approaches but rather require an approach that utilizes interpersonal considerations as well as intrapsychic ones. In essence, he sees the development of phobias as being the result of interpersonal misperceptions, communicative malfunctioning and informational distortions, all of which he traces to the maladaptation and malfunctioning of the nuclear family unit. His therapeutic approach basically involves dealing with the patient's family psychodynamics and helping the patient learn to decode the family's warped method of communicating.

In order to provide the reader with a sense of continuity between the closely related disorders of phobias and obsessive-compulsive neurosis, the editor felt it would be best to also have someone with a basically Sullivanian approach discuss the treatment of obsessive-compulsive neurosis. This should more clearly highlight the similarities as well as the differences between those two related disorders. The authors are broad enough in their perspectives and theoretical contributions to prevent a problem of redundancy from occurring. In Chapter 4 the author distinguishes the various types of obsessive and compulsive disorders and she discusses the various kinds of difficulties which typically arise in trying to conduct psychotherapy with these kinds of patients. The author also discusses in detail the typical patterns of communication and behavior which helps the therapist identify the essential pathological theme that has to be dealt with in psychotherapy with each kind of obsessive or compulsive patient.

Chapter 5 deals with a disorder which is also historically related to the anxiety states, but which currently goes under the labels of conversion reaction and dissociated reaction. The psychoanalytic approach was developed as a function of its application to the treatment of hysterical conditions and therefore it was felt that this area should be represented by the psychoanalytic approach. Most therapists still agree that the psychoanalytic approach is probably the most effective method for the treatment of patients with hysterical conditions because of the necessity of dealing with repressed material, unconscious symbolization of the body and the importance of early childhood influences. The author presents not only a detailed discussion of the historical development of the treatment of hysterical patients but brings it up to date and discusses some of the more current types of hysterical characters in our society. He offers some new advances in theory in regard to the mechanism of conversion symptoms and illustrates his thesis through the use of case illustrations. His discussion of the psychodynamics of hysterical disorders is quite extensive because he believes that the disorder cannot be treated successfully without an extensive knowledge by the therapist of the theoretical and psychodynamic bases for the development of hysterical symptoms. He is adamant in his belief that some form of psychoanalysis is essential for the treatment of hysterical disorders because of the necessity for uncovering and reconstruction of the personality.

Chapter 6 focuses primarily on the neurotic and character disorder forms of depression, but there is also some new theoretical formulations presented in terms of the essence of psychotic depressions. The author also presents some new theoretical formulations, in regard to the nature and function of depression, which are in an existential vein, and these formulations are interspersed with a psychoanalytic interpretation of psychodynamics. Much of his discussion of the treatment of persons with depressive reactions and his case illustrations highlight many of the major points in regard to the essence of psychotherapy that he makes in Chapter 1. He offers a number of practical suggestions in terms of working therapeutically with depressed patients and their families and he consistently emphasizes the importance of the affective quality of the therapeutic relationship as being essential in achieving therapeutic results with depressed patients.

The treatment of patients with suicidal potential is a great challenge to the therapist and usually a very frightening one. Very few therapists have ever received any kind of training at all in regard to dealing effectively with such patients, and material in the literature has also been sorely lacking. The author of Chapter 7 presents an extensive discussion of the various psychodynamic factors which can precipitate a suicidal attempt. His presentation appears to be a blend of existential and psychoanalytic theory. He offers many practical as well as theoretical guidelines for the treatment of such a patient, and he deals with some very essential issues such as when to treat and when to hospitalize such a patient. He also offers some very helpful hints on how to utilize the initial interview to determine a patient's suicidal potential and particularly helpful is his discussion and suggestions of how to deal with a patient when suicide is imminent. His therapeutic approach emphasizes the importance of establishing a meaningful therapeutic relationship with the patient.

The author of Chapter 8 presents and integrates most of the new and relevant research findings in the area of cause and treatment of psychosomatic disorders. He presents a detailed discussion of the nature of each major psychosomatic disorder and contrasts the various theories that relate to each. He also brings a wider perspective in regard to the mind-body issue in describing their interrelatedness. He takes a definitive stand in putting down the psychoanalytic notions of a psychosexual type for each particular psychosomatic disorder and insists that there is no common personality makeup in patients with similar psychosomatic symptoms. He presents some new theoretical formulations in regard to the treatment of psychosomatic disorders. In essence, his therapeutic approach emphasizes the importance of the transference relationship because he contends that psychosomatic symptoms seem to inevitably occur in these persons when there has been a threat to key family relationships which produces the loss of dependency gratification.

The authors of Chapter 9 clearly demonstrate that what was once considered to be the untreatable patient is in reality quite treatable. They demonstrate that the patient who acts out his pathology in the form of unacceptable and antisocial behavior can be helped through the use of psychotherapy to behave more constructively and no longer has to be relegated to a penal institution as a hopeless case. The authors use an approach that can best be described as being eclectic. They use a combination of traditional and newer approaches which seem to contain strong elements of reality therapy, rational-emotive therapy, gestalt therapy, behavior modification and group therapy. They also utilize a particularly innovative approach, which they call therapeutic acting-out, as a means of helping the patient achieve a greater sense of reality-testing in terms of the inappropriateness of self-defeating aspects of his behavior. They also utilize a very creative but practical approach in regard to establishing a therapeutic relationship with those patients which historically has always been the major problem in the successful treatment of these kinds of patients. The case illustrations they present are quite detailed and illuminating of the major points they are emphasizing in the text.

Even though there is a chapter devoted to the treatment of acting-out disorders it was felt that because of the legal and social implications of sexual disorders and the difficulty that most therapists have in treating these disorders, this area, therefore, deserved to be represented by a separate chapter of its own. The author's basic thesis in Chapter 10 is that because the sexual act involves an interaction with a member of the opposite sex, there is, therefore, no such thing as a sexual disorder, as such, but rather these sexual disorders are just manifestations of a more basically underlying interpersonal and personality disorder. He contends, therefore, that no single approach can be always appropriate and effective in treating these disorders but that an understanding of the nature of the disorder in each case is essential. Essentially, his therapeutic approach is psychoanalytic but he goes beyond the classical use of the transference and the counter-transference in treating these patients and discusses this in detail. His work tends to be much more active and immediate goal oriented than the classical analytic approach. Also of particular value is his discussion of the significant social and legal issues involved in the treatment of sexual disorders.

Schizophrenia is another disorder that many therapists have felt, and many still do feel, cannot be treated successfully with psychotherapy. The author of Chapter 11 makes it very clear to the reader that this is not the case. He takes a very optimistic attitude in regard to the effective treatment of schizophrenics and feels that it is only the limitations of the particular therapist which make such treatment difficult. His approach is basically a modified psychoanalytic model to which he adds his own theoretical formulations in regard to the importance of interpersonal factors. He calls his own approach interactional psychotherapy of which the core seems to be the therapist's unconditional willingness to give and help, which he terms the "vectorial attitude." He not only offers the reader many specific and practical guidelines for the treatment of schizophrenic patients in individual therapy but also offers much help and discussion of group therapy procedures with schizophrenics. He also makes some significant contributions to the theoretical understanding of the nature of schizophrenia which are also particularly noteworthy.

Theory and practice is so diverse in the area of schizophrenia that it was felt that no single chapter could do justice to this topic and be representative of what is actually being done in the field. Therefore, a second chapter has been included. Whereas the previous chapter presented some rather structured procedures for dealing therapeutically with schizophrenic patients, the author of Chapter 12 approaches the treatment of schizophrenic patients in a much more subjective manner. The author's approach clearly stems from a client-centered point of view but seems to be moving much more in an existentialist direction. Probably no system has done as much research or studied the therapeutic process with schizophrenics as much as have client-centered therapists, and therefore they deserve to be represented in this volume. The author presents some material in working therapeutically with nonverbal psychotics which is particularly noteworthy and valuable. The warmth, caring and understanding of the therapist comes through to the reader quite readily and the therapist's capacity to risk himself with the patient through his own creativity and spontaneity should teach the reader much about how to establish a meaningful therapeutic relationship with the psychotic patient.

With people living longer and having to adjust to a rapidly changing world, psychotherapists are more and more finding themselves challenged to find effective means of dealing therapeutically with older persons. This is another area that has lacked adequate representation in psychotherapy books of the past probably because of the old bias which used to exist that "you can't teach an old dog new tricks." The author of Chapter 13 takes a strongly optimistic approach in this regard but does realistically point out the various difficulties that exist in therapeutic endeavors with the aged. The author's approach is basically a blend of psychoanalytic and existentialist points of view, but he offers much that is very practical in dealing therapeutically with aged patients and their families as well as how to use community resources to assist in the therapeutic process. He discusses the elimination of the middle-age model as the standard for the measurement of adequacy and makes some proposals for a new measure of adequacy and fulfillment which could more appropriately be applied to the aged. Also particularly noteworthy and valuable are the suggestions that he offers to help both the therapist and patient deal with their own death anxiety.

In the last chapter the author presents some guidelines for determining the effectiveness of a therapeutic process. He discusses the many problems inherent in constructing a therapeutic process that will be acceptable to therapists with differing theoretical approaches to the nature of man and ends his discussion by suggesting the importance of studying the effective therapist. He makes a prediction about the future of psychotherapy and makes a plea for the development of a new kind of psychothera-pist. He encourages the reader to make his own self-discoveries in regard to the essence of therapy and recommends that the reader go beyond this book in his pursuit of self-knowledge.

To utilize this book most profitably the reader should come to each chapter almost like he would approach a patient—that is, without a prior bias or commitment. Being uncommitted, he is then optimally open and receptive to be sensitive to hear and be impressed by all that the particular author is attempting to com-municate. He should take a creative and reflective stance toward each contribution and permit the various similar and contrasting approaches and theoretical points of view to operate upon him and impress him as they will, without any prior design or pre-commitment on his part. This kind of creative stance will per-mit him to develop the kind of understanding and level of so-phistication about the nature and essence of psychotherapy which will ultimately enable him to creatively do his own thing in his own unique way, rather than being just an imitator, role-playing someone else's formula. In this way is he most likely to make a personal contribution to the advance of the field of psychother-apy.

I would like to express my appreciation to the contributors for their very fine cooperation and their commitment to the pur-poses of this volume. I am also grateful to those who helped to type the many drafts and manuscripts, especially my wife, Clara, and my secretaries, Gloria Anderson, Gloria Greer, Mary Girard and Minnie Leavitt. I am also indebted to my students, whose provocative and perceptive challenges helped me to recognize the need for such a book, and to my patients, who live in many of these pages.

Max Hammer

CONTENTS

THE THEORY AND PRACTICE
OF PSYCHOTHERAPY
WITH SPECIFIC DISORDERS

Chapter 1

To Students Interested in Becoming Psychotherapists

MAX HAMMER

Be not like the lame selling crutches;
And the blind, mirrors.

KAHLIL GIBRAN

THE CURRENT STATE OF THE ART

FROM MANY recent studies, it has become clear that the primary determinant in regard to therapeutic effectiveness is the therapist himself. Certainly it is helpful if the patient is subjectively uncomfortable, highly motivated for change, intelligent, verbal, in relatively good contact with reality and nonimpulsive in a sociopathic sense[4, 7, 14, 16, 21, 22]; but most of all, the kind of person that the therapist is will be the primary determinant of whether or not there will be therapeutic results. This fact has been well documented by the research findings over the last few years. Consistently, researchers have pointed out that successful outcome in therapy is related to the empathic ability and understanding of the therapist.[3, 5, 29, 30] There appears to be a direct relationship between the effectiveness of therapeutic outcome and the personal psychological health of the therapist.[1, 2, 5, 6] These studies point out essentially that the therapist who is more anxious, conflicted, defensive or generally "unhealthy" is least likely to promote change in his patients. Other studies have determined that therapeutic results tend to be most favorable when the therapist is warm, genuine, congruent and one who sincerely likes his patient.[15, 23, 24, 28]

Other significant studies relating the characteristics of the therapist to therapeutic outcome confirm that in general, the more

3

experienced the therapist is, the more effective and successful he tends to be; inexperienced therapists may actually cause their patients to deteriorate.[3, 7, 8, 11-13] All these studies plus the studies relating effectiveness of therapeutic outcome to various techniques, systems or schools of psychotherapy[10, 12, 13, 25, 26] lead to the obvious conclusion that positive therapeutic change by the patient is not related to any particular kind of school, technique or theory of psychotherapy but is definitely related to the therapist's own psychological health and capacity to understand his patient regardless, apparently, of whether this understanding is a function of some natural empathic ability or comes through years of experience as a psychotherapist. One can assume that it is probably not just the number of years of experience, as such, that leads a therapist to develop the empathic ability to understand his patient but likely those that had this ability to begin with are more successful and remain longer in the career of psychotherapist, whereas the less empathic and less successful therapists are more likely to move into other than psychotherapy positions such as administration, research or teaching.

HEARING: THE ESSENCE OF PSYCHOTHERAPY

At this point, it should be clear to the student that being an effective psychotherapist does not involve a specific kind of doing or performance, such as a role that one has to play or a formula of some kind that has to be followed and mastered. Psychotherapy is not a recipe that is recited, rather it involves the therapist's capacity to be sensitive enough to clearly and deeply hear and understand in the patient those rejected truths that have become disassociated from himself and have caused his disintegration and which, when heard and understood by the patient, lead to his reintegration, growth and liberation from his conflicts, fears and tensions. This kind of sensitivity in the therapist, which is basically a keen sense of awareness and contact with reality, is developed as a function of the therapist's openness to his own moment-to-moment experiential reality. This, in my view, is really the essence of the psychological health process and the antithesis of the pathological process which is essentially the escape from the actuality of one's personal experiential reality and the pursuit of what one ought to be, conceptually and ideally.[18] This kind of sensitivity and openness comes as a function of just practicing a continuous nonjudgmental and nonanalytical self-awareness.[19]

Being an effective psychotherapist then requires that the therapist himself be psychologically healthy, which means being nondefensive and totally open to the moment-to-moment reality of himself. This kind of sensitivity liberates him from the distracting tension and self-preoccupation which exists ordinarily when one is in conflict trying to escape from some inner truths. A mind that is quiet and not distracted by one's own conflicts or by needing to move somewhere (because the therapist is ambitious for the patient to achieve some kind of predetermined objective or goal) is able to hear with enormous sensitivity. This capacity for awareness enables the therapist to be in a state of communion with his patient—a state in which he is totally present and fully attuned at all levels to what the patient is trying to share or avoid. This is the essence of empathy, understanding or what I refer to as the ability to hear. It is this kind of empathy or hearing which produces what is called *movement* in therapy and which ultimately leads the patient to self-discover and commune with those rejected and painful experiential realities of himself which culminates in that self-integrating, healing and liberating effect which is called *growth*.

Hearing really involves two basic elements. It includes empathy but also goes beyond it. First, there must be the clear and full *awareness* of the patient's subjective reality, which is called empathy. However there must also be the additional factor of the immediate perception and *understanding* of the *why* of that particular moment-to-moment subjective reality. Empathy involves being totally attuned, or one with, the patient's *individual* moment-to-moment experiential reality, but hearing also includes the immediate integrative perception and understanding of the thread which ties together that complex of thoughts, feelings and behaviors with which the therapist has been individually empathic. It is that basic experiential truth or thread which gives rise to the individually manifested thoughts, feelings and behaviors and which must be understood for there to be a liberating effect. This kind of understanding cannot be obtained through logical deduction. It involves a total, direct and immediate perception of the whole of the thing as a result of a mind which is passively and creatively open and uncommitted and in a state of communion with the moment-to-moment experiential reality of the other person. This capacity for total and integrative perception which is called understanding is the essential ability of which the therapist must be capable, if he is to be effective as a psychotherapist.

To really hear, a state of communion must exist between the listener and the verbalizer, between the observer and the observed. It is the therapist's own self-preoccupation that prevents his total absorption in the patient (the state of communion) and instead fosters the state of duality which separates and isolates one behind his own self-enclosed ego boundaries. When awareness of the sense of self is absent then the observer and the observed merge into a state of true communion. The potential for producing a state of communion and hearing the patient is optimal when the therapist has transcended his identification with all self-concepts and images and therefore is one with his moment-to-moment awareness. Being no entity self and having no sense of self-awareness, he then is fully attuned to whatever is in his awareness. This permits him to be in direct communion with whatever the patient is saying and feeling. A self-concept demands constant self-attention and efforts toward confirmation of that self-concept. As a result the therapist's attention becomes split and the patient receives only part of the therapist's attention while the other part of the therapist's attention is on himself, devoted to confirming some image of himself, such as being an effective therapist. When there is no identification with a self-concept, then attention upon the self is reduced and the therapist can then become locked into the patient's moment-to-moment experiential reality with unwavering attention (for that is his only awareness) and thereby be in a position to hear every subtle nuance of the patient's thoughts and feelings.

This state of communion is necessary, not only for the therapist to really be fully attuned and hear the patient but also because it is the basic therapeutic state or state of integration which may be referred to as the state of *quiet mind*[19] which the patient must be in relative to his own experiential realities, if he is to make the full contact with himself which yields self-understanding, self-integration and growth. This state comes into being when there is no longer an active or deliberate thinker that is attempting to initiate, judge, control or direct the content and movement of thought—that is, when one just permits thought to come to awareness and watches it without any kind of interference. Then the thinker becomes merged into thought and there then exists only the process of *thinking,* which I refer to as the process of *free-flowing consciousness* or the *state of creative understanding.* In this state, because it is unimpeded by the existence of any countercathecting censor, in the form of the deliberate thinker, and because in this state of psychic integration there is no longer any sense of duality, internal contradiction or opposition to prevent the integration of rejected truths, thought flows directly to its source of most immediate conflict and liberates itself. Awareness of the truth which liberates is immediate because there is no active thinker present to serve as an influence to distract attention away from the direct perception and understanding of the contents of consciousness.

In essence then, when the deliberate thinker is unactivated and quiet—that is to say, when the ego, in its role as deliberate thinker, is not deliberately or purposefully introducing conscious thought in order to capture the mind's attention—there is no chattering noise on the surface of consciousness to superimpose itself upon and distract the mind's attention away from clearly hearing and following the soft whisperings of unconscious thoughts, feelings or impulses. The ego, in its role as the deliberate thinker and defender of its own sense of integrity, acts as the censoring wall of separation and division between consciousness and unconsciousness and prevents the free flow of consciousness from integrating material from the repressed unconscious into conscious awareness. The most basic drive of consciousness is to flow freely and to heal itself by making itself integrated and whole. The contents of consciousness which are repressed always push for intrusion and discharge into conscious awareness in order to drain its pent-up energy and tension; therefore, psychopathology develops when the ego, as deliberate thinker and censor, invests psychic energy toward the goal of inhibiting that free flow of consciousness. When the ego, as obstacle, is absent, then consciousness is free to integrate itself and reduce the tension accumulated through the repression of unconscious material and its accompanying psychic energy, and so it flows freely to the source of conflict and repression or, to put it another way, the source of conflict and repression is free to flow directly to the surface of conscious awareness. For example, a rubber ball, kept submerged under the water through the countercathecting force of your hand, flows freely and directly to the surface as soon as the obstacle of your hand is removed. Thus, no purposeful pursuing of insight or understanding is necessary; it comes of its own, immediately and directly, to your conscious awareness, if you just do not purposefully activate the deliberate thinker. Essentially then, psychotherapy is not the process of the active pursuit of the repressed but rather is the result of the elimination of the barrier between conscious and unconscious awareness which then permits that which is repressed to surface of its own accord.

Freud tried to create this integrated psychic state and free-flowing consciousness process with his method of free association, but he apparently failed to recognize that in his process of free association, thought is quite often not really free because it is not free of the influence and control of the ego. The ego, operating as the entity of the thinker, is still in a position to be outside of and separate from its thought and therefore still in a position to have an element of control over thought which prevents a true sense of integration from developing and prevents the energy of consciousness from having the opportunity to flow freely to the source of its own conflict and inhibition and thereby resolve it. Furthermore, in free association, because the ego is still in control of thought, the ego can use thought as the means of defense and escape from contacting the rejected experiential realities through the means of presenting to awareness distracting concepts or intellectual insights.

What does self-understanding or self-integration really mean then? It should be obvious that it does not refer only to an intellectual comprehension. Rather it refers to a state of realization in which one makes real or brings into concrete existence formerly rejected aspects of self. It is knowing by becoming one with, as the word "knowing" was used in the scriptures to mean having intercourse with. One must have a true intercourse with the rejected aspect of self, by becoming one with it, in order to really hear, know or understand himself. He must be in immediate and direct contact with himself. This is the essence of integration which produces liberation from conflict.

Liberation involves resolution and is not to be confused with the seeking of a solution to a conflict or problem as a means of escaping from it. A solution can bring about a superficial *change* by altering one's awareness through some form of distraction, but only resolution can result in liberation and *growth*. Liberation cannot be the result of any solution which involves forms of escape such as suppression, distortion, avoidance or withdrawal. Rather it involves resolution and transcendence.[18] Thus, for example, if I feel an intolerable sense of loneliness, one way that I might try to solve this problem is by attempting to escape from my awareness of it by going to the movies or taking a drug. However, as soon as the movie ends or the effects of the drug wear off, my awareness of my loneliness as a problem returns. I have not resolved or transcended the problem and will not until I fully understand why loneliness to me is intolerable and why it is interpreted by me to be something more than just aloneness; for example, do I feel abandoned? empty? worthless? vulnerable? unaffirmed as a particular identity such as a male? and so forth. To really understand and resolve this problem, I must permit myself to be one with the loneliness instead of running from it by one means or another.

Thus, resolution of a problem lies only inside of the problem and never outside or away from the problem. By remaining inside the problem the kind of total perception and understanding which liberates can come; but by seeking some kind of solution away from the problem, there results only a kind of transitory distraction of awareness away from the problem but the problem, as such, is still preserved. Understanding is its own sufficient action to bring liberation, but no amount of effort away from the problem can bring liberation. One does not become released from a problem by the effort and struggle to free oneself through some form of escape from it. Rather, the problem must be confronted and faced head-on and not just glanced at as though through the corner of one eye, and then, through the contentedness just to be fully emersed in communion with it, the kind of total perception and understanding of the problem that brings full release and transcendance of the problem will come.

Thus one should learn to totally explore and understand the problem or question and in that total understanding of the question lies the answer. The answer or resolution to any question is never the result of a solution which is brought to it from outside of it but rather lies just in the total understanding of the question. A problem is just the result of an incomplete perception and understanding, and when it becomes focused into direct and total perception, the problem disappears.

Understanding leaves no trace remaining of the problem, and therefore there is true liberation from the problem; on the other hand, solutions and escapes keep you tied to the problem because they leave a trace of bound-up energy tied to the parts of the problem not yet acceptable, revealed or understood. In seeking its release, that bound-up energy captures thoughts in the attempt to gain some expression and discharge into awareness and as a result you cannot be free of the problem or its preoccupation. Understanding is its own action, sufficient to bring release from the problem because it brings the full release of the pent-up energy, as the rejected truths which contain it are released into awareness.

Therefore, helping the patient learn how to inquire into himself for the truth of himself is more essential than providing him with any solutions or answers to his problem which he finds intolerable and from which he wants to escape. Such solutions only take him away from his problem, and even worse, they teach him to look outside of himself and away from his problem for its resolution. They condition a process of escapism which is the essence of the pathological process and which is the essential thing that the patient learns from that kind of "therapy." On the other hand, self-inquiry provides the self-integration which itself is therapeutic. It is both the process and the outcome of therapy. It is both the means and the end of therapy. It is the necessary self-integration process that leads to the self-integration outcome referred to as growth.

Thus, the patient is in the state of creative understanding when he comes to recognize that he *is*, for example, his anger, his fear, his depression or whatever the experiential reality happens to be and not just the *observer* of these from the outside. Then the observer has become the observed and the basic pathological state of duality and self-disintegration is transcended. In this integrated state of creative understanding, insights come to you in flashes of vivid clarity without any effort to seek them out. Therefore, the state of creative understanding is the basic self-healing state of integration that the patient needs to learn before he terminates psychotherapy for it is the means by which he learns to heal himself in the future rather than having to keep coming back to the therapist for "patchwork" every time he finds himself in an uncomfortable conflict.

The process of therapy must have as an intrinsic part of it the means of achieving the ends desired. If therapy seeks as an end the greater integration and growth of the patient, then the process by which this is to be achieved must also permit integration. The means and ends of psychotherapy are not really separate. If the process of therapy always keeps the patient outside of himself, then it cannot expect to lead to the patient being integrated in the end. The patient must come to recognize that his symptoms are not something that must be studied and explained away but rather they are aspects of himself with which he must have communion. He must blend himself into the symptom and be one with it, and in that process lies the essence of liberation, healing and growth.

In addition, to really be effective, the therapist needs to know from *personal experience* what the "path" is that leads from internal conflict and contradiction to liberation. If you do not know how to liberate yourself from an internal conflict, fear or pain, then you are not in a position to help others do it either. If what you do does not work for you, it will not work for the patient either. What right does the therapist have to ask the patient to face his rejected truths and anxiety and to take risks in terms of exposing himself and making himself vulnerable, if the therapist is not willing or able to do so? You cannot instruct a patient to be vulnerable. You can only be the model for that kind of vulnerability through your own openness and spontaneity. The therapist must know from personal experience that honest self-confrontation leads to growth and liberation; otherwise his encouragement of the patient to confront himself will not be genuine and will certainly lack conviction, and the patient, at some level, is bound to be aware of that and no growth will take place.

In essence then, the two basic factors which distinguish the therapist from the patient is the therapist's ability to be open to hear and accept painful realities without resorting to some form of suppression, disguise, withdrawal or escape and his ability to permit himself to be vulnerable and take risks for growth. Because of these factors the therapist is continuously becoming more and more open to and in full contact with all the internal and external realities which confront him, so that he is constantly self-integrating and growing, whereas the patient is not.

The patient cannot grow unless he is willing to take the risk of making himself exposed and vulnerable. Only then can greater integration take place with that which is real, but rejected, within him. Fears of being vulnerable usually are related to the concern of there being a threat to the dissolution of the sense of integrity of the ego. The loss of that feeling of integrity is experienced, subjectively, as the psychological death of self.

Threat tends to be experienced as being greatest when one feels helpless and vulnerable in the face of emotional or physical pain, which the ego fears will overwhelm it and destroy it, and also when the ego is in the position of recognizing rejected truths about itself which have been disassociated from the ego because they were experienced as being in contradiction to the feeling of consistency and integrity of the ego's sense of identity; and were they to become conscious, they would also threaten the ego with dissolution. Thus, for example, if I am basically identified as a "male," then I reject and repress all aspects of myself which I consider to be "female"; and therefore because all that I am aware of about myself I consider to be "male," I feel a sense of being an integrated and consistent personal entity self. However, I feel severely threatened if I am confronted with aspects of myself which I label "female" for how can I be both "male" and "female" at the same time? Thus if I were to accept these "female" traits as really being part of me, I then would become very frightened that perhaps I was not really anything at all in terms of a consistent and integrated psychological identity. This would threaten me with psychological extinction.

Thus, the term "ego strength" really represents the ego's capacity to tolerate inconsistency and contradiction within its own sense of identity, and the tension and pain which results, without feeling threatened with anxiety which is essentially the ego's reaction to feeling threatened with extinction. In the face of inconsistencies and psychological pain, ego strength is reflected by the ego's ability to say, "this, too, is me." Therefore ego strength is basically the ego's capacity to confront and endure psychological pain without having to distort or escape from the source of that pain for fear that the pain will overwhelm and destroy the ego. Where there is psychological growth, ego strength has been enhanced. There can be no real growth without it. Thus the reader can see that ego strength is not enhanced through intellectual awareness, alone, but only when the ego is confronted with the painful aspects of its rejected self in the form of repressed memories, feelings, emotions, impulses, etcetera. It should be clear from this discussion that psychological pain exists only where there exists an identification with a self-concept which feels threatened with being diminished or extinguished.

Thus, it is a clear psychotherapeutic principle that *regression always precedes real progression or growth.* All other forms of "growth" are only conceptual in nature—that is, one feels one-self to be making progress toward becoming some kind of conceptual self or imaginal ideal and concludes, therefore, that he is growing. In reality, however, it is only through that form of regression in which the patient first takes a backward step, so to speak, by permitting himself to enter into full communion with those repressed and painful aspects of his rejected self which then permits the forward advance—in terms of a greater sense of integrative wholeness, liberation or growth—to really take place. It is only when the patient recognizes that he is nothing more than just his moment-to-moment experiential self, that he then is in a position to permit himself to immediately become sensitively aware of and one with that moment-to-moment experiential reality as soon as it arises and thereby live in that integrative and psychic energy liberating process which may be referred to as the process of *growing* or *psychological health.* In this way nothing lingers unresolved in the mind to become repressed into unconsciousness and thereby distort the functioning of consciousness and its contact with reality.

However, as long as he is identified with some kind of fixed conceptual or imaginal entity, he must be faithful to that conceptualized entity self and reject and repress from conscious awareness other aspects of himself which appear to be inconsistent with and in contradiction with that particular self with which he has become so strongly identified. It is identification with such imaginal selves which is really the essence of the pathological process because it is the essence of what produces a state of disintegration and schisming of the self. Thus, the patient is not fully integrated and healed until he has transcended his identification with any and all conceptual and imaginal selves, even those which he judges to be highly positive in nature, and is content to be nothing except his moment-to-moment experiential reality.

Another basic reason why the patient fears being vulnerable is that the realization of his vulnerability feelings will also trigger the awareness of the weak, helpless and fearful child in himself which he has tried to deny is a reality in himself through repression, escape and various means of distorting this reality. Through past experience he has learned that being a vulnerable child is associated with being helpless in the face of intolerable pain which produced, and still does produce in him, an intense state of apprehension, anxiety or panic. Therefore, he maintains an unconscious inner commitment to avoid, at all costs, ever realizing that he is truly in a vulnerable position. His compensatory attempts at power and need to deny his helpless vulnerability is a basic contributor to what is referred to in psychotherapy as the problem of *resistence.* Resistence is a phenomenon, which is encountered either directly or subtly in probably all systems of psychotherapy, in which the patient seems to consciously or unconsciously resist the therapeutic overtures of the therapist. In essence what is occurring is that the patient is resisting relinquishing control of the interaction to the therapist in order to resist acknowledging himself as being vulnerable and so he tries to deny his feelings of vulnerability and gain a compensatory sense of potency by entering into a kind of power struggle with the therapist and defeating him by not permitting himself to be influenced or changed by the therapist. This usually takes the form of resisting confronting his own real feelings and of denying the truth and appropriateness of the therapist's insights or suggestions. By so doing, the patient is also preventing the therapist from understanding him because he feels being understood is extremely threatening—the same as the therapist having penetrated his defenses— and therefore it makes him feel exposed and very vulnerable. Therefore, when resistance exists, psychotherapy becomes basically a fencing contest in which the patient parries every thrust that the therapist makes.

Essentially the patient is resisting being vulnerable because he is committed to resisting being confronted with psychological pain due to the fact that he is inwardly convinced that his ego is too weak to endure such pain and therefore his ego would be overwhelmed and destroyed. At some level the patient understands that the goal of the therapist is to make him confront the pain from which he is trying to escape and therefore he feels that he must resist every overture on the part of the therapist to remove his defenses against the experiencing of that pain. Most patients really do not come for psychotherapy to face the painful realities from which they are escaping but really they come hoping to find some new gimmick which they can use to insure that their escape and their defenses against such pain will be more effective. When they come to the therapist for help, they tend to have the same expectations which operate under the medical model in which one goes to the doctor when one has pain and is given something for the immediate removal of that pain. Most patients come to psychotherapy hoping to learn how to gain a sense of mastery over psychological pain. They want a sense of confidence of having power and control over pain so that they will be able to conquer it at will. In essence they are hoping to attain a form of psychological invulnerability and omnipotence.

Unfortunately many systems of psychotherapy attempt to supply the patient with forms of escape from having to experience his psychological pain, but in actuality this form of "treatment" really encourages the intensification of the pathological process. The essence of psychopathology is the process of attempting to escape from one's own psychological pain by rejecting and repressing particular realities about oneself which threaten to bring pain. This produces a state of psychic disintegration and an inner conviction that one is weak and unable to endure pain without being overwhelmed, and so the ego builds defenses in its struggle to escape from feeling helpless and vulnerable in the face of pain. The defenses operate to distort not only one's contact with the rejected and painful inner experiential realities from which one is trying to escape but also operates to distort those various aspects of the external reality which could possibly trigger the repressed painful inner realities if they were given full conscious recognition. Thus, if one can face pain and no longer hide the truth from himself, then it is no longer necessary to distort and escape from reality and the pathological process is ended.

Growth, therefore, depends on the ability to risk facing pain and results, in essence, from the patient's greater capacity to confront and endure painful reality without having to distort or escape from it in some way. Intellectual insight alone, if it does not lead to the arousal of rejected painful feelings and the conscious confrontation and integration of those painful feelings by the patient, can never be effective in producing a sense of liberation and growth in the patient. Thus what the therapist has to essentially hear and help the patient integrate with are not just the intellectual truths which the patient must deny to himself but rather those feelings which are the consequences of accepting the reality of those rejected intellectual truths. It is the experiential reality rather than the verbal reality that needs to be the focus of integration.

Therefore it should be clear that analysis of the patient's problem can have no real therapeutic effect because analysis is only an interpretive theoretical hypothesis applied to the patient's problem from outside the patient by the analyst who is trying to bring an intellectual understanding and synthesis to the problem. But the patient's real problem, most basically, regardless of how it is verbally presented to the therapist, is his inability to confront and integrate with the painful rejected realities of himself from which he is committed to running. That is the essence of his psychopathology.

Analysis is intellectual in nature and only serves to carry the patient away from contact with the painful subjective realities which he must confront in order to grow. Knowing *about* oneself is not the same as knowing oneself. Knowing oneself comes about through direct perception and experience, by actually being there at the place where the pain is at and being totally immersed in it. Then, instead of speaking for the pain or symptom as analysis would do, the patient through his reuniting and integration with the pain permits the pain to speak for itself until it runs its course to the end and exhausts itself. By reuniting and integrating himself with his pain, instead of identifying himself as just the observer or controller of it, the patient has taken the first essential step that leads to his becoming integrated with those former aspects of himself which he has rejected and repressed because their acknowledgment brings him pain. This greater sense of wholeness and integration is what is real psychological growth. Thus, for example, by being with the pain of what I call my loneliness, I am then in a position to integrate with that rejected part of me and essential reality which lies beneath that label of loneliness which may be, for example, the child in me, which feels so helpless and vulnerable and is so frightened of abandonment when left alone, and which I have longed repressed and denied is really part of my self.

In essence then, the basic commitment that the patient has to make to therapy involves the recognition that he is not coming for assistance by the therapist to help him escape from pain or help him discover some means of mastery over it, but rather the commitment must be to face the pain of one's rejected experiential realities because he understands very clearly that it is the only means of really growing and liberating himself from the pain and therefore liberating himself from the pathological process which involves his need to distort both internal and external reality in order to escape from the threat of experiencing what he believes to be the annihilating capacity of that pain. Thus, it should be readily apparent to the reader that the therapist who cannot face his own psychological pain is really not in the position to ask the patient to accomplish something which in the therapist's own personal experience is not accomplishable.

Another essential factor that can help the patient to expose himself and permit himself to be vulnerable to the experiencing of psychological pain is the patient feeling a deep sense of trust toward the therapist. This sense of trust convinces him that should he permit himself to be vulnerable, the therapist will not take advantage of his vulnerability to hurt him. More specifically he must have trust that the therapist will not make him confront painful realities and then abandon him emotionally to face this threat of annihilation alone. It is this factor of lack of trust, probably more than any other, which serves as the basic deterrant to successful therapeutic outcome. It is the patient's clear conviction that the therapist is trustworthy which ultimately brings an end to the therapy-defeating process of resistance.

There are several basic ingredients which contribute greatly toward the patient feeling the kind of trust toward the therapist that will permit him to lower his defenses, feel vulnerable, confront pain and therefore to grow. One major factor is the therapist's own ability to take risks and make himself vulnerable when he is with the patient through his own openness and spontaneity of his own thoughts and feelings without concern for the preservation of any idealized image of self. Another factor is the honesty and sincerity of his responses to the patient. A third factor is his ability to really hear the patient which forms a bond of alliance with the patient and also tells him that he is really understood and appreciated. I find that compassion or love is the natural and spontaneous consequence of being in communion and really understanding the other person. Love is not a volitional act on the part of the ego but rather is, on the contrary, the result of the loss of the sense of self-awareness and is the natural consequence when one makes full contact with another human being even if at the moment of communion the patient is expressing extremely negative feelings. If the therapist is free of any self-concept identifications for himself and enters into the relationship with the patient as an unlabeled whole, then he will find that without it being a volitional act, feelings of compassion will flow spontaneously from him toward his patient. This is for me the true meaning of what some refer to as having unconditional positive regard for your patient or what others call the I-Thou relationship. This kind of communion relationship is not only the essence of what produces optimal hearing of the patient's moment-to-moment experiential reality by the therapist but is also the essence of what is necessary to produce the kind of therapeutic atmosphere and therapeutic alliance between the therapist and patient which has to exist for the patient to venture forth into his own self-exploration.

The kind of love that brings security to the patient is not to be confused with giving the patient a strong feeling of being valued or liked. These latter feelings are the result of an evaluative personal judgment of only some part of the patient. The patient, as an unlabeled whole, cannot be valued or judged. The patient intuitively knows that such evaluative judgments by the therapist are really subtle forms of rejection of him as a whole and it makes him feel very insecure because he knows that such positive judgments can quickly turn to negative evaluations if the patient ceases to personally satisfy the therapist and therefore they cannot produce any real sense of security and trust. But a nonjudgmental, compassionate form of love which flows as the natural consequence of fully understanding or knowing the patient contributes significantly to his development of a real sense of trust. The patient now feels free to be even his most negative self without the threat of being condemned or rejected. There is a real sense of security in knowing that the therapist has heard him and seen his most negative and rejected self and has not disliked him or used it against him; so there is no longer a great need to defend himself and therefore he is free to explore himself more fully. However, the therapist's capacity to hear and accept the rejected in the patient depends upon his openness to the negative in himself. If the therapist cannot bear to face his own psychological pain, then he is not in a position to hear and be empathic with the patient's pain, for that empathy would only serve to trigger his own pain and threaten him with being overwhelmed. Therefore in running from contact with his own psychological pain he must also run from full contact with the patient.

One other major factor that probably contributes more than any other to the mistrust of the therapist by the patient is the patient's recognition, at whatever level of consciousness, that the therapist himself is emotionally disturbed and needful in regard to the patient. This recognition is very threatening to the patient and makes him fearful that if he does not defend himself at all times that the therapist will manipulate him and use him for the gratification of his own needs. This makes it impossible for the patient to ever permit himself to be vulnerable and therefore it closes the door to the possibility of his achieving any real growth. Thus, it is absolutely essential that the therapist be free of any major psychopathology and of any need to use the patient as an object for attaining his own gratification or elevation in his self-esteem. Quite often students choose psychotherapy as a career precisely for these reasons. If the student is to really be an effective therapist it might be well for him to honestly explore his basic motivations for becoming a psychotherapist and thereby be in a position to prevent his inappropriate needs from having a deleterious effect in therapy. It is toward this end that the next section is presented.

MOTIVATIONS FOR BECOMING A PSYCHOTHERAPIST

For the most part, students choose a career in the field of psychotherapy for honorable and noble reasons. They tend to have a deep sensitivity and empathy for persons who are experiencing psychic pain and difficulties in living. Most of these students also feel a sincere yearning to personally involve themselves in the process of helping to relieve these persons of their suffering and difficulties. Their sensitivity and empathy frequently grows out of their own related personal experiences, and also, in the Jungian sense, they tend to be persons to whom the assuming of the archi- typal roles of the nurturant parent, teacher and healer comes eas- ily and naturally.

However, in assuming these roles the student is frequently unwary of the many pitfalls and traps that he may inadvertantly permit himself to fall into as a function of his individual person- ality and needs. As a result, in many cases in which psychother- apists attempt to help patients with their problems it becomes a matter of the "blind leading the blind." As the Scriptures (St. Luke 6:39-42) admonish: Can the blind lead the blind? Shall they not both fall into the ditch? The disciple is not above his master. . . . And why beholdest thou the mote that is in thy brother's eye, but perceivest not the beam that is in thine own eye? . . . Thou hypocrite, cast out first the beam out of thine own eye, and then shalt thou see clearly to pull out the mote that is in thy brother's eye.

In the same vein we need to recognize that the patient probably cannot grow beyond that level of emotional health and maturity achieved by his therapist. What the therapist cannot permit him- self to be aware of in himself, he likely will also not be able to be aware of in the patient. Having conditioned himself to be insensitive and defensive toward himself in order not to have to confront certain unacceptable aspects of himself, the therapist then tends to carry over this conditioned insensitivity into his relationships with others. If the therapist is really to be effective, he must first eliminate those psychological problems within himself which are likely to result in distorted perceptions of his patient and of his psychotherapeutic endeavors.

After working closely for a long time with students in training to become psychotherapists, I have come to recognize some basic personality needs in students that are more likely than others to lead the student into the kind of pitfalls and traps that make it difficult for him to utilize the constructive motives that originally led him to choose to become a psychotherapist. These needs tend to make it extremely difficult for the therapist to be effective in his therapeutic endeavors with his patients.

The Need To Dominate

Some students have been so severely dominated and controlled by their parents that they seek a career that will offer them opportunities to be in the dominant and controlling position. They envision patients as being very needful and dependent, which they feel will offer the therapist a great opportunity to gratify his own basic need to dominate. These students are determined to be the superior one in a relationship, and they equate the inferior role with humiliation. They are trying to undo all of the humiliation they felt toward themselves for submitting and permitting their parents to dominate them and for this reason they harbor a secret revulsion toward all their patients for putting themselves in the inferior position of having to ask for help.

These therapists frequently become extremely antagonistic toward their patients, especially toward those in whom they expect to put some "backbone," and it is not unusual for them to quite often ridicule those patients who continue to remain passive and dependent. Some of their revulsion toward passive-dependent and submissive patients is usually related to the fact that these students have unconsciously come to equate submissiveness with femininity and dominance with masculinity. Those persons whom the student feels are trying to dominate him he also feels are trying to "castrate and feminize" him and by the same token he is unconsciously perceiving all submissive persons as being castrated; for this reason he is revolted by them. This kind of therapist finds it almost impossible to endure silences during therapy or any other behavior on their part which they could possibly construe as being passive; for this reason they tend to be almost compulsively active and penetrating in their therapeutic approach toward their patients regardless of the therapeutic system or school to which they say they adhere.

The need to dominate is also observed in students with strong sociopathic and/or paranoid tendencies. Their need to control, manipulate and exploit others is basically a function of their worship of power. This craving for power and superiority which contributes toward their motivation to become a psychotherapist serves basically as a compensatory defense against their own despised feelings of weakness, fearfulness and vulnerability and also serves as a defense against their basic inability to trust and relate meaningfully and deeply with people.

In essence then, these students are busily engaged in a one-upmanship game with their patients. If they feel successful in influencing the patient and getting him to submit, then they feel that their compensatory need for power, which is used to offset their more basic feelings of weakness, helplessness and vulnerability, has been confirmed. If they cannot influence the patient, they become very upset because unconsciously it tends to confirm their more basic conviction of their impotence and vulnerability. The methods they adopt for therapy usually are consistent with their need to influence and tend to offer them an opportunity for almost absolute control over their patient. Because the therapy relationship to most patients reflects a parent-child relationship, most patients tend to be very sensitive in regard to being overpowered and influenced because it confirms, for them too, that they are weak, helpless, vulnerable and impotent. It is for this reason that this kind of therapist usually is confronted with a great deal of resistance in his patients throughout the course of therapy.

Should the student who needs to dominate be confronted with

a very aggressive patient and one who, similar to himself, needs to dominate, then the therapeutic interaction becomes extemely competitive and the therapist may utilize every possible interpretation and device in order to disarm the patient and make him finally submit. If the therapist cannot achieve this victory he will usually discharge the patient with some type of admonition that he had not been a good patient and probably cannot be helped in psychotherapy by anyone.

I find that a great many students are attracted to the field of psychotherapy out of a need for power. This need for power makes them become very hard and insensitive people, which destroys their capacity for hearing and truly empathizing with their patients. They essentially become manipulators of their patients and are incapable of really caring about them or seeing any beauty in them.

These students find it extremely difficult to accept supervision or undergo their own personal psychotherapy because they perceive these relationships as involving a forced passivity on their part which makes them feel extremely anxious and vulnerable, and as a result they tend to aggressively resist these kinds of forced passive or submissive relationships.

The Voyeurist

Some students seek to use the therapeutic relationship as a way of peeking into the private lives of others. They are especially interested in sexual matters, but any kind of secret may hold erotic excitement for them. They are forever looking for such secrets in the patient's life, and the way they conduct therapy reflects their morbid curiosity. They frequently ask prying questions usually related to highly erotic and perverse sexuality. They usually become quite bored with patients who do not provide them with such discussions.

This kind of morbid curiosity may often stem not only from sexual voyeuristic tendencies but also from an environment in which parents habitually withheld certain information from the student when he was a child, which led to his feeling very insecure unless he "found out what was going on." Not knowing becomes equated with helplessness and vulnerability and in order to reduce anxiety the student grows up with a morbid curiosity and "need to know" which eventually moves him in the direction of seeking a career as a psychotherapist.

The Exhibitionist

There are some narcissistic students who are so identified with and enamored by their physical appearance that they need to display themselves to others and require a steady stream of patients who, because of their needful state, will usually supply the therapist with an overexaggerated reaction as to his desirability. There are other therapists who attempt to exhibit themselves via their wisdom and intellect and are unconsciously equating the potency of the head with a kind of phallic and masculine potency.

These therapists are forever offering interpretations to the patient and expecting him to reflect to them their admiration of their wisdom and potency of mind. They are unconsciously quite competitive with their patients because when the patient is talking, the therapist projects his own needs onto the patient and feels that the patient is trying to display himself. The therapist can hardly wait for the patient to stop talking so that he can have his turn to talk and thereby display himself again. The therapist is therefore quick to interrupt the patient, which in a sense, by abruptly cutting him off, is a kind of castration of the patient; at the same time the therapist is really unconsciously "knocking the patient off the stage" and assuming the spotlight for himself. This kind of therapist also enjoys group therapy a great deal because the larger the audience he has, the more he enjoys displaying himself.

A Need for and Fear of Intimacy

I have progressively become more aware that there are many students and therapists who crave intimacy yet fear it, either because they are greatly apprehensive about emotional involvement for fear of getting hurt or because it is equated with union and therefore loss of self. Because their own identity or sense of self is not clearly established they unconsciously fear that intimacy will produce a state of fusion which will result in the loss of their individuality. The therapeutic relationship, they feel, will offer them a controlled type of intimacy. They envision that they will be in full control of the relationship which they expect will permit them to satisfy their need for intimacy and yet, because they control it, will prevent the overinvolvement or loss of self which they fear. They cannot handle intimacy unless it is this controlled type of intimacy.

For those therapists in whom the *fear* of intimacy is greater than their *need* for intimacy, the therapist's stance in his role as a professional, rather than as an involved other, limits the degree of intimacy and puts the control of this factor in his own hands. Other therapists, whose *need* for intimacy is greater than their *fear* of intimacy, tend to become overinvolved with their patients and lose the distinction between self and other and thereby become overly identified with the patient. They tend to suffer when the patient suffers and in general become overwhelmed with all kinds of countertransference feelings toward their patients. This distorts their perceptions of reality and greatly hampers their effectiveness as a psychotherapist.

Much intimacy of a sexual nature also goes on at the fantasy level with patients of the opposite sex which, for some students, provides a kind of vicarious sexual relationship which is highly erotic and stimulating. Some need this kind of sexual intimacy in order to confirm a sense of masculinity and sexual potency which they are unconsciously questioning in themselves, and they see all positive transference and valuing of the therapist by the opposite sex patient as such confirmation.

The Omnipotent Healer

Some students are unconsciously driven into choosing psychotherapy as a career by what may be called a "savior complex." The "savior complex" is based primarily on an unconscious striving for a sense of omnipotence which is a reaction to an enormous inner feeling of fearfulness and helpless vulnerability. They have a great need to exert their potency and prove their power by influencing others. They perceive themselves as being able to heal all those who come to them for help. Sometimes the first patient confronted who does not respond in a positive way or does not grow or change can traumatize the student seriously because he has come to identify himself with this role of omnipotent healer. The failure to fulfill the role can make him doubt the substance of his own identity and existence. Without this ideal to live up to, his life is disrupted immeasurably.

Many of these students will project the blame for the lack of therapeutic success onto the patient for having no capacity for growth rather than accept the reality that perhaps their capacity to help has some limitations. To some students the reality of the first nongrowing patient can be extremely disturbing because they have the need to maintain the illusion of their own omnipotence which they unconsciously hold as being essential in order to feel a sense of security. These therapists envision therapy relationships as providing them with an opportunity, via the patient's adoration, reverence and growth, to substantiate the illusion of their own personal worth and omnipotence. Their need for omnipotence may also be revealed in their need to demonstrate to the patient that they have all the correct answers and also in their need to be able to condition and influence the patient's thinking and living. Many of these therapists also indulge their need to feel omnipotent by maintaining the attitude that the fate of their patient's psychic life and happiness lies in their hands.

Another aspect of the "savior complex" found in some students and therapists is the belief that all the patient requires to get well is love and that they have this healing, loving capacity. I find that many of these students have come to believe that the only reason they were unhappy in life is that their parents did not love them enough. They therefore conclude that all anyone needs to be happy is sufficient love. When some patients fail to grow, in spite of the student's "love," the entire thread which has woven the meaning of his life together begins to unravel and he responds with great emotional disturbance.

The People Addict and the Lonely One

Some students in psychotherapy have led very lonely lives as children. They may have been an "only child" who always longed for companionship or lived in a neighborhood where friends were scarce. These people tend to grow up with an intense hunger for companions. They are constantly on the lookout for a pal. They tend many times to make personal friends of their patients and project that it is the patient who needs it and that the patient cannot grow without it. They envision a career as a therapist as providing them with a constant source of interpersonal relationships to relieve their panic of being lonely and isolated. Basically they need to use others as a confirmation of their own worth and existence. When one has had for many years no significant other to relate to, unconsciously one comes to question the worth and viability of one's own existence.

The same thing is basically true of the "people addict" who also unconsciously feels that without someone to relate to, he does not exist. These are people with a poor sense of self because they were either always surrounded by a large number of family members and felt "lost in the shuffle" or else they always had to please some significant other, usually a parent, in order to feel safe and secure, and they thereby learned to localize the sense of self in the other instead of within themselves. For these kinds of students, to be alone is their greatest fear and they perceive the role of the therapist as being perfect for filling this basic need for a constant flow of interpersonal relationships.

The Need To Hurt and Be Hurt

I have encountered many student therapists with strong sado-masochistic features to their personality. Some are attracted to the field of psychotherapy because of their own heightened state of fearfulness which makes them unconsciously want to see other more frightened people than themselves and in some cases even contribute toward the intensification of the patient's fearfulness. The sadist is particularly attracted by helpless and vulnerable persons, which makes working with emotionally disturbed people so attractive to him. I have seen many students rationalize their destructive anger toward their patient by calling it "good clean anger" and therefore insist that because it is honest, it is therapeutically helpful. Essentially they are trying to control and make the patient feel frightened of them in order to try to cloak their own interpersonal fearfulness.

Other more masochistic therapists tend to provoke their patients into abusing them. They invite attack by the patient upon them in numerous ways. Typically they will invite attack by their unconscious but deliberate failure to understand the patient, which makes the patient feel much more confused and frustrated, which then tends to make the patient direct his exasperation and anger onto the therapist. In essence, these therapists tend to provoke and encourage the negative transference. Some therapists achieve masochistic gratification by suffering along with the patient when the latter is suffering. This, of course, makes it impossible for the patient to "let himself go" and confront all of his own repressed feelings because he is afraid that the therapist will not be able to tolerate it. The patient then has to become concerned with protecting the therapist from hurt and is therefore unable to grow.

As is true in the field of nursing, medicine, social work and other related professions, students choose psychotherapy as a career because it is one of the "helping professions," and in so doing, they can, via reaction formation, deny to themselves and others their basic sadistic need to hurt others.

The Need To Be Loved and Needed

Some students who desire to become therapists are trying to compensate for very low feelings of self-esteem related to unconscious feelings of worthlessness which were usually precipitated by the fact that they never felt loved or valued by their parents. As their sense of self-esteem drops, their feelings of worthlessness increase and the unconscious equation that they make is that being totally worthless is the same as being totally nothing, and therefore a severe threat to their self-esteem is really a threat to their feeling of existence as a psychological self. They envision being a therapist as the optimal means of gaining love and thereby boosting their self-esteem. Such therapists tend to overly encourage the positive transference by continuously offering supportive, reassuring and complimentary remarks to the patient hoping that these will make the patient feel obligated to return to the therapist some kind of mutual admiration and affection.

Just as some students have a compulsive need to receive in the form of being loved, there are other students who have a compulsive need to give of themselves to others in the form of some kind of nurturant assistance, and therefore they have an intense need to be needed. This kind of student quite often uses his image of himself as the "unselfish giver" as the primary means of elevating his low sense of self-esteem. He basically becomes the prototype of the nurturant mother who takes in and protects all the strays and underdogs of the world. This kind of therapist also tends to have a history of being unloved by parents and quite often what he is doing is identifying with his patient and giving him the kind of nurturance and love from a loving parent that he never received. By so doing, he feels as though he is making up for his own early years of deprivation. I have also observed this need to be the nurturant parent in students who have identified with an overly loving and doting parent.

As a result of his need to be needed, this kind of therapist unconsciously tends to keep his patients quite dependent and needful by continuously and forcefully offering the patient advice and suggestions. He is forever coming to the patient's "rescue" when he is having difficulty with some aspect of his life or is very uncomfortable. To do for another what he is capable of doing for himself prevents the patient from ever growing and becoming aware that he is capable of dealing with life effectively on his own. These kinds of students become therapists because it is a "helping" profession and although they consciously are quite devoted to helping their patients to grow, they guarantee that just the reverse occurs through their compulsive ministrations of "help."

These therapists can never satiate their need for self-esteem, for it only seems to be as high as their last success, and therefore, because it is so tenuous and precarious, their need for it becomes compulsive and insatiable.

The Self-Cure Seeker

There are many students who desire to become therapists because they feel that in the process they will learn enough about themselves to cure themselves of their own emotional disturbances. They secretly hold the conviction that they are severely disturbed and they are afraid to reveal their problems to anyone for fear that this illness will be exposed. They are determined that they can cure themselves and somehow they convince themselves that they can do so if only they can gather enough information in the area of personality, pathology and psychotherapeutic theory. When they find that they are unable to cure themselves just by the use of the intellectual knowledge which they have accumulated, they then unconsciously seek to work with patients similar to themselves and hope that by curing these patients they will somehow have found the cure for their own problems.

In many ways they are similar to the medical student who chooses to become a physician in order to deny and counter his unconscious but intense fear of death. The fantasy that is being acted out is the one that holds that if he can keep a patient from dying then maybe he will be able to do the same for himself. Some students of psychotherapy are living out a similar fantasy in regard to mental illness.

The Need To Escape from Oneself

Another prevalent need found in many psychotherapists is the need to escape from their own unpleasant thoughts and problems. Similar to the gossiping neighbor, the therapist seeks to get involved in the problems of others as a way of escaping from the confrontation with his own very unpleasant existence. His life lacks meaning, sensitivity and intensity because he lives only on the surface of his own consciousness, always afraid to confront himself in regard to his own realities, so his mind becomes dull and insensitive. Needing to feel a sense of vitality, intensity of experience and meaning to his life, he becomes absorbed in the intensity of life of his patients and lives vicariously through their experience.

As a result of their alienation from themselves, the sense of identity in these therapists is very vague. Consequently they become overly identified with their role as professional psychotherapist, to the relative neglect of almost all other aspects of their lives, in order to fill their own inner emptiness. Their professional commitments usually become overly extended and they lose themselves in their professional work and in their patients; this kind of escape may become the basic pattern of their lives.

THE IMPORTANCE OF A PERSONAL GROWTH EXPERIENCE

Ideally, the most constructive and effective therapist is one who has gone through a meaningful growth experience of his own and knows directly the joy and peace that comes with liberation and the deep beauty that is within oneself and in one's capacity to love. Then there results a great unselfish need to want others to also have such an experience and to want to contribute in some way toward others achieving such a similar experience. The existence of any other selfish need will tempt the therapist consciously or unconsciously to use the patient for the gratification of the therapist's own needs. This does violence to the patient because it makes of him an object which is a form of destruction of him as a person.

Even if the therapist does not use the patient to fill his own unmet needs, these needs will probably still serve to distract him and thereby severely impair his capacity to be totally present to, and hear, what the patient is really trying to communicate. When the therapist with strong unmet needs becomes aware of a strong emotion or impulse within himself, he cannot be sure whether he is reacting to something in the patient or something solely in himself. The therapist is not in a position to trust himself, and therefore he cannot trust what he is hearing in the patient.

Thus, for example, if a therapist has strong doubts about his masculinity he will probably need to have his masculinity confirmed by the admiration of his attractive female patients. Consequently, if he finds himself experiencing strong sexual feelings toward one of his female patients, he cannot be sure if it is an indication that he is surrendering his controls in regard to his sexual needs or if it is rather an indication that the patient is really deliberately trying to seduce him as a function of her own particular needs. Not being able to trust himself, he will not be sure of what is really happening and as a result of his confusion he will likely repress or consciously ignore awareness of the entire issue and thereby not have to deal with it in the patient or in himself. This impaired capacity to be aware of certain truths must then serve as a severe obstacle to the likelihood of a successful therapeutic outcome.

For these reasons I recommend that any student or therapist who recognizes that he is burdened by some kind of incapacitating need or problem or anyone who has not himself ever achieved a meaningful growth experience should consider getting involved in a personal psychotherapeutic experience if he is ever to become a truly effective psychotherapist.

PATIENT TRAPS

Just as the therapist's needs can serve as a trap which can ensnare him in a net of resistance and nonconstructive interactions with his patients, so too can the patient's needs. The therapist must be alert to the fact that the patient has a devotion and commitment to obtaining basic gratifications that have long gone unsatisfied and of reviving previous traumatic situations in the hope that by reliving and reexperiencing the emotional event he may achieve some kind of mastery, resolution or integration of certain feelings which at the time they occurred were intolerable. Over and over again, they subtly force persons into playing certain roles with them and try to arouse certain behaviors, reactions or feelings in these persons which enables them to react in a way which they hope will resolve the situation, but unfortunately they usually tend to react in the same old way and so they are compulsed to repeat this event over and over again.

The therapist should learn to be alert to these forms of what may be called transference and repetition compulsion, because unless he is sensitive to what is happening he can frequently end up aggravating the patient's pathology. The student should not be misled into believing that these reactions by patients occur only to therapists who are pathological themselves or who are themselves involved in some kind of countertransference reaction to the patient. Even a therapist without large areas of significant pathology in himself can fall victim to these kinds of maneuverings by the patient.

The therapist should be constantly watchful and sensitive to what is happening within himself as a clue to what it is that the patient may be trying to accomplish with him, which probably relates to the patient's basic problem. What is happening in the interaction between the patient and the therapist is quite often more important and significant than the content of what is being discussed, which is quite often used by the patient as a diversionary vehicle for camouflaging what he is really saying or doing to the therapist, such as making the therapist feel, for example, like a child, like a parent, angry, fearful, sexually aroused, stupid, impotent, neglectful, rejecting or elated.

The therapist should also recognize that not only might he fall into one trap with one patient and another trap with a different kind of patient, but even for any one patient his various needs and the various needs of the patient can entice him into many different traps and if he is not alert to these, then therapy can never be effective for it only encourages the perpetuation of the irrational acting-out that is taking place.

IS PSYCHOTHERAPY AN ART OR A SCIENCE?

An issue which is much discussed and frequently fought over, not only by students but also by faculty members and clinicians, is whether psychotherapy is really an art or a science. The answer to this question seems vital to many people in the field of psychotherapy because it seems to determine the way students are trained and the psychotherapeutic methods and philosophy that students will use. Quite often the stand that one takes in regard to this issue is not based so much on what the individual has personally explored and found to be really true but tends rather to be based much more on the particular individual's need to be consistent with his particular conceptualization of the nature of man and life, which itself quite often stems from more basic personality needs. Thus, for example, those who need to see life as something to be mediated through the mind and senses and as something that is to be mastered and controlled tend to react to man in general and patients in particular in the same way; and those who need to conceptualize life as a work of art will tend to react to man and patients in terms of the pleasure of immediate experience and appreciation.

Probably both of these rather exclusive and absolute conceptualizations are a gross oversimplification of what is really true. I would have the student consider the likelihood that both are necessary and complementary to provide a full and complete understanding of any phenomenon. For example, the scientist will contribute a great part toward the understanding of the nature of an apple by studying its size, shape, color, texture and its other physical characteristics, and the artist will contribute too, but his approach to understanding the apple may be to take a bite out of it and taste it; this analogy applies to psychotherapy as well.

Unfortunately, not all those who purport to identify with the scientist's stand are really scientific and not all those who purport to identify with the artist's stand are really artistic, but rather each tends to use his approach to life and man as a way of confirming an image of himself with which his personality needs require that he strongly identify. The student of psychotherapy who needs to identify himself as being an absolute scientist is usually one who needs to see himself as being powerful, masterful, intellectual, self-controlled and masculine, rejecting all traits of weakness, passivity and emotionality. He is usually someone who values having a strong will and enjoys feeling capable of doing battle with life and being victorious over it and in some cases superior to it as though looking down upon life as if from some godly perch. He unconsciously uses this illusion as the means of gaining a sense of security by identifying with a sense of being an omnipotent power. He basically feels that life and man are objects which have to be subdued and conquered, and he has to see himself as the conqueror in order to maintain the illusion of great power and deny his more basic conviction of great weakness and vulnerability or, perhaps, femininity, and so he uses the discipline of a science as the vehicle for domination and control over the elements in his life and for the purpose of self-concept confirmation.

On the other hand, the student who has strongly identified himself as the absolute artist tends to try to gain a feeling of personal superiority by trying to confirm an image of himself as someone who is tender, gentle, affectionate, emotional, sensitive, intimate, noncombative, esthetic, altruistic and nonmaterialistic. He identifies with all of these feelings as a value but does not really experience them or live them as a reality. One is not an artist in the true sense of the word without having an inner sense of beauty and inspiration which serves as the generating source for artistic creations. Most of these students do not possess any significant degree of such feelings. In fact, quite often this identification serves as a cover for, and denial of, more unconscious and unacceptable destructive impulses. But in its absolutism it is similar to the absolutism of the scientist in its goal of attempting to achieve a sense of security through the pursuit of a form of omnipotence, but it differs in its identification with the loving attributes of godliness rather than the power attributes, which is the case for the absolute scientist.

Obviously psychotherapy must involve more than just the artistic component because it is not sufficient just to fully appreciate a person in psychic pain, whereas for the artist it is an end in itself just to be totally sensitive to and in full contact with the reality of that person and his pain. The therapist goes beyond just the artistic when he concerns himself with an understanding of the process of growth and makes a commitment to being in a profession which is devoted to helping the person who comes to him with a desire to achieve a sense of liberation from his pain.

To the degree that psychotherapy is an art, it is a creative art rather than an imitative or interpretive art. An analogy would be in the field of music in which the creator of a composition engages in a creative art, whereas the concert pianist who plays the composer's work, however masterfully, is engaged in an imitative or interpretive art in the sense that his self-expression is primarily dominated by a patterned, external influence, whereas for the composer the self-expression is primarily a manifestation of his own creative inner experiential reality.

I see creativity essentially as being that *state of mind* in which there exists the absence of the deliberate thinker. It is that state of mind in which consciousness is free flowing without the intrusion or interference of a censor which initiates, controls or attempts to direct the content and movement of thought and feeling. It is also that open and passively receptive state of mind in which consciousness meets a confronting challenge without a rehearsed or predetermined conditioning, expectation or commitment to that challenge. It involves permitting the stimulus to operate upon you and trigger in you whatever it will, without any interference on your part to predetermine what your reaction or response should be.

When consciousness is uncommitted or not put in a mental straitjacket, then it is open and receptive, not only to all kinds of influences from the outside but also influences from the unconscious; and as a result, one has available, to meet any challenge or problem, relevant elements from both consciousness and unconsciousness. When one's consciousness alone is brought to bear on a challenge or problem, then the ability to deal with it is always incomplete and fragmented. It would be as though a ship traveling at night were to consider only the surfaced part of an iceberg to be a relevant threat but take no account of the submerged aspect of the iceberg. Thus, when you are in a creative state of mind you are bringing more of yourself than your conscious awareness to every problem and challenge in life. You come to every situation with a potential for integration of both conscious and unconscious relevant factors.

When the mind is precommitted, then it is a closed mind and unreceptive to a wide variety of relevant external stimuli and also closed to elements from the unconscious that could also possibly be relevant to the situation. The mind is uncommitted only when consciousness is not trying to move to get somewhere. It is not committed to becoming or achieving any special thing. Therefore, approaching a situation with the hope of attaining some kind of specific goal or objective prevents a creative interaction with that situation.

You cannot be taught to be creative and spontaneous any more than you can be taught to be sensitive or to love, for these states exist only when the mind is not rehearsed or patterned in any way. So no path, method or formula can ever lead you to creativity and spontaneity. No one can teach you the loss of the sense of self-consciouness in the absorption of communion with the moment-to-moment actual reality, which is necessary if one is to be creative and spontaneous in living. It can never be the result of some deliberate or contrived act for all such acts stem from the self as the one who acts (that is, the doer) which only serves to arouse and heighten self-consciousness. For that reason the more effort you make to be creative, the less creativity can result. Creativity is not something that can be pursued, but rather it is something which *comes to you* when all effort-making and pursuing ends, for only then is the sense of self-consciousness put to rest.

Effective psychotherapy is creative in the sense that reality is created from moment to moment as a function of the noncontrived and nonpredetermined interaction between the therapist and the patient. The therapist never knows in advance what the patient is going to say nor does he know in advance what his reaction will be, and in that sense reality is created from moment to moment and from that creative reality comes real hearing, understanding and integration.

Many therapists hide behind their professionalism as a way of avoiding a real creative human encounter with the patient. Because of his "professionalism" he conceptualizes his role as a master technician and tends to be more interested in the "case" than the person, more interested in following his formula to the letter than in the challenge of the patient's problem and moment-to-moment reality, and more interested in *his* truth than in *the* truth. When the therapist is lacking an affective appreciation of what the patient is experiencing and has only an intellectual appreciation, there tends to result a basic intolerance for the patient's suffering and his understanding of the patient must always be incomplete. He is always outside the patient's range of contact. The therapist may say "I understand you" or "I care about you," but the patient could make the same response as the boy did to his father who while spanking him reflected, "This hurts me more than it does you." "Yes, but not in the same place," was the boy's reply.

Psychotherapy cannot be absolute in its scientific or artistic aspects because man is not. The patient is a synthesis of intellectual, sensory and experiential components and psychotherapy must correspond and be the same. It cannot treat only part of the man and hope to be a real, effective therapy. A whole, integrated man cannot be the end, if the means involves only dealing with the partial man. The therapist must come to his patient as a blend of the artistic substance and the scientific form. As any artistic creation is the result of a blending of the artist's deep inner feelings of beauty and inspiration which serve as the substance, essence or source of the creation, as well as his training in theory and practice which serves to mold the specific form and manifestation of the creation, so too must the psychotherapist and psychotherapy be a blend of these same aspects.

To be able to be fully attuned and sensitive to the patient in order to really hear and understand him, the psychotherapist must have his theories of psychodynamics, psychopathology and psychotherapy as well as an inner sense of inspiration, beauty and warmth, but these all must be synthesized into a creative whole from which then flows his spontaneous responses of that which he creatively hears. Ideally, the therapist should be not only a synthesis of what man is but also participant in the highest of what man can be so that he will know how to arouse and elicit the highest in the patient.

In psychotherapy, as with any other art, when the quality of feeling is lacking, the art is then prostituted; for example, for an artist to paint a picture of a tree without having some kind of deep inner feeling of beauty or love for that tree or toward what trees in general represent to him prostitutes the work, for then his painting is little more than a picture of a tree that can be captured accurately in its formal qualities with just a camera. The same is true for some therapists who work with patients and have not the available capacity to love them or see beauty in them but rather mechanically attempt to dissect the patient in order to understand him intellectually. This is a prostitution of the art of interpersonal relationships and psychotherapy because his intercourse with the patient is without real affective investment. He is just going through the motions of relationship.

Just as painting, music or poetry requires some kind of inspiration as the source for these artistic manifestations, in order to be considered as creative and meaningful, so too psychotherapy requires inspiration on the part of the therapist to be creative and meaningful. This inspiration is based on the therapist's capacity for loving and possessing an inner sense of beauty. To sing, one must have a song in his heart. To help the patient to have his own "song" requires that the therapist have one of his own. The therapist's own inspirational feelings, more than any other factor, contributes toward arousing that same thing in the patient. Beauty begets beauty and warmth begets warmth.

It is from such a state of inspiration that the total action of all therapy needs to emanate. Unfortunately most training centers in psychotherapy concentrate mostly on teaching therapists what to *do* because they are at a loss as to how to teach a therapist how to *feel*. They are not in a position to inspire and elevate the therapist because they themselves are basically uninspired.

Many universities offer courses in art appreciation but can the appreciation of art really be taught? For an appreciation of art to be taught one must be able to teach the appreciation of beauty. But just the intellectual appreciation of form, structure and composition is not the appreciation of beauty. Beauty emanates from love and inspiration and that cannot be taught but it can be developed as a result of continuous self-sensitivity. Art is beauty, shared or made manifest, but beauty is never the manifested but only that which gives rise to the manifested. As Gibran[17] puts it, "Where shall you seek beauty, and how shall you find her unless she herself be your way and your guide?"

Without those inspirational feelings of beauty the therapist enters into the human encounter with his patient deprived of his most basic and potent tool. In the training of psychotherapists we must become more interested in helping our students to be beautiful people, in the true sense of the word, and then maybe they will know something of how to help others really be happy. Psychotherapy must amount to more than just being a process for symptom removal; it must begin to study and understand the essence of the nature of joy, beauty, and warmth and the inspirational mother of these offspring—love. If *we* do not do it, who then will?

This entire discussion is succinctly yet profoundly reflected and summarized in a simple poem by E. E. Cummings,[9] which reads as follows:

> While you and I have lips and voices which
> are for kissing and to sing with
> who cares if some one-eyed son of a bitch
> invents an instrument to measure Spring with.

PSYCHOTHERAPY: THE ART OF THE INTERSUBJECTIVE

Basically, psychotherapy may be defined as the art of the creative intersubjective relationship. In contrast to the intersubjective relationship is the interpersonal relationship. An interpersonal relationship involves just an objective interaction between two persons. The word "person" comes from the Latin word "personna," meaning mask. An interpersonal relationship then is one in which each of the two members of the relationship is relating to the other *as* the mask or social role which he displays to his interpersonal world; he is relating only *to* the mask or social role of the other.

On the other hand, in the true intersubjective relationship each is relating to the other with what is subjectively most real in himself and to what he sensitively feels to be most subjectively real in the other. The intersubjective is a getting-through to the other's deepest aliveness. The intersubjective is the light, heat and energy generated in the interpersonal. If someone goes into a store and asks for a container of milk, that is interpersonal; but if he senses that the clerk feels depressed and says something supportive to cheer him, then that is intersubjective. It is the difference between seeing only the grades or seeing also the eyes of the child who is presenting his report card.

Two friends may meet, both smile sweetly, each asking about how the other is, each replying "fine"; they are only just going through the motions of relationship for it really is more an interaction than a relationship, no matter how long they have known each other, because the intersubjective has not been stirred. Yet it may be that the eyes of strangers may meet only momentarily and it is immediately clear that the intersubjective has been awakened and involved. There is an old Chinese story about a man who asked his friend

> "Do you love me?"
> "Yes, of course, I love you," said his friend.
> "Do you know what's bothering me?" the man persisted.
> "No, how can I?" demanded the friend.
> "Then you don't love me," the man said sadly.

In the same way patients in psychotherapy equate caring and concern on the part of the therapist with the therapist's being sensitive to his (the patient's) subjective. The basic concern on the part of the patient (and the Chinese man in the illustration) is not so much, "Do you know what's bothering me?" but rather "Do you *care* to know what's bothering me?" To really care about another is to hear the subjective of the other. One cannot hope to demonstrate concern and caring for another by just the giving of supportive and flattering words but only by the intersubjective hearing of the other. As the therapist hears and speaks to the subjective of the patient, the patient learns to be sensitive to and hear his own subjective, and by so doing, he comes in contact with that which is most real in himself and integrates himself as a real person instead of some imaginal or conceptual ideal.

In both casual contacts and established relationships, intersubjective caring is the step out of our narrow, egocentric preoccupation and turned-off isolation. Both for the carer and cared for, it redeems the world in all the little daily transactions. Intersubjective hearing and caring is the first step out of solitary confinement and is the essence of the therapeutic relationship.

Therefore, a meaningful definition of a good therapist is not just one who has published a large number of books and articles or one who has given many therapy workshops or one who has received many awards or holds high office in professional organizations, for the capacity to be therapeutic is not related to how renowned one is but is much more related to how sensitive one can be to the truth of the patient's moment-to-moment subjective reality. Regardless of the profoundness and uniqueness of one's theories and techniques, you will never be effective as a therapist if you cannot hear the truth of the patient's moment-to-moment subjective reality. Therefore, the judgment of whether or not you are a good therapist is one that can be made only at any given moment in therapy and is not some kind of an absolute, enduring or final judgment. This means that at any given moment in therapy, even the most naive student, in terms of degree of experience, can be better than the most experienced and "sophisticated" therapist if he can be fully attuned and clearly and precisely hear the truth of the patient's moment-to-moment subjective reality and has the sensitivity, openness and courage to respond honestly with his own subjective reality. At that moment he is the very best therapist that anyone can possibly be, and therapy is as effective as it can possibly be.

REFERENCES

1. Arbuckle, D.: Client perception of counselor personality. *J Counsel Psychol, 3:*93-96, 1956.
2. Bandura, A.: Psychotherapist's anxiety level, self-insight, and psychotherapeutic competence. *J Abnorm Psychol, 52:*333-337, 1956.
3. Barrett-Lennard, G.: Dimensions of therapist response as causal factors in therapeutic change. *Psychol Monogr, 76 (No. 43),* 1962.
4. Barron, F.: Some test correlates of response to psychotherapy. *J Consult Psychol, 17:*235-241, 1953.
5. Bergin, A.: Some implications of psychotherapy research for therapeutic practice. In *Psychotherapy Research,* edited by G. Stollak, B. Guerney, and M. Rothberg, Chicago, Rand McNally, 1966, p. 118-129.

6. Bergin, A., and Solomon, S.: Personality and performance correlates of empathic understanding in psychotherapy. *Am Psychol, 18:*393, 1963.
7. Cartwright, D.: Success in psychotherapy as a function of certain actuarial variables. *J Consult Psychol, 19:*357-363, 1955.
8. Chance, E.: *Families in Treatment.* New York, Basic Books, 1959.
9. Cummings, E. E.: *Six Non-lectures.* New York, Atheneum, 1967, p. 47.
10. Fey, W.: Doctrine and experience: Their influence upon the psychotherapist. *J Consult Psychol, 22:*403-409, 1958.
11. Fiedler, F.: The concept of the ideal therapeutic relationship. *J Consult Psychol, 14:*239-245a, 1950.
12. Fiedler, F.: A comparison of therapeutic relationships in psychoanalytic, nondirective, and Adlerian therapy. *J Consult Psychol, 14:*436-445b, 1950.
13. Fiedler, F.: Factor analysis of psychoanalytic, nondirective and Adlerian therapeutic relationships. *J Consult Psychol, 15:*32-38, 1951.
14. Fulkerson, S., and Barry, J.: Methodology and research on the prognostic use of psychological tests. *Psychol Bull, 58:*177-204, 1961.
15. Gardner, G.: The psychotherapeutic relationship. *Psychol Bull, 61:*426-437, 1964.
16. Garfield, S., and Affleck, D.: Therapists' judgments concerning patients considered for psychotherapy. *J Consult Psychol, 25:*505-509, 1961.
17. Gibran, K.: *The Prophet.* New York, Alfred A. Knoff, 1923, p. 56.
18. Hammer, M.: The hopelessness of hope. *Voices: The Art and Science of Psychotherapy.* Winter 1970, Vol. 6, No. 3, p. 15-17.
19. Hammer, M.: Quiet mind therapy. *Voices: The Art and Science of Psychotherapy.* 7 *(No. 1):*52-56, Spring 1971.
20. Hollingshead, A., and Redlich, F.: *Social class and mental illness.* New York, John Wiley & Sons, 1958.
21. Kirtner, W., and Cartwright, D.: Success and failure in client-centered therapy as a function of client personality variables. *J Consult Psychol, 22:*259-264a, 1958.
22. Kirtner, W., and Cartwright, D.: Success and failure in client-centered therapy as a function of initial in-therapy behavior. *J Consult Psychol, 22:*329-333b, 1958.
23. Rogers, C.: The necessary and sufficient conditions of therapeutic personality change. *J Consult Psychol, 21:*95-103, 1957.
24. Rogers, C.: A theory of therapy, personality and interpersonal relationships as developed in the client-centered framework. In *Psychology: A Study of a Science,* edited by S. Koch. New York, McGraw-Hill, 1959, Vol. III, p. 184-256.
25. Shlein, J., Mosak, H., and Dreikers, R.: Effects of time limits: a comparison of two psychotherapies. *J Counsel Psychol, 9:*31-34, 1962.

26. Strupp, H.: An objective comparison of Rogerian and psychoanalytic techniques. *J Consult Psychol, 19* (No. 3):1-7, 1955 a.

27. Strupp, H.: The effect of the psychotherapist's personal analysis upon his techniques. *J Consult Psychol,* Vol. *19* (No. 3):197-204, 1955 b.

28. Strupp, H., Wallach, M., and Wogan, M.: Psychotherapy experience in retrospect: Questionnaire survey of former patients and their therapists. *Psychol Monogr, 78,* No. 11, 1964.

29. Truax, C.: A scale for the measurement of accurate empathy. *Psychiat Instit Bull* (Wisconsin Psychiatric Institute, University of Wisconsin), *1* (No. 10), 1961.

30. Truax, C., and Carkhuff, R.: For better or for worse: The process of psychotherapeutic personality change. In *Recent Advances in Behavioral Change.* Montreal, McGill University Press, 1963.

Chapter 2

Psychotherapy with Patients with
Anxiety Reactions

JARL E. DYRUD

Anyone who wants to make a living from the treatment of nervous patients must clearly be able to do something to help them.

SIGMUND FREUD

A NXIETY IS our primary topic here. Phobia, one of the many ingenious ways man has found to relieve his feelings of anxiety, will be referred to from time to time in this chapter because anxious people act phobic too when the opportunity presents itself, but usually they do not look that far ahead. True phobics should be categorized with the obsessionals, who can smell anxiety a mile away and take evasive action; so I will leave them properly to be dealt with in the appropriate other chapters.

Very few psychotherapists have not experienced the reality of feeling anxious themselves. The vast majority of our patients spend a fair amount of their time feeling just that way. Thus, it is not surprising that we have placed "feeling anxious" at the heart of our psychopathologies and the relief of such feelings as at least one measure of our therapeutic successes. We probably should call it the management of anxiety rather than its treatment, because to be without anxiety altogether is to be hit by a car or to find that one has become "unexpectedly" pregnant. Like food, we have to have it, but anxiety is really only helpful in moderation. Our problem then is to keep it within reasonable bounds while maintaining its signal function, so that we can draw

Note: Some of this thinking was done with the support of the U. S. Army Medical Research and Development Command, 1966-67, Behavioral procedures in psychiatric practice, DA-49-193-MD-2638, and 1967-68 Metaphorical Communication—Its uses and changes when psychotic patients receive psychotherapy, DA-MD-49-193-67-G9240.

upon experience to set an appropriate criterion for our performance.

For the sake of making a few points I have invented an evolutionary story we can share.

It might be fair to say that signal or expectant anxiety has been with man from the day he developed a bit of forebrain and some capacity for a bit of foresight. Perhaps an equally enlarged subcortex adds an increment of foreboding. Somehow I suspect that in the evolution of man, this heightened capacity to sense impending danger and respond to it flexibly has provided the basis not only for our survival but for our extraordinary development of secondary process thinking as a way of coping with our pervasive uneasiness about what is going to happen next. Both morbid and simply expectant anxiety then can be described as a response sequence set in motion by a present stimulus. We have one fundamental criterion to judge its morbidity—that is, if its signal elicits a response sequence quite out of keeping with the average expectable response of such an environmental event. Here we can account for a variety of idiosyncratic behaviors, including the category of "acting anxious," when anxiety so far overshoots its signal function that it preempts the stage and thus leaves no room for corrective search and response sequences, by inferring that they all are responses to a peculiarity of the individual's foresight.

From the standpoint of safety, primitive man found it imperative, if not certainly convenient (and I think desirable), to live in groups, as do many of our relatives in other primate groups to this day. Then, as now, the preservation of the group was crucial. For this purpose one of the group's important functions is to control prediction to encourage and constrain the individual's own predictions such that they fall within the limits of what is good for the group. This avoids the risk of idiosyncratic predictions which when acted upon hazards the group as a whole. This group function has a developmental consequence in view of our long period of dependency in childhood; thus the family group must be considered the primary transmitter of a child's reasonable expectancies or what Jerome Frank[11] calls the child's "assumptive world."

As the group became larger than a single family unit, some method for achieving consonance may have needed to be devised among families which still took into account individual survival. This may well have been the beginning of the development of the role of priest or shaman. His task was to structure those predictions for the individual that could come in conflict either with a prudent man's definition of reality or with the good of the larger group. The evidence that myths in the oral tradition have evolved in every preliterate society strongly suggests that they developed in consonance with man's ethology and are as characteristic of social man as is the development of language. Such myths might best be considered not as tales spun on a long winter's evening but as analogs for predictive behavior using language as a mnemonic device.

Myths' subjects are birth, death, life transition—all anxiety foci. We have no reason to think that myth-making decreased in the literate societies but rather that literacy simply increased our mnemonic capacity—that is, our capacity to store and retrieve information. This development of longer and more complex mythically sanctioned behavioral sequences serves as convenient guiding referents for prediction, "templates" to interpret and prescribe action which could be achieved by rational prediction but would not be as convenient and orderly if they did.

Myth functions to sanction "packages" of socially significant time and effort which are not to be questioned; for example, anxious rites of passage like our residency training, mixtures of ritual and education which are to be taken for granted. This is for the benefit of the group, but, as you may well imagine, it also relieved the burden of choice for the individual on these larger issues, just as a daily routine permits us to get up and go to work without the agonies of existential choice. Thus, perhaps the age of faith, which bridges the unseen and unknown, was born and lasted a million years.

Now we are told that the age of faith has given way to the age of anxiety. Our myths worn thin, we shiver in the cold light, not of reality necessarily but of uncertainty. Some say we are now free of the myths that controlled us, and now we can see the face of reality. I share Levi-Strauss'[19] idea that mythic thought is an essential component of mental life. The notion then (that we are without myths at all) may be the most damaging myth of all, especially if it provides no assumptions on which to proceed! It seems unlikely that self-evident good has changed. We still value health over (physical) illness; wisdom over ignorance (although the defense of innocence has its faddish moments); hope over despair; love over hate; productivity over indolence. But how to achieve them seems to call for some new or reaffirmation of some old behavioral sequences.

All of our present-day shaman are not on Madison Avenue cueing us from our television sets. A fair number of them are called psychotherapists. They come from a variety of the helping professions, including medicine, the clergy, clinical psychology, sociology and so on. Diverse though the academic backgrounds may be (psychodynamic or behavioral psychology), a common set of assumptions creates strong similarities in theory and technique. This common set of assumptions includes the notions that we are all more alike than we are different; that differences exist on a continuum along which the patient may be induced to move; that, with a half-hearted sort of determinism, we hope that by bringing into awareness the past assumptions controlling our present behavior, we may achieve some degree of freedom of choice. Underlying all is a strong bias in favor of verbal interaction as the vehicle for treatment.

Far from being a handicap, this diversity of backgrounds can bring to the psychotherapist's training a wide variety of behaviors that add richness to the metaphor of whatever theoretical system with which he is identifying his work. We might feel sorry for the impoverishment of the hypothetical student trained in only one discipline, having read in only one discipline, who encounters a patient or a series of patients who do not fit his system.

Relatively few of our customers come to us because they represent any real and present threat to the group. Their trouble with the group is that what seems to work for others fails them or they fail at it. In fact, in contrast to our ancestors, they may have little or no sense of authentic group membership. Our society is so mobile today that group membership is no longer conferred and retained automatically as in one's family and community of origin. It must be defined, identified as to what is congenial and convenient; indeed frequently it must be intentionally sought out as part of our growing up. With all its hazards, this greater possibility of developing individual potential and choice of groups is where our civilization is at. Our patients have all, to a greater or lesser degree, failed at both group membership and individuation. Even though we treat them as individuals we must recognize the need for their entry into an authentic and congenial group as one of the goals of treatment. This is not to be confused with group therapy which has its own special advantages and economies for some patients and may be very inappropriate for others. We cannot digress at this point to consider the timing in therapy of optimum group or therapeutic community experience for our patients. If we are to adequately canvas our resources for treatment, however, we must consider what training is better done in a group and what is done better with the therapist alone, while also acting as a representative of the healthier group toward which the patient is moving. Our uneconomic use of individual therapy is not in all cases a bad choice dictated by theory. Our theory itself is a response to our greater individualization in comparison to the average Sea-Dayak of rural Sarawak where group therapy has been the mode of treatment for centuries.[22]

Most of our patients come self-referred because in the ordinary course of events, they find their lives difficult to live. Their needs are not different from those of others, but their success in getting their needs met leaves something to be desired. For many of them, the avoidance of anxiety has become such a major undertaking that the pursuit of pleasure seems to be irrelevant. Harry Stack Sullivan[25] pointed out in his *Conceptions of Modern Psychiatry,* just how much of our daily activities are security operations—that is, the avoidance of anxiety rather than the active pursuit of pleasure. Pleasure itself is hard to define in positive terms. Reduction of tension in a need system is not very far removed from the reduction of anxiety. Put positively, it might come out that pleasure is simply the affect accompanying performing well under favorable conditions.

I wish to discuss those portmanteau terms, psychoanalytic psychotherapy and behavior therapy—both of which theoretically center upon relief of anxiety—from the standpoint of their complementarities rather than their differences. It is my view that there is no real contradiction in the theoretical polarities with which we are being presented. It is more a matter of what is covert in one system while being overt in the other.* It puzzles me why we strive for such purity of doctrine when it is the combination that works. Certainly the combination includes not only the relief of anxiety, which is a negative concept, but the training of new behaviors which can be performed well and the identification of favorable circumstances in which the patient can experience pleasure. Why not assume, rather than having two competing ideologies, each may have a different piece of the picture, neither complete nor irrelevant. Psychotherapists have abundant knowledge of the doctor's and patient's mental states and the vicissitudes of a therapeutic relationship but a narrow range of acknowledged techniques. Behavioral psychologists have an impressive array of techniques for observing and modifying behavior—verbal, overt (motor) and visceral—but a curious lack of interest in the relationship other than viewing the therapist as a potential reinforcer of desired responses. We may be able to describe what they are doing in a way that heightens their effectiveness, just as they may be able to help us look at what we are actually doing in the treatment session. A final common pathway of theory and technique strikes me as logical, if not inevitable.

---

*Fiedler's[10] study of the behavior of beginners and experts during psychotherapy, with three very different theoretical orientations, demonstrated that there was a high correlation among the behaviors of the different experts as there was among the beginners but essentially no correlation between beginner and expert holding the same theoretical views. This supports my impression that as we develop more skill in our healing craft, we are brought closer to the actual myths we and our patients live by, needing the secondary elaborations less in our practice while still persisting in them in our fraternal activities.

We analysts must admit that we have tended to refine and complicate our theory, possibly beyond its utility in doing psychotherapy. This behavior need be viewed neither as essential nor as perverse and capricious. It might be profitably viewed as part of man's pattern-making or myth-making propensity, an ethological sink-hole into which we tend to slip, much as the Breland's[7] raccoons tended to slip into food-washing behavior at the expense of persisting in a more useful behavior sequence when the program of training ran too close to their innate food-washing sequence.

We have tended to ritualize our method. In our efforts to heighten our effectiveness or deepen our analyses, we have lengthened the period of dependency in treatment until it approaches the length of the original period of dependency in childhood. At the same time, we have been recommending such treatment for increasing numbers of patients in spite of Freud's[13] endorsement of a wide variety of simpler psychotherapeutic measures which he would not hesitate to use in appropriate circumstances. Horrified as we may be at treating a patient without the polite effort of making his acquaintance, as in Peter Lang's "automated densensitization procedure,"[18] we need to become more alert to the likelihood that a fair number of patients are probably waiting for some face-saving way of dropping a symptom. In our fascination with the unfolding of the patient's mental life, we may have tended to rely on the mysterious workings of his unconscious, perhaps even at the expense of good clinical observation and a responsive technique. It is for all these reasons that I suggest we broaden our view.

B. F. Skinner[23] has been foremost in the efforts to establish a language and method of behavioral analysis which is based upon observable data generated from the close study of the individual over a relatively long and open-ended period of time. Rather than statistically comparing end results, he emphasizes clarifying the point-to-point relationships between the behavior of the experimenter and the behavior of the individual under study, with the assumption that out of such scrutiny some useful generalizations can be made. His method has been used in the operational study of a variety of transactions, including education, various forms of psychotherapy, as well as drug effects on the intact organism. This analytical approach is not to be confused with a system of behavior therapy based upon the discovery that a nod of the head means yes. Nor is it be equated with Eysenck's[9] "learning theory" or Wolpe's "conditioning theory." They have their own language of intervening variables, drawn in the main from the laboratory of Pavlov with the behavior considered as reactive to controlling stimuli, in contrast to the Skinnerian concept of behavior governed by its consequences.

It has become a convention in the numerous articles and summaries to refer to behavior therapy in general as "direct," as opposed to the "indirect" method of psychoanalysis. "Indirect" seems to be used in the sense of seeking to remove the underlying cause, rather than addressing one's attention to the presenting complaint. From my point of view Wolpe's use of fantasy as a vehicle for reciprocal inhibition can hardly be described as more direct than analyzing a dream or a slip of the tongue, unless we consider it more direct to be inhibiting the report of a maladaptive response rather than eliminating a conflict by interpretation. In any event, both approaches use verbal exchanges in a therapist's office in an attempt to influence the patient's behavior outside the office, and they are both, in that sense, indirect. It seems rather that "direct" would imply addressing oneself to the symptomatic behavior *in situ* and modifying it, as has been done in some research settings with children; however, these authors present themselves as investigators rather than as behavior therapists.[4, 5, 20] It would appear then that "behavior therapy," as it is commonly defined, is not, in that total sense, direct, but rather follows the procedural method of Wolpe's[29] "systematic desensitization" method.* When we contemplate the dynamics of the curative effect of a technique such as systematic desensitization,

---

*Definition of systematic desensitization: Neuroses are persistent, unadaptive learned habits of reaction that have been learned under conditions of anxiety and can be unlearned by presenting stimuli for the neurotic response under conditions of deep relaxation. This is done in a systematic sequence beginning with the least anxiety-provoking stimulus, mastering it and proceeding to the next in its hierarchy.

all protestations to the contrary, it would seem highly improbable that the transferences (the individual's unconscious carry-over of specific inappropriate learned patterns of response) which insinuate themselves into all relationships should not be present in the behavioral therapist's office. Indeed, Eysenck and Rachman's[9] book on therapy introduces as parameters all the devices of conventional psychotherapy which leaves their definition of "behavior therapy" as a form of psychotherapy with the essential element of systematic desensitization, just as psychoanalytic psychotherapy may be defined as a form of psychotherapy with the essential element of interpretation (including interpretation of the transference as contrasted to psychoanalysis which focuses on the analysis of the transference neurosis).

Is interpretation the necessary, if not sufficient, ingredient of psychoanalytic psychotherapy? Given a technique which rests upon the fundamental notion of interpretation rather than relaxation as the therapeutic tool, what can we do to demonstrate a significant relationship between interpretation and behavioral change in the patient during the process of analysis itself, as well as subsequent to it? What is characteristic of a mutative interpretation? Is it "direct" or "indirect"? We have been taught that it includes three elements: (a) consideration of the transference, (b) consideration of the current life situation and (c) consideration of the patient's past experience. We have also been taught that when timely it works, and when it works, we can state only that there is a higher degree of congruence between the patient's witting and unwitting behaviors, that the move has been toward a higher degree of appropriateness in the here and now.

The interpretation itself may well be dependent on a careful scrutiny of the patient's statements about past behavior and experiences with others to define the nuance of the behavior currently under study. Many authors express a critical concern with the historical truth of such interpretation.[28] This correctness or truth of the interpretation is, however, actually validated not by extra-analytic attempts at historical research but by its consequences in modifying the patient's behavior—either interrupting ongoing behavior or instating new behavior. What is often lost sight of is that the nature of preliminary interpretations and working through is such that whatever truth is established is tautological truth. Thus the question of validity is more properly addressed to the behavioral change rather than the ultimate historical truth of the concept used in bringing it about. Recognizing this aspect of interpretation is important in another sense, in that we tend to be mysterious about it rather than curious. Interpretation is directive at least in the sense of cognitive focusing. We select, we have something in mind, even if we profess unawareness we specify what new behaviors may be engaged in and what behaviors are prohibited. This adaptational aspect of interpretation is often ignored because our theory suggests that new, appropriate behaviors simply appear once the unconscious conflict has been brought into awareness. This is also a weakness of Wolpe's theoretical position, with his emphasis on removing the maladaptive response rather than on the teaching of appropriate responses.

We are led then to ask how do we choose our way of engaging this common misery? If we consider "feeling anxious" to be an epiphenomenon of certain performances, then our technique can be at least as varied as the performances themselves. For example, the evolution of Freud's thinking about anxiety suggested three very different therapeutic strategies. In 1895, his definition of anxiety neurosis was that of actual neurosis. That is, in response to a present stimulus, there is an inadequate discharge of sexual excitation that remains in the body, seeking alternate somatic routes of discharge. Common sense observation indicates that incomplete drive behaviors produce an altered psychophysiological state.*

In 1917, Freud's lecture 25 of the *General Introduction to Psychoanalysis* is entitled "Anxiety." Here, he defined three cate-

---

*When I was a boy on the farm, it was the practice to bring in a cheap stallion to "warm up" an expensive mare so that she would be receptive to the expensive stallion and not kick him. At the auspicious moment, we would lead the cheap stallion away and bring in the valuable one. Out behind the barn the loser would stand and sweat and shiver, pupils dilated—having to all appearances a full-blown anxiety attack.

gories of anxiety: reality or expectant anxiety, bound or phobic, and free-floating anxiety. The latter two are defined as reactions to internal danger—namely, id impulses which threaten discharge.

In 1936, when he wrote *The Problem of Anxiety*, his view had again changed somewhat. His position here, which is derived from the analyses of Little Hans and the Wolf Man, is that morbid anxiety is an affect of the ego rather than arising in the id and secondly, that anxiety precedes repression rather than following it. Freud notes that in all of the psychoneuroses there is one motivating force behind the ego's troubles. This one force is anxiety, which Freud describes as castration anxiety, derived from a situation which is perceived as a danger far out of proportion to what we might define as a rational expectancy. All symptoms, inhibitions and defenses are means which the ego uses to ward off this anxiety; that is to say, the symptoms, the inhibitions and the defenses are behaviors—behaviors which are developed to avoid anxiety reactions to a situation which is perceived as threatening. If these behaviors are not developed effectively (or, as we said earlier, in moderation), anxiety becomes predominant in psychic functioning and paralyzes effective behavior.

The three therapeutic strategies to meet Freud's definitions of anxiety might be as follows. With regard to the actual neuroses, it would appear that by advice and guidance one might put an end to the abuse and allow its place to be taken by normal sexual activity. In the 1917 theory, anxiety is a response to repression. Therefore, it would seem that the appropriate way to alleviate anxiety would be by therapeutic catharsis or loosening of the repressed energies. In the 1926 theory, morbid anxiety is a signal-like expectant or reality anxiety; however, it is a response to a misperception. Therefore, it would seem that the appropriate mode of alleviating such anxiety is to develop more adequate perception. Now, if our goal were to develop a unitary theory, we would have to choose which formulation is preferable. However, if we consider anxiety to be an affect accompanying certain performances, we are free to retain all three, using one or another strategy as the patient's performance indicates. We might take courage from

Freud, who wanted a unitary theory as much as any of us and yet said in his 1926 paper:

> It might still be true, therefore, that in repression anxiety is produced from the libidinal cathexis of the instinctual impulses. But how can we reconcile this conclusion with our other conclusion that the anxiety felt in phobias is an ego anxiety and arises in the ego, and that it does not proceed out of repression but, on the contrary, sets repression in motion? There seems to be a contradiction here which is not at all a simple matter to solve. It will not be easy to reduce the two sources of anxiety to a single one. We might attempt to do so by supposing that, when coitus is disturbed or sexual excitation interrupted or abstinence enforced, the ego scents certain dangers to which it reacts with anxiety. But this takes us nowhere. On the other hand, our analysis of the phobias seems to admit of no correction. Non liquet. [It is not clear.]

It is this lack of clarity of which Freud complains that we should actually welcome, because it dispels any notion that the presence of anxiety dictates any single treatment strategy and throws us back directly to the observation that anxiety is an affect accompanying certain performances, because the patient's performance, not his anxiety, is the interface at which we meet. It is also important for us psychoanalysts to recognize that understanding the dynamics of a performance is not identical with the treatment of choice.

Robert White,[26] in his monograph "Ego and Reality in Psychoanalytic Theory," laid much of the groundwork for a sound rapprochement between psychoanalytic ego psychology and the behavioral psychologists with his emphasis on competence and the need for the development of a general theory of action. He points out that classical psychoanalytic theory and method, so superbly adapted to uncovering unconscious processes, is very limited in helping us learn about reality and how to be effectively active in it. If this is so, we have several alternatives. We can confine ourselves to the psychoanalysis of a very select group of patients, for whom simpler measures fail in other people's hands, or we can see what other methods and theories there are which may have something to contribute to our own repertoire. Assuming that we are all willing to give sound advice to the actual neurotic, help him relax if need be, present an opportunity for catharsis when appropriate, what more can be said about the treatment of anxiety as an affect of the ego? Because I am inclined to agree with White that what the ego is concerned with is competence, I also see the ego as primarily a control device concerned with the appropriate staging and phasing of behaviors. Our assumption is that even seemingly erratic behavior is in fact consequential, often at a level below awareness, and that the elucidation of its consequences is our major vehicle for treatment (making the unconscious conscious). For this reason I am confident that behavior analysis along Skinnerian lines can be helpful to us (Goldiamond and Dyrud, 1966). Such an approach in no way precludes our investigation of the roots and multi-level relationships of a symptom, it simply gives greater precision to our descriptions.

At any event, when we turn to the study of the functional relations of the human organism with his environment, if we are not to credit ESP, we must devise some language of observables in which to make our observations and validations. Our criteria must be defined in terms that can be specified and observed. For this reason I like Joseph Brady's[6] description of anxiety: "If we draw two lines on a graph, the upper one called expectations and the lower one called performance, the distance between them may be called a measure of anxiety." Phobia then may be described as staying off the graph. Simple as this may seem, the model gives us two handles on the problem of anxiety: we can treat it by either raising the performance or lowering the expectations. A good psychotherapist of any school very likely reduces anxiety initially by the latter method. His warmth and acceptance suspends contingencies for the time being and permits the patient to experiment with raising his performance level, along with an almost imperceptible rise in expectations. All of our emphasis on trust and understanding as a basis for successful psychotherapy may well relate to this necessity of overriding the patient's initial criterion, which is, at the moment, too high and substituting for it responses which support uncertain and inadequate moves in the right direction. If this fails to happen, the patient has only the choice of bitter disillusionment or chronic attachment to the therapist, because nothing outside the sessions improves.

Any effort I know of to improve performance of alienated people without this ingredient of trust or social reinforcement, to put
it minimally, has failed to persist.*

It is true that punishment can knock out an aberrant behavior
when one is dealing with an acute disruption of an otherwise fairly
adequate repertoire of behaviors. One of the problems with it
is that it not only suppresses the target behavior, but it tends to
suppress behavior across the board, and if the patient is not emit-
ting a wide range of behaviors to begin with you might find you
have very little left to work with. It is also true that the prospect
of punishment must be maintained indefinitely unless a different
behavior is developed which better achieves the goal of the aberrant behavior. Ayllon and Azrin's schizophrenics[1] on their token
economy ward showed perfect A-B-A reversals because their behavior was rigorously linked to the token economy, without the
phasing in of social reinforcement. Such rigor was essential to
test the model, and later work has demonstrated the success of
phasing in social reinforcement as a way of maintaining the new
performance level in the community.[8]

In the office, we may not need behavioral gimmicks like a token
economy, but we do need a good start. Don't we all start out
with a few simple techniques first without violating any of our
theoretical principles? For instance, the initial history-taking takes
the form of helping the patient identify his up till then private
and subjective misery as something the doctor feels competent
to help him with. Wolpe finds phobias; psychoanalysts find a
broader history of maladaptation. In either case it is critical that
doctor and patient together feel successful in identifying something they can work on. If the patient has some capacity for trust,
the work can focus quickly on his specific behavioral deficit and
the more we know about techniques for discrimination training,
relaxation training or just plain sound advice, the faster he will
be relieved of his need for treatment.

*Lang's[18] subjects, who responded well to automated desensitization procedures,
happened to be university students selected as paid subjects from a nonalienated,
or at least nonhelp seeking group, so we may assume that their capacity for trust
was higher at the outset.

A 45-year-old physician came in with an intense concern over his "cardiac symptomatology," palpitation and shortness of breath, although he assured me there were no physical findings to support a diagnosis of heart disease. As he sat leaning forward in his chair in a mixture of eagerness and embarrassment telling his story, I was impressed by the fact that he was holding his breath. I suggested that he lean back, drop his shoulders and exhale. As he did so he began to cry. With some encouragement to let himself feel the emotion he sobbed for a time, then reported that the tightness in his chest was gone. Reviewing some of the fleeting thoughts he had had while crying, he reported that it seemed so sad that his condition might lead to his leaving his wife and newly adopted son alone in this world. He left feeling much better.

During the next two visits his sadness turned to fury over the little intruder's presence, and his wife's insistence on adoption when after many years she had failed to become pregnant. As he turned these thoughts over in his mind he recalled the birth of a younger brother and some of his feelings at that time. Throughout this period of review the fury eased and a warmth and regard for both the baby and mother were evidenced. We stopped by mutual agreement.

This fleeting encounter of three visits seems profane in our day of long-term treatment, but it was over eight years ago and the family has grown and prospered. He was ready to trust another person to help him discriminate past from present, perhaps ready for confession and absolution, in any event he was relieved of his distress.

There are many patients for whom such a trusting relationship needs to be developed and examined before they can profit from their new performance level by becoming part of a congenial social group. I think what we actually do first in developing a relationship of trust needs to be spelled out a bit, to clear up the possible misconception that some therapists simply have it and others do not. Whitehorn and Betts'[27] type A and type B therapists, rather than being immutable diagnoses, may have more to do with our inchoate theories of technique rather than with innate limitations of the therapists. Their type A therapist was three times as successful as their type B therapist in eliciting improvement in schizophrenic patients. The two groups were indistinguishable in their results with depressive and neurotic patients.

If we assume, as they did, that the schizophrenic patients had a greater problem with trusting another person, we can learn from their data some of what we have to teach. The type A therapists were more interested in the patient's personality than in his psychopathology. They were actively involved in their relationship with the patient rather than applying treatment to him. Their treatment goals were defined in positive terms of personality growth, often quite specific, rather than in terms of eliminating symptomatology. In other words they were located toward the evocative end of the therapeutic spectrum, whereas the type B therapists were located toward the directive end. I wish to emphasize the notion of a single spectrum of psychotherapeutic approaches with classical psychoanalysis at the evocative pole and behavior modification at the directive pole. Assuming some sort of a normal distribution curve between trust and distrust in our patient population, we might then assume that the vast majority of our therapeutic efforts should be an optimum mixture of directive and evocative techniques. Ian Stevenson's[24] description of such an approach is very much to the point here.

When expectant trust is high, it may not be too critical what technique is used; directive techniques may be the fastest. When trust is deficient, directive therapies falter and evocative therapies take a longer time. In such a case the therapist is strongly drawn toward polarizing his technique—to become more purely directive or purely evocative in order to strengthen his own conviction and thus maintain his own behavior. I am of the opinion that usually this is an unfortunate security operation on the part of the therapist. Our task is to build that deficient trust by a patient and diligent attention to the patient's need for the kind of emotional arousal that emerges from discovering with the therapist that in some small ways he can be successful.

> Some years ago I saw an alcoholic, childless woman who was entering the menopause. Her marriage was crumbling and her mother was dying of cancer. Scanning the field to find something to work on, I found that in her general apathy there was a small peak of unhappiness over her mother's unwillingness to eat that was hastening the elderly lady's death.

Following Arthur Bachrach's[2] prescription for anorexia nervosa, I suggested in her daily visits to the hospital, which were greatly prized by her mother, that she go at mealtime and stay only as long as her mother continued to eat. The experiment was successful. Not that the mother recovered, because in spite of the weight gain she died, but the daughter felt effective and also felt that she had been helped. This was the beginning of her opening up with me to examine many other ways of being more effective, and over a period of several years she was. Later on in treatment she described that early episode as one of being "recognized" by me as a really decent and capable person in spite of all appearances.

I am not concerned here with the charismatic healer's magic touch, but rather with a relationship of trust growing out of and responding to the alienated patient's need to be "known"—known in the sense of being permitted to be with the therapist more than the bearer of a familiar symptom complex. Once I had glibly written to a nonpsychiatric friend, Arthur Stratton, that therapy works because we are more alike than we are different. He wrote back, "yes, but aren't you always surprised by the people once they have done their best, or worst, to strip themselves bare for your help, aid or succor? They are the more mysterious for standing revealed, not mother-naked, but as bare as bare can be. Which is to say, with their hair on, clothed in scars." This is true in my experience. The new beginning of which Michael Balint[3] speaks is based upon mutual acceptance of this core of mystery in each participant. That is how trust is born in those who lack it. Much of our work with alienated patients from the very beginning must be toward removing obstacles from the path to this sort of intimacy.

Here history-taking transcends the statistical sheet to become part of the process of the patient's making himself known to another. In addition to factual recall, it calls for organizing one's inner experience into an intelligible communicable thought which requires an interaction with the therapist about what is consensually valid—meaning, not on the therapist's terms in a didactic sense but in terms of what they together can comprehend. In spite or rather because of the terrible personal and unique character of such an interchange, the therapist must remain clear as to his role of change-agent and representative of the prospect that the patient can find his way into meaningful community of his own. This process tends to gravitate toward the puzzling or distressing aspects of experience, which are seen to form fairly characteristic repetitive patterns as diverse as anxiety attacks, stomach distress or a temper tantrum. In most instances, these aspects of experience have a quality of inevitability for the patient, stemming from the lack of alternatives within the patient's awareness, a lack enduring over a period of time sufficient to permit question and answer alike to drop out of awareness. In the process of becoming "known," some of these troublesome behavior-controlling patterns become conscious and explicit. Then the repetition comes in as these patterns are tested verbally in many ways. Being "known" gives strength to leave a shared question open until a new and more adequate answer develops. In the hands of a tyro, psychoanalytic theory or behavior theory may interfere when the therapist introduces a new system of causality rather than helping the patient transcend his need for a pat answer. This type of "working through" is the crux of therapy—that is, giving the support to prevent premature closure. The person who has been "analyzed" but unimproved has often simply learned a new set of answers by repetition of these same answers. The one who does not move in therapy may be dealing with a therapist who tries one answer and if the question comes up again, he tries a different answer; thus, the point of reference is lost and the patient is deprived of even the doubtful good of learning a new set of answers.

I have taken this rambling approach to our subject because I must admit to being rather bored with the mind-body dichotomy, which is represented by the humanist versus mechanist, psychotherapist versus behaviorist of today. All very reminiscent of the nature-nurture controversies of the 1930's which still flicker on from time to time. I say this because we have enough data at hand now to know that one cannot really be comfortable in either camp.

Behavior analysis can be of significant help to us in the opening moves of therapy which have more to do with ease than with intimacy, reliability and regularity of response rather than sub-tlety. We must also recognize that a fair number of patients can make it on their own from there. For those whose loneliness is more established, however, a return to the "old self" is a goal I question. In this respect I agree with Ronald Laing[17] that the patient's symptomatology may be a creative attempt to enrich his barren life, but one that miscarries. In that sense, he cannot go back through the same door he entered without a real sense of failure. For these people there is that need to be known rather than understood with all its reductive implications. They need openness rather than closure. Perhaps technicians can help the easy ones, but the others require our broadest training and our best effort.

The patient who both requires and profits from this experience has reached the point of needing fewer simple cause-and-effect explanations and has some capacity to live with unsolved prob-lems until sufficient relevant data is in to come to a conclusion. This is not a solitary strength but a confidence forged in a pro-totypical relationship with the therapist which generalizes to the patient's interpersonal environment. His foresight has become both prudent and reasonably benign; he will have begun to find his authentic group.

In summary then, the anxious patient may need advice and direction to reduce the ambiguity of cues which make it difficult for him to proceed. He may need to be helped to relax to reduce the psychophysiological concomitants of his anxiety. He may need discrimination training to identify the stimuli as well as his inappropriate responses to them, whether called interpretation or something else. Verbal psychotherapy is important to discrimi-nation training as well as in labeling of inchoate experiences. However, a large part of psychotherapy, though unrecognized, is simply a sharpening up of the patient's expressive behavior. He must learn to discerningly trust himself and the other person, but not all within awareness. Awareness is simply never large enough to take care of all the responding required, and for this we have no vocabulary at all.

REFERENCES

1. Ayllon, T., and Azrin, N. H.: The measurement and reinforcement of behavior of psychotics. *J Exp Anal Behav*, 8:357-383, 1965.
2. Bachrach, A. J., Erwin, W. J., and Mohr, J. P.: The control of eating behavior in an anorexic by operant conditioning techniques. In *Case Studies in Behavior Modification*, edited by L. P. Ullman and L. Krasner. New York, Holt, Rinehart & Winston, 1965.
3. Balint, M.: *Primary Love and Psychoanalytic Technique*. New York, Liveright, 1953.
4. Bandura, A.: Social learning through imitation. In *Nebraska Symposium on Motivation*, edited by M. R. Jones, Lincoln, University of Nebraska Press, 1962.
5. Bijou, S. W.: Behavior Therapy in the Home: Amelioration of Problem Parent-Child Relations with the Patient in a Therapeutic Role. Mimeographed paper, 1966.
6. Brady, J.: Personal communication, 1965.
7. Breland, K., and Breland, M.: *Animal Behavior*. New York, Macmillan, 1966.
8. Cohen, H. L.: Educational Therapy: The Design of Learning Environments. In *Third Conference on Research in Psychotherapy* (1966), edited by J. Schlein. Washington, American Psychological Association, Inc., 1968.
9. Eysenck, H. J., and Rachman, S.: *The Causes and Cures of Neuroses*. San Diego, Knapp Press, 1965.
10. Fiedler, F. E.: A comparison of therapeutic relationships in psychoanalytic non-directive, and Adlerian therapy. *J Consult Clin Psychol*, 14:436-445, 1950.
11. Frank, J. D.: *Persuasion and Healing*. Maryland, John Hopkins Press, 1961.
12. Freud, S.: On the grounds for detaching a particular syndrome from neurasthenia under the description 'anxiety neurosis.' In *The Standard Edition of the Complete Psychological Works of Freud*. London, Hogarth Press, vol. 3, pp. 87-113.
13. Freud, S.: On psychotherapy. In *The Standard Edition of the Complete Psychological Works of Freud*. London, Hogarth Press, vol. 7, p. 259.
14. Freud, S.: Introductory lectures on psychoanalysis. In *The Standard Edition of the Complete Psychological Works of Freud*. London, Hogarth Press, vol. 16, pp. 392-411.
15. Freud, S.: An autobiographical study. In *The Standard Edition of the Complete Psychological Works of Freud*. London, Hogarth Press, vol. 20, p. 16.
16. Freud, S.: Inhibitions, symptoms, and anxiety. In *The Standard Edition*

of the Complete Psychological Works of Freud. London, Hogarth Press, vol. 20, pp. 77-175.

17. Laing, R. D.: *The Divided Self.* London, Tavistock, 1960.
18. Lang, P.: Fear reduction and fear behavior. In *Third Conference on Research in Psychotherapy* (1966), edited by J. Schlein. Washington, American Psychological Association Inc., 1968.
19. Levi-Strauss, C.: *Raw or Cooked.* New York, Harper & Row, 1969.
20. Lovaas, O. I.: Some studies on the treatment of childhood schizophrenia. In *Third Conference on Research in Psychotherapy* (1966), edited by J. Schlein. Washington, American Psychological Association Inc., 1968.
21. Rukeyser, M.: Effort at speech between two people. In *Selected Poems New Directions*, 1951.
22. Schmidt, K. E.: Folk psychiatry in Sarawak. In *Magic, Faith and Healing*, edited by Ari Kiev. Glencoe, Free Press, 1964.
23. Skinner, B. F.: *Cumulative Record.* New York, Appleton-Century-Crofts, 1961.
24. Stevenson, Ian: Direct investigation of behavioral changes in psychotherapy. *Arch Gen Psychiatry, 1*:99-107, 1959.
25. Sullivan, H. S.: Conceptions of modern psychiatry. Reprinted from *Psychiatry, 3 (No. 1)*, 1940; *8 (No. 2)*, 1945.
26. White, R.: Ego and reality in psychoanalytic theory. *Psychol Issues*, Monograph II, 1963.
27. Whitehorn, J. C., and Betts, B.: A study of psychotherapeutic relationships between physicians and schizophrenic patients. *Am J Psychiatry, 111*:321-331, 1954.
28. Wisdom, J. O.: Testing on interpretations within a session. *Int J Psychiatry, 48*:44-52, 1967.
29. Wolpe, J.: *Psychotherapy By Reciprocal Inhibition.* Stanford, Stanford University Press, 1958.

Chapter 3

Psychotherapy with Patients with Phobias

GERARD CHRZANOWSKI

PHOBIAS ARE familiar phenomena of everyday life as well as manifestations of mental disorders. A phobia is a morbid fear of objects or situations which realistically do not constitute a genuine danger to the person. In a clinical descriptive way, phobia denotes a phenomenon which ordinarily cannot be dealt with in an objective or rational fashion. The morbid fear has become attached to objects or situations and is usually recognized by the phobic person as not being a source of danger. Nevertheless, there is a compulsion to stay away from the imaginary threat. There may even be physiological responses characteristic of facing an actual danger such as tachycardia, rapid breathing, sweating, gastrointestinal symptoms, tremor and so forth. The victim of the phobic reaction is ordinarily aware of the relative harmlessness of the situation. He frequently does not know what he is actually afraid of. Nevertheless he feels compelled to avoid phobia-producing situations. His insight into the inappropriateness of his phobic response does not protect him against acting irrationally.

There is little doubt that many people have been plagued by some irrational fears which they may have concealed from outsiders or rationalized to themselves and others. They may have dealt with their excessive concern either by attempting to cope with it somehow or by permitting themselves to yield to unreason. Conditions of the above-described nature qualify technically as phobias, but they usually have little clinical significance. On the other hand, some phobias may veil the existence of moderate or even severe psychopathology.

In classical psychoanalytic theory, phobias are grouped with anxiety hysterias. The concept is closely linked to the framework of libido theory, whereby "the libido which has been liberated from the pathogenic material by repression is not converted but set free in the shape of anxiety."[7] It is postulated that the anxiety hysteria develops into a phobia when the effort of psychically binding the released anxiety fails. In phobias the anxiety is cut off from reconversion into libido and cannot be attached to the complexes which were the source of the libido. In other words, all avenues connected with the formation of anxiety are foreclosed by erecting mental barriers in the nature of precautions, inhibitions and restrictions. "It is these defensive structures that appear to us in the form of phobias and that constitute to our eyes the essence of the disease."[6] Freud did not make a definitive statement concerning constitutional versus experiential factors in the formation of phobias. However, he stated that to his way of thinking phobic states were least dependent on a constitutional predisposition and of all the neurotic disorders were most easily acquired at any time of life. Freud also felt that the cure of a phobia could not be accomplished by forceful intervention. He cautioned against depriving the patient of his defenses and leaving him prey to the liberation of his anxiety. At the same time he stressed the necessity of having the phobic patient face the feared situation rather than avoid exposure to the dreaded situation or object.

The concept and treatment of phobias have undergone some significant modifications since Freud's initial exposition which will be discussed in some detail later on in this text. Generally speaking there has been growing criticism of the mechanistic and nonpsychological hypothesis of the libido theory with its major focus on quantitative, physiochemical factors as a primary basis for human behavior. Instead of viewing human attitudes as being mainly governed by biophysiological forces, the emphasis has shifted to adaptational disturbances in response to environmental influences. Our major field of interest here is in the complex interplay or transaction between the organism and its total surrounding milieu. The waning of the topographical point of view with its main goal of making the unconscious conscious has contributed to this reorientation by paving the way for interpersonal considerations. There is no longer a need to trace a thought from its origin in the dark recesses of the unconscious to its emergence into conscious awareness. Greater appreciation can now be given to the actual experience of person-to-person encounters. Transference then emerges less as an inherent repetitive compulsion but rather as an open-ended channel for interpersonal experience. In addition, the growing focus on structural aspects has placed the defenses of the ego, or the adaptational factors, in the foreground. Along with this evolution, concepts of ecology and information theory have gained a foothold in modern psychoanalytic thinking. The ecology principle relates to the interdependence of human as well as environmental transactions. It rejects the concept of a purely intrapsychic process and stresses the constant interplay between the inner and outer life of a person without a stable line of distinction between them. Another consideration in classic theory is the fact that energy (libido) is considered to be a decisive factor in regard to a person's actions and activities. The available amount of energy determines the degree of tension which is built up either to initiate activity or to accumulate energy to the point where pressure is created as a result of psychological or external barriers which prevent its release. Thus there is no potential for activity unless energy is stored up. Modern information theory, on the other hand, is much less concerned with quantities of energy. It has been shown that the vital event of exchanging information takes place with a minimal expenditure of energy. The important aspect of our newer concept is the rearrangement of forces within a field which occurs in the process of coding, decoding and transmitting information without major energetic requirements. In other words, many events of major significance involving the organism and the environment are not primarily dependent on the absence or presence of energy. For example, an individual may feel magnetically drawn to another person of the opposite sex. The person may account for his intense emotions and desires with the explanation that he has "fallen in love." It may be possible to demonstrate to this individual that his state of heightened energy may actually be the result of a malignant rather than a healthy process. The data may indicate that he has found the "perfect partner" to perpetuate his neurosis.

One may be able to document to him that his powerful attraction to the other person is part of a pattern designed to lower his self-esteem, and a thoughtful therapeutic dialogue may shed light on the irrationality of his behavior. The person may now have a chance to correct his attitude on the basis of additional information made available to him. There is no guarantee that he will use the information constructively, but it provides an incentive for a different course of action. The point is that there has been no change in any respect regarding the available energy level. Rather, there has been a transmission of information which enables the person under certain circumstances to rearrange his interpersonal field in a positive manner.

In this chapter, phobias will be discussed mainly as thought disorders which are closely related to the obsessional states. The opinion will be advanced that it seems appropriate to view phobias and obsessions as one clinical entity, contrary to the classic point of view. Phobic and obsessional phenomena will first be discussed independently before concentrating on the common features of both conditions. The metaphoric nature of obsessive-phobic communications will be explored with particular attention to the existence of faulty perception and distortions in communication. Faulty perception refers predominantly to a pattern of certain recurrent distortions which interfere with an objective evaluation of what the patient thinks of himself in regard to other people—that is, the way he imagines others look at him (the patient's reflected image of himself in the eyes of others). Although perception is, of course, a much larger field, it is this aspect of perception which I believe is most relevant to phobias. In regard to distortions in communication, attempts will be made to show how in obsessive-phobic people important messages were transmitted through a warped, familial network of communication. It is suggested that certain phobic symbolisms can be directly traced to the maladaptation and malfunctioning of the nuclear family unit.

In regard to treatment, the revival of behavior therapy with its methods of desensitization has paved the way for dealing with certain uncomplicated phobic symptoms. However, the treatment of the majority of phobic-obsessional symptoms has not been affected by the behavioral approach. The task of accomplishing durable characterological and perceptual changes is formidable and some suggestions for improving the technique will be made later on. Significant modifications in the treatment approach center on a different understanding of the phobic process as well as on concepts of the nature of anxiety.

CULTURAL FACTORS

It can be said that phobias and depressions are probably among the most widespread psychological manifestations in daily life as well as in the realm of psychopathology. Certain phobias enjoy a high degree of social sanction despite the irrationality that may be involved. Phobic attitudes toward snakes, for example, are so common that they are rarely considered to be phobias as such. Among the more than two hundred phobic patterns, I have not encountered names for children's fear of the dark or phobic reactions to rats, mice, snakes and so forth.

Many cultures and societies tend to foster phobic reactions by imposing exaggerated threats of punishment on basically harmless infractions of the prevailing code. Our training and information are richly interspersed with misconceptions about the alleged danger of certain attitudes, actions and thoughts. It is fairly common, for instance, even among well-educated Europeans to be afraid of ice-cold beverages as health hazards. The cultural phobia of, for example, the supposedly dangerous qualities of "outsiders," "foreigners," "deviants," etcetera, is often a means of exploiting underlying prejudice. Thus, it is not an easy task for a child to know who is friend and who is foe, what is a genuine hazard and what is relatively safe.

Every culture has a host of irrational tabus about noninjurious practices and activities pertaining to eating habits and sexual, social, religious, political, economic and other aspects of life. Traditions are a powerful factor in governing human behavior and many fears are engendered because there is a clash in the culture between conventional and nontraditional behavioral patterns. An example may be found in the phobic attitude of the present older generation toward all drugs and the reckless antiphobic attitude of the younger generation in that respect. For instance, marijuana smoking is considered by many elders as being highly dangerous. There is good reason to believe that the degree of the actual danger is frequently exaggerated and not based on the best evidence available today. On the other hand, the younger generation takes it for granted that they are dealing with a perfectly harmless substance without having proof that this has been clearly established. It is this sharp clash between two polar opposites, each irrational in its own right, which in my opinion forms a frequent basis for a culturally prepared foundation for phobias. However, in order to develop the clinical disorder of phobia, we need the additional component of a particular family disturbance as will be discussed in some detail later on.

HISTORICAL REVIEW

Clinical descriptions of phobias and obsessions have been with us for a long time. According to Zilboorg,[20] it was Hippocrates in the fourth century B.C., who first gave an excellent description of what appears to have been a psychoneurosis with phobias. The French psychiatrist, B. A. Morel, is usually credited with the first clinically valid illustration of an obsession (1861). Kraft-Ebing (1879) made reference to compelling, persistent thoughts (*zwangsvorstellungen*) which could not be eradicated from the mind and whose pondering quality defied reason. Griesinger (1870) included in the term "obsession" a compulsive need to ask questions. Autochtonous ideas were coined by Westphal (1877) to describe obsessional impulses which seem to intrude from the outside as if they had been thrust upon the patient by demonological forces.

Charcot (1885) used the term "onomanomanic" in reference to an obsessional preoccupation with names and words where, in extreme situations, the victim would feel compelled to shout the names or words. Ladame (1890) referred to phobias and algias as part of the obsessional syndrome. Janet (1903) linked obsessions with psychoasthenia and hypothesized a morbid diminution of psychic energy as a causal factor. This in turn led to a ruminative, obsessive-compulsive tension state with a concomitant disturbance in reality perception. The result was a state of mental anarchy without adequate control over higher functions. According to Janet, the phobic reaction is closely related to hysteria, since both conditions constitute avoidances of feared situations.

Historically speaking, phobias and obsessions were grouped together as one clinical entity until the advent of psychoanalysis. Freud exhibited an early interest in obsessions and phobias in a paper entitled "Physical Mechanisms and Their Etiology."[8] In this paper, he insisted that a clear distinction be made between phobias and obsessions; that they were separate neuroses. According to Freud, the obsession is actually a thinking disorder with doubt, remorse, anger, ambivalence, etcetera, as the basic associated emotional states. Obsessions are genetically related to the anal-sadistic phase. Freud postulated the principle of displacement in obsessions as a dynamic factor. In true obsessions, the original idea connected to actual painful experiences in the sexual sphere has been displaced. The obsessional person attempts to forget the memory of the primal scene by repressing the disturbing sexual aspects. Focal attention is diverted from the painful area to a peripheral, obsessional preoccupation. Freud added other psychic mechanisms in order to account for obsessional behavior. These were ambivalence, an unresolved conflict of loving and hateful impulses; doubting, an ever-present manifestation of indecision; and isolation, a neutralizing device designed to obscure the affective origin of a thought. Freud uses the term "isolation" when he speaks of the separation of an idea or memory from its affective cathexis.* Finally, Freud used the constructs of regression, omnipotence and ellipsis to describe the obsessional people as a way of substituting thinking for acting, as a "compromise formation" between two antagonistic impulses which, when it comes to action, leads to a self-centered, infantile frame of reference. Ellipsis is a distortion by omission. It refers to a thought process which is distorted because a central issue is left out.

---

*This is in contrast to Sullivan who means by isolation a form of withdrawal from people.

In contrast, phobias center exclusively around the emotional state of morbid anxiety. The typical emotional state in phobias occurs only when the person is confronted with the alleged danger. It is not present as long as the seemingly dangerous situation is avoided. We must appreciate here that Freud's initial concept of anxiety was based strictly on a chemical, physiological process. It meant that people with inadequate sexual outlets would build up toxic substances in their system. The cure for this so-called actual neurosis, or as Ferenci named it "physioneurosis," was exclusively to have a more active and a more satisfactory sexual life.

Later on, Freud expanded the concept of anxiety by making it a predominantly psychological phenomenon. In the later theory, anxiety represents a warning from within when impulses based on wish fulfillment clash with censorship mechanisms. Current psychoanalytic thinking transcends this concept in many areas. It runs the gamut of existential, humanistic, nonpathological anxiety and other considerations. A significantly different point of view is injected by the tenet of anxiety as postulated in interpersonal theory. Anxiety in this frame of reference is not part of the human, constitutional makeup but is acquired by means of exposure early in life to people who suffer from anxiety. Accordingly anxiety is postulated as an experience which is basically alien to the human organism since it has no particular anatomical pathway to deal with it. The consequence is that according to Sullivan,[16] anxiety, once it is imprinted in a person, remains there as a lifelong experiential ingredient which cannot be removed or minimized.

Eventually Freud settled the problem of phobia with his classic presentation of "Little Hans." He considered the principle of substitution and displacement to be central in the phobic reaction. The boy's ambivalence toward his father is displaced onto the horse, which seemingly becomes the main threat in the boy's life. It is possible for the boy to avoid the horse which obscures his fear of his father as a castrating figure.

It seems to me that Freud unwittingly moved closer to a rapprochement between obsessions and phobias than he realized. In the obsessions it is the primal scene which is displaced, while in the phobia there is a displacement which consists of a shift of object from the father to the horse. The fact remains that both the victim of the phobia as well as of the obsession is unaware of the underlying fear and that he is warding off the confrontation with a conflict. In the obsession he supposedly wants to forget a painful sexual memory, while in the phobia he is afraid of the consequences of his unconscious wishes. There is little doubt that the causal assumptions in both instances are unproven and highly speculative.*

To my way of thinking there is no valid theoretical or clinical justification for splitting the obsessive-phobic complex into two separate entities. For one thing we have ample evidence of a common thought disorder in both conditions. Obsessional and phobic patients alike suffer from a mild delusional distortion in spite of the frequently glib rationalization of the phobic person. Neither obsessional nor phobic patients have the capacity to perceive themselves in relation to other people with any measure of accuracy. Both rely on a coded, metaphoric language which is similar to dreams. It defies logic to believe that the phobic patient has a pinpoint anxiety which he can manipulate by avoiding the anxiety-producing situation and that except for this particular foible he is emotionally intact.

I prefer to view both phenomena as one nosological category. Both obsessions and phobias are states of preoccupation whereby the focus of attention is diverted from the relevant aspects of a particular interpersonal situation. For instance, I have observed in patients with hypochondriasis a distinct tendency to combine

---

*It is of historic interest that the boy's father was the therapist in this case, in spite of the fact that he was the principle source of the boy's fear. There is another significant aspect to the situation which, to the best of my knowledge, has not been commented upon. In a postscript to the case of Little Hans, Freud casually mentions that the boy's parents were eventually divorced. It would be inconceivable in modern psychiatry to ignore the effect which the parental marital disturbance must have had on the boy's evolving anxiety. A study of family dynamics in the case of Little Hans would have shed considerable light on threatening components in the family's relational structure. A detailed knowledge of the integrational familial patterns might have lead to a different formulation of Freud's famous case illustration in regard to the genesis and dynamics of phobia.

both obsessive and phobic phenomena. The hypochondriacal person is obsessed with thought of ill health and is phobic about the malignant nature of his alleged illness. Similar considerations apply to some paranoid and to many algolagnic conditions.*

We can understand how Freud's genius went astray in separating obsessions and phobias. Freud was committed to a primarily internal conceptualization of neurotic conflict. He was convinced that the basic threat in phobias came from instinctual demands as illustrated in the following quotation: "The ego behaves as if the danger of an outbreak of anxiety threatened it not from the direction of the instinct but from the direction of perception."[9] The thesis of this chapter reverses this concept by placing the perceptual disturbance in the foreground of both obsessional and phobic conditions.

POST-FREUDIAN DEVELOPMENT

It is remarkable that Freud's ingenious theory of phobia has remained virtually unchallenged for sixty years. Furthermore, little attention has been given to the work of others who have made significant observations concerning the nature of phobias. In this connection, certain clinical studies of Sullivan's merit consideration.

Sullivan did not consider phobias a specific clinical entity nor an isolated manifestation of psychopathology. Rather, he grouped phobias with obsessive phenomena and with compulsive doubting. He viewed severe phobias as an enduring warp of the personality which he traced to a very early developmental period. It was his belief that the phobic pattern had its origin at a time when the infant's spontaneous self-exploration was disrupted by the mother's overwhelming anxiety. The infant's needs were regarded by Sullivan as being insufficiently gratified as a result of

---

*The term "algolagnia" is derived from the Greek word *algos* and refers to people who have a compulsion to expose themselves to painful situations. It is a particular form of sadomasochism which clinically forms part of a complex that includes obsessional, phobic and paranoid syndromes. There is a link between all four of the above-mentioned conditions and under certain circumstances the same patient can manifest all these symptoms.

personal and cultural misperceptions of the mother. That is, the mother was seen as being extremely vulnerable as to what she perceived to be society's expectations of her, thus having an exaggerated feeling of social responsibility. Sullivan conceives of two elementary human requirements which he calls needs and satisfactions respectively. The former are related to the basic biological requirements of the organism while the latter pertain to sociocultural necessities. Ordinarily the infant's needs evoke tender feelings in the mother which provide a satisfaction giving give-and-take between mother and child. In the presence of major difficulties on the mother's part there is inadequate gratification of the infant's needs and a resulting lack of satisfaction for those needs.

Using the example of a primitive genital phobia, Sullivan illustrated his point. He postulated the existence of zonal needs which call for satisfaction or gratification and ordinarily bring forth an appropriate response. A mother who is abnormally concerned with anal or sexual matters may become increasingly vigilant about any movement on the part of the child which threatens her—that is, she is overwhelmingly anxious about sexual and anal contamination of the body. The result will be strong, forbidding gestures whenever the child penetrates this sphere of anxiety. In response to the mother's anxiety, the infant experiences what Sullivan called "uncanny sensations,"* which impose strange taboos on the genital region. Accordingly, the genitals do not become part of the child's feelings of "my body." There arises a lack of sensations in conjunction with appropriate experiences pertaining to the genitals.

Sullivan's formulation, as described above, may be illustrated by the following case presentation. I interviewed a 9-year-old boy and his mother during a psychiatric consultation. The boy suffered from an extreme degree of phobic and obsessional disturbances. His mother was a nurse who had rigid notions of cleanliness and a morbid concern about contaminating certain parts of

---

*Experiences of awe, dread, horror and loathing attributed to the abrupt intervention of severe anxiety.

the body with anal, genital, oral, nasal and other excretions. She had devised a system of having a different colored washcloth reserved for a particular region of the body. One washcloth was to be used exclusively for the anal area, another for the genital region, a third for the neck, and so on. It so happened that the boy would occasionally mix up the colors and, for example, wash his neck with the washcloth reserved for the anal region. Such a step would evoke immediate panic on the part of the mother, who would become livid with rage and describe horrible consequences for this harmless transgression. As a result, the boy developed an extreme degree of inhibitory phenomena and a throttling of all spontaneity. The result was a case of severe phobia.

As previously noted, Sullivan did not consider phobias as a separate category but grouped them together with obsessions and doubts. The basic dynamic principle is referred to by him as obsessional substitution, a conspicuous and distressing difficulty in living. It refers to an individual who guards against experiencing severe anxiety by engaging in ritualistic, unproductive ruminations and thoughts. To this individual, spontaneous feelings of self-affirmation, affectionate impulses toward others or an encounter in which he is genuinely approved of only lead to the intervention of anxiety. Tender impulses are readily transformed into hostile operations (malevolent transformation),* and spontaneous gestures of friendliness and acceptance are responded to in a highly defensive manner. The underlying core for this dilemma is postulated by Sullivan as a recurrent doubt on the part of the person as to whether the significant person in his life is basically accepting or rejecting him; the evidence always being divided in such a fashion that there is never any clarity as to predominant acceptance or rejection by the key figure.

Thus, it seems to me that Sullivan has added one important dimension to our understanding of phobic and obsessional disorders. He has stressed the basic distrust and self-doubt which the phobic and obsessional person experiences toward his own

---

*The need for tenderness has been transformed into a feeling of hostile anticipation.

impulses and emotions and has emphasized a basic distrust of affirmative experiences as one of the primary factors in phobias and obsessions. In an operational way, phobias and obsessions are described by Sullivan as preoccupations which are a way of dealing with anxiety-producing situations or the threat of punishment. However, the concept does not stop at the level of an avoidance operation.* It also considers phobias and obsessions as isolating techniques. They isolate the person from any of his own emotions (that is, tenderness, anger, resentment) and create a powerful barrier in person-to-person contact. Interpersonal situations involving phobic and obsessional components tend to minimize intimacy and foster a hostile integration. The result is a style of life in which tenderness and affection are repressed and concealed while preoccupations drain off a great deal of emotional spontaneity.

In recent years, some attempts have been made to reexamine our thinking about phobias. Arieti[1] is of the opinion that phobias represent a general principle of psychopathology. He takes an existential point of view in speculating that human existence has become increasingly precarious and that man is constantly concerned with his fear of being in the world. Arieti suggests that concretization rather than displacement is the primary phobic mechanism. The concretization is an effort to symbolize experiences of profound anxiety. As an example, a sexual phobia may obscure the difficulty in sustaining loving relationships, a travel phobia may conceal a fear of venturing out into life, and so forth. In addition, he ascribes certain characteristics to phobias such as a "dehumanization of the emotional object, alteration of the emotional status, retention of active role and of reality test which can be correlated."

Salzman[15] believes that psychologically phobias and obsessions "are more closely related to one another than would appear to be the case in view of Freud's position." He reinforces Sullivan's theory by stating that they frequently develop around the need

---

*Avoidance operation refers to activities designed to avoid exposure to a dreaded situation or object.

to defend oneself against tender impulses or the potential threats against feelings of pride or self-esteem. He also points to the necessity for distinguishing phobic avoidance operations from ordinary avoidance tendencies. According to Salzman, it is the failure to separate ordinary avoidance reactions from genuine phobias which is responsible for the markedly discrepant reports of success or failure in treating them.

Another significant point of view has been expressed by Spiegel,[16] who has concerned herself with the vicissitudes of communication in various emotional disturbances. She has also called attention to a warp in the thought processes of obsessionals. Spiegel describes the intellectual thought disorder of obsessionals by stating, "The mesh of rationalization is often so firm and finely knit that it, surprisingly, often passes for genuine thought. The rationalization is actually comparable to a very mild delusional system with a faulty frame of reference." I would add to this that the faulty frame of reference is often to be found in the patient's familial pattern of thinking and frequently has its roots in the family dynamics.

Barnett[2] places disordered cognition as central in the obsessional style of life. He views this type of person as a decidedly ineffectual thinker who suffers from inferential distortions.

The classic distinction between phobias and obsessions on the basis of overt or covert anxiety has little meaning to me. Both reactions may be associated with morbid anxiety or the relative absence of it. The principle of displacement is not the specific property of phobic phenomena, nor is avoidance or manipulation of the environment an essential goal of people suffering from phobia. I agree with Arieti that phobias are concrete representations of more abstract anxiety-provoking situations and relationships. However, I consider the basic fears of the phobic person to be related to specific familial transactions. Accordingly, I do not accept the hypothesis that phobias are manifestations of the general psychopathological phenomenon of concretization. It is my opinion that phobias are similar to the night terrors experienced by troubled children who utilize such symbols as thunder, lightning, loud noise, bright light, unpleasant smells, etcetera, to refer to reactions to people they are afraid of. On the other hand, the symbols may refer to the network of confusing and threatening communicative messages within the family unit. It must be realized that these symbols are coded systems of communication representing disturbed interpersonal transactions. There is reason to believe that the symbols evoking terror in children are connected with powerful threats from the interpersonal environment. Freud showed us the way to appreciating the displacement of intense fear from a key person to a peripheral object. He demonstrated in his case history of Little Hans how the boy came to be afraid of a horse since he could not cope with his fear of his own father. However, Freud considered infantile sexuality and the Oedipus complex to be the basic dynamic factor involved. Today we assume that there are many additional factors which play an important part in the presumed shift from a person to a symbolic representation by an animal or an inanimate object. The displacement is not from the father to a horse or from the mother to a mushroom cloud. Rather, it is from a pathologically charged field of communication to animate or inanimate phobogenic object. The basic threat lies in the menacing nature of the informational message and the morbid atmosphere of the family which does not permit alleviation of the anxiety. For example, a child may have been subject to extreme stress and strain by the milieu of a destructive marriage, a profound family pathology or by the exposure to a psychotic parent. Parental wrath may become so charged with anxiety that it assumes an independent representation by the child in symbolic form. The situation may best be illustrated by the following example. I had an opportunity to interview the mother of a young patient who suffered from numerous phobias. It turned out that the mother had undergone a psychotic episode when the boy was less than one year old. During her acute disturbance the mother experienced powerful impulses to kill her child, drop it "accidentally" or harm it in some other fashion. The patient had numerous nightmares in his preschool and early school years which undoubtedly were connected with his mother's menacing behavior at an earlier time.

In classical concepts, the initial threat originates inside of the person because of instinctual demands which conflict with the reality situation. The result is a profound fear of punitive action if the underlying desire were to be pursued. Neoclassical concepts focus a great deal more on actual life experiences as the foundation for later difficulties. To my present way of thinking the phobic phenomenon is rooted in disturbed familial relations. The phobic symbol then becomes a metaphoric transposition of a morbid family atmosphere. The basic threat lies in the menacing nature of the informational message and the morbid atmosphere which does not permit alleviation of the anxiety.

Furthermore, there are indications that familial thought disorders have permeated the phobic person's thinking and have created disturbances in the realm of cognitive, perceptual and emotional processes. This particular formulation is similar to the concepts expressed by Spiegel and Barnett, except that I address myself directly to the origin of the thought disorder and trace it to particular family dynamics.

Other references appear in the literature which deal with the selection of phobic objects,[12] the phenomenological point of view,[5] the adaptational[13, 14] and behavioristic[19] concepts of phobias. The reader is referred to the above references for a more detailed exposition of these points of view.

In summing up the prevailing psychological thinking on phobias, I would like to add some additional thoughts. There has been a general shift in psychoanalytic thinking from focusing on intrapsychic processes to a transactional point of view. Even within the classic frame of reference the advent of egopsychology has placed greater emphasis on adaptational and environmental factors. However, traditional psychoanalysis has attempted to embrace the best of two possible good worlds by maintaining the libido theory while becoming increasingly more conscious of here-and-now phenomena. The result has been a peculiar hybrid with a biological determinism on the one hand and a milieu-oriented concern on the other hand. The egopsychology of Fairbairn, Melanie Klein, Schultz-Henke and others[3] has stressed the central position of the ego and frequently emphasized the principle of introjection. The last mentioned concept represents an internalized process of an adaptational nature. It refers to experiences with other people which have been incorporated by the person. For instance a child may have taken on a mother's punitive attitude as if it were her own characteristic pattern.

A similar point of view is expressed in Sullivan's interpersonal theory. However, additional elements are added here. They may be condensed for brevity's sake into four interpersonal postulates: the ecology, anxiety, similarity and tenderness principles.[4]

The ecology principle refers to the interdependency and interpenetration of the organism and environment. It postulates the necessity for a never-ending active interchange between the human organism and it is essential milieu. The storage capacity for specifically human characteristics is limited and isolation from a specifically human surrounding is tantamount to mental illness. The ecologic principle also uses the construct of a transactional field as a central frame of reference.

The anxiety principle according to Sullivan specifies anxiety as a predominantly social phenomenon which is related to the encounter with other people. It is largely governed by the approbation or the lack of it by key persons who played a major part in the upbringing of the individual.

The similarity principle refers to Sullivan's much quoted statement, "We are all very much more alike than we are different, whether we are mentally ill or well."[18]

The tenderness principle conceptualizes tenderness as a constructive, reciprocal mother-child transaction. It negates the instinctual aspects by focusing on the way a mother affects her child and vice versa.

The above constructs can be applied to the understanding of a variety of mental disorders. They represent certain fundamental conceptual postulates and must not be mistaken for everlasting truths about human nature. When applied to the phobic-obsessional disorders these basic interpersonal tenets lead to the following concept.

The ecology principle is closely related to focusing our therapeutic attention on family dynamics. The interdependency of the child and its familial environment are viewed as the arena in which the foundation for faulty thinking and warped communication is laid. We find here the early medium through which the larger world is interpreted. There is frequently a misuse of words in families producing obsessive-compulsive disorders. Words tend to conceal true feelings and to distort many events in these settings. Thus, simple communication is rare and the transmission of information is frequently faulty. We also find in the family a sensitive system with its own equilibrium which tends to create images of all family members depending on the solidity or disturbance of the system. In troubled families irrational fears impinge on some members of the unit depending on the overall constellation of the family, on the distortions which are transmitted and a host of other factors. The ecology principle points to multiple variables which contribute to the formation of a phobic-obsessive disorder.

Next we encounter the anxiety principle. Here we are dealing with a very early aspect of the mother-child relationship whereby a highly insecure mother who may have inadequate emotional support from her husband transmits her own lack of self-esteem to the growing infant. The mother may have been disadvantaged by her own parents, a sibling, spouse or other person and her "externally" induced anxiety then is passed on to the infant. Once anxiety is imprinted in the child it is there to stay as an ever-present factor of low self-esteem. The particular experience of anxiety distorts the child's self-image and its perception of other people which takes on a particular character in the obsessive-phobic difficulty.

In regard to the similarity principle, we tend to approach the patient through familiar channels of common human experiences rather than emphasizing the gulf between the patient's psychopathology and the therapist's alleged superior mental health.

The tenderness principle applies to the understanding of the early mother-child relationship with particular emphasis on the mother's capacity to respond to the child's expressed needs in an appropriate fashion.

In conclusion I want to reiterate that I consider the genesis of phobias to be usually traceable to the network of communicative channels reflecting the relationships within the nuclear family.

I tend to view phobias as communicative difficulties in the presence of disturbed cognitive, perceptual and emotional processes. It is my contention that phobias have their origin in particular forms of familial misintegration. Each individual family member constitutes a subsystem with its own components, devices, goals and activities which, in turn, is connected with the structure of the overall familial integration. This system has been referred to as *family dynamics* which, according to R. D. Laing,[11] is "the interexperience and interaction of people living together united by affinity and kinship."

It can be very helpful in the treatment of phobias to focus primary attention on the warped method of transmitting information to the phobic person. In many instances, neither the sender nor the receiver of the message has a workable key for decoding the nature of the communication.

CLINICAL ILLUSTRATIONS

The above described conceptualization of obsessive-phobic phenomena forms the basis for a therapeutic approach to these disorders. To illustrate the treatment aspect, I offer some clinical vignettes pertaining to the topic under discussion.

Case I

A young married woman who is endowed with unusually high intelligence and a most pleasing appearance suffered from a severe phobia which had numerous manifestations. Her mobility was extremely curtailed by her fear of leaving her house. In addition, she had a major travel phobia, could not spend any time away from her husband, and went into a state of panic when he had to be out of town even for a single night. On such occasions, she would hire a private nurse to spend the night with her. When she went to the theatre, she had to sit on an outside aisle near an emergency exit. She never permitted herself to go to a movie and took extreme precautions in all her activities.

Furthermore, she suffered from severe psychosomatic disorders and lived in constant fear of death. There was a distinct suspiciousness on her part in regard to all medications and to all medical doctors.

Her analysis was stormy but turned out to be successful in terms of her phobia. In the early part of treatment, she suffered an extreme degree of separation anxiety. She resented the analyst's absence, even for short periods of time and went into a decline when he went on a vacation. During his absence, she took to bed and did not once get up until he returned. A dream she had around that time illustrates her predicament by highlighting the extreme feeling of precariousness of her situation. She dreamt that she was on top of a high tower of a giant suspension bridge. There was a tentlike structure far up in the sky which was connected to the tower by a very narrow plank, and she required her husband's assistance to walk the "tightrope" back and forth between the tent and tower. The thought of having to make the crossing filled her with horror and panic.

The initial work consisted of reconstructing the family dynamics. It had been the patient's impression that she had been doted on by her family. She had always felt very close to her mother to whom she was very attached. There were numerous memories of sitting in mother's lap even as a teenager, having her hair stroked and being treated as mother's favorite child. The father was described as being extremely fond of her; he lived away from home for a year's time when the patient was five years old. His absence was explained as having been necessitated by the unavailability of a suitable job in the community where the family lived. She recalls having missed her father greatly during that time.

The patient is the youngest of three siblings. She was born when her sisters were ten and twelve years old respectively. There was a close bond between the patient and the middle sister, who was always in very poor health and eventually died after a chronic illness. She identified a great deal with her and frequently felt in a superstitious way that she was also destined to die prematurely. The older sister became a kind of assistant mother to the patient.

As the analysis progressed, the concept of the nature of the family constellation changed considerably. Mother emerged as a chronically unhappy woman who felt trapped in her marriage. The mother became increasingly bitter and toward the end of her life unmistakably paranoid. We learned that one sibling had died as an infant and that the mother had blamed the father for not taking appropriate action to save the child's life. From that time on the marriage deteriorated to a state of open hostility. There was also a state of constant warfare between the mother and the older sisters. Both girls were beautiful and had many suitors. Mother interfered with their romances and broke up one engagement after the other.

The patient had one previous marriage which ended in divorce. It never became quite clear why the marriage did not endure. What emerged, however, was the lack of an adequate motivation for having married in the first place.

In her early twenties, the patient spent a brief period away from home when she was relatively successful. However, she developed a major sexual phobia which broke up a promising relationship. Furthermore, she was extremely fearful of her health and suffered an episode of profound emotional and somatic disturbance prior to her second marriage.

Her second marriage encountered many difficulties; but in recent years has evolved as a basically sound relationship. In the early years of her second marriage the husband mothered her a great deal which evoked negativistic and outright hostile feelings on the patient's part.

As the analysis progressed, we observed a major change in her attitude toward her parents. She had a dream in which the mother and father were both trying to kill her. Another time she dreamt that her mother was psychotic, and at a later point the father appeared in her dream as a dilapidated alcoholic who pleaded with her to be his sexual partner. About this time she came to feel much closer to the middle sister but had many anxiety dreams in which she suffered the sister's fate and died of consumption. Her attitude toward the older sister became more hostile.

Another crisis occurred when her husband became ill and required hospitalization; this forced her to stay by herself over a fairly long period of time.

The therapeutic relationship evolved into a situation of increasing trust. However, there were recurrent periods of severe doubt when she felt I had basically misled her and had failed to appreciate her genuine needs. These episodes were usually of short duration.

In the meantime, her freedom of movement has increased greatly. She is able to travel with a minimum of fear, and she has stayed by herself for long stretches of time without undue anxiety. It can be said that for all practical purposes, her phobia no longer exists; but she still has her share of difficulties in sustaining a close relationship. Nevertheless, the outlook is bright, and her overall state of well-being is remarkably good. There have been no recurrences of her frequent somatic episodes which paralyzed her and made her bedridden for considerable periods of time.

COMMENTS. In reviewing this sketchy history, it should be clear that the patient's self-image and her role concept within her family were quite faulty. She saw herself as everybody's darling who had been particularly doted on by the mother. There was almost no awareness on her part of her morbid dependency on the mother. She did not appreciate the intense hostility between her parents which occasionally spilled over and made her the target of their violent impulses. While she was able to observe the mother's malice toward her sisters, she felt falsely immune to it. She came to realize that the middle sister died not only as a result of tuberculosis but just as much as a result of deadly familial interferences. Her fear of the oldest sister was an element she was slow to realize. The father's emotional and erotic involvement with her was illustrated by several events in recent years. Also, the mother's profound mental disturbance was not recognized by her until the time of the mother's death. Soon after she was able to reconstruct past experiences which indicated outright paranoid ideation on the mother's part, as well as direct physical threats against the patient. She recalled an episode where the mother displayed a murderous rage towards her when she was a young child.

In reviewing the salient factors in this phobic patient's life, I would like to stress the following points:

The patient grew up in a family atmosphere in which she experienced herself as the favorite child. She had no awareness of the deep-seated difficulties between her parents, the mother's discontent and suspiciousness, the father's instability and erotic preoccupation with her. Her own morbid dependency on her highly suspicious mother obscured an appreciation of the mother's violent anger. Furthemore, she was used by both parents in a destructive way as an object to divert attention from their own misery. Her alliance with the middle sister made her fear that she would suffer the sister's unfortunate fate. There was not one reliable ally in her early life. Her actual environment was filled with numerous threatening undercurrents which for the better part were carefully camouflaged. The phobias then seem to be a response to the inherent dangers in the family situation. What confronted the patient was a wall of misrepresentations and warped communications. She reacted to the situation as it actually was rather than to an inner impulse, relatively independent of her environment. Freud was disappointed when he realized that some of his patients had fabricated early traumatic situations. In our situation the opposite was true. The patient had great difficulty in recognizing the realistic basis for her seemingly irrational fears. She was largely unaware of the great hostility between her parents, the disturbance between the mother and her siblings as well as the father's maladjustments. She did not appreciate the faulty, familial network of communication and the resulting perceptual distortions on her part.

Case II

This patient is a pleasant young mother with two small children. She had been plagued by morbid fascinations of a highly disturbing nature. When alone with her children, she would suffer from agonizing obsessive thoughts which tended to increase in severity. For instance, her gaze would become fixed on the edge of a knife while she was cutting potatoes, and she would then experience an almost overwhelming urge to grab the knife and stab her children. It required every ounce of strength in her possession to resist the destructive impulse, and she would become exhausted from the effort.

Another problem consisted of an irresistible urge to read about crimes in the newspaper with the resulting compulsion to repeat the crime or place herself in the role of the victim. At such times she had to overcome the impulse to take a pair of scissors and stab herself in the throat. She became a self-imposed prisoner in her own home. Her phobia reached such severe proportions that she could leave the house only if accompanied by her husband or one of her sisters. In addition, she developed a claustrophobia; this prevented her from attending church which, in the past, had given her a feeling of solace. Neither could she attend social functions of any kind or visit with friends or relatives. It became necessary for her husband to bring her to my office for each visit.

She was one of four sisters, all of whom were victims of phobic-obsessive reactions. It was a case of *folie a quatre*. Her oldest sister was the most phobic of the quartet; she was also possessed by an obsessive-compulsive mania. She insisted that her husband remove his shoes before entering the house; so also her two preteenage children. Her house was kept similar to the way in which a sterile operating room should be maintained. Everyone in the household was subjected to the most irrational cleansing rituals. It should be noted that this sister eventually developed an ulcerative colitis and died in an overtly paranoid state. The two younger sisters had severe phobic-obsessive difficulties. All four sisters were married and lived in close proximity to each other in a small suburban community where they had been raised.

The patient was seen in psychotherapy on a once a week basis for a period of about eight years. At present, she is still maintaining contact with me, averaging two to four visits per year.

She developed a childlike, dependent relationship with the therapist. There was a magical form of transference improvement in the beginning. I realized that I was dealing with a borderline psychotic state; but there was never evidence of decompensation on the patient's part. Her most severe symptoms subsided in a very short period of time, while her phobic symptoms remained relatively intact.

The first phase of therapy consisted of a variety of explanatory comments pointing to the concentration camp atmosphere in which the girls had been raised. We were able to understand her repressed hateful impulses based on the constant fear of reprisal and brutal abuse. The fatherless home, with an intimidated widowed mother, necessitated the oldest sister's maternal role; it also explained the closeness between the sisters and the symbiotic ties to the oldest one. Another fact emerged as time went on. The oldest sister had been placed in the position of the protecting, maternal wing; she had also assumed the role of scapegoat, who was often beaten for minor misdeeds of her sisters. The three younger girls worshipped the oldest one, and she became increasingly suspicious, for understandable reasons. However, her emerging paranoid ideation penetrated the thoughts of her siblings. The closest tie existed between my patient and the most severely traumatized oldest sister. We had to work through a morbid empathy which made her see the world through her sister's eyes. Progress in this respect was relatively slow. There was a temporary setback when the sister died. The patient had a difficult time separating her own feelings and thoughts from her powerful ally in childhood and her unwitting tormentor in adult life.

The final phase in treatment centered around the patient's dependent relationship upon her husband. Many of her ties to her sister had found their way into this relationship. She harbored numerous resentments toward her husband, who had become "her eyes and ears" in regard to the outside world. It is of interest that the husband became markedly disturbed when the patient loosened her symbiotic ties to him. He began to drink heavily and came close to assuming the uncle's role. The situation has been resolved reasonably well. There is no longer evidence of the original morbid obsessions; her phobia has subsided, and the only remnants of her emotional difficulties are brief periods of moderate depression.

COMMENTS. A review of the therapeutic process indicates that the initial task consisted of establishing a mode of communication which bypassed or transcended her anxiety-fraught preoccupations. It became necessary to link her morbid ideation, her obsessions and phobias, to environmental, familial events. I did not hesitate to point out behavioral and attitudinal patterns within the framework of the familial situation. The husband was invited to participate in several sessions, as were the patient's sisters and some of their respective husbands. We were able to pool information with her siblings and learn a great deal more about the mother and her relationship to the uncle, as well as about the more durable alliances in the family unit.

Case III

The patient is a young single woman who embarked on a successful career immediately after leaving college. She entered analysis in a state of profound depression. There was evidence of marked obsessive doubting which reached a state of outright confusion. The patient had resigned from her job and could not make a decision about choosing one boyfriend or another. Her plans were to get away from it all and travel around the world.

The patient had had a sheltered childhood and was considered to have been a beautiful and highly intelligent youngster. She was never really denied anything by her mother, who centered her life around her and called her "Princess."

At the time of puberty, the patient developed an acute school phobia which kept her at home for a period of many months. She had always been an outstanding pupil and could not explain her phobia about attending school. Combined with this, she developed several other phobic reactions. For instance, she insisted that all venetian blinds in the house be closed so that nobody could look inside. Furthermore, she would lie flat on the floor of the car when she went out with her family. Her fear was that people would see her; but she could not explain why

she thought that people should not see her. She recalled a recurrent nightmare which she had at that time in her life. It
consisted of the appearance of a withered, clawlike hand with
very long, sharp fingernails. There was something infrahuman
about this hand which caused eerie sensations. It is interesting
to note that her well-to-do family did not see to it that she
received professional help at the time of her severe disturbance.
Eventually, her symptoms subsided and the patient went back
to school.

There is still today an air of unreality about this episode which
has never been clearly understood by the patient. She has many
rationalizations in retrospect; but there is a basically ego-alien
quality to her phobic reaction. A fugue-like character is present
in the quality of the psychopathological phenomena which occurred at the threshold of adolescence.

The patient is a highly competent person with a tendency
toward fragmentization. Many of her emotions and thoughts
are relegated to compartments without the existence of an obvious nexus. She gives the appearance of an independent person
which, on closer inspection, proves to be a faulty impression.
Her family ties are deep and complicated.

There is one older sister who always had an alliance with the
father, while the patient was overly involved with her mother.
The parents have never been very happy with each other; the
mother confided in the patient on many occasions that she lived
exclusively for her two children. It became clear to the patient,
however, that mother had eyes only for her and treated her the
way a lover would behave toward his love object. There were
constant clashes between the patient and her father over financial
matters, attitudes toward way of dressing, behaving, etcetera.
These were undoubtedly fostered by the mother, wittingly or
unwittingly. As far as she was concerned, the patient could do
no wrong. Father tended to be cautious about money, and
mother would deceive him about the sums she spent on her
daughter. They would secretely take taxis together without letting
father find out or buy expensive clothing for the patient and
make it appear as if little money had been spent for the dresses.

Mother had made it known to her daughter that she did not have respect for the father, who was highly dependent on the mother. In addition, the mother was very close to her own mother, who lived in the same household with them during the patient's childhood. The grandmother was a domineering woman who did not get along with the patient's father. She was a most distrustful woman, with numerous superstitions and prejudices.

The patient's sister married at an early age in order to get away from home; the patient remained single until her middle thirties, in spite of frequent marital proposals. She had a phobic attitude toward marriage and had a great deal of difficulty in sustained contact in love relationships. There is an almost total absence of personal rapport between the patient and her sister.

In the analytic situation, the patient found it difficult to be productive or relate in a personal manner. There was also a considerable degree of passivity which constituted a formidable resistance.

It was in connection with the analysis that some tension developed between mother and daughter. The mother overstepped her boundaries and had her first major fight with the patient. Shortly after this upsetting encounter, the patient had a revealing dream.

The main character in the dream was a woman who had been a neighbor when the patient was growing up. This woman had a flower garden which she guarded jealously. One day the patient, at the age of five, went over and picked one little flower, whereupon the woman turned into a witchlike creature who displayed a rage of probably psychotic proportions. The incident frightened the patient to the extent that she could still recall the details of the episode as an adult. In the dream, Mrs. Brown (the neighbor) appeared, her face contorted with rage, and she shouted very unpleasant things at the patient.

Her association to the dream was to link Mrs. Brown and her mother. It came as a genuine surprise to her that her mother was capable of being irrationally angry. There is little doubt that she must have encountered mother's uncontrolled rage as a child; however, she had pushed this memory out of her awareness. She had seen mother become very angry at father but had not re-called having been the target of mother's wrath in the past.

COMMENTS. The above-described patient had a major phobic reaction during her early adolescence. In adult life, she was relatively symptom free in terms of phobia, but she suffered from a severe obsessive neurosis. She did not receive any kind of treatment for her phobia. It stands to reason that every therapist, regardless of his school of thought, would have claimed success in treatment (if the patient had gone to see such a person). Be that as it may, there is no doubt about the severity of her obsessional disorder. Treatment is still in progress; the results up to this time are somewhat disappointing. There is a deeply entrenched schizoid core which has combined with the obsessional dynamism and resisted a major breakthrough thus far.

SUMMARY

In this chapter phobias have been presented as thought disorders which are closely related to obsessional states. It was suggested that phobias and obsessions be viewed as one clinical entity rather than two separate conditions. Subsequently, the obsessive-phobic syndrome was discussed in terms of (a) its interpersonal misperceptions, (b) its communicative malfunctioning and (c) its informational distortions. The underlying obsessive-phobic thought disorders were traced to the maladaptation and malfunctioning of the nuclear family unit.

Particular emphasis was placed on the warping of the self-image as well as on the inaccurate evaluation of how the obsessive-phobic person is seen by other people.

Phobias and obsessions were viewed as a particular lack of basic trust with a corresponding conflict as to whether the most significant person in one's life is friend or foe. As part of the chronic doubting and ambivalence, phobic-obsessional people distrust spontaneous feelings of tenderness in themselves and others. They are easily prey to malevolent transformation which represents a defensively hostile reaction to feelings of affection and intimacy. Another interpersonal characteristic of this disorder is a masking and denial of a highly dependent way of relating to other people.

Impairments in the process of communication and cognition were pointed out resulting from faulty communicative channels in the initial, familial setting. The difficulties pertain both to the way in which messages are communicated as well as to the content of the message. Accordingly, obsessive-phobic thought disorders are related to miscarriages in familial communication.

Some obsessive-phobic manifestations are discussed with particular reference to faulty information about family relations in the initial recollection of early life experiences. The presence of realistic danger in the past is pointed out which is not recognized in the patient's awareness.

In the discussion of treatment, reference was made to Freud's famous case of Little Hans. It was pointed out that Freud did not consider the subsequent divorce of the boy's parents as a significant factor in the dynamics of the child's phobia. Our present frame of reference emphasizes the disturbed, marital relationship as a key element in the formation of the boy's irrational fear. Today there is less stress on the intrapsychic, Oedipal conflict as the central, neurotic disturbance compared to the reactive, adaptational manifestations within the malfunctioning of the familial unit. Therapy focuses more specifically on the family network of communication and the resulting warpings in perception. The therapeutic task includes an appreciation of the underlying thought disorder with its concomitant relational, cognitive and emotional distortions. A thorough reevaluation of the explicit and implicit roles within the family unit is also necessary in order to understand potential miscommunications and misperceptions among the family members. Many reality factors are stressed which may account for certain deviations in thought, attitude and behavior.

Three clinical illustrations were offered which were designed to highlight various aspects of treating phobias. In all instances, an effort was made to place the family dynamics in the center of the therapeutic approach. An attempt was made to decode the complex symbolic messages in terms of familial experiences.

The problem of dependency came in for its share of attention. Much time was devoted to exploring the nature of communicative patterns in the analytic situation as well as in daily life. Under certain circumstances, relatives, friends and other persons of significance were invited to meet jointly with the patient and analyst. It was found that once the phobia yielded to therapeutic intervention, other personality difficulties came to the fore. One case was reported in which there was a spontaneous recovery from a severe phobic reaction in adolescence, with the emergence of a pronounced obsessional disorder.

REFERENCES

1. Arieti, S.: A re-examination of the phobic symptom and of symbolism in psychopathology. *Am J Psychiatry, 2:*118, 1961.
2. Barnett, J.: On cognitive disorders in the obsessional. *Contemporary Psychoanalysis, 2:*2, 1966.
3. Chrzanowski, G.: The independent roots of ego psychology and their therapeutic implications. In *Science and Psychoanalysis,* edited by J. Masserman. New York, Grune & Stratton, 1967, vol. XI.
4. Chrzanowski, G.: The utilization of family dynamics in individual analytic treatment. (In press)
5. Frankl, V.: *Theorie und therapie der neurosen.* Wien: Urban und Schwarzenberg, 1956.
6. Freud, S.: Analysis of a phobia in a five-year-old boy. *Collected Papers.* London, Hogarth Press, 1953, vol. III.
7. Freud, S.: A case of obsessional neurosis. *Collected Papers.* London, Hogarth Press, 1953, vol. III, p. 357.
8. Freud, S.: Obsessions and phobias: Psychical mechanisms and their etiology. *Collected Papers.* London, Hogarth Press, 1953, vol. I.
9. Freud, S.: Obsessions and phobias: Their psychical mechanism and their etiology. *The Standard Edition of the Complete Psychological Works of Freud.* London, Hogarth Press, 1962, vol. III.
10. Freud, S.: The unconscious. *Collected Papers.* London, Hogarth Press, 1953, vol. IV.
11. Laing, R. D.: Family and individual structure. In *The Predicament of the Family,* edited by Peter Lomas. New York, International Press, 1967.
12. Lief, H.: Sensory association in the selection of phobic objects. *Psychiatry, 4:*18, 1955.
13. Ovesey, L.: The phobic reaction, a psychodynamic basis for classification and treatment. In *Developments in Psychoanalysis at Columbia Univer-*

sity, edited by Goldman and Shapiro. New York, Hafner Publishing Co., 1966.

14. Rado, S.: Achieving self-reliant treatment behavior: Therapeutic motivations and therapeutic techniques. In *Science and Psychoanalysis,* edited by J. Masserman. New York, Grune & Stratton, 1960, vol. III.

15. Salzman, L.: Obsessions and phobias. *Contemporary Psychoanalysis, 1:* 2, 1965.

16. Spiegel, Rose: Specific problems of communication in psychiatric conditions. In *American Handbook of Psychiatry,* edited by S. Arieti. New York, Basic Books, 1959.

17. Sullivan, H. S.: Anxiety in everyday life and in psychiatry. *Psychiatry,* 1950.

18. Sullivan, H. S.: *Conceptions of Modern Psychiatry.* New York, W. W. Norton, 1953.

19. Wolpe, J.: *Psychotherapy by Reciprocal Inhibition.* Stanford (Cal.), Stanford University Press, 1958.

20. Zilboorg, Gregory: *A History of Medical Psychology.* New York, W. W. Norton, 1941.

Chapter 4

Psychotherapy with Obsessive-Compulsive Patients

ROSE SPIEGEL

THEORETICAL CONSIDERATIONS RELEVANT TO PSYCHOTHERAPY

MOST OF US have obsessional traits and lead an obsessional way of life; we are preoccupied with clock time and with problems of order and orderliness in our paper subculture. In a sublimated way, obsessional values are part of our middle-class social character. At their best, the operation of these values gets things done, particularly the routine ones, makes the world move more smoothly—so to speak, the trains run on time.

We need to understand the normal functioning on which obsessionalism is based in order to begin to understand its miscarriage in the clinical syndromes. We need to understand the traps we fall into with obsessional patients, often out of our own obsessionalism. We need to recognize banal, acceptable forms of these syndromes that yet are extremely powerful, for instance in the patient's family. These everyday aspects of obsessionalism, often ignored, should be added to our concern with the more severe and even bizarre, obsessional symptomatology.

Not surprisingly, it was the bizarre extremes of obsessive-compulsive functioning that captured the attention of the early psychiatrists, whose descriptions go back as far as 1840. A most telling and concise account is this one given in 1884—pre-psychoanalysis—by Ribot,[17] the French psychiatrist:

> ... In works of insanity we find recorded many instances of persons who, tormented by the impulse to kill those who are dear to them, take refuge in asylums, becoming voluntary prisoners.
>
> The irresistible though conscious impulse to steal, to set fire to houses, to commit suicide by alcoholic excess, belongs in the same category. ...

The transition from the sane state to these pathologic forms is almost imperceptible. Persons that are perfectly rational experience insane impulses, but these sudden and unwanted states of consciousness are without effect, do not pass into acts, being suppressed by opposite forces, by dominant mental habit.

. . . Or again, a person is given to acts that though not seriously compromising are nevertheless mischievous. . . .

Sometimes fixed ideas of a character frivolous or unreasonable find lodgment in the mind, which though it deems them absurd, is powerless to prevent them from passing into acts. . . .

These disorders were placed under the rubric "diseases of the will" and, in distinction to psychotic confusion, were also designated as *folie lucide.* The feeling of being taken over by a force from within regardless of one's consciously approving will is typically the characteristic of obsessive-compulsive patients, but does not apply to the entire range of syndromes. The concept of will and willfulness is not identical with that of ego support (a theme evocative of modern views on will—Rankian and existentialist).

An Overview of Obsessionalism

As Rado[15] pointed out, Freud's term "zwang" was translated as "obsession" in London and "compulsion" in New York. However, "compulsion" lends itself more in application to irresistibly driven behavior with some quality of impulsivity and "obsession" for preoccupation with thoughts and feelings and even for the performance of private rituals. It is as though *compulsion* has the quality of physical force.*

The presenting and most tangible operation in obsessional states is overpersistence in behavior, thinking or feeling or the impulse to take an action; even obsessional vacillation is persistent—experienced as subjugation to the superimposed will. However, in some individuals whom we designate as obsessional, the persistence (and/or meticulousness, frugality) has the full sanc-

---

*The writer, in general, uses "obsessionalism" to signify "obsessional states" (Sullivan's term), "obsession" for the particular pattern and "compulsive" for the drive to an action.

tion of the ego, regardless of whether they feel themselves helpless or powerful.

More subtle and characteristic presenting cognitive operations
are overconcentration with a narrowed range of thought, association and imagery with elimination of everything but what is being
focused on, including the alternation of doubt. The alternations
in behavior may be the well-known doing and undoing, as in the
case of Freud's "Ratman,"[5] who felt compelled first to remove a
stone from the road lest it hurt the lady and then to replace it,
so that "her carriage might come to grief against it."

The extreme tidiness or orderliness and the fussiness with details, familiar expressions of obsessionalism, often are at the cost
of loss of the larger context. In Rorschach terms, the d's and dd's
(details and minutiae respectively of blot figures) are seen, but
not the W's (the blot in its entirety) and often not any M's (movement perceptions). In interpersonal communication we often
experience as obsessional the hammering away at a point, with
a struggle to control the situation, to win, or the compulsive talker,
who cannot let go of talking even at the appeal of another. The
general personality quality may come across of someone on an
inner treadmill, lacking spontaneity, plasticity and the freedom
to change.

We are accustomed to thinking of obsessional patients as "the"
obsessional character or "the" obsessional personality. This is
far too simplistic. It is more accurate to think of obsessional *characteristics* which may occur in a wide range of personality con-
figurations and psychopathology, from a richness transcending
the obsessionalism to engulfment by that condition entirely within
the terms of an approved social character. Besides the clinical
conditions in which it dominates, obsessionalism may be involved
in other psychopathologic conditions—depression, schizophrenia,
addictions, the paranoid delusions, the compulsive eating of
obesity or the compulsive denial of eating in anorexia nervosa.
Obsessionalism is intimately connected to phobias, both in their
similar tenacity and in the setting up of counterphobic rituals.
There are modes in which obsessionalism operates as an effective
adaptation, as life style, even with sublimation into devoted ser-

vice to a cause. It is recognizable culturally in some of the demands made on us for performance, whether in work, play or ritual.

Basic Obsessionalism

It is suggested that obsessionalism as psychopathology has its origin in a normal prototype, that it is a miscarriage of a normal capacity. The basic functioning is manifest in the tenacity and concentration that characterize the drive for mastery and accomplishment, epitomized by the child's struggle to walk in spite of repeated falls. It is involved both in self-assertiveness and in the normal aggressivity that enter into holding one's own vis-a-vis the human and nonhuman environment or of more aggressively imposing one's will on it. There is an early suggestion of this in the game of the baby who repeatedly throws out toys for the adult to retrieve. Classically, the burgeoning of obsessionalism is placed later in early childhood, at the time of toilet training and the so-called anal-erotic phase. However, the salient fact is that this is the age at which the young child can implement his will with physical as well as psychologic resources in an attempt to individuate from his mother.

Intrapsychically, as an ongoing mode of functioning beyond childhood, basic obsessionalism operates in the effort not to forget by means of an inner holding on in the mind—repeating to oneself an idea, goal, feeling. This holding on may involve a pleasant feeling, such as a glow of accomplishment. Often it is to "unfinished business," a problem still unsolved or something immediate to be done or not forgotten, which intrudes on sleep until closure is secured. Release from this holding on may be obtained by writing out the memorandum as external reminder. However, when the achievement cannot keep pace with the aspiration, the list-making itself becomes an obsessional self-harassment. (Compulsive list-making in order not to "forget" is a symptom long familiar to physicians of hypochondriacal patients.) There is no area of experience with which obsessional concern may not be involved as a drive to problem-solving. In the field of ideas, the problem-solving preoccupation may continue into sleep and be rewarded by resolution, perhaps even by creativity.

The imposition of order belongs to the realm of normal obsessionalism. Freud, in "Civilization and Its Discontents,"[7] describes the quest for order as

> . . . a kind of repetition-compulsion by which it is ordained once for all when, where, and how a thing shall be done so that on every similar occasion doubt and hesitation shall be avoided. The benefits of order are incontestable: it enables us to use space and time to the best advantage, while saving expenditure of mental energy.

We can discern here, in the quest for order, the basis for habit formation, related to the normal, basic obsessionalism. Control and orderliness of course involve time. There may be pleasure in the correlation between acomplishment and time, as a skill in itself, a game with time. In psychopathologic obsessionalism the race with time is carried to tension and unresolved anxiety often to a freezing, a stalling of action.

Normal obsessionalism, as persistence until something is completed—as pressure for problem-solving, routinization, orderliness—involves processes that enter into the usual meaning of work. The closure by achievement reenforces the sense of self and releases the tension of the drive to perform. In such respects, the normal prototypic obsessionalism is related to the ego functioning of mastery and the development of skills. It offers a refuge from painful emotion; one can get lost in the routine, in the effort and concentration demanded by work; one can get reassurance from the order of one's life and from a sense of accomplishment. These routines, as in work, can provide a kind of meaningful ritual. Intrapsychically, this obsessional drive to escape painful emotions forms the basis for the psychopathologic use of obsessionalism as an inadequately functioning substitute that does not achieve its goal.

A whole important area exists in which ritual and normal obsessionalism are linked through symbolism. Susanne K. Langer,[14] in *Philosophy in a New Key*, discusses ritual from the standpoint of symbolism and its meaning, but it seems to me, she depicts the normal obsessionalism in her concept of man's need to superimpose order over chaos.

This presentation of the normal prototype for obsessionalism attempts to point out the basic functions in their own right and to indicate where their miscarriage enters into psychopathology. It is hoped that this may help in the understanding and greater ease in the actual therapy of patients who are often experienced as resistant.

Evolution of Psychoanalytic Theories on Obsessionalism

One's working hypothesis for the psychogenesis of obsessionalism may predispose the therapist to limit therapy to the terms of that hypothesis. A review of the milestones in theory should cast light on both the contribution and the limitations of their correlated therapeutic approaches.

The psychoanalytic era immediately introduced dimensions beyond the surface phenomena accurately described clinically and opened the door to far subtler observation. Freud's 1895 paper,[8] entitled "Obsessions and Phobias: Their Psychical Mechanisms and Their Aetiology," is the entering wedge in this subject. Though there was still the simplistic one-to-one equating of disorder with symptom, the paper established that the obsessional symptom is a substitution for an "original" idea and that the substitution itself prevents release of the original associated emotion. The "original" idea of the obsession was some fairly recent, fortuitous, sexually significant experience, and "cure" was obtained by "reinstatement" of the "original" idea and its affect. In connection with phobias, an independent syndrome—obsessional ideas and practices—served to defend against the phobic anxiety. Freud's enthusiastic efforts to "cure" obsessions by ascertaining the presumed sexual "original" idea which was being "substituted" were not effective in the long run and many years later, with broader conceptions of obsessionalism and therapy, Freud became pessimistic about the effectiveness of psychoanalysis as therapy for obsessional conditions. However, the idea of substitution and also of defense against phobic anxiety has stood the test of time.

In 1907, in "Obsessive Acts and Religion,"[9] Freud declared that both obsessional and religious ceremonials share in the objective of the warding off of fears, anxieties and guilt feelings, which in the obsessional are sexually based, whereas in religion they are based on destructive egoistic drives. Obsessional ritual, he said, is private and on the surface seems silly and devoid of meaning, whereas religious ceremonial is public and communal with rich and explicit symbolic meaning. Obsessive acts "serve important interests of the personality and . . . they give expression both to persisting impressions of previous experience and to thoughts about them which are strongly charged with affect. This they do in two ways, either by direct or by symbolic representation, so that they are to be interpreted either historically or symbolically." Freud maintained his original view that the obsessive act is based on sexual experiences. For both obsessional and religious ceremonials Freud's attribution of purpose is to the warding off of guilt feelings and not to the expression of normal symbolization in rituals, as in Langer's discussion. Regardless of this issue or even of the therapeutic merit of this theory, in this paper Freud added another dimension, that of *meaning,* to a symptom pattern and correlated it to broader aspects of living.

In 1908, in "Character and Anal Eroticism,"[6] Freud took the first step toward understanding the obsessional personality as well as character in general. Cleanliness or orderliness, parsimoniousness and obstinacy, which have become the classical triad of the obsessional character, were linked to the presumed fixation of the libido to the anal-erotic level of development. That is, because of their rectal pleasure in retention and defiance of toilet training, Freud inferred that in these children (and adults) there is an innate constitutional predisposition to a heightened erotogenic significance of the anal zone, which is submerged in the later sublimatory triad of traits. Further he believes that reaction formation, such as generosity or overcompliance, depends on whether the "instinctual" expression or the countermanding force prevails.

Important though this paper is historically, the concept of anal-erotism, particularly in connection with obsessionalism, is dis-

puted. Its acceptance or challenge and rejection is a good indicator of a basic difference in orientation to the therapy of patients
with this condition.

In his long and labyrinthine paper of 1909, "A Case of Obsessional Neurosis,"[5] Freud gave a superb account of the psychoanalysis of a young man suffering from an extremely distressing
obsessional neurosis, which included the preoccupation with cutting his throat with a razor, a neurosis which had been precipitated
by some highly emotional encounters with his sadistic army cap-
tain. Interestingly, the patient had suffered from a prototype
episode of obsessional preoccupation at age seven, consisting of
guilty erotic wishes which had actually been provoked by his
seductive young governess; fear that he might have betrayed
these wishes to his parents and that they were reading his mind;
fear that some disaster would occur because of these wishes—
namely, his father would die. Protective measures against these
preoccupations and wishes developed, which made for later episodes of variants in obsessionalism.

The interesting theoretical points that Freud made on the basis
of this case gave more meaning and function to the symptomatology with implications for directions in therapy. Indeed, Freud
considered that this young man had been restored to mental
health. The footnote adds a timeless lament: "Like too many other
young men of value and promise, he perished in the Great War."

To summarize the points he made in this paper: Freud compared the overt obsessional content with the manifest content of
dreams and suggested a similar approach to interpretation. With
modifications based on different approaches to dream interpretation this is often helpful therapeutic strategy. Freud stressed that
obsessionalism involves unresolved unconscious conflict between
love and hate—that is, ambivalence, which with this young man
involved his father and also the lady he admired. The concept
of ambivalence is a revealing descriptive term, but in the writer's
experience is not of itself reward in therapy unless its basis interpersonally is explored.

Freud's remarks on the cognitive processes in the obsessional
combined what was already known with fresh observation and

ideas of his own. He said, "The capacity for being illogical never fails to bewilder one in such highly intelligent people as obsessional neurotics." He noted the vacillation between superstition and enlightened thinking, that the former (later designated as "magical thinking") is sophisticated, taking the form of a belief in one's own dreams, hunches and intuitions as prophetic. This he considered as compensatory to the severance of causal connections between ideas and affect, particularly by displacement. The sense of the obsessional that his wishes, especially the hostile ones, can simply by their force be actualized (that is, the "omnipotence of wishes"), Freud considered a persistence of the childhood sense of omnipotence. There are, however, some analysts, including the writer, who believe that the child's sense of omnipotence is compensatory for his basic feeling of insecurity and is also partly attributable to the exaggerated response, often punishment, evoked by his behavior.

The function of the obsessional doubting, Freud said in this paper, is to render the person out of touch with reality in order to avoid a decision. His young man avoided any knowledge that would help him resolve his conflict about marriage to the lady or the lovely rich girl his mother had picked for him; what was particularly confusing to him and added to the indecision, was that his father had made the latter type of choice in his own marriage. Preoccupation with death was considered by Freud to be another device for avoidance of solution of conflict and of making decisions, covertly, death was to be the solution. By these devices, the obsessional remains incapable of coming to a decision, especially in matters of love.

Freud's next paper on obsessionalism, in 1913, entitled "The Predisposition to Obsessional Neurosis,"[10] develops the theme of the "option" of the neurosis. Freud arrived at the position that the option of the neurosis is basically derived from "the nature of dispositions" rather than from "experiences that operate pathogenically" and that these dispositions are manifest in "disturbances of development. . . . The question of what factors produce such disturbances of development . . . we must leave" to biological research. The constitutional basis here suggested introduces a climate of therapeutic pessimism. Clearly at this point the psychoanalytic schools which place far more emphasis on life experience in the shaping of personality and its disorders move away from the Freudian approach.

Freud in this paper reiterates that obsessional neurosis is based on "sadistic anal-erotism" and that in bouts of recurrent obsessionalism, regression occurs to this point in libido development.

A helpful clinical distinction is made between character development and the mechanism in neurosis—in the former, the repressed impulses are replaced by reaction formations and sublimations; in the latter, there is "miscarriage of repression and the return of the repressed." This distinction implies an explanation for the unruffled quality in the person with the obsessional character in contrast to the unease in the person with the neurosis.

A notable contribution was made by Karl Abraham within the framework of Freudian theory of libido development. He gave a rich clinical picture of obsessional questioning in his paper of 1913 on transformations of scoptophilia.[1] He wrote extensively on the symbolic meaning of obsessional rituals. In his 1924 paper, "A Short Study of the Development of the Libido, Viewed in the Light of Mental Disorders,"[2] he demonstrated a clinical relationship between manic-depressive states, melancholia and obsessional neurosis. He drew obsessionalism and melancholia together as related to stages of anal-erotism. A particularly meaningful point directly relevant to therapy is Abraham's interpretation that in melancholia the patient is undergoing the experience of loss of the love-object, while in obsessionalism the person is holding on tenaciously to the love-object in the face of the threatened disappearance. Abraham considered the obsessional quality that patients with melancholia have to be a manifestation of the ambivalence, the love and hate toward the lost "love" object that characterizes them.

The concept of "cure" had changed from symptom removal in the early days of psychoanalysis to the recall of infantile repression of sexuality, coupled with "insight" and symbolic interpretation, still in Freudian terms. In spite of Freudian formulations of obsessional character and obsessional neurosis in terms of sexual symbolism, classical analysis of such patients, did not achieve satisfactory results, as their therapy became obsessionally prolonged and slow moving.

A new approach to the psychoanalytic therapy of obsessional conditions—still within the framework of the libido theory—was introduced by Wilhelm Reich. In 1933, in his book *Character Analysis*, Reich[16] presented his concept of character, resistance analysis and orgone therapy, of which the first two are within the scope of this discussion. Rather than Freud's stress on dissociation of affect from a related idea, Reich emphasized flattening of affect, "affect-block," from a more holistic view of personality. He interpreted the flattening to a persistence of extreme self-control from the time of toilet training, and appearing like the "good adjustment" that is socially acceptable. This control, he stated, is actually a repression of aggression and is manifest in analysis as a kind of resistance which is expressed somatically in "chronic hypertonia" of the muscles. The repression, resistance and hypertonia are components of what Reich termed "character armor." He pointed out the futility of holding the compulsive to the primary rule of free association and of offering him early interpretations, which, he held, accounted for the admittedly poor results of Freudian analysis of these patients. Instead of avoiding the resistance, he "analyzed the resistance" by means of tackling the affect-block.

His analysis of resistance involved the therapeutic strategy of focusing during sessions on verbal, tonal or bodily modes of the patient's expression. In one example, he drew the patient's attention to the defensiveness in his supercilious smile and his ridicule of the analyst and worked through to his recall of the early events from which his style of expression was derived. Indicative of the intensity of the resistance to free association was the patient's reluctance to associate to his dream.

An interesting theoretical point that Reich made was that in the Freudian style of analysis, the ambivalence was not mastered and was therefore wrongly interpreted as biological instead of the outcome of experience.

In an article, "Obsessive Behavior," Sandor Rado[15] presented his experience and interpretation in terms of his adaptational theory. From the cluster of elements in Freud's concept of obsessional character and anal-erotism, Rado singled out "the battle of the chamber pot" as the starting point. The prototypic experience of obsessionalism, Rado considered to take the following course: *defiant rage* at the pressure in toilet training, by which the mother makes the child feel *guilty* and implants in him the *need* for *reparative expiatory behavior,* often manifest in *obedience and compliance.* The child involved in the battle of the pot is caught between his inner need for self-assertiveness and the realization that his parent's loving care is at the price of compliance. This dilemma, of being caught between the need for self-assertiveness and the need for parental love at this price, according to Rado, accounts for the phenomenon of ambivalence and not the pull between love and hate, which is Freud's explanation of obsessional ambivalence. The maladaptation in the child's efforts to cope goes beyond repression of rage to the point of a precautionary turning of the rage against himself in the "retroflexed rage." This retroflexed rage is later manifest in the undue punitiveness and vehemence of the adult's self-reproaches.

In terms of Rado's classification, obsessionalism falls into the category of overreactive disorder with "emergency dyscontrol." Consistent with his attempt to assimilate psychiatric syndromes to a biologic approach, Rado invoked a hypothetical genetic limitation of the capacity for genital pleasure, which, by the absence of its "power to soften rage," also contributes to the obsessional's grimness of conscience. Though there are temperamental and constitutional differences in personality, this assumption to account for attitude or basic mood may too easily be misused by the therapist to explain away failure or the still inadequate state of our knowledge and understanding. Actually the "grimness of conscience" in both obsessional and depressive patients often does dissolve with psychotherapy.

Rado (and Sullivan in a different frame of reference) considered stammering as a speech disorder closely related to obsessionalism and based on (the assumed) "early illusion that (the) most powerful weapon is the mouth; (and) rage is channeled into speech." It is interesting that this idea of an obsessional dynamic goes beyond the narrow meaning of anal-erotism and involves the role of aggression and orality. Also recognizable is the element of the struggle for power.

The therapeutic strategy Rado devised is one application of his "reconstructive therapy," which he said required special training. In principle, first the patient is helped to break up the mechanisms of retroflexed rage and its derivatives by learning to face his full rage in recall of its original context; second, after the patient regains his composure, an exploratory analysis follows, conducted in simple terms of motivation, showing him why he behaved in the reported situation the way he did, and, by contrast, how healthy people would have behaved.

This program is patiently gone through again and again. However, Rado voiced some cautious pessimism about the results.

Karen Horney and Harry Stack Sullivan were contemporaries whose orientations overlapped, and yet they had distinctive differences. Briefly, they rejected Freud's theories of instinct, libido and character formation. Horney did not actually deal with obsessionalism in the usual sense of a dominant symptomatology or of a seeming resistance nor, as did Sullivan, in a more operational mode. In her "holistic" concept of personality she conceived of "compulsive drives" as really a quality of a whole personality and as a way of life, which in some fashion is shared by *all* neurotic individuals.

In *Our Inner Conflicts*,[12] published in 1945, Horney presented her views on the meaning of compulsive drives, as characterizing *all* neuroses. The motor power behind the compulsivity is anxiety; the manifestations are in the neurotic craving for affection and for power and their aim is not satisfaction of needs, but a sense of safety. She also stressed that compulsive drives represent "a basic attitude toward others and the self, and a particular philosophy of life." She included indecisiveness, ineffectuality, a cutoff from the self by means of a false "idealized image" of the self, cravings for affection and for perfection, all among the characteristics of compulsivity.

In *Self-Analysis*,[13] published in 1942, Horney had pointed out how she analyzes a patient whose neurotic personality she interpreted as having hidden compulsive drives. We are given the picture of a young woman, Clara, which certainly is not the clearly etched obsessionalism that the other major contributors have discussed. Nor is Clara the classical obsessional personality which functions with mastery. As Horney described the movement in analysis, the trends were recognized in three phases: the discovery of her compulsive modesty; the discovery of her compulsive dependence on a partner; and finally, the discovery of her compulsive need to force others to recognize her superiority. This approach seems to be particularly applicable to the muted character of an unobtrusive but basic obsessional inhibition. Certainly Horney's approach is very idiosyncratic; we might engage in the exercise of translating her discussion into the language of the different schools of psychoanalysis.

A qualitatively new approach to obsessionalism was introduced by Harry Stack Sullivan, whose interest in obsessionalism was an outgrowth of his long concern with schizophrenia. Incidentally he expressed an admiring puzzlement at the ingenuity of obsessional defenses.

Instead of the libido theory with its concept of anal-erotism, Sullivan proposed the concept of a developmental maturation of body zones which serve as boundary with the outside world and are accessible to manipulation by others and by the individual: thus the oral, anal, urethral and genital zones. Also, rather than a basic hostility in the obsessional, Sullivan stressed the presence of a basic anxiety evoked by specific operations within the family. As stated in *The Interpersonal Theory of Psychiatry*,[22]

> . . . quite often an irrational and . . . emotional way in which parental authority is imposed on the child, teaches the child that the preoccupation with some particular onetime interesting and probably . . . profitable activity is very valuable to continue . . . (not) for satisfaction of new abilities but . . . to ward off punishment and anxiety. When this type of performance is rewarded by approval and affection, the child's direction may well be set toward the complexity of obsessionalism.

Sullivan saw obsessionalism as a substitutive process by means of which one conceals vulnerability and anxiety and attenuates contact. This interpersonal defense shows up more often, Sullivan stated, vis-a-vis anyone with whom the obsessional integrates in intimacy. The other direction in which the defensiveness works is to keep the anxiety out of one's own awareness. The emphasis on defensive substitutions gave as one strategy of therapy the search for the hidden anxiety; sooner or later the therapist could address the patient for collaboration in this search.

Sullivan pressed the distinction between the obsessional personality and the obsessional neurosis. The former individual maintains his comfort in his mode of integrating and rarely experiences anxiety. The latter person suffers from his own obstructionism, difficulty in communication, obsessional fears of either committing violence or suicide and difficulty in achieving closeness. The latter is the sicker person, presenting volatile challenges and varying symptomatology.

Sullivan considered some hypochondriacal obsessionalism as substitutive for schizophrenic symptomatology. He stated that some obsessional neurotics become schizophrenic, passing through to schizophrenia through the substitution of rumination for more effective adjustment.[21] Perhaps the substitution is a defense against inordinate anxiety which would break through as panic. It is noteworthy that Sullivan's linkage of the extreme panic underlying obsessionalism with schizophrenia contrasts with Abraham's linkage of obsessional operations with the depressive syndromes. Bleuler,[4] some years before Sullivan, had made a similar observation, but without offering any therapeutic application.

As application of the principle of the analyst as participant-observer, Sullivan noted the interpersonal interaction between the obsessional patient and himself—what the ploys were between them and what happened when he himself became caught in the patient's obsessional "flypaper."[21] Sullivan particularly stressed the obsessional's use of language as a magical tool, stemming from the time of the child's realizing its power in the interaction with his parents, so that language began to play an even more intricate, subtle and powerful role in the tactic of the obsessional. Sullivan encouraged the patient to observe when his verbal obsessionalism became intensified and to note any defensiveness against anxiety; he was very patient in listening to the repetitiveness for some clue of anxiety or of anxiety-laden experience, past or present, to make its appearance. He suggested that the obsessional musing about doubts and the appeal for their resolution are among the most baffling and tempting encounters for those in his environment, including often his therapist.

Sullivan handled that most distressing symptom, the obsessional fear of perpetrating violence or sexual assault, or of committing suicide, on the basis of the substitutive function of obsessionalism. In this he differed markedly from previous analysts. Rather than stress and explore the assumed (or actual) hostility in the content in a literal sense, he would state to the patient that the function of this plaguing was to distract oneself from awareness of unwelcome inner conflicts held in repression. This view, which Sullivan maintained and shared with the patient, I have found has the additional advantage of not reenforcing the patient's sense of guilt and low self-esteem, which otherwise take on a life of their own as a problem in therapy.

Sullivan considered the ongoing obsessional ruminations to be based on a hostile interpersonal integration with a significant person in the patient's childhood with whom he had not been able to cope either interpersonally or by freeing himself inwardly, other than by the fantasy. Clinically then, this can serve as a pointer to an important relationship with someone and a mode of interaction, which otherwise is not easily brought to light.

Reference needs to be made to Sullivan's way of handling suicidal threats made by his obsessional patients,[23] which, he said, were "in retaliation for my alleged brutality to obsessional neurotics." He cited some biting comments he had made which had served as deterrent. Sullivan's style was coupled with an intuition which was very special and unusual. I have great reservation about taking over his mode as a routine in handling suicidal threats.

To sum up: In his explication of obsessionalism, Sullivan clearly presented first, implications of interpersonal theory both for the genesis and the therapy of a personality disorder; second, his concept of anxiety as a central issue for every personality to cope with in whatever mode of interaction he had best available—here in the obsessional mode; his eschewing of a libidinal concept of character formation.

Paradoxically, the interpersonal operations can actually be discerned in the case reports and discussions given by his predecessors, but without regard for their potency in psychopathology and for a therapeutic leverage. In contrast to Freudian thinking which placed ambivalence as the nuclear emotional state in obsessionalism and to Rado's centralization of rage, Sullivan put anxiety as the emotional state against which obsessionalism defended.

CLINICAL CONSIDERATIONS AND TECHNIQUES

It is often remarked that since Breuer's and Freud's *Studies in Hysteria*,[11] obsessionalism has replaced hysteria as a dominant syndrome. This has been attributed to the increasing sophistication of the culture, and with more general awareness that hysteria is a psychologic disorder, its secondary gains have diminished, whereas in social classes that have had less exposure to this general information, hysterical ailments still occur with high frequency. It is a fact that obsessionalism is a more acceptable defense to the individual and to those about him because of the logical and seemingly sensible (or more thoroughly rationalized) surface over the neuroticism. Another reason for the greater number of obsessional persons who come to therapy may be the actual intensification of obsessionalism in the culture itself. Still another factor in the actual or apparent increase may depend on the greater clinical skill in recognizing obsessionalism in its more banal form, while in the early days of the psychoanalytic era only the bizarre symptoms drove the individual to seek professional help. Finally, people nowadays have greater expectations for their gratification in living and are more likely to come to therapy seeking an answer to their discontent, whether with themselves or with the course of their lives, and not only for alleviation of specific psychiatric ailments.

In present-day psychotherapy we are most likely to encounter the *obsessional character,* the *obsessional neurosis* and also, in the course of therapy, a transitory obsessional mode of interacting with the therapist as a *form of resistance.* We are less likely to meet the patient with the *single obsessional or compulsive symptom* which seems bizarre clinically and inexplicable to the sufferer. In this group, the obsessionalism plays the central role and dominates the clinical picture. In another range of disorders, the obsessionalism is overshadowed by the encompassing condition. Such is the obsessionalism functioning as *masking syndrome* for schizophrenia or depression and in still a different way as an intrinsic part of these disorders when there is decompensation. In still another major category is the element of *compulsivity in addictions,* whether to food, alcohol or narcotics. Obsessionalism has a special and essential psychodynamic linkage with *phobic reactions.* All of these varieties have the quality of resistance.

The range of obsessional syndromes may be schematized in the following spectrum:

1. Social character and cultural pressures toward obsessionalism.
2. Normal obsessionalism. Basic obsessionalism.
3. Obsessionalism as a life style.
4. Obsessional personalities and character neuroses.
5. Syndromes of obsessional neuroses.
6. Obsessionalism and other psychopathology.

As part of or as defenses against

Depression

Schizophrenia

Phobia

Addictions

Obesity/Anorexia Nervosa

Paranoid delusions

Basic obsessionalism has already been extensively discussed and to some extent also obsessionalism in relation to both social character and life style. In this section will be presented issues and examples of the writer's direct experience in psychotherapy of patients with various syndromes of obsessionalism.

Application of Theories to Clinical Practice

How do you select from the array of theories the proper theory(ies) to apply to clinical situations? My suggestion is to center on the patient as figure-in-the-ground and to allow theories to be present but in the background of one's thinking. Without taking a polemic position nor assuming that all theories are saying the same thing but in different words and that all therapists are functioning in the same way, we can recognize in the description of the empirical experience of the various authors of the theories one or another of our patients who at least meets one of the descriptions. The therapeutic approach recommended by the theorist remains pragmatically within the evaluation and implementation by the therapist. Every patient presents a fresh constellation of personality difficulties, assets and potential and should be viewed with freshness. How this rather open-end approach works out will be illustrated in the clinical discussion in general and specifically in the hypothesis of anal-erotism. For convenience, the different theoretical views concerning the basic psychogenesis and psychodynamics of obsessionalism are given in the following condensation:

Freud—anal-eotic libidinal fixation with sexual symbolization in the obsessional symptoms.

Abraham—(the above, plus) tenacious retention and possession of the love object in contrast to the depressive's submission to loss.

Reich—character armor.

Rado—repressed rage evoked by "the battle of the pot" superimposed on constitutionally diminished capacity for pleasure.

Horney—(not in the usual clinical phenomenology of obsessionalism, which in her special sense is based on alienation in the personality.)

Sullivan—substitution for anxiety, at times a defense against schizophrenia, with characteristic interpersonal modes of relating, including power operations in language and communication.

Clinically I have found the concept of anal-erotism only occasionally suggested in the analytic uncovering. More accurately, there were themes of preoccupation with bowel function that varied from person to person.

Two patients had parents who were obsessionally focused on stools and enemas. For one of these patients the frequent enemas became a symbol of tenderness and caring and had been experienced with rectal pleasure. The other patient became oppositional and rebellious to that particular invasiveness as well as in general and had experienced herself as helpless and powerless during the enforced procedure.

One patient was preoccupied with attempts at self-mastery and self-control, which included inhibiting his response to the signal for stool.

One patient was phobic about "germs" (the predominant symptom) and was also hypochondriacal; she was particularly anxious about breaks in control of defecation and was obsessional about cleansing herself and the bathroom.

Three patients had dreams about producing stools which were inordinately large and out of control. One of these patients was extremely fastidious as well as controlling, obsessional hypochondriacal, phobic and depressive (not the above-cited patient). Another, in her dream, was involved in an endless doing and undoing—there was the overflow and the cleaning of the toilet. In waking life, out of her low self-esteem she was often lax about personal grooming.

Some patients in their mode of behavior leave the therapist feeling affronted, "crapped upon." One such instance was reported to me of an obsessional man who had set up his private ritual of beginning his session by half-squatting and carefully emptying his pockets with a backward movement of the hands into the analyst's wastebasket. Is this a symbolic anal aggression?

Several of these instances clearly point to fixation on bowel function as the outcome of interpersonal interaction between parent and child involving the specific physical zone, as Sullivan stressed. In others, the predominant significance, not necessarily contradicting the above, was on control to symbolize a self-image of the self as dirty and to be discarded or to convey aggression. In the practice of psychotherapy, the tried and true strategy when incidents or imagery of preoccupation with bowel function are presented is to explore them for the meaning to the particular patient in his particular life experience—a principle of far wider application.

General Problems in the Psychotherapy of Obsessional Patients

At one end of the spectrum obsessionalism may be a life style with considerable effectiveness; at the other, a Sisyphus of striving and failure. Even in the extreme miscarriage of its effectiveness in agitated depression, a goal is present, generally outside the patient's awareness. It may be to express rage and destructiveness toward the one held responsible for the depression or to work out a problem in living. Getting a sense of what the objective of the operation is enhances the patient's appreciation of himself as less constricted actually than he appears.

To the stubbornness included in Freud's triad of traits, I would add the characteristic involvement with problem-solving, distorted though it often is. It is the stubbornness and this problem-solving drive that arouse the hope of the therapist that these operations will be directed to "work" in psychotherapy. However, the patient may remain oppositional, particularly as the painful emotion of anxiety, depression, anger or even love is touched on. In defending against these feelings and also holding on to a sense of inner structure and of power vis-a-vis the other person, the obsessional operations may culminate in the impasse of resistance. Indeed, *any* inner experience may touch off defensiveness. We might say that there is a phobic flight from inner experience.

The obsessional person's alienation from his experience may actually be a restriction of articulation, a belief that feelings are not to be talked about, and at times also a lack of cognitive clarity of such processes, while the feelings are running their course. Barnett[3] terms the obsessional's mode of experiencing affect as "affective implosion," "a mechanism by which affect is forced inward on the psychological processes and disorganizes these processes. Impression can be said to occur to the exclusion of expression."

Whatever the presenting picture, the core approaches involved getting a sense of the whole person behind the obsessional operations and ascertaining other significant pathology in connection with the function of the latter. Of parallel importance is the therapist's self-perception of his participation and countertransference.

The psychotherapy of obsessional patients requires not only the more usual modes of approach but also focuses on the obsessional operations themselves, in order to resolve them and not only move around them as obstacles. The interaction with the therapist and others is explored both for the purpose and the impact. The interpersonal bases of the defensiveness, past and present, are uncovered, as are also the emotions or affects, events, interpersonal experiences that are being substituted for. Also, the patient has the difficult task of realizing when he is being pseudorighteous or pseudocorrect in his logic.

Focus on such operations alone can fall into the patient's sense of guilt, despair or obsessional system, making therapeutic change slow or come to a halt. A desirable complement is the cultivation of other styles of inner experience—permissiveness to self-awareness of bodily perceptions, dreams and associations to them—which leads to more spontaneity in communication.

Communication in the Therapeutic Situation

There is no royal road to resolution. One element in therapy, more than with most other categories of difficulty, is the ability of the therapist to sustain the particular kind of stress that the patient engenders without being caught in counterobsessionalism or of snapping in irritation with the feeling of lost self-control. A patient one can work with knowledgeably and well when one is fresh may become an irritating, frustrating challenge when one is stale and weary, and this is not a matter of liking or disliking the patient as a person. The patient's insistence that his formulations, often a priori, have right of way is particularly provocative to the therapist who is earnestly engaged in arriving at his interpretation. I recall a patient who had been self-recriminating about feeling hurt at an extreme inconvenience she had been subjected to; to my astonishment, when I pointed out that the other person had indeed been inconsiderate and that understandably she felt offended, rather than relief she felt dejected that she "could never win an argument" with me. I had thought the issue of self-esteem was involved in the *incident,* but with her, self-esteem had been involved in her *contest* with me.

Obsessional patients often appear to have steellike durability and even the fuzzy vacillation seems peculiarly impenetrable. Yet they have unexpected fragility and may suddenly leave therapy, feeling reproached, criticized or disappointed in the absence of the covertly longed-for magic or because of an obsessional impasse between therapist and patient beyond the point of return. Spurts of mutual frustration and exasperation as well as of tedium occur in most endeavors of psychotherapy with obsessional persons, and rather than termination, these should be worked out to fuller understanding and ventilation of feeling. Rather than hostility in the full meaning of the word, the patient takes refuge in intellectual pride and dogmatic finality, with a tinge of depressive affect, which may be the basis for stopping therapy.

The discussion has centered on the characteristic obsessional interpersonal communication between patient and therapist. Another area of communication difficulty in the therapeutic situation is the withholding of information about family and relationships that the patient thinks, or rather fears, is important to him or to the analyst. The withholding sometimes is deliberate in the game of testing the therapist's ability to "understand" him and "not his family"; sometimes it is the "forgetting" characteristic of resistance and, early in therapy, is carried almost to the point of amnesia. Even the bare externals of information are bypassed by reiteration of obsessional content, including "I don't know what to say" or "that isn't important" generalizations or pat stereotypes which for a long time the patient does not care to explore. In addition, the very quality of the family relationships out of which his obsessionalism developed lends itself to being overlooked or taken for granted. The slow, grinding, nagging control, with the premium on repression of affect and emotion, only rarely is dramatic, though dramatic occurrences also are "forgotten."

Obtaining written autobiographic details, though restricted, sometimes is helpful as a starting point. The therapist's hunch (as with the "compulsive talker" to be described) may point up a clue to a person or happening that is extremely important and encouragement to discuss more fully, or even presenting a tentative hypothesis, may open up the area significant for the development of the syndrome. Occasionally asking, "Against whom was it necessary to (argue or . . .) in this way?" will elicit recall of the person or situation.

Cognitive Style Involved in "Magical Thinking" and Dreaming

Characteristic of the *cognitive style* of the obsessional person are "magical thinking" and/or "omnipotence of thought," often mentioned as obsessional symptoms and attributed to so-called infantile omnipotence. If the thought content is bizarre, one tends to consider a schizophrenic process as potential in the patient. For therapeutic purposes I find working with the operational role and function of this thinking pattern helpful as part of the total personality rather than focusing on it just as being of prognostic importance. The omnipotence of thought does not necessarily take on the pattern of magical thinking but rather that of responsibility for events, particularly for damaging events rather than in the open grandiosity of paranoid thinking. (This will be illustrated by a case vignette of a depressive, obsessional woman in the section, "Obsessionalism in Connection with Other Syndromes.")

It has long been recognized that the obsessional patient has difficulty in "free-associating." He may either block, be repetitive or present obsessional ruminations as associations. Though sometimes these ruminations have the imagery suggestive of free associations, generally he is distrustful of imagery and of making contact in depth with inner experience. He generally appeals to reasoning, which may be faulty, and to pseudo common sense. A young man, who was talented in the visual arts, had had terrifying nightmares as a youngster and recent fleeting terrifying experiences of dissociation and distrusted fantasy and imagination outside his field and also spontaneity as a break in "control." An-

other young man, a college dropout, had recourse to intellectuali-
zations, actually of good quality, whenever he was threatened by
the rise to awareness of sexual impulses and emotions. Nitrous
oxide in his dentistry was a terror because of the "loss of control."

The anxiety which may verge on terror at the break on "control" is compounded by fear of the unknown emotion behind the
scenes, whether it be sexuality, aggression, love, intimacy, fear of
the unstructured and whatever does not fall into the pattern of
syllogistic logic or common sense; there is shame at being "caught"
outside these confines.

The dream experiences and attitudes toward dreaming and
associating also fall into special styles. Though no simple one-to-
one correlation is offered here, I have observed the following:
The dreams themselves at one extreme are just as obsessional in
content as the waking verbal content and behavior with repetitiveness and prosaic symbolism. Anxiety is symbolized in some
repetitive experience. For instance, one patient's dream was of
a dangerous tour through empty rooms and attics of a vast broken-
down abandoned house with insecure roof beams; a woman
dreamt of endless jars of preserves she was dusting and putting
on shelves and also of endlessly unrolling toilet paper. A young
man dreamt of moving from one scene to another on campus,
where a miscellany of classmates, one after another, were doing
chores such as loading trucks, from which he drove away in a
new car with an advanced motor that has not yet been invented.

The meaning under the symbolic pattern of repetitiousness of
the first two was despair and a dry depression at the futility of
their activities. The last one, in form obsessional, turned out to
deal with the young man's growing sense of power in driving away
from the repetitiousness of the mundane tasks.

On the other hand, some have characteristic dreams consistently
that are highly imaginative and symbolic, with the meanings
obscure and the patterns not neat and quasirealistic and prosaic.
Most of the patients simply presented these dreams as enough,
leaving them entirely alone or proceeding to get involved in details additively rather than getting the themes in the dream and
latent content. Some worked at disowning the dream as an indul-

gence without much light. Many distrusted any interpretation, their own or mine, because dreams are foolish and "you can say anything about them," though they did not in fact come up with other associations. Some few did engage in associating and interpreting. Part of my efforts in therapy are directed to helping the patient respect his dreams and permit the play of meaning and symbolism.

It is quite clear in this section that a pervading problem in the psychotherapy of obsessional patients involves his communication and cognitive style, which is characteristic intrapsychically and interpersonally and which operates no less in the interaction between therapist and patient and as barrier to the process as "resistance." It is also indicated that every so often the therapist gets caught in both his own and the patient's obsessionalism.

Specific Obsessional Patterns and Syndromes

Patterns Involving Verbal Communication

The *compulsive talker* suffers from a dominating behavior style which actually is part of his personality as a whole and which involves speaking as part of interpersonal communication and not language per se. What these individuals present, which not all are aware of, is a competitive interrupting or drowning out of the other person by the rising din or tempo of their own speech. Not only is the voice of the other dinned out, but he is left with the sense of not hearing himself in the contest for the air waves. Sometimes the compulsive talker does this with a speech style that is soft-spoken outside of the moments of drowning out.

I have noted that this urgency developed out of several kinds of childhood experience—namely, the child's anxious endeavor to communicate with a parent who himself is a compulsive talker; to race the parent in order to get ahead with a verbal argument; or to please a parent with achievement in language by talking in inordinate quantity (and other experiences where speech seems to be at a premium to the child).

As one patient described it, she held herself ready to pounce as her mother drew breath in talking so that *she* could get some attention for what had happened in school. What brought this woman to therapy was the effect her obsessionalism was having on the children, along with her perfectionism and taking away of their initiative.

In contrast to compulsive talking is the *obsessional blocking in uneasy silence.* In some instances, this is based on the following sequence of interpersonal difficulty in communication: the childhood dread that pleasing with language is impossible, because the parent never admitted an accomplishment had been achieved; the child's struggle then being expressed in the obsessional seesaw between performance and inaction, between failure and success in talking, language and thought.

Reference has already been made to stammering as an obsessional syndrome, particularly from the interpretations given by Rado and Sullivan which center around the magic and the power operation of spoken language.

Obsessional Character

Individuals of obsessional character often are fairly comfortable with themselves and turn to psychotherapy out of a general discontent with their relationships with others or because of a sense of constriction in living. At times they come motivated by the pressure of others whom they make uncomfortable. With these patients psychotherapy involves first of all helping them become aware of what operations of theirs disturb people. This awareness often is experienced with emotional detachment or as though it is the other person who has the problem of oversensitivity.

The cultivation of self-awareness includes capturing, at first fleetingly, what the flick of emotion or attitude was in the interpersonal transaction. To illustrate, the patient just referred to was actually unusually content with her life, husband, children and career and had occasional twinges of disbelief and unreality that life could be that kind to her. She came to therapy for the reason generally unacceptable to analysts that "it would make my husband happy if I cleared up a problem in communication." This "problem" involved her endless interrupting and verbal anticipation of anyone's talking, followed by a shy little girl smile.

She would also try to impose her pseudo-efficient obsessional organization of time and tasks on her family—"why shouldn't he do these errands on his way to work?"

Involved in the development of her obsessionalism, in addition to communication with her mother, the compulsive talker, was also the need to prove herself "right" and clever. (Another obsessional young woman said, "Clever! That's the word!") It also was uncovered that it was important to prove herself to her older sister for whom she was almost amnestic and whose initiative and imagination she envied. Emulating her sister, she had pulled herself out of their childhood life situation of hard times and parental indifference. Her life style of drive, ingenuity and organization continued compulsively into her present-day comfort and was experienced by her husband as harassing. It was awhile before what had started out as my working hypothesis could be used by the patient and therefore was not presented until she had prepared the ground. This is another instance of the importance of the "forgotten" relative of relationship.

The therapeutic direction was as follows: first, helping her appreciate that imposing her life style on her husband disregarded his ideas and way of doing things. This then moved her to recognition that under her disarming amiability was a competitiveness, as toward her sister. Some time later she could become aware of the pangs of anxiety and despair she had suffered in the early days in her struggle to pull herself up by the bootstraps, which had involved the normal obsessionalism of coping.

After some months in therapy this patient was able to say, after some silence in which she became flushed and a little teary-eyed, that she was afraid that if she did not rush to say "something bright," she would find out that she was empty, that she was not as imaginative as her sister. Encouraging the patient to permit experience in its immediacy, in the moment of process, instead of outracing time and process was helpful. Later she said in enjoyment of paradox, "I am doing less and enjoying it more. Even if I do it just for myself, I don't need reasons, and before, there were reasons, even if I really made up reasons."

Some Patterns of Intimacy of Obsessional Individuals

Two obsessionals who mesh with each other in some intimacies, especially marriage, are prone to mutually lacerating experiences as one tries to impose his system on the other. Each bounds from one tangent of logic to another in arguing, the original issue is lost, there is wrangling to the bitter end in the name of principle. The amount of hostility and *ad hominem* arguing is consuming of time, ingenuity and preoccupation beyond belief. The fact that there had been mutual attraction or that there is underlying affection is lost to recall and awareness.

In therapeutic work with couples with such interlocking problems, one of the targets is to get one or the other partner to step out of the obsessional system in addition to other approaches which are appropriate. If neither can achieve this, they may find themselves at the point of no return. The same person, living with someone who is not threatened by his obsessionalism and can stay out of it, may live in a much happier state of intimacy.

Sexual relationships are variously affected by obsessionalism, depending on the defensive function. For some obsessional persons who use their operations effectively in work or career, their sexual relationship can be immune and be experienced with enjoyment and affection. For many others, the obsessionalism invades the sexual relationship, as for example when there is a perfectionism about the "right" number of times per week for intercourse, the "right" number of times for orgasm and the interpretation of fatigue, illness or reluctance on the partner's side as being the result of either inferior performance or withholding what is due the other. Sex may be approached as a kind of work, test or performance to be accomplished, rather than as spontaneous expression or as an interpersonal experience. Obsessional preoccupation or little chores that just must be done around the time of intercourse often interfere with emotional and physical closeness.

One mode of relating of obsessional persons is in the "love-hate ambivalence," which mainly appears as a stark inner contradiction, the peculiar distinction of these individuals. However, on closer and more discerning view of the intimacy of "love-hate" is a dynamic flux, an intricate sequence of phases, which then recycles as follows: the brief "honeymoon" of love and acceptance; accumulation of stress from "intolerable" faults and frictions; mutually lacerating criticism, rejection or withdrawal; fleeting relief from tension with subsidence of the obsessional mode of operating; depression at the loss of the "love-object" (regardless of the basis); the quest for him; coming together afresh with the emotionality that initially bonded them; the beginning of the obsessional interaction—and the cycle resumes.

The cycle may be condensed into a very short span of time, in "love" and out in a few days, or take about six months. The repetitions may characterize the course of a longstanding marriage, indeed provide the excitement if the marriage goes on; they may finally just break up the intimacy and change partners. In several couples I have had the opportunity to study, there were indeed facts which made for the attraction and others which could be distressing, if the partner was going to be intolerant and unaccepting. At times what was more important than affection was the feeling of power or its pursuit. One element in the coming together after the pulling apart is the fear of loss of the love-object, reminiscent of Abraham's description of the tenacity of the obsessional in contrast to the relinquishing of the depressive.

This discussion is offered to be suggestive and to leave the subject of ambivalence open ended and also to exemplify the interplay of theory and clinical observation, which may give correlations that were not necessarily predictable.

Obsessional Neuroses

In the person with the obsessional neurosis we are faced with a different order of difficulty from that in the obsessional personality. The contrast hinges on the ego strength of the whole personality and on both the intrapsychic role and the interpersonal use of the obsessionalism. In the obsessional neurosis the person feels himself harassed by himself and by the demands on his attention made by the compelling symptom and not by the other person. He has a quality of ineffectuality and of poor ego strength and feels himself inadequate—that *he* is failing and not that the other person is failing him. He may consciously experience diffuse anxiety as well as the obsessional symptom that partially defends against it. The persistent repetitive thought does not make sense to him. The repetitive doubts or self-questioning are undiminished by either his own repetitive answer or the common-sensical ones offered by others to allay his distress. The compulsive bit of behavior may make sense to him the first time around, but it is the repetitiveness that does not and which is disquieting.

The specific dominating obsession is the top of the iceberg of an obsessional personality, and psychotherapy involves the dimension of working with the person as a whole, beyond the single-minded confrontation with the presenting obsession.

Understandably the therapist as well as the patient is puzzled and seeks the meaning of the obsession itself, as in the classical paradigm that Lady Macbeth's handwashing is to wash out her guilt. Clinically, however, ascertaining the symbolic meaning does not relieve the obsessional operation, or it may be used to exchange another operation for the early one. That is, to the obsessional person, the formulation of the meaning of the obsession falls into the obsessional system; as it were, it embellishes the system and is not experienced in terms of the therapist's intent. The so-called insight, chalked up as a failure of true insight, actually had not revealed in depth what the obsession was substituting for. Reassurance for the associated sense of guilt also gives only fleeting comfort.

After giving us a chance at the direct examination of the obsession, I have found it productive to move on to the uncovering of the patient's life, in the broad design of psychoanalysis but with specific modifications for obsessionals. To recapitulate, there should be much more activity on the part of the therapist to involve the patient outside his reiterated obsession by asking him to describe current interpersonal experience, past experience, moods and emotions and thoughts other than the obsessive ruminations, difficult though this may be. Also—though this can not always be maintained—stay out of hassles with him. Reenforcement of the expression of any feeling, regardless of whether it specifically underlies the obsession, encourages a widening of such experiences.

These patients often try to impose their obsessional rules on the therapist. Examples may be "urgent" phone calls of crises that are not even mentioned the next session, letters of explanation as running supplement to the sessions or peculiar ways of paying bills (one man had a routine of emptying his pockets into the analyst's wastebasket at the beginning of every session). These foibles, often with a pseudosensible facade, may be tolerated long enough to recognize them and then it is effective to pull out from being subject to the system.

The following thumbnail sketch will illustrate some of the points about therapy.

> A youth had an obsession based on a sexual advance to a girl, which was the reiteration: "I shouldn't have said 'suck.' I said it and that's why I am sick!" He also was depressed and had brought his life to a standstill. His verbal productions were sparse and consisted essentially of the obsessional reiteration and a plea to be made happy. He wrote me, "Would I have developed an obsess (sic), if I had said, 'would you like to perform fellatio?' do you think? . . . are my obsessions irrational in the sense that they do not relate directly to the depression. In other words is it correct that the obsessions are not normal?"—formulations whose meaning is befuddled.
>
> The acknowledged turning point in getting out of his minute obsessional orbit was the growing awareness of emotion that emerged in response to the approach I have described. His frustration, anger and rage with the girl became more open. The girl he "liked" did not meet his standards of status. He had selected her for his initiation into sex, and her lack of acceptance precipitated in him both rage and a sense of inadequacy that even someone "not worthwhile" rejected him. He then entered a phase of flaring up angrily and lustily at mild provocation—from other drivers, his parents, myself. In addition, participation in group therapy with his age peers helped mobilize him.

This case vignette is also noteworthy for the presence of severe obsessionalism in the encompassing depressive syndrome.

Obsessionalism in Connection with Other Syndromes

PHOBIAS. The phobias themselves have an obsessional tenacity coupled with intense anxiety, but they also alternate with the obsessional counterphobic ritual of control. The phobia is comparable to the specific obsessional symptom in the obsessional neurosis, though it is associated with a far greater intensity of anxiety in awareness. Comparably, the phobia has its immediate symbolic meaning which accompanies the anxiety experience, and ascertaining this meaning has only a limited therapeutic usefulness, in contrast to ascertaining the broader underlying significance. For instance, in the case of a young woman whose activity was severely restricted by a phobic anxiety about germs and by a counterphobic obsessionalism about sterilizing, the phobia and the obsessionalism turned out to be substitutions for a rageful killing off of human "enemies" with whom she felt powerless and inarticulate. The direction of therapy then was to help her in her self-assertiveness and the awareness of anger, so as to diminish the necessity for displacement.

The meanings of the phobia and obsessionalism emerged indirectly after attempts to reach it directly had failed. The clue was given seemingly in an unrelated way by my growing awareness that any comment I offered to her request—whether to help her cope with a life situation, understand a relationship or penetrate to the meaning of her distressing symptoms—was dinned out. Then it was established that accompanying the pseudo-reasonable questions and challenges she presented me with was the feeling "she thinks she knows it all and that I know nothing" and a determination not to be overridden. Thereby the greater my earnest efforts, the greater her countering.

This partial insight, which of itself resolved nothing, opened up her awareness of rage at me which gave more vigor to her cleansing obsession immediately after a session. The transferential basis lay in her impotent rage at each member of her family who had tried to "improve" her, to give her "advantages" in order to compensate for a congenital defect. Further exploration disclosed her sense of power in killing "germs" as symbolic of the rageful destruction of human "enemies" with whom she felt powerless and inarticulate. The direction of therapy was to have her accept the confrontation and to develop the courage involved in becoming more self-assertive, to become aware of her anger and what precipitated it, in order to diminish the necessity for displacement.*

SCHIZOPHRENIA AND DEPRESSION. Obsessionalism functions in various ways in the context of schizophrenia and depression, indicative of the complexity of the constellation of processes that give it its character and also linked to the particular state of integration or decompensation in these particular conditions. Obsessionalism may be an intrinsic part of the disorder and operate *within* it; it may be part of the decompensation, a defense against it or a masking syndrome.

As part of the schizophrenic process, the tenacity with which a stereotype of language, gesture or ritual is maintained meets the criteria for obsessionalism or persistence, substitution and/or symbolic meaning. As an example, a schizophrenic youth's monotonous repetition of "I have a vagina" led to the disclosure of its meaning, which was not what we would tend to assume— namely, loss by castration—but his longing for a vagina as belonging to the favored sex, as did his sister, his mother's favorite. Similarly the paranoid delusion in schizophrenia is characterized by tenacity and substitution, but the bizarrete and grandiosity, the open pleasure and sense of power, contrast with the sense of guilt that characterizes the obsessional.

As part of the depressive process, in agitated depression, the obsessional preoccupation and utterances circumscribe the individual in every avenue of functioning; they prevent him from making full emotional contact with his world and from cohesive efforts; they set up formidable barriers to communication, including being reached by the therapist. The schizophrenic obsessive idea is more likely to be bizarre while the depressive thought is most often a declaration of self-reproach or reproach to others and of pessimism and hopelessness backed by pseudologic. Ref-

---

*For a general discussion of phobias, see reference 10.

erence has already been made to the type of magical thinking entering into the obsessionalism which is part of depression. The following is an illustrative case vignette:

> One patient, a chubby little woman of fifty, with bouts of depression beginning with her second pregnancy and with obsessional self-berating for the low stature of her middle son and the allergies of the two others, blames herself for having read and acted upon dietary experiments on rats in the feeding of her infant sons. There is denial that any hereditary factor about stature may apply. Her refusal to accept any assuagement of presumed responsibility for damage is defended with obsessional intensity of arguing. Her description of longstanding ineffectual efforts to please her mother and a critical, dogmatic older sister suggests a linkage with her inordinate disappointment in her son and her inordinate sense of the power to damage. At least she is distinguished by a negative monument of low self-esteem. Though this is the translation of the meaning of her sense of guilt and self-berating, to use this directly in therapy is ineffectual. The larger scope of the underlying psychodynamics for the obsessional omnipotence for damage and for the recurrent depressions involves far more than the meaning factor and includes her ambivalent competition not only with the sister but with intellectual authority in general and her sense of having some power, even if it is hidden and negative. It is noteworthy that what had appeared as a mysterious omnipotence of thought in the patient's wording in the first session began to lose its quality of mystery and of bizarrete as these various factors were disclosed.

There is one special connection between obsessionalism and depression—the obsessive's constriction of experience leaves the person with the sense of ego diminution which contributes to a feeling of depression; so does the sense of failure when the individual cannot achieve his obsessional goals.

In both *schizophrenia* and *depression,* the *masking obsessionalism* serves as an integrative defense in that it gives a sense of self-control, power and coping vis-a-vis the outside world. In the schizophrenic masking, the protective obsessionalism is the great emphasis on reasoning and logic to prevent immersion in fantasy and the autistic world.

In the depressive masking there is frequently routinized compulsive action designed, often consciously, to combat the inertia of depression. In both these compensatory uses of obsessionalism, a fairly well-functioning adaptational goal for maintaining the integrity of the psyche is achieved, but this often is at the cost of not resolving the underlying or latent disturbance. An example is the flight into an obsessional type of working and into frenzied smoking of a business executive who admitted he did not dare face the depression of impending retirement. Particularly in men with the cultural value of pride in work, obsessionalism is used as a mask in a flight from therapy.

Where one has reason to believe that the obsessionalism is a mask for depression or schizophrenia, one should be prepared to cope with the undefended pathology disclosed. This then is a matter of therapy of the underlying schizophrenia or depression. Whether it is more therapeutic to work toward removing the mask or toward helping the individual build some inner strength before challenging the serviceable defense must be determined with each patient. We are really concerned here with the therapy of the underlying condition rather than of the obsessionalism. The same problem applies to the addictions in which also an obsessional style is present as part of a complexity of factors beyond the scope of this chapter.

Obsessionalism ranges from normal functioning and mastery through a variety of miscarried effort and aggression involving thought, language and feeling. Into its understanding and treatment have entered trial, error and achievement from the various psychoanalytic approaches.

REFERENCES

1. Abraham, K.: Restriction and transformations of scoptophilia in psychoneurotics. In *Selected Papers on Psychoanalysis,* edited by J. D. Sutherland. London, Hogarth Press, 1968.
2. Abraham, K.: A short study of the development of the libido, viewed in the light of mental disorders. In *Selected Papers on Psychoanalysis,* edited by J. D. Sutherland. London, Hogarth Press, 1968.
3. Barnett, J.: On cognitive disorders in the obsessional. *Contemporary Psychoanalysis,* 2:130, Spring 1966.
4. Bleuler, E.: *Textbook of Psychiatry.* Translated by A. A. Brill. New York, Macmillan, 1924, p. 409.
5. Freud, S.: A case of obsessional neurosis. In *Collected Papers.* London, Hogarth Press, 1946, vol. 3, pp. 296-372.

6. Freud, S.: Character and anal eroticism. In *Collected Papers*. London, Hogarth Press, 1946, vol. 2, pp. 45-51.
7. Freud, S.: Civilization and its discontent. In *Civilization, War and Death*, edited by J. Rickman. London, Hogarth Press, 1939, p. 40.
8. Freud, S.: Obsessions and phobias: Their psychical mechanisms and their aetiology. In *Collected Papers*. London, Hogarth Press, 1946, vol. 1, pp. 128-138.
9. Freud, S.: Obsessive acts and religion. In *Collected Papers*. London, Hogarth Press, 1946, vol. 2, pp. 25-36.
10. Freud, S.: Predisposition to obsessional neurosis. In *Collected Papers*. London, Hogarth Press, 1946, vol. 2, pp. 122-133.
11. Freud, S., and Breuer, J.: *Studies in Hysteria*. New York, Basic Books, 1957.
12. Horney, K.: *Our Inner Conflicts*. New York, W. W. Norton, 1945.
13. Horney, K.: *Self-Analysis*. New York, W. W. Norton, 1942.
14. Langer, S.: *Philosophy in a New Key*. Cambridge, Harvard University Press, 1957.
15. Rado, S.: Obsessive behavior. In *American Handbook of Psychiatry*, edited by S. Arieti. New York, Basic Books, 1959, vol. 1, p. 324, 345.
16. Reich, W.: *Character Analysis*. New York, Orgone Institute Press, 1949.
17. Ribot, T.: *The Diseases of the Will*. New York, J. Fitzgerald, Publisher, 1884, p. 21 (165).
18. Salzman, L.: Obsessions and phobias. *Contemp Psychoanal* 2:1-26, Fall 1965.
19. Salzman, L.: *The Obsessive Personality*. New York, Science House, 1968.
20. Spiegel, R.: Specific problems of communication in psychiatric conditions. In *American Handbook of Psychiatry*, edited by S. Arieti. New York, Basic Books, 1959, vol. 1, p. 928-1930.
21. Sullivan, H. S.: *Clinical Studies in Psychiatry*. New York, W. W. Norton, 1956, p. 237, 256.
22. Sullivan, H. S.: *The Interpersonal Theory of Psychiatry*. New York, W. W. Norton, 1953, p. 211.
23. White, M. J.: Sullivan and treatment. In *The Contributions of Harry Stack Sullivan*, edited by P. Mullahy. New York, Hermitage Press, 1952, p. 136-137.

Chapter 5

Psychotherapy with Patients with
Hysterical Disorders

IRVINE SCHIFFER

THE SUBJECT of hysteria is historically important in the field of psychiatry because of the role it originally played in the development of psychoanalysis. The technical procedures employed by Freud and Breuer in studying and treating hysterical patients paved the way for Freud's invention of his instrument for examining the human mind, wherein a succession of obstacles to treatment was discovered, including the amnesia that is characteristic of the hysterical patient as well as other "resistances" to the uncovering of infantile sexuality and the Oedipus complex. Freud was able to discover the important role that sexuality played in the pathogenesis of hysteria and in the motive for "repression." Earlier[8] the two men had felt that the splitting of consciousness, so striking a finding in their well-known classical cases, was a rudimentary dynamism in every hysteria and that this tendency to dissociation, along with the emergence of abnormal states of consciousness which they termed "hypnoid," was the basic phenomenon of the hysterical neurosis. Their early thinking on the etiology of hysteria included Breuer's concept of the habitual coexistence of two heterogeneous trains of ideas operative in the human psyche. "We are also capable of what is undoubtedly psychical functioning while our thoughts are busy elsewhere—as for instance when we read aloud correctly and with the appropriate intonation, but afterwards have not the slightest idea of what we have been reading."[9] Breuer felt that the capacity to acquire hysteria was linked with some idiosyncrasy of the person concerned, some peculiarity of his nervous system and his mind. The inability to tolerate boredom, the craving for sensations which drove the hysteric to interrupt the monotony of his life by all kinds of "incidents," these features he felt led the patient further and further along a road that required that he be ill, a trait which Breuer felt was pathognomic for hysteria. He postulated that hysterical emotional excitations invariably had a sexual content. He considered other characteristics of such individuals to be their high degree of suggestibility and their tendency to autohypnosis. He felt that the psychic content of these "hypnoid" states consisted in those ideas which were fended off in waking life and repressed from consciousness; the mental state of the hysterical patient Breuer likened to that of a hypnotized subject. The splitting of the mind then was the consummation of hysteria, a splitting that for Breuer explained the principal character of the disorder; one part of the patient's mind he saw as being in a "hypnoid" state—always prepared for a lapse in waking thought and ever prepared to assume control over the whole person. This "hypnoid" mind he felt was in the highest degree susceptible to suggestion.

Freud,[14] with his attention on symptom formation itself, observed that the sexual function of the human was liable to a great number of disturbances, most of which exhibited the characteristics of simple inhibitions. He classed these together as "psychical impotence." He also underlined disturbances in the function of nutrition, locomotion and work, as inhibitions in the expression of "restriction of an ego function." He further recognized that physical organs could become too strongly eroticized and that an ego function of an organ would become impaired if its erotogenicity (sexual significance) was increased. "It behaves, if I may be allowed a rather absurd analogy, like a maid servant who refuses to go on cooking because her master has started a love affair with her." He saw that the ego renounced organ functions so as not to be obliged to undertake fresh measures of repression— in effect, to avoid a conflict with the instinctual impulses (id). He also observed that there were certain inhibitions that served the purpose of self-punishment, such as those placed on professional activities. The ego was not allowed to carry on these activities because they would bring success or personal gain that the severe conscience (superego) forbade. He contrasted these renunciations to more generalized inhibitions of the ego brought about as the result of an impoverishment of energy, such as in states of depression. Basically he viewed the hysterical symptom as a sign of and a substitute for an instinctual satisfaction held in a state of abeyance. It was the consequence of a process of *repression,* a repression specifically created to remove the ego from a situation of danger. A generating of anxiety setting the symptom formation in motion was seen as a prerequisite to hysteria, in that if the ego did not arouse the pleasure-unpleasure agency by generating such anxiety, it could not obtain the power to arrest the process which was preparing in the id and posing a danger to the ego. Thus such symptom formation put an end to a threatening situation that had two aspects, one hidden from view—the operation in the id; the other presented openly—a demonstrable creation in the place of the instinctual process—the symptom itself. Repression then was seen as serving the same purpose as flight; the ego was perceived as withdrawing its energy charge (cathexis) from the instinctual representation to be repressed and using that cathexis for the purpose of releasing unpleasure (anxiety). Freud recognized the ego then as the actual seat of anxiety. By making use of this signal of unpleasure, it could attain the complete repression of the instinctual impulse which of necessity was obliged to find a substitutive channel of expression, very much reduced, displaced and inhibited and no longer recognizable as a satisfaction—a substitute impulse which on overt expression no longer afforded any sensation of pleasure, but instead had taken on the quality of a compulsion. Freud saw that in repression, the ego exercised its power in two directions, acting in one manner upon the instinctual impulse itself and in the other upon the psychic representative of that impulse (the symptom).

Freud became aware that the mental process which had been turned into a symptom owing to repression could maintain its existence outside the organization of the ego and independently of it. This process and all its derivatives could enjoy a privilege of extraterritoriality; and when such derivatives came into associated contact with the ego organization, they were in a position to draw a part of it over to themselves and thus enlarge themselves at the expense of the ego. Freud likened this to the reaction of tissue to a foreign body which keeps up a constant succession of reactions in the tissue in which it is embedded. He saw it as only natural that the ego should try to prevent symptoms from remaining isolated and alien by using every possible method to bind them to itself in one way or another and to incorporate them into the ego organization by means of these bonds. A classic instance of this he saw in those hysterical symptoms which were a compromise between the need for satisfaction and the need for punishment. Such thinking led to his understanding of "secondary gain" from illness. This gain was seen as coming to the assistance of the ego in its endeavor to incorporate the symptom and increase the symptom's fixation; treatment then aiming at helping the ego in its struggle against the symptom would be met by the opposing conciliatory bonds between ego and symptom—bonds operative on the side of *resistance*. The symptom being the true substitute for and the derivative of the repressed impulse would carry on the role of the impulse, continually renewing its demands for satisfaction, and thus oblige the ego in turn to give a signal of unpleasure and put itself in a posture of defense. This secondary *defensive struggle against* the symptom, a struggle that takes on many different shapes, is in fact the *clinical picture* of the *hysterical patient* who presents himself for treatment.

With this brief historical background, we are now in a position to take a look at those varied clinical shapes and entities that are encompassed by the term "hysteria," and we might well begin with *phobic disturbances*. Here the motive force of the repression is a fear of castration. The signal of anxiety, which is the essence of the phobia, comes not from the process of repression nor from the libidinal energy of the repressed impulses, but as I have indicated from the repressing agency itself, the ego. Phobias then are related to an anxiety felt by the ego in regard to the demands of libido. They do not arise from repressed libido. Freud grouped together all phobias under the term *"anxiety hysteria."* The substitute formation in phobia—namely, a castration anxiety displaced toward a substitute object and in a distorted form—has two obvious advantages: it avoids the conflict due to the ambivalence relative to the original object and it enables the ego to cease generating anxiety, because the anxiety belonging to the phobia is conditional, only emerging when the object of it is perceived. What happens in phobia then is that one external danger is replaced by another. The anxiety of phobia differs in no respect from the realistic anxieties which the ego normally feels in situations of danger except that its content remains unconscious and only becomes conscious in the form of a distortion. For example, a boy may develop a castration anxiety relative to his father as a result of the Oedipus complex and by means of repression, in substitution for the terror of his father, evolve a phobia for an animal such as a dog, wherein the youngster's anxiety is only felt in the presence of the animal, the boy having now become oblivious of his original fear of his father. An additional element in phobia relates to the existence of "anticathexis," a mechanism more characteristically operative in the obsessional neuroses, where an alteration in the ego called reaction formation serves to reinforce an attitude which is the direct opposite of the instinctual trend that is to be repressed. Such anticathexis also occurs in phobia, where reaction formations unmistakably serve to further disguise the object of ambivalence and in some circumstances represent the principal symptom of the patient; a hatred of a loved one for example may be submerged by an exaggerated amount of tenderness. In phobics, such reaction formations do not have the universality of character traits as they do in obsessionals but rather are confined to particular relationships. Reaction formations in hysterics tenaciously cling to particular objects and never spread throughout the ego as they do in obsessional neurosis. There is yet another form of anticathexis peculiar to hysteria in the nature of a special vigilance which, by means of restrictions of the ego, allows external situations to be avoided. Such restrictions are especially noticeable in the phobias.

Any meaningful treatment of phobia (or anxiety hysteria) would of course require an uncovering, not only of the original object of fear but of the castration complex revolving around that particular object (commonly the Oedipus complex). For this reason, depth analysis is the treatment of choice and other more superficial therapies such as conditioning, supportive and others can at best be only temporary and afford but symptomatic relief without dealing with the underlying conflict and its resolution. Yet supporting a patient's fixated infantile sexual solution by superficial therapeutic techniques is still the practice of many therapists even in this day. It can only be justified when extenuating circumstances contraindicate depth exploration.

Abraham described *hysterical dream states*[2] wherein the dynamic power of the repressed wishes was so strong that the patient's available means of repression was unable to cope with such instinctual trends. In such cases, the neurosis itself subserved the instinctual tendencies exclusively. Abraham observed the hysterical dream state as one of a variety of phenomena by means of which the multitude of repressed wishes found expression. He saw in such states a domination of sexual fantasies, on the surface appearing nonsexual, yet arising from sexual wishes through the process of sublimation. Such fantasies, by their admission to consciousness through the censorship, were seen to serve as a medium for the representation of repressed sexual wishes and derived their energy from the latter source. Here again, treatment should desirably aim at dealing with the unresolved sexual conflict underlying such dream states, otherwise the therapist can be led down the garden path by such dramatic, colorful and seemingly endless chain of sublimations emanating from early sexual conflicts. A student of physics, "obsessed" with florid fantasies ostensibly dealing with the refraction of light rays through different sized apertures, revealed in analysis the underlying sexual impasse he had never surmounted in his earlier years relative to certain penetration fantasies of his phallic period of sexual development.

Helene Deutsch, in her observations on hysterical states, wrote on *"fate neurosis."*[6] She saw this type of neurosis as a form of suffering imposed on the ego by the outer world with a recurrent regularity. The diagnosis of fate neuroses can be ascribed to people for example who in their early infantile sexual development have become libidinously enmeshed with a parent to such a degree as to be doomed in later life (ostensibly by fate) to a repetitive substitution of love objects carrying ingredients of personality identical to the original parental object. Oftentimes such parental objects may be untrustworthy, unfaithful, sadistic or psychopathic and so the patient embarks (unconsciously) on a lifelong quest for untrustworthy, unfaithful, sadistic or psychopathic love objects. To illustrate, one of my female patients could only allow herself a sexual involvement with men who eventually abandoned her in the manner that her father had abandoned her mother (and her) for a mistress. Deutsch saw such fate neuroses as hysterical when they could be traced back to repressions which arose in that period of childhood in which infantile sexuality had reached the stage which corresponds most nearly to the genital sexual life of the adult. In such cases, the libido did not regress to earlier stages of development; the unsuccessful repression affected the choice of object and the conflicts which resulted from the fixation in the infantile genital phase of the libidinal development. Like hysterical symptoms, the hysterical fate neurosis acts as an alien body organized against the ego in its entirety. Fortunately, the fate neurotics are quite adaptable to treatment because the blows of "fate" are conditioned by the same inner motives as neurotic symptoms. Hysterical fate neurotics can be described as having a disorder wherein clinical conditions are lacking; "healthy" patients so to speak, healthy in the sense of being free from symptoms, yet pathological in their perpetual conflict with the outer world. Such patients do not come for therapy because of symptoms, but because of unhappiness and a search for a helping hand. They commonly resist depth analysis of their "loser" complex until through the transference of their therapy, they begin to recognize the repetitious bondage of their sexual life and likewise begin to discover a capacity for exercising an option that their sexual choices never permitted as long as the original conflict remained buried from conscious volition and appeared under the duress of "fate."

Freud never ceased to search for the "mysterious leap from

the mind to the body," from a mental process to a somatic enervation; and in this respect Felix Deutsch[4] continued in Freud's footsteps. For his cornerstone of psychosomatic theory, he used Freud's concept[12] of the sense of reality—namely, something that originates from the projection of sensory perceptions of one's own body onto objects outside of it, the external objects being perceived as if severed from the body and lost. Deutsch[5] became impressed with the importance of the process of symbolization stemming from the continual wish of the infant to restore this loss of the body wholeness; by observing how the physiological functions of those body parts which had taken on the representation of such symbolized objects came to be modified because of such symbolizations, he developed his concept of the somatic symptoms characteristic of *conversion hysteria*. Deutsch considered symbolization the most important factor in conversion and recognized how it fused together the body parts so that the unconscious became infiltrated by such symbolizations, which formed a bridge to consciousness; though they faded into the unconscious, nonetheless when reevoked, they became the precursors of the conversion symptom. Deutsch saw the beginning of symbolization as a happening at the earliest period of one's life and identified a rudimentary body ego, using nonsexual energy and in fact an antecedent to the process of identification. "Only when the fantasy and dream world is imbedded in the reality of the body does the process of symbolization begin. Previous to that, however, the body or body parts of the lost object are searched for in one's own body." Deutsch perceived that sense perceptions evoked by this search were forerunners of dream symbolization. Just as Freud postulated a knowledge of dream symbolism as unconscious in the dreamer's mind, so Deutsch saw organ symbolism as unconscious in the waking state. He recognized the development of a body ego as contingent upon the incorporation of others into itself. The process of symbolization was seen in this respect to be similar to identification, but nonetheless differing in that it originated in one's need to make good for the earliest loss of the body's integrity by a reintegration into the body ego of adequate substitutes. Further, Freud[12] had observed that we become aware of the living objects around us by perception complexes which came forth from them but which are fused with memories of similar perceptions of our own body; Deutsch clinically confirmed how patients used such sensory perceptions to become reunited with the lost objects in the process of symbolization. He recognized how certain sensory stimuli emanating from different objects—a voice of a father for example, or the aroma of a mother's bath powder—could serve as a trigger signal to revive the mechanism of retrieval of such lost objects into one's body ego via the reactivation of one's earlier network of symbolizations. Thus, for example, the bronchial contractures of an asthmatically disposed individual could become triggered by an olfactory stimulus linked with a parental object.

Conversion hysteria differs from conversion in more "average" individuals insofar as its development seems to be based on a constitutional or predispositional inability to ward off emotional tensions which the healthy individual masters without apparent disability and which in the hysterical individual leads to an inevitable transformation of great amounts of libido into organic manifestations. Yet conversions can be viewed as necessary forms of a continuing psychodynamic process in all individuals, playing a part in any normal or neurotic condition as they attempt to adjust the individual's instinctual drives to the demands of his culture; the most suitable targets for conversion seem to be those body parts with an organic pathology. In the absence of such, the organ systems selected for transitory conversion are those most appropriate for their symbolic suitability. The individual, by choosing this conversion means of defense against certain stimuli, renounces the adequate discharge of his emotions via the proper channels, and the continual repetition often leads to psychologically induced organic disturbances in ever widening and less related body parts. The residues of incompletely discharged emotions then continuously keep alive this process in conversion hysteria. Such emotions, though prompted to a significant degree by the aggressive instincts and though strongly linked with early identifications, are nonetheless predominantly initiated by conflicts in the area of sexuality.

Analysts following Deutsch's lead such as Ludwig, Mann, Mushatt and Silverman[15] have given particular attention to the nonverbal communication of their patients—their gait, their posture, their body movements and their sensory experiences. Their work has offered considerable data corroborating Deutsch's views. I reported clinical findings[16] of a woman in analysis with conversion hysteria; her body parts strongly reflected the early environmental objects that had become symbolically incorporated into her body imagery. In her midthirties at the time when she sought treatment for a problem of frigidity, she presented herself as a not unattractive, well-built woman with an embarrassed blush, restless agitated hands and constant picking of her fingers. Her anamnesis revealed her to be a strongly controlling, envious woman, the "ugly duckling" and oldest of four daughters of an unhappily married middle-class couple. She had assumed the role of family "hostess" from the time she was thirteen until her mother's death and her own marriage at twenty-two. She maintained a stranglehold on her husband and five children throughout her marriage. She recalled intruding herself between her parents in the parental bed at the age of three and this power to "divide and conquer" stayed with her throughout her later adolescence and adult life. She was convinced that it was because of her that her mother and father separated for a period of time when she was a child. In the course of her analysis, this woman was able to bring into view an extensive pattern of her body representation. Her legs symbolized her parents, her left leg her father, her right leg her mother. When threatened with loss of these figures or their surrogates, she developed symptoms in her lower extremities, the laterality depending on the particular figure involved in loss. A threat to her control over one of her sons achieving a shift from adolescence into early manhood (a threat of loss) was met with somatic symptoms in one of her thumbs— her body symbolization of this particular object. Her analytic associations to her frigidity in sexual relations revolved around early pregenital experiences which were noteworthy by the repression of erotic elements. Through the investigation of her conversion symptoms, the analysis afforded not only an understanding of her body symbolization but also of her mechanism of splitting phallic sexual strivings from deeper pregenital cravings of an especially oral nature. It was possible to forecast which family figures were to appear in her verbal content by the conversion signals given somatically. Trends initiated in her childhood were faithfully repeated in the transference, dictating the manifest content of her dreams and the associations to her symptoms. The symbolizations of hands and legs as representations of parental and sibling objects demonstrated a clear splitting of laterality (left representing male objects, right female) and was heavily determined by the patient's early handling of the primal scene. With her parents as accomplices, she had managed a "divide and conquer" dynamism from her earliest years that was destined to account for a strong bisexual dissociation, a markedly dissociated right and left body image and a concomitant splitting of phallic sexuality from deeper maternal oral cravings. Further observations reported by me on the mechanism of conversion symptoms[17] included the hypothesis that the lost object in the conversion process was symbolically taken back into one's body in a "defective" state in order to fulfill and perpetuate the symbiotic needs basically motivating the process. My particular addition to Deutsch's concept of the conversion process has been further elaborated in more recent papers yet to appear in print, but for now, I will only mention clinical cases I have already published. One involves a 32-year-old man whose laryngeal function was strongly eroticized. His profession involved public speaking. He used his voice to demonstrate his aggressiveness and his masculinity as well as to seduce audiences to his ideas. He undertook treatment for a symptom, an almost total loss of his voice. Physical investigation by a specialist had failed to reveal other than slight inflammation of the vocal cords. Features shedding light on this man's problem included his constant reference to his symptoms as "loss of control." Once in treatment, it was soon clear that he was a very manipulating and controlling homosexual. An early homosexual object was his brother whom he envied earlier for his larger penis and later for his stronger speaking voice and his greater success in his profession. Analysis of my patient's psychopathology revealed that shortly following his renunciation of a guilt-laden homosexual relationship wherein he resisted performing fellatio on his partner, he psychologically and symbolically incorporated this man's phallus (a substitute phallic brother) in a defective state, the patient abruptly developing a damaged voice (vocal phallus). His laryngeal conversion symptom not only represented a "borrowing" of his brother's envied phallus but further served to elicit secondary gain—sympathy from his professional associates as well as his therapist, all of whom became objects for exploitation in this man's acting-out of his oral-phallic conflict.

Another patient, a lawyer in his midthirties, consulted me for incapacitating twitching, pain and stiffness in his buttocks and legs of such severity as to make standing and protracted sitting while at work almost impossible. Extensive medical work-up over a period of months for brain or spinal cord disorder failed to reveal organic pathology. His history included a voyeuristic preoccupation at puberty with young girls' legs, beginning with his 8-year-old sister who aspired to the ballet. Earlier, he had idolized a famous track athlete who had overcome polio involving both legs. He recalls how at that time, he developed a transient limp in one leg in order to appear heroic to his classmates. A later idol was Franklin D. Roosevelt. At age eighteen he developed a perverse interest in young women's buttocks and began indulging in what he called "frottage." This involved unobtrusively brushing his flaccid penis against the buttocks of women in streetcars or in other crowded situations. On one such occasion in a department store, he was apprehended by the store detective. At age six or seven, there was a history of sadistic sexual excitement while impaling imprisoned butterflies on a sharp pin or needle and gleefully watching the twitching of the antennae and the slow oozing of brownish fluid. He recalls embalming the butterflies in formaldehyde to "preserve" them. A character trait of fickleness this man described as his "butterfly tendency." His father was a passive, ineffectual man dominated by a phallic, compulsive woman who was to be the model for this man's marital choice. It was following the near-loss of his son through infantile diarrhea that this patient developed his hysterical conversion symptoms. Coincident with their appearance, he once again impregnated his wife as insurance against the death of his only son.

This man demonstrated how the anal-sadistic content of his repressed sexual fantasies also played a vital part in the quality of his conversion symptoms where in his early symbolizations were reevoked, his legs becoming eroticized to complement the twitching "butterfly" buttocks that were the symbolic representations of his young sister. His "frottage" was the acting-out of his incestuous anal fantasies surrounding his sister. The conversion symptom was also an expression of the need to guard against his fickle "butterfly" identification with his "impaled and embalmed" sister who remained permanently symbolized in his petrified buttocks and spastic legs, an unconscious imprint always in readiness for reactivation. The treatment of these cases of conversion hysteria rested on the detailed exploration of the body symbolizations involved and a reconstruction of the sexual conflicts surrounding the early objects represented in these symbolizations. The aim of such analytic work was to permit the patient to belatedly free the libido tied up on these infantile sexual attachments, allowing a discharge of emotions to take place along more appropriately adult channels no longer linked with organ systems such as vocal cords, legs and buttocks. This effort at belated genitalization is by no means an easy task, but one thing is certain, any treatment of conversion hysteria that fails to take into account the symbolization of the body and the reconstruction of a patient's dealings with early lost objects and the struggle for reunification is only palliative at best and on a par with the temporary results of hynotherapies or other transference "cures."

No clinical discussion on hysteria should exclude description of that character type whose personality ingredients are basically derived from and reflective of all the afore-mentioned hysterical mechanisms because such are secondarily defended, embellished and disguised by a superstructure of reaction formations. They take on a personality cast that can best be labeled the *hysterical character*. This clinical picture is of special significance in that it has become one of the commoner shapes in which the hysteric patient presents himself in the modern-day psychiatric setting for treatment. The days of the "grand hysteria" appear to be more or less numbered. Sociological factors presumably have played a role in their gradual disappearance from the clinical scene. Gross hysterial palsies and other similarly incapacitating bodily afflictions now play only a relatively minor part in most psychiatric practices. It is true that in the past, the interest in hysterical disorders was focused primarily on body symptomatology; now with the broadened knowledge of contemporary psychiatry, the focus of interest on both the physician's part as well as that of the patient has turned toward the deeper elements of the neurotic disturbance. Moreover, with many more people coming to therapy these days, the incidence of gross hysterical symptomatology may only appear to be reduced, since such cases are proportionately in much smaller numbers within the overall spectrum of the diagnostic categories of neuroses. Nonetheless, hysteria—1970 style—appears to be significantly comprised of the hysterical character types. What exactly are such types? The essence in the hysterical character, true to Freud's dictum, is the systematic repression of genital and adult elements of sexuality. The cause of such is usually castration anxiety. Instead of an overt neurotic conflict, one finds a substitute personality development which has a qualitative stamp that ranges from acting and theatricals to outright imposturing. Such patients behave "as if" they had certain meaningful emotions—"as if" they were anxious to consummate a love affair, "as if" they were caught up in an involvement with people, community and global society. Yet because there is a wholesale repression or discarding of the genital elements of sexual expression and development, one discovers in these patients a wholesale rejection of genuine independent feelings, thoughts and impulses. Such people are often capable of dual or multiple personalities. As I have indicated, they give the impression of experiencing great depth of emotional commitment, yet closer scrutiny identifies their emotionality as a shallow and flimsy structure, which to be maintained must find constant corroboration in one form or another from the outside world. Lacking a basic sense of autonomy, hysterical characters commonly go out of their way to gain attention, recognition or notoriety. Their symbiotic need is in depth of immense proportions and the objects for their dependencies are usually selected from those considered strong or socially prominent. The fear of losing their carefully nurtured substitute personality joins with a fear of losing the borrowing power afforded by their symbiotic attachments to prestigious objects and results in most possessive and parasitic liaisons which such patients frequently refer to as "love." Their overdramatizations, including their "show" of supersensuality are indicative of the impoverished substratum on which such superstructures have been built. Their imposturing, charlatanism and disturbed sense of identity provoke a chronic state of fear of being unmasked. This accounts for the extreme forms of secretiveness and vigilance that many such people harbor toward an outer world that for them is potentially humiliating; their fear is for the shame and ridicule, not for the experiencing of any guilt, an indication of their poorly defined ego ideal—yet another deficiency in such hysterical disorders. In hysterical characters there are often strong outer layers of a negative reactionary nature to their personality. Many behave as if constantly threatened with a loss of integrity, of being invaded by the very external influences they secretly admire and envy. Strongly resentful of authority or coercion, they defend heavily against such external forces that in depth they would absorb like a sponge if they were not in fear and conflict. In effect, their negative resistance is but a defense against their own suggestibility. Likewise, in the intellectual area, such people often show a peculiar mixture of extreme credulity and extreme skepticism. Hysterical characters often react against their tendencies toward excessive repression of mature adult drives by a zealousness wherein it becomes impossible for them to postpone gratification of their hypertrophied infantile wishes and impulses. Actually they hold little hope for any meaningful gratification and their impatience of a "now or never" variety is based on their conviction that there are very few opportunities left for them. The objects in their stunted sexual fantasies are often real persons but ones who are most unlikely to reciprocate realistically in these compensatory infatuations and are, therefore, hardly in a position to challenge the impoverished and limited sexuality of these hysterical characters. The other common fantasy elements in such people relate to the omnipotence of their narcissism, which takes the form of protracted family romance complexes that further indicate the infantile scope of ego ideal structure. On the group level, the beatniks, the hippies and the yippies seem in many instances to be appropriate representations in our modern society of the hysterical character. Angyal[3] has offered a fine descriptive outline of this personality type under the heading of "the pattern of vicarious living."

Hysterical characters are more difficult to treat than hysterics with overt symptomatology because their motive in seeking psychiatric help is commonly as superficial and flimsy as their created personality superstructures. Status or "prestige analyses" is in the same category for such people as expensive limousines and mink coats. However, when in their treatment their "bubble bursts" as the initial resistances are overcome, such hysterical characters often become earnestly disgruntled neurotics, desperately struggling to overcome their early repressions and impoverishments and capable in many instances of using their previously dissipated creative talents and energies towards the mobilization of more genuine and basic affects, impulses and ideas.

The *treatment of hysterical disorders* in general has improved consistently over the years through the increasing understanding of the psychology of the ego. Earlier, Freud[10] observed: "we found, to our great surprise at first, that each individual hysterical symptom immediately and permanently disappeared when we had succeeded in bringing clearly to light the memory of the event by which it was provoked and in arousing its accompanying affect. . . . It brings to an end the operative force of the idea which was not abreacted in the first instance, by allowing its strangulated affect to find a way through speech, and subjects it to associative correction by introducing it into normal consciousness (under light hypnosis) or by removing it through the physician's suggestion, as is done in somnambulism accompanied by amnesia." Many are of course familiar with Freud's changing techniques in the treatment of hysterical disorders, such as the cases of Emmy Von N., Elisabeth Von. R. and Dora, studies which remain classics to this day.[11, 13] Today it is still safe to state that difficult though the resistance in hysterics may be, what with the overdramatized, hyperemotional yet amazingly shallow transference features which such patients exhibit, psychoanalysis continues to provide the only situation in which the hysterical defensive reaction against the early narcissistic injuries of childhood can be stripped away to expose the infantile conflict and allow it to be worked through and adequately resolved.

Very often, hysteria is only positively identified diagnostically through the treatment situation itself. Abraham's notations on hysteria[1] are helpful in differentiating the more clouded and bizarre hysterical syndromes from schizophrenia. He observed that with neurotics in general, the sexual impulse is distinguishable from that of a normal person by its excessive strength and the fact that the component instincts are incompletely subjected to the heterosexual one which is repressed; with the outbreak of the neurosis, the repressed material emerging into consciousness becomes converted into hysterical symptoms, serving as a discharge for such impulses, often of a perverse nature. Unlike hysteria, he saw schizophrenia as destroying the person's capacity for sexual transference and for object love; a revulsion of the libido from an object upon which it was at one time cathected with particular intensity Abraham saw as an irrevokable vicissitude in schizophrenia. Although such patients were often very suggestible, he saw such suggestibility as of a different order from that of the hysteric; in the former, the patients failed to struggle against outside influence because they were too indifferent to oppose such influences; they suffered a disturbance in the capacity for attention. It seemed then to Abraham that such suggestibility was an absence of resistance, yet, nonetheless, very easily changed into resistance. The negativism of schizophrenia was an antithesis to transference. In further contrast to hysteria, the patients were only to a slight degree susceptible to hypnosis. In the psychoanalysis of schizophrenics, he discerned an absence of transference. The strong presence of autoeroticism was yet an additional feature that for Abraham distinguished schizophrenia from hysteria; in the former, the libido was seen as withdrawn from objects, while in the latter, it cathected objects to an excessive degree. Further, he discerned a loss of capacity for sublimation in schizophrenics, whereas in hysteria there existed an increase in this capacity. Abraham's differential remains an invaluable yardstick in assessing the therapeutic prognosis of hysteroid conditions in depth therapy.

Easser and Lesser[7] have described some of the difficulties in working with the transference of hysterical patients. They underline the zealousness with which the hysteric approaches the therapeutic situation, seemingly more than ready to absorb insights yet trying to obscure his vicarious posture of onlooker, observing and reacting to the analyst at work rather than working himself with his own problems. These authors have underscored the dangers confronting the analyst and his own countertransference problems. "The analyst finds his day enlivened by this patient's hour, courted and flattered . . . the analyst's expectations of his curative powers are mobilized by the apparent simplicity of the defenses." By far the major tactic through which the hysteric achieves his secondary gain is his ability to evoke in others strong emotional reactions of responsiveness and pleasure; such undesirable countertransference reactions in a therapeutic situation invariably produce a repetitive neurotically gratifying experience rather than corrective analytic insight; thus the patient continues to sustain the very inhibitions and repressions that allow him his neurotic manipulations, his stock in trade from early childhood, wherein infantile sexuality can be exploited in an endless repetition of seductions; in hysterics, the infantile repression of their own genital sensations continued into their adult lives leaves them with limited outlets for sensual expression, forcing them to resort to an evoking of sensuality in others.

A middle-aged woman, married to a mathematics professor and the mother of an infant child, came to analysis because of a symptom of sexual disappointment in her marriage. Though she "loved" her husband, she found little satisfaction in intercourse, a sense of impoverishment also experienced in sporadic extramarital affairs. Her transference in therapy was keynoted by monotonous infantile efforts at arousal and seduction of the therapist, wherein she repeated all the games and tricks in her limited arsenal of hypertrophied genitalless sexuality. Only through detailed working through of the heavy superstructures of these compensatory offerings did this patient ultimately risk the revealing of her underlying conflict, including her strong envy of all men and her punishment of herself and them by an identification with a similarly envious and theatrically seductive mother.

The hysterical patient brings into her transference a faithful repetition of her way of relating to many figures, including the earliest ones. Such attitudes and posturings, laden with shallow hyperemotionality, overdramatization and game-playing—defenses and resistances against the primary narcissistic hurt in the patient's core—are the stereotyped patterns of the transference of the hysterical patient for better or for worse; as such, they require patient and thorough analysis until they are ultimately abandoned, so that the underlying infantile conflict of the patient can be exposed and the freeing of the genital strivings of the patient toward a pathway to maturation effected. This is the aim in the treatment of all forms of hysterical conditions, whether they be primarily problems of frigidity, impotence, conversion, character disturbance, fate neurosis, phobias or inhibitions in work or other aspects of normal living.

In conclusion, the treatment of choice in hysterical disorders is psychoanalytic intervention. Any modification of such a procedure by psychotherapists should be advisedly a therapy of an uncovering and reconstructive nature. Other therapies, whether basically drug oriented, hypnotic, behavioral or reconditioning, are at best palliative and offer only a temporary resolution of the more superficial manifestations of the hysterical problem.

REFERENCES

1. Abraham, Karl: The psychosexual differences between hysteria and dementia praecox. *Selected Papers on Psychoanalysis.* New York, Basic Books, 1953, pp. 64-79.

2. Abraham, Karl: *Hysterical Dream States: Selected Papers.* 1910, pp. 90-124.
3. Angyal, A.: *Neurosis and Treatment. A Holistic Theory.* New York, John Wiley & Sons, 1965, pp. 136-155.
4. Deutsch, F.: Zur Bildung der Konversionsymptoms. *Int* Ztschr. Psa., *10:*380-392, 1934.
5. Deutsch, F.: *On the Mysterious Leap From the Mind to the Body.* New York, International Universities Press, 1959, pp. 75-79.
6. Deutsch, H.: *Hysterical Fate Neurosis. Neurosis and Character Types.* New York, New York International Universities Press, 1965, pp. 14-28.
7. Easser and Lesser: *Transference Resistance in Hysterical Character Neurosis—Technical Considerations: Developments in Psychoanalysis at Columbia University.* New York, Hafner, 1966, pp. 69-80.
8. Freud, S., and Breuer, J.: On the psychical mechanism of hysterical phenomenon. Preliminary communication. *The Standard Edition of the Complete Psychological Works of Freud.* London, Hogarth Press, 1962, vol. 2, pp. 3-7.
9. Freud, S., and Breuer, J.: Theoretical. *The Standard Edition of the Complete Psychological Works of Freud.* London, Hogarth Press, 1962, vol. 2, p. 185-251.
10. Freud, Sigmund: The psychotherapy of hysteria. *The Standard Edition of the Complete Psychological Works of Freud.* London, Hogarth Press, 1962, vol. 2, p. 255.
11. Freud, Sigmund: Case histories. *The Standard Edition of the Complete Psychological Works of Freud.* London, Hogarth Press, 1962, vol. 2, p. 48-181.
12. Freud, Sigmund: The interpretation of dreams. *The Standard Edition of the Complete Psychological Works of Freud.* London, Hogarth Press, 1962, vol. 2, p. 550-577.
13. Freud, Sigmund: A case of hysteria. *The Standard Edition of the Complete Psychological Works of Freud.* London, Hogarth Press, 1962, vol. 7, pp. 7-122.
14. Freud, Sigmund: Inhibitions, symptoms and anxiety. *The Standard Edition of the Complete Psychological Works of Freud.* London, Hogarth Press, 1962, vol. 20, p. 77-174.
15. Ludwig, Mann, Mushatt and Silverman: In *On the Mysterious Leap from the Mind to the Body: A Workshop Study on the Theory of Conversion,* edited by Felix Deutsch. New York, International Universities Press, 1959.
16. Schiffer, I.: The psychoanalytic study of the development of a conversion symptom. *Int J Psychoanal, 63 (Parts 2-3):*169-174, 1962.
17. Schiffer, I.: Psychoanalytic observations of the mechanism of conversion symptoms. *Psychoanal Rev, 5 (No. 2):* 33-42, Summer edition 1964.

Chapter 6

Psychotherapy with Depressed Patients

MAX HAMMER

A DEPRESSIVE reaction is basically an acute feeling of despondency and dysphoria of varying intensity and duration. It is a response which is highly subjective in that what causes one individual to become depressed may leave another relatively unaffected. In this chapter the neurotic or pathological states of depression will be dealt with rather than the psychotic states or those transient states of mood typically referred to as dejection, pessimism or disappointment which are relatively common to all.

ONSET

A depressive reaction usually follows some unpleasant experience or event. Usually the event is unanticipated and therefore is experienced as being relatively traumatic. What marks the dysphoric reaction as pathological is that either the event is not one which typically evokes a dysphoric reaction in people or else the event may be realistically capable of precipitating a feeling of despondency but the person's reaction to it is overly intense and incapacitating or more prolonged than the usual response to such an event. Pathological depression is also marked by the fact that the person appears helpless to overcome it through his own efforts.

Among the events which may typically precipitate a depression are illness or death of a close relative, illness or loss of certain capacities in oneself, loss of love or narcissistic supplies (that is, all kinds of compliments, attention, concern, etcetera), a financial setback or moving to a new location.

At a more conscious or preconscious level, depression is invariably the result of the experience of frustration that comes

156

with the recognition that one wants something very badly but, at the same time, is helpless to do anything about being able to possess or achieve that which is craved and valued but is continuously being denied to oneself. However, at a deeper, more unconscious level this feeling of frustration is being experienced as a loss which tends to intensify an already existing inner feeling of deficiency, emptiness and worthlessness. Basically then, a depression is potentially capable of being precipitated by any event which produces a significant feeling of loss. The loss may be one of various types. For example, it may be the loss of a sense of security, a loved or needed person, self-esteem or some idealized image, valued possessions or something with which one has become identified, control or influence over the elements and events of one's life or some kind of adequacy, ability or sense of potency. The loss tends to be unconsciously interpreted as a diminishing of the self in one way or another. In essence, depression can result whenever the self is experienced as being significantly diminished. The experience of the diminishing of self tends to provoke an unconscious fear that one is moving in the direction of confirming the unconscious conviction of oneself as basically a worthless nullity. Therefore, intrinsic to an experience of a diminishing of self is the deeply unconscious fear that one is moving in the direction of becoming totally nonexistent as a personal entity self.

Thus, whereas depression and other dysphoric states signify an experience of the diminishing of self, the elational states signify that one has had the experience, at some level of consciousness, of an accretion, aggrandizement or affirmation of the self. In the same vein, anxiety may then be understood basically as the reaction of fear that such a diminishing of self is *about to occur*, whereas depression may be understood as the reaction equivalent to the experience that the diminishing of self has *already* taken place.

SYMPTOMS AND EQUIVALENTS OF DEPRESSION

In addition to the dysphoric affect, one most conspicuously finds in depressed persons some, although not necessarily all, of the following: all activities and interests are highly constricted (including sex); affective response is significantly diminished; there is lowered self-assurance, apprehension, tears, heavy sighing, avoidance of people, guilt, fear of impending doom, feeling of intolerable anxious distress, somatic complaints, slowing down in psychomotor functions (although in some cases we find a motoric restlessness), impaired appetite, highly restricted narcissistic involvement with little interest in one's home or personal appearance, inability to enjoy simple pleasures, hobbies, social contacts or one's work. Usually even the simplest routine task seems to require Herculean effort and is seen as a major endeavor by the depressed person.

Rather than the overt depression, many times one will see what is referred to as depression equivalents. To the somatic equivalents of depression especially belong fatigue and pain, the latter of varying localization and intensity. Fatigue is often the result of internal tensions created by deep-seated emotional conflicts. The tension is usually a consequence of the patient's intensive efforts to neutralize his upsurging aggressive impulses. Pain, usually generalized, vague and rheumatoid, or localized (for example, a headache), is another sign of the patient's attempt to neutralize inner aggressive trends. In other cases the pain may be the result of the ego's attempt to relieve or expiate the intense dictates of a guilty conscience via self-punishment.

Other equivalents of depression which may be observed are dyspepsia, nausea, a bad taste in the mouth, constipation and general irritability. In an attempt to escape from the extreme tension caused by an impending depression, persons with an especially weak ego may turn to artificially induced states of elation produced by such things as alcohol, drugs, compulsive eating, buying sprees, gambling, etcetera. When a sense of euphoria is achieved, then it tends to elevate feelings of self-esteem and security which serves to inhibit the depression.

In other instances, especially in the adolescent or in the adult with a weak ego, the attempt is to escape from the depression by draining the tension associated with it through some kind of antisocial acting-out such as speeding in automobiles, petty thievery, aggressive outbursts, sexual promiscuity and the like.

Other depression equivalents that are frequently observed involve various forms of hyperactivity such as when one becomes overinvested in civic and social affairs. This type of person seems to be continuously "on the run." Compulsive smiling or laughing is still another frequently observed manicky reaction formation defense and equivalent of depression.

Whereas depression has many equivalents of its own, depression itself may at times also serve as a substitutive equivalent in the form of a pseudo-emotion in order to cover up some other, more basic emotion such as anger, fear or sorrow. These more basic emotions, for one reason or another, are intolerable to the self and must be defended against being consciously recognized and experienced.

PSYCHODYNAMIC FACTORS

In my experience, I have found it convenient to subsume the basic psychodynamic causes involved in depression within five major factors. Essentially, I find one of these five basic psychodynamic factors operative in almost every case of depression. Several of these may occur together in any single case of depression. One factor involves an attempt to regain self-esteem which was lost or is threatened as a function of the withdrawal, or possible feared withdrawal, of love or narcissistic supplies. Another basic factor which is found centers around the depression being the result of hostility or sadistic impulses which are being blocked from expression and then turned back upon the self in a rather masochistic fashion. A third factor which is frequently found in depression relates to events, feelings or thoughts which have produced a great deal of guilt, and the depression reflects the attempt to expiate this guilt through the discomfort that it brings. A fourth factor is a mourning reaction due to the loss of a loved one. The fifth factor, which to some degree is also involved in the first four, relates to the depressed person's need to reaffirm his control and lost sense of omnipotence which is the primary means by which he achieves a sense of security. Each factor will now be discussed in more detail.

Depression and Self-Esteem

Fenichel[1] points out that depression is based on the same predisposition as addiction and pathological impulses. A person who is fixated at the oral passive-dependent stage of psychosexual development is fixated at the stage at which his self-esteem is regulated by how much he is given by others in his environment, and if his narcissistic needs are not satisfied, his self-esteem diminishes to a danger point. He is ready to do almost anything to avoid this.

This kind of depressed person goes through life in a condition of perpetual greediness. He is, in a sense, a "love addict." The personality of the object or provider of love and narcissistic supplies is of little importance to him. He needs the narcissistic supplies desperately for the maintenance of his self-esteem; it almost does not matter who provides these. It does not necessarily even have to be a person; it may be a drug, alcohol or an obsessive hobby. As with any addictive personality, the basic drive which motivates this kind of depressed personality can be termed "the search for euphoria." He is basically in pursuit of the nirvana-type state which the infant experiences when he is well fed. In this search for euphoria he tries to coerce some person in his environment to "feed" him the narcissistic supplies and if he is unsuccessful in finding someone he will then usually attempt to feed himself by taking something orally which will produce the euphoric effect, such as drugs, alcohol, food, etcetera.

Early in life, due to the nurturant feeding process, being fed or given to becomes equated with being loved and therefore with a sense of worth or self-esteem. Being hungry or not being fed or given to becomes equated with fears of annihilation and later self-depreciation and unlovableness. Later in life the tension and insecurity of not being loved is therefore capable of triggering the unconscious threat of not being fed, and as a result, fears of annihilation become aroused. I have consistently found that this kind of person unconsciously makes the basic equation that having no self-esteem means that he is totally worthless and if he is totally worthless he feels that he will have been reduced to being *absolutely nothing* and therefore he feels threatened with the extinction of his psychological self when his sense of self-esteem is lowered.

Still later the superego or conscience develops and takes over the inner regulation of self-esteem. No longer is the feeling of being loved the sole prerequisite for a feeling of well-being, but now the feeling of having done the right thing is also necessary. Conscience operates as a warning function. A punitive conscience creates minor annihilations or small diminutions in self-esteem in order to warn against the danger of a complete loss of narcissistic supplies. Thus, for example, the conscience says, "You have been bad, I shall have to punish you to warn you that if you keep on being bad something much worse will happen—mommy and daddy may cease to love and protect you."

A distinction can be made here between neurotic and psychotic depressions. In the neurotic condition the depression represents the attempt to induce some person in the environment to provide narcissistic supplies in the form of love, sympathy, concern and the like. The receipt of these supplies enhances self-esteem which thereby reduces the threat of annihilation. In psychotic depressions, however, the complete loss of the love object in the environment has *already taken place* and the depression represents attempts to gain the narcissistic supplies exclusively from the superego.

Depression and the Feeling of Loss of Self

Some depressed people tend to react very strongly to loss of love not only because of the loss of narcissistic supplies and self-esteem but also because they become so overly identified with the love object that the loss of this person is experienced as a loss of self. Typically in these cases the overidentification with the love object is the result of a long-standing pattern which started early in the patient's life in which he first learned to feel secure by identifying with the most dominant, controlling parent through introjection and incorporation. This was considered to be necessary by the patient due to the fact that he felt that he had no self unless he incorporated the self of the parent within him to guide him and help him make judgments and decisions. The depression in these cases represents the loss of the introjected object with the resulting feeling of inner emptiness and nothingness; as though one were basically a void and therefore did not exist at all. In essence then, this kind of depression is a form of death anxiety.

Typically, the parent of this kind of depressed individual is usually a very critical parent who does not see her child as a separate self but only as an extension of herself and she proceeds to do most of his thinking and decision-making for him. As a consequence, the child comes to feel that he has no self or mind of his own. He then "swallows up" the parent which serves to fill the emptiness of self and proceeds to live by the dictates, values and directions set down by the parent. In addition, early in his life, he was usually convinced by the parent that self-direction would ultimately lead to his own self-destruction. As a child he usually tests out the parent's admonitions and at some point decides to follow his own will instead of the parent's will but invariably it turns out badly in some way. The child ends up being traumatically hurt either physically or emotionally. He thus comes to conclude that he is not able to protect himself and that if he is to survive he must incorporate this "all-knowing" parent as his guide through life. The will of the parent then takes on the security of omnipotent protection. His thinking goes something like this: "My parent knows everything. She said that if I tried to do this thing by myself I would fail and get hurt and I did. The only way to be safe is to do only what she tells me is right to do and never to allow myself to have a will of my own. My parent and I will become basically one."

This attitude is perpetuated into adulthood and with other parent surrogates. He just does not dare to govern his own life. He feels, "I need a wiser and stronger one to govern me in order to feel safe and secure." Certainty and safety comes only with having an introjected parent figure directing and guiding him. He continues to try to escape from his feeling of inner emptiness by continuing to "swallow" love objects who serve basically as parent surrogates.

These depressed patients tend to react very possessively toward their love object because to lose the other is felt as a loss of self and complete abandonment to a helpless vulnerability and fear of nonbeing. They tend to be compulsively driven in their search for and accumulation of love objects. They usually want one permanent one and also the freedom to go out and collect others too in order to guarantee that they will never feel empty. It is also not unusual to find compulsive eating or alcoholism serving as a depression equivalent in these persons. The orality serves to defend against the depression by attempting to fill the perceived inner void.

Depression and the Need for Protection

Basically the depressed person craves safety and protection. His attempts at securing love and narcissistic supplies is his way of converting these into believing that because he is loved and valued, he will be protected. All this usually stems from the early emotional rejection by parents and also the sensing of their hostility toward him. Their emotional abandonment of him left him feeling extremely helpless and vulnerable. At first he tries to regain a sense of security by asserting his omnipotence, but when his attempts to totally control his environment fail, he recognizes that he is not omnipotent and cannot guarantee his own security by himself and so he turns to the coercion of the environment to protect him by overplaying his suffering.

He demands demonstrable evidence of love and protection; verbal assurances of regard by others are insufficient because the early rejection by his parents has led to his own self-hate. He projects out his own self-hate and believes that others must be hating him; he is so involved with self-hate that he is unable to feel anyone's love for him.

Self-esteem by itself offers little protection to the depressed person and is therefore not his ultimate goal. He wants to feel protected, and the self-esteem is only a means to this end. It leads him to believe that because he has worth others will value and want him. The self-esteem is also necessary for him to protect his ego against the sadistic accusations from the superego. Thus, his intense demands for love and esteem really represent his craving for protection and security.

Case Illustration

Mrs. Black was doing relatively well until her husband lost his job and told her he could not work any more due to a progressively deteriorating arthritic condition. This meant that for the first time in her life she would have to go out to work full time. She became very threatened at the prospect of relinquishing her dependent role and just could not let herself accept the reality of her husband's illness. She felt that her husband was competing with her for dependency and was just deliberately making himself helpless so he could lean on her. She became extremely depressed and could not take care of the house and children. In this way she tried to coerce her husband to take care of her.

When he persisted in asserting that his illness was making him just as incapacitated as she was, she became more desperate and attempted "suicide." She took a small overdose of aspirin knowing that it really would not seriously harm her, and she did so in her husband's presence in order to be sure that she would receive immediate medical attention. When even this gesture failed to move him into returning to work and showing her more concern, she put herself into a pseudopsychotic catatonic condition. She expected that he would send her to the state hospital where she hoped to receive the care and protection which she craved. She thought that going to the hospital would also remove her from the situation of having to go back to work.

He compromised by sending her to me. I was not what she wanted, and as a result she was extremely resistant to communicating with me. It soon became clear that she intended to hold on to her symptoms at all costs. I finally got the background of the situation from the husband, and when what was happening became obvious to me, I confronted both of them with the subtle "war" that was going on between them. She soon became much more communicative. When she was finally able to express her extreme hostility toward her husband her depression lifted noticeably.

Much of her hostility was related not only to the subtle competition between husband and wife for dependency gratification but also to the fact that she married him without love because he seemed to be in a position to be a good financial provider. She had married him for security and now she felt that he was reneging on this role. She was also attracted by the fact that he was big and strong and she felt that he would be someone she could lean on and be protected by.

In addition, when she married him he did not drink and she had always resented males who drank because her father drank and could not then be in a position to fulfill her dependency needs. She felt that her husband had begun to change in this respect as well. She became convinced that he was denying her everything for which she had married him, and as a result, she felt terribly deprived, cheated and angry—all leading to her depression.

The husband was subtly aware of her control of him and also her not loving him and he proceeded to reject her needs as a way of punishing her. When some honest confrontation was finally brought to the situation and both expressed themselves cathartically, her depression lifted. In addition, after the release of all of the pent-up negative feelings, they each came to recognize that there also lay, underneath, some warm and positive feelings toward each other.

This case illustrates the importance of also working with the patient's mate or whoever the patient is looking toward for the basic gratification of his needs. I find that this expedites therapy quite significantly.

One of the most basic factors involved in treating depressed people is the vicious circle that causes them to be self-defeating in terms of the needs which they want satisfied. Because they feel so insecure, they become extremely coercive and demanding for love, attention, consideration, appreciation and all the other elements that typically comprise narcissistic supplies for depressed people. As a function of these extreme demands, the narcissistic or love object soon begins to feel overly controlled and manipulated. He comes to feel that he must reject the demands not only because they are excessive, but also because he needs to feel that when he gives love it is because he wants to and not because he is forced, threatened or tricked into it.

If the husband submits to his depressed wife's demands and threats, he comes to see himself as weak and submissive, which threatens his feeling of masculinity. He also typically feels that the more he gives in, the more she will demand from him and so he recognizes no choice but to reject her. The more the depressed individual is denied her narcissistic supplies, the more demanding she becomes; and the more demanding she becomes, the more she is rejected, *ad infinitum*. It is therefore crucial that the therapist help the depressed patient recognize how the vicious circle into which she has put herself is operating. The therapist especially needs to point out how it has become self-defeating for her.

I also try to point out to the patient that even if her husband gave her attention when she demanded it, it would do her very little good because a part of her would always know that she had to work for it rather than having it freely given to her. Attention and support, thus coerced, could never serve to alleviate her diminished self-esteem or her fears of not being loved.

Depression and Repressed Hostility

What is the cause of the experience of depression itself? Essentially the experience of depression is caused by the turning of a great intensity of energy upon the ego. This energy is usually destructive in nature. In simplified terms, depression is oftentimes experienced when the energy of anger is turned toward the self instead of being expressed toward some object or the symbol of some object in the environment. This destructive energy is turned toward the self rather than externalized because somewhere along the way the patient has learned that such expression could lead to the destruction of some other person, feared retribution, loss of love and security, abandonment or the loss of a highly invested idealized image.

Case Illustration

Mrs. Jones was referred to me because of her depression and recurring headaches. The physician who referred her could discover no organic cause for her condition. She had previously been a nurse, but for the last five years, since her children were born, she had been home with them. She hated being home with the children not only because she preferred to be working in order to gratify strong masculine achievement strivings but also because her children were very boisterous and very hard to control. She admitted that she could not control her children because for a number of reasons she could not permit herself to get angry with them. She had a great need to be needed and was very fearful that if she got angry with her children they might not love her. Most of all she feared the loss of control of her anger. This fear related to an event that had occurred early in her life. She was a very tall and powerful girl and one day she lost control of her temper and nearly killed another girl.

For many years she had repressed her hostility toward her mother who was extremely controlling. Her mother selected what clothes the patient was to wear and later on in life even told her what career to select. All the other siblings in the family were boys. She noticed that her mother disliked aggressiveness in her boys, so the patient competed for attention by becoming the "good little girl." She never got angry, and never did anything naughty.

Her husband, who seasonally was out of work, would take out his frustrations on her and she would rationalize it away by saying that she knew he really did not mean it but that he just naturally had to get it off his chest. She had come to see that she had adopted the role, for the world, of the "human punching bag."

Her consistent and intense repression of her anger eventually caused her to become depressed. At first she tried to escape from her depression by compulsively becoming involved in civic and social affairs in an almost manic fashion, but soon she withdrew and seemed to lose interest in all of her affairs.

This need to block hostility from being expressed, which is so frequently the case in depressions, leads the body to assist the mind in holding the angry feelings in check, producing all kinds of physical complaints (for example, the headaches here). It is also typical that in this kind of depression, due to the severe over-control which these patients impose upon themselves, they are also unable to achieve sexual release, for all "letting go" is experienced as dangerous. The blame for this sexual frustration is usually projected onto the husband and may lead to sexual fantasies about other men, aggravating the depression by the guilt that it engenders. This was also true for Mrs. Jones. In addition, her masculine identification made it almost impossible for her to cry, which would be a sign of weakness, femininity, vulnerability, etcetera. Thus she had no outlet for the release of her tension which had built up due to the repressed hostility and ungratified sexuality. As a consequence, her enormous tension, without an opportunity for release, was being turned in toward the self, resulting in the depression and the headaches.

Therapy with this kind of patient should aim at helping her to learn to express negative affect, at least verbally, without feeling guilty. Sometimes the establishment of a negative transference toward the therapist may be necessary in order for the patient to learn that her hostility is not destructive and that people will not necessarily reject or abandon her just because she expresses herself honestly. For therapy with this kind of patient to be successful, of course, it is necessary that the therapist be secure about his own worth, so that he will not have to hurt her in any way when she starts to express her pent-up angry feelings onto the therapist.

Helping the husband to accept negative expressions from his wife is also helpful in the same way. It is not unusual, as was the case with Mr. Jones, that the husband is actually quite pleased with his wife becoming more assertive because her "good girl" role made it very difficult for them to communicate honestly and have a close relationship. Many times his anger toward her was a baiting of her in the hope that she would express the hostile feelings that he sensed were within her. He recognized that she was also making him feel very guilty by not responding to his anger.

Depression and Guilt

In some cases, depression represents self-punishment in an attempt to expiate guilt feelings related to a real or fantasied event or to unacceptable impulses usually of a sexual or destructive nature.

Case Illustration

Mrs. Brown was sexually molested at the age of twelve by her father and felt very guilty about this event for several reasons. One reason for her guilt feelings was that she had unconsciously wished for this to happen because her father's extreme seductiveness toward her had heightened and intensified her sexual fantasies. She also felt guilty because she enjoyed the experience much more than she felt she should have. However, she felt most guilty about the fact that this event ultimately destroyed the marriage between her parents. Her depression was her attempt to produce the suffering necessary to expiate her guilt. For the most part, as an adult, she was never able to permit herself to respond and enjoy sex with her husband. However, on those rare occasions when he performed in such a way as to overly arouse her sexually she would respond the next day with a depression.

Depressive episodes also ensued after she would come from a visit with her mother. At those times when she visited her mother and found her to be especially unhappy it would trigger her earlier guilt. She felt responsible for her mother's unhappiness, and as a result, a depressive reaction would ensue. Once the patterns that were serving as the triggering events for the depression were discovered, it was not much longer before the reasons behind these episodes of depression came out and the patient experienced symptomatic relief. (Once the "secret," so to speak, is discovered by the patient and shared with the therapist, the patient usually feels relieved almost immediately.)

Where guilt is the problem there is usually an id versus super-ego conflict. It is crucial but sometimes very difficult to identify those id impulses that have been, or secretly desire to be, gratified. In those instances where the triggering patterns for the depression are not clear or where the source of guilt is too well hidden or defended, then it may be helpful to turn to projective personality tests and/or dream interpretations for clues.

In some cases of guilt it is more important to discover the source of the patient's understanding of the concept of sin than it is to focus on an id impulse. This is especially true of patients reared in an overly strict Catholic or religiously Fundamentalist home where the subject of "sin" is continuously discussed. For some patients almost every act or thought produces some kind of feeling of guilt. The normal sexual interests and fantasies during the growing-up period sometimes cause tremendous guilt and may even produce the conviction that the patient is a sexual pervert. The suffering involved in the depression is felt by the patient to be necessary in order to expiate the guilt.

These patients have usually been taught that angry or sexual thoughts are sinful. They are fearful that God will punish them unless they try to placate Him by making themselves suffer. This attitude is a projection of the perception of a strict and punitive parent onto God, making Him a wrathful and exacting Old Testament Jehovah. Also, the suffering is necessary because they feel worthless and sinful which leads to a strong masochistic-like need for punishment. The superego is unrealistic and savage and needs to be altered. Yet for some, their religion and the way they interpret it is so basic to their personality that to challenge any of their interpretations of dogma makes them feel that the therapist is attacking the very essence of their being. They become identified with their basic religious convictions, and to try any reconsiderations and reconstruction of these would threaten them with loss of self.

In such problems, it is sometimes necessary to enlist the aid of some clergyman whom the therapist knows to be liberal and sophisticated in these matters and who can help these patients restructure their religious convictions. In some cases only then can the therapeutic work begin, and in some instances therapy is no longer necessary because the depression lifts with reassurance from the clergyman that the patient is not as sinful as she believed and that God will not punish her for her bad thoughts or misdeeds.

If the patient's religious convictions are not too intransigent, then the goal is to have the patient incorporate the therapist as the new "alter-superego," so to speak, via identification with the therapist's loving and forgiving nature until the patient can reconstruct his own superego along less punitive lines.

Pathological Mourning

To mourn over the death of a loved one is a normal reaction. Pathological mourning exists when there is either an excessively intense or violent reaction to the loss of a loved one or if the process of mourning is unduly prolonged or unduly retarded in its onset and development. Persistent absence of any emotion may signal undue delay in the beginning of the work of mourning. It may sound strange that the absence of grief can be considered pathological, but the reality of the death of a loved one is inescapable and must be felt. The grief may be disguised in many ways: it may be transformed, hysteriform, obsessional or schizoid.

In most cases of pathological mourning I find typically that the grieving mate has always basically considered herself to be a "nothing" and considers her spouse to be "everything." The meaning and substance of her life had come essentially through her identification with her husband. When he dies, she is traumatically confronted by her nothingness again. She drastically attempts to avoid the conscious recognition of her emptiness and nothingness by becoming totally involved in obsessive thoughts and reminders of the lost loved one. In essence, she attempts to substitute for the lost husband a total involvement with his memory through obsessional thinking. Both basically serve as escapes from the real problem of her own inner emptiness and feeling of nothingness from which she has been trying to escape all her life.

Many times she will turn to alcohol or compulsive eating after the death of her spouse, not only to help her forget the grief of her loss but to fill her and to help her escape from the feared reality of her own lack of identity and inner emptiness. Various escapes only prolong the mourning process but helping her confront the real problem of the fear of her own nothingness speeds the resolution of mourning very rapidly.

In mourning reactions the patient essentially seeks relief not from the recurring pleasant memories but rather from the painfulness of the obsessional morbid thoughts. These morbid thoughts keep returning causing the patient to suffer because they were not fully acknowledged and integrated when the events first occurred. Thus, for example, as the patient was experiencing how the loved one died, the funeral, the burial and so forth, the mind was blocking out and filtering these events because a part of the mind was rejecting and attempting to deny the reality of the event. Because these events were not fully faced at the time of their occurrence, the memories of these events become separated from the self and are rejected as a not-self. As a result, they keep returning in an attempt to force the mind to put attention upon them so that they can be integrated and drained. However, each time the memories return the patient continues to try to escape from them by taking drugs, turning to friends or a variety of other distractions. Thus it is clear that the most expeditious means of resolving the morbid aspects of the mourning and preventing a prolongation of its effects is to encourage the patient not to try to escape from these memories but rather to look at them full-face, head-on. In a relatively short time, they lose their potency and the healing process takes effect. Unfortunately, the tendency is to look obliquely out of the corner of our eye at problems and at painful memories instead of confronting them head-on. As long as the patient continues to try to escape from these morbid memories, she retards the integration and healing process and her suffering is prolonged.

Therefore the patient should be encouraged not to try to escape from the pain of her grief but rather to immerse herself fully into it and let that grief express itself as it will. She may cry and cry until there are just no more tears left to cry and the wound will be healed and the mourning is over. There may still be a scab on the wound but at least the bleeding has stopped. It isn't that the patient decides that the mourning is now over, it is just over. The pain of the feelings related to the loss of the loved one have been confronted (for example, feelings of abandonment) and integrated into her awareness and so the grief has been worked through and resolved. But if the patient does not permit the full confrontation and expression of the pain of the grief to occur, then the wound is preserved and never heals and is later triggered by related kinds of conscious or unconscious reminders.

Mourning becomes even more complicated if the relationship of the mourner to the lost object was an extremely ambivalent one. In this case the incorporation of the lost loved one then not only represents an attempt to preserve the loved object but also an attempt to punish the hated object. If a hostile significance of this kind is in the foreground, the incorporation will then create new guilt feelings.

Case Illustrations

Mrs. Blue, aged fifty-nine, was referred to me by her family physician who was concerned about her because it had been over a year since the accidental death of her grandson Donald, age nine, and she was still suffering extreme grief.

Mrs. Blue found it almost impossible to talk about her grandson without weeping bitterly. She indicated to me that she cries nearly every night since the boy was struck and killed by an automobile. She told me of a dream she had recently in which she noticed that there was no snow on Donald's grave but all of the other graves were covered with snow. In the dream she had said to her husband, "No wonder Donald has no snow on his grave, he was always so warm and loving. He was my whole life." Then she remembered that she screamed and awakened herself.

She related that some fifteen years ago she had suffered a "breakdown" when her first husband abandoned her and left her alone to care for her young son. She expressed the concern that she "never had much luck with males." In addition to her grand-son dying and her first husband leaving her, she indicated that her younger brother hated her, her son turned against her when his father left home, and she never had a satisfactory relation-ship with her current husband. However she did admit that since the death of her grandson her present husband has been very comforting and supportive of her. She acknowledged that she was implying that perhaps she is a curse or jinx to males and felt that whomsoever she loved would in some way suffer. For this reason she has feared letting herself love anyone and indicated that when her grandson, Donald, was first born, she was afraid to touch him for fear that she might drop him or hurt him in some way.

She reported that since the boy's death she has had recurring visions of seeing the boy and confessed that she still believes that Donald is somehow still alive. She admitted that she had let herself get very close to Donald and was really blaming her-self for the boy's death; because of this she could not let herself believe that he was really dead for then she would also deserve great punishment. She came to recognize that her mental anguish was her attempt to expiate her intense guilt feelings. However, she admitted that there were many times when she felt extremely hostile toward the boy because he would not let her control him. She was able to further admit that she has needs to control oth-ers and that she turned to Donald for the gratification of these needs because her son and daughter-in-law and her present hus-band all resented her need to control their lives.

It was only after I labeled the guilt that I felt she was hiding that she finally confessed her secretive feelings and soon after this her grief lifted. She was also able to establish a better rela-tionship with her husband. She remarked, "No wonder my hus-band was angry with me. I turned all my attention to Donald and left him out in the cold. I must have been blind not to see that."

I have also used the directed daydream technique[2] with in-transigent cases of prolonged mourning and find it to be an ex-tremely helpful tool. One 17-year-old girl whom I was seeing in therapy in a woman's reformatory continued to deny the reality of the death of her brother. She kept insisting that her brother was waiting for her at home. After her brother died, she attempted to run from the reality of this event by "losing herself" in all kinds of acting-out, primarily sexual activity with boys who in some way reminded her of her brother. Eventually, this behavior landed her in the reformatory.

Suzi and her older brother by five years were both abandoned by their parents when the children were quite young. They lived with several different sets of foster parents and because of their mutual insecurity they became very close to each other. They repeatedly reaffirmed their vow that neither one of them would ever marry and that they would always take care of each other. The brother died suddenly in a car accident when Suzi was fifteen years old. When I first saw her she was extremely hostile about everything. She claimed that she was now unable to love anyone and enjoyed making fools of men by laughing in their face and showing them how stupid and inadequate they were, especially sexually.

In the directed daydream technique used with her, the symbolism will be readily apparent to all sophisticated therapists. With her eyes closed and quite relaxed she spontaneously pictured a beach and an island (representing a distantiated part of her psyche) far off from the mainland. I encouraged her to take a boat out to the island. She did so, but she found the water extremely rough, tossing and tumbling her small rowboat from side to side. When she finally arrived at the island she was exhausted and just felt like quitting everything and going to sleep forever. When I encouraged her to explore the island, she wandered lost for a long time in dense forest and then suddenly she saw a clearing up ahead. When she approached it she saw a casket lying there. At this point she wanted to terminate the daydream but I encouraged her to continue. She went over to the casket and I encouraged her to open it and describe what she saw within. She offered much resistance in regard to this but when she finally opened the casket she let out the most mournful scream that I have ever heard. "It's Harold," she repeated over and over, "It's my brother Harold and he's dead." She cried with profuse tears for the first time since her brother's death. When she finished crying after many minutes, she remarked, "I'll be all right now. I know he is dead. It hurts to think about him like that, but I feel that I can make it okay now." Her adjustment, in the institution, after that cartharctic confrontation was quite noticeably improved and about two years after this experience she became engaged to marry and is currently making an excellent adjustment outside of the institution.

Depression and Omnipotence

An infant's existence and security is affirmed because he feels himself to be the only principle in the universe and so he feels omnipotent. However, as he matures he comes to recognize that there are elements, both internal and external, in his world which he cannot influence or control. With love from his parents he can give up his need for omnipotence because he feels that he will receive from them the necessary protection and security which he needs to have. However, without such love and a feeling of being valued, he loses his sense of security and feels very vulnerable. As a result, he needs to continue to maintain the illusion of his omnipotence in order to feel secure. But when the events in life clearly point up to him that he cannot always control and influence it, he becomes severely traumatized and regresses into a dependent and depressed state in an attempt to get persons in his environment to protect him.

This kind of depressed person adds to his suffering by taking the blame for all that happens not so much because he likes to suffer but primarily because he needs to hold on to the omnipotent belief that nothing could possibly happen to him that is somehow not under his direct influence and control. A classic case in this respect is described by Smucker[3] of a woman who had convinced herself that she had murdered her own child. The child had died of a childhood disease but she was unable to accept the fact that the child could have possibly died without her wish and agency (not only wanting it to happen but in some way actually making it happen). So, even though she made herself suffer with terrible guilt and convinced herself that she had murdered her child, in so doing she preserved the more important illusion that she was still omnipotent.

In addition, because her therapist was a very loving and accepting man she set out to make him hate and reject her in order to affirm her capacity to control. The more accepting the therapist was, the more depressed and desperate she became. The more he encouraged her not to feel guilty about the death of her child, the more this would disturb her because she felt the therapist was threatening her sense of omnipotence. She finally had to declare her "love" for the therapist before he was able to give her the kind of response that she could interpret as rejection. Only then, because she felt in control again, could she relax her demanding attitude and only then did her depression lift sufficiently for her to get along without further intensive help.

This kind of depressed patient is by far the most seriously disturbed of those discussed and it is not unusual for them to move in and out of periodic psychotic episodes precipitated usually by some confrontation of loss of omnipotence which drastically undermines their security. As stated earlier, most depressive reactions are brought on by the onset of some sort of traumatic experience. It is traumatic to the depressive personality because the ego, which tends to protect and defend itself via the use of its anticipatory function, is caught off-guard and is shockingly confronted with an event which was totally unanticipated. The ego is then inundated with energy it cannot contain, avoid or deny and it regresses in an attempt to escape.

The essence of the trauma then lies in the patient's unconscious realization that her omnipotence, which she has secretly been holding to, is just illusory. At this point all security is undermined by the recognition that she is not omnipotent and the patient then searches for a parent-type figure to provide the protection that she needs. She projects on to this parent figure all kinds of omnipotent qualities as she formerly had done with her parents earlier in life. That is why doctors are so often chosen for this role by depressed patients. There is a tendency on the part of the population and also some doctors to see omnipotent qualities in the knowledge and healing capacities of persons in the helping professions.

These depressed persons are almost continually bitter because life is such that trying to prove one's omnipotence in the everyday world is futile. Thus they are always "hurting." The bubble of this illusion must eventually burst, and depression or worse becomes inevitable. They live only with phantoms of security in the form of the belief that the fates protect them. They require some real sense of security, which makes it necessary to work very closely with the immediate members of the family.

Depression and Existential Issues

Apart from the more pathological forms of depression there is another form of depression worthy of discussion because psychotherapists are encountering it with a rapidly increasing rate of frequency. I am referring to depressions which appear to be related to existential issues. In some part the presence of these existential issues can be attributed to the progressive complexity and depersonalization that one experiences in society today but there are many other important reasons as well. One such reason relates to the fact that in generations past, much of one's felt insecurity was attributed to the realistic lack of economic security. The prevailing tacit attitude and assumption that existed in those days was that economic security, once attained, would serve as a panacea for all of the mind's insecurities and needs. However, in today's world, many persons in their hierarchy of needs have fulfilled their need for economic security and therefore their current insecurities reflect other, more complex, kinds of issues and needs, some of which may be classified as being basically existential in nature.

A patient suffering from depression related to existential concerns is likely to bring into therapy one or more of the following typical complaints: life has lost its personal meaning or direction; a chronic feeling of boredom or inner emptiness; a loss of all motivation and ambition in regard to a career that once was held to have extreme value; a deep sense of confusion or anxiety concerning his most basic identity; feeling burdened with vague fears of deterioration or death; a feeling of being trapped, with an accompanying fear that it may already be too late for his current situation or condition to be changed, or the related feeling that life has somehow passed him by; concerns that his marriage or family life has lost its vitality and meaning; a profound sense of loneliness or alienation from others; or he may report only an indistinguishable malaise, restlessness, or sense of desperation.

The onset of this kind of depression most usually occurs around the age of forty or at a time which the patient equates with the beginning of the second half of life. Quite often it occurs when the patient seems to be at the pinnacle of his career. In women it may typically occur when her last child has grown up and has left the home or when a parent that she has long been caring for has died.

What is generally at the base of all of these existential depressions is that the early long-range ego enhancing and ego affirming ideals or career goals that the patient had set for himself, as the anticipated means of attaining a sense of absolute worth, fulfillment, identity, security, or meaning to his life, although fulfilled failed to bring with it a real sense of fulfillment in terms of the specific absolute benefits that he expected that the attainment of these goals would bring. As a result the patient feels a tremendous sense of despair because he believes that his entire life has basically been a waste. In addition, he feels very angry because he believes that he has been misled and deceived by persons important in his life in regard to the rewards that would accrue to him as a function of his attaining those goals which they laid out for him to pursue. Early in his life he was implicitly or explicitly led to believe, by society, parents, church, etc., that if he surrendered and subjugated his own real and spontaneous inner yearnings, interests, and abilities, and replaced them with a set of pursuits, values, ideals or direction in life more in accord with those who were trying to influence him that his life, in the future, was certain to be highly rewarded with a sense of joy, fulfillment, esteem, security, identity, meaning, and the like. The future has now become the present but he finds that the goals that he strived for and attained returned no big payoff. There was "no pot of gold at the end of the rainbow."

His depression begins to arise the moment he attains the clear conscious recognition and conviction that his life, as he is currently living it, will never offer him any of the rewarding consequences that he thought would be his when he finally achieved his ideals and goals. He finds, for example, that he still feels basically empty inside, or confused about his identity, worth, security, or the meaning of his life. His resulting sense of helplessness, hopelessness, frustration and anger all contribute significantly to the development and maintenance of his depression. How some of the specific existential issues relate to depression will now be described in more detail.

For many of these kinds of patients the depression symbolically represents the death of what he holds to be the most basically real part of himself. Essentially, the existential issue or problem is one of an identity crisis. He identifies his real self with those most basic experiential realities and personal yearnings which he felt compelled to ignore or surrender earlier in his life in order to pursue the externally imposed ideals or values. He feels that he has sacrificed all of the essentially real and important aspects of himself on the altar of his great need for acceptance by others. Now he has suddenly awakened to the realization that the personality that he has molded himself into is just not real nor is it anything that he really wants to be. He was never able to discover this truth before because he always held to the belief that if he achieved all of his goals that he would then be a totally fulfilled person. Now that he has achieved his goals he discovers that it is not true. It seems to him to be too late now to ever express and fulfill his true yearnings and abilities. In a sense he feels that something in himself has died or is irretrievably lost and that he has closed the lid over his own coffin. His deep sense of frustration and hopelessness and his mourning over what he feels that he has lost precipitate his depression. His anger toward himself for permitting himself to be so manipulated and misguided by others and the unexpressed anger that he feels toward

those he holds responsible for his current state of loss and confusion also contribute significantly to the development of the
intensity of his depression.

For other patients the depression and existential issue is related not so much to a problem of identity as it is to a problem
of needing to find a sense of absolute worth and meaning in one's
personal life. This problem quite often manifests itself as a concern or preoccupation with the meaning of the whole of life, for
one's personal life cannot be deemed to be meaningful unless
the whole of life is first established as being meaningful. One
typically finds in this kind of patient that for one reason or another the meaning or feeling of significance has gone out of his
career which once was invested with very great meaning and
significance. Quite often this kind of person is also involved in
a marriage or family life which is loveless and which he also perceives as being meaningless so that his entire life seems to him
to be totally empty and devoid of any meaning or significance.

At a deeper level one discovers that this kind of patient is
extremely fearful of death and one who is desperately searching
for some means of denying his own impermanence. He operates
under the assumption that if he could find some personal meaning
to his life that he would then be able to face his own termination
in death without his extreme fear and trepidation. He generally
concludes that the best way to establish that his life has meaning is through some kind of absolutely meaningful and uniquely
personal contribution that he hopes to make to the enhancement
of mankind. His fantasy is that his meaningful contribution will
endure long after his death and that this would preserve a sense
of continuance of his own existence through his identification
with the enduring contribution that he has left behind or through
the memory of him which will endure in the minds of many
people as a function of their association of his name with his lasting good works.

However, he must first attempt to establish that life as a whole
is meaningful for if life as a whole is not meaningful then there
will be no way for him to establish that his own personal life has
meaning. His first impulse is usually to read widely in areas such

as philosophy, psychology and religion in the hope of establishing the validity of some kind of deeper conceptual meaning to life or he may instead seek to join some kind of social movement, cause, or organization that he feels is already involved with doing meaningful things and making significant contributions to the well-being of mankind. However, after some period of time this kind of activity usually palls and he begins to feel a deep sense of despair and total loss in terms of where else to turn to find meaning in life. Some of these persons will then seek out psychotherapy in the hope of resolving their doubts and questions in regard to this existential issue as well as their fears and depression.

Concerns around fear of death are quite often also at the root of the depressed patient who feels that having reached the pinnacle of his career he has run out of significant goals to achieve or significant challenges to conquer. In these persons living has become equated with the striving toward some kind of becoming, that is, movement toward some kind of goal of self-enhancement. Its opposite, stagnation, becomes equated with death. It is not unusual to find in many of these cases that here, too, there is a marriage and family life which seems to have lost all of its sense of vitality and excitement and the feeling of boredom associated with the stagnation in the home life intensifies his unconscious fear that his psychological self is dying. This kind of patient requires an almost continuous sense of excitation and self-enhancement striving for him to feel that he is really living. In an attempt to engender such feelings in his life he may typically get involved in extramarital sexual affairs, compulsive traveling, or in some kind of recreation or hobby by which he can continue to feel that he is enhancing himself such as improving his golf scores, learning a musical instrument, or the development of some other kind of new skill, or, as many do, he may go on some kind of self-indulgent buying spree. However, after a while, frustration and boredom inevitably set in again and his depression is the resulting unconscious symbol that he feels that his psychological self is dying.

The last such patient to be discussed in terms of existential depression is the person whose depression results not from the fulfillment of career or long-range goals but rather because of the frustration of such fulfillment. His feeling is that the time is now too late for him to fulfill his life-long ambitions and he still holds to the belief that without the fulfillment of his goals that he will be affirming that he is absolutely inadequate and worthless. He feels himself to be rapidly deteriorating or "going down-hill" and he desperately would like to make time stand still so that he could accomplish all of his major goals. He sees his life, essentially, as amounting to zero, as though he had never lived at all. Analogously, he feels that the sun of his life has risen, passed its apex, and is now past noon and beginning to set but his harvest has not yet been brought to market. He feels tortured and panicked by the realization that his efforts and goals will likely never reach fruition and that sense of hopelessness along with strong feelings of self-condemnation results in his becoming severely depressed.

In summary, one finds three basic factors underlying the development of existential depression. One is a long-standing self-alienation and rejection of what has been real in oneself, and an identification with conceptual and imaginal ideals. After a long period of time the self-alienation becomes extremely painful, especially when one comes to the belief that it is now too late to give expression to those realities of oneself. A second factor relates to one's awakening to the realization of the tenuousness and impermanence of one's personal existence. The third factor seems to relate to the need for some persons to find some higher motivating principle for their life than just the devotion to one's own ego-enhancement in order to achieve a real and deep sense of fulfillment in life. The psychotherapist would do well to reflect deeply on these issues himself first before considering taking on such a patient in psychotherapy.

On the whole the prognosis in psychotherapy for these kinds of depressions, as with most forms of depressive reactions and other neurotic disorders, is usually quite good. The prognosis is good because in these kinds of disorders the ego is relatively strong, otherwise the patient would be exhibiting some kind of habitual acting-out or character disorder rather than a depression, and also because the extreme discomfort of the depression tends to maximize motivation for change. Spontaneous recoveries are also relatively frequent in depressions usually due either to some kind of expiation of guilt feelings through interpreted "punishments" that spontaneously occur in the patient's life or perhaps through the appearance on the scene of a new source of self esteem such as a new job or love object which can greatly enhance feelings of worth and security.

A MEDICAL EXAMINATION IS ESSENTIAL

Prior to any psychotherapeutic work with depressed patients it is essential that the patient have a complete and thorough medical examination because the affective state of depression can quite often be the result of some hormonal or other organic dysfunction. When one is not feeling well physically, there is a greater tendency for dysphoric states to also be present. I had one such case referred to me by a physician after a rather cursory medical examination. Apparently he felt certain that the patient's depression was psychogenic in nature due to the fact that her depressed affect seemed to be cyclical. After a few sessions with her she one time casually mentioned something about having frequent colds especially during the time of year in which she also seemed to get depressed. This corresponded with the time of year when the pollen count was highest. The possibility of some allergic condition made me refer her back to her physician even though she insisted that she had never been diagnosed as having such a problem although she did remember always having frequent "colds." The physician subsequently diagnosed her as being allergic to a wide variety of substances.

Apparently what was happening was that the allergic condition was clogging her breathing apparatus making it difficult for her to ingest sufficient oxygen. This tended to make her feel very tired and listless making it very difficult for her to do her chores around the house. This produced self-depreciatory attitudes which were further aggravated by her husband's criticism of her for not being able to handle her household chores. Relatively soon after the treatment for her allergies was initiated her depression lifted and did not return. She has now passed two seasons during which she had previously developed a depression and has not, as yet, experienced any such episodes.

It should be made clear, however, that although metabolic complications are often implicated in the etiology of depressions, psychotherapy can still be valuable in dealing with its psychological affects.

GENERAL COMMENTS IN REGARD TO PSYCHOTHERPY WITH DEPRESSIVES

Prolonged orthodox analysis is hardly ever required to cope with most cases of depressive reactions. Some form of brief, active psychotherapy is usually the therapy of choice. The most basic ingredient in working successfully with depressives is the establishment of a trusting and honest relationship with the patient, toward which a sincere, empathic attitude on the part of the therapist is an essential contributor. The meaningful relationship in which the patient is valued as a human being contributes more than anything else to the achievement of a sense of personal worth and importance. Because they usually have experienced a long history of rejection, they feel themselves to be as "valuable as feces which ought to be flushed down the toilet." For this reason, logical arguments on the part of the therapist, in an attempt to prove to the patient that she is not as worthless as she feels that she is, are basically a waste of time. The patient's experiences in life have conspired to convince her that she is valueless.

Only the therapist's sincere valuing of the patient can begin to overcome her deeply entrenched conviction of her worthlessness. Thus when the patient discusses her most recent rejection, the therapist ought not to come out with a statement to the effect, "there are other fish in the sea." This kind of statement does not comfort because it lacks empathic understanding and also fails to recognize that one of the things that frightens the patient most is the thought of being rejected again. This kind of statement also communicates to the patient that she ought to quickly put away her hurt feelings or that she is foolish for harboring hurt feelings—both of which only contribute all the more to her feelings of humiliation.

Because a good, empathic relationship is so crucial to the success of working with depressed patients, the major deterrents to this success are the therapist's own negative countertransference feelings toward the patient. If the therapist is to work successfully with these patients, he must not be overly sensitive to feeling manipulated and used by them. Otherwise he will surely react negatively to the patient as soon as he recognizes that he is subtly coercing him into giving narcissistic supplies. Depressed patients can be extremely demanding and the therapist has to expect this from them.

Many therapists become upset when they begin to recognize that the patient has lured them into taking responsibility for their depressed condition. Essentially the patient is saying to the therapist, "It's up to you to get rid of my depression. There is nothing at all that I can do about it." Many therapists become extremely resentful when they finally come to discover that the patient is not coming to therapy to change or give up symptoms, but only to get his dependency and narcissistic gratification. The therapist has to be careful not to yield to the temptation of using insight as a "club" against the patient in an attempt to force him to giving up his depression.

I am not one who readily encourages the depressed patient to turn to medication of one kind or another, except in extreme cases. Medication can certainly be an important adjunct in the treatment of psychotic cases. However with less severe cases I find that medication tends to "feed" the patient's dependency needs and later it becomes very difficult for him to give it up without feeling a kind of abandonment which can precipitate an even more intense depressive reaction. I have also found that suggesting that the patient take medication communicates to him that I think that he is weak and needs a crutch. It is very important for the patient's ego strength that he recognize that he is getting better and it is very difficult for him to feel that he, not the pill, has achieved the growth and improvement. In a sense, medication may cheat him out of an opportunity to take credit for his own achievement undermining his self-esteem and confidence in himself.

However, most importantly, I try to explain to the patient that the depression is part of him and is being produced by some aspect of himself and that he ought not to treat the depression as a not-self. Resorting to a pill is forcing the patient to take sides between the conscious part of his functioning which declares that the depression is bad and "I don't want it" and the unconscious part that says, for example, "I need to be depressed in order to get relief from guilt or to achieve the gratification from others that I need."

I feel that it is a great mistake to encourage the patient to distantiate a symptom from himself and then set out to rid himself of it, in a sense, forcefully. This only intensifies conflict and tension. I find it extremely helpful, therapeutically, when the patient begins to recognize the importance of accepting all feelings, thoughts and behavior as part of self. It contributes greatly toward the integration and wholeness of personality which is essentially what the therapist is attempting to help the patient achieve.

Essentially the depressed patient is encouraged not to try either to escape from or fight to overcome the depression. Fear invariably occurs when one tries to run from what is. To contest the depression and try to overcome it is also inappropriate because it only heightens the patient's state of tension and conflict. The unconscious desire or need for the depression becomes pitted against the conscious desire to eliminate it. The more one fights a problem, the more life and strength one gives to that problem. Depression or discontent of any kind is painful only when it is resisted. When the patient is depressed he *is* the depression and not just the experiencer of the depression. This duality only heightens conflict and the depression. To fight the depression is to fight oneself. To become one with the depression and not outside of or separate from it is to end conflict and produce the integration necessary for the creative healing process to take effect.

This is the essence of the entire creative process. When a person is in the state of experiencing—that is, when the experiencer and the experienced are one—then the person is in the state of *creative understanding*. When the experiencer or awareness of self is eliminated by the patient's total attention to the problem, without making any effort in regard to escaping from, contesting or solving the problem, then the hidden aspects of the problem become immediately revealed because there is no longer any barrier of the self interposed between conscious and hidden aspects of the problem. The problem then is seen in its totality and a direct and immediate understanding of the problem occurs.

The patient needs to understand that in a passive way, he needs to permit the depression to operate upon his mind rather than to force his mind to operate on the depression. It is crucial to understand that freedom from the depression comes only through the patient seeing for himself the truths behind his depression rather than through any effort he might make to escape it. This realization or self-discovery by the patient of the truth and understanding of his depression is *the* essential ingredient in producing a release from depression.

In addition to helping the patient understand the content of his problem, the therapist who works with depressed patients must also have a quality of inspiration about himself and the way he perceives life. In dealing with persons with severe depressions, logic and reason alone are generally insufficient tools. It is the inspirational quality which reaches the depressed patient at the level at which he needs to be reached. It makes contact with a void in him which can be filled only by inspirational feeling. Even when the patient does not hear every word the therapist is saying, he is still moved by the feeling tone of what is being experienced. A mechanical, intellectual approach reaches and remains only at the surface of the patient's consciousness and by itself can never move the patient away from his morbid preoccupations. Inspiration helps to lift the patient away from morbidity on the wings of its own intensity. The source of this inspiration can only be love; that heightened sensitivity, openness, inner feeling of beauty, tenderness, compassion and unselfish concern toward all struggling humans beings which can come into being only as the result of the therapist's profound self-discovery of the highest in himself.

REFERENCES

1. Fenichel, Otto: *The Psychoanalytic Theory of Neurosis.* New York, W. W. Norton and Co., 1945.
2. Hammer, Max: The directed daydream technique. *Psychotherapy: Theory, Research and Practice, 4 (No. 4):* 173-181, 1967.
3. Smucker, Leonard: *Spring: A Therapeutic Relationship.* Scottdale (Penn.), Herald Press, 1967.

Chapter 7

Psychotherapy with Suicidal Patients

MAX HAMMER

PSYCHODYNAMICS

ALTHOUGH SUICIDE is frequently a reaction to a feeling of intolerance to one of the depressive reactions discussed in the previous chapter, this is not always the case. It is important to recognize that not all suicides manifest depressive symptoms and that the psychodynamics of depression are not always sufficient to account for all suicide attempts. Some of the most typical psychodynamics involved in suicide will be discussed. It is important to recognize that several of these psychodynamic factors may be operative at one time, in any one suicidal reaction.

Suicide as Appeal and Threat

It is clear that not all apparent suicide attempts are genuine. That is to say, the urge to destroy oneself is not always present in some "suicidal attempts" but rather represents an attempt on the part of the patient to coerce some person(s) in the environment to provide narcissistic supplies.

As an example, Mrs. Black, after twenty years of marriage, was feeling that her husband was beginning to lose interest in her. He was spending more and more time at his job and less and less time with her. When he was home he sat in front of the television and almost completely ignored her. The more he ignored her, the more demanding she became and the more demanding she became, the more he ignored her as a way of showing her that he was not going to submit to her demands for fear that if he did give in to her demands that this would reward her into becoming even more demanding. Her children had grown older and did not seem to need her any more. It seemed to her that no one even knew that she existed or cared if she lived or died.

I have come to recognize that many dependent persons require acknowledgment and recognition by some significant other, not only as a source of narcissistic supplies for their self-esteem, but even more importantly they begin to doubt their own existence if persons no longer need them or react to them in a meaningful way.

In order to find out if she had any value to anyone and to force a reaction of loving concern toward her, one night after feeling particularly hurt and rejected by her husband, she ran to the medicine cabinet shouting and insisting that she was going to commit suicide because no one cared about her anyway. Fortunately, her husband ran after her and when she put a large handful of aspirin in her mouth, he smacked her across the face and knocked the aspirins out of her mouth. She later confided to me that she really had no intention of killing herself and did not intend to swallow the aspirins and even if she had accidentally done so she knew how to quickly prepare an antidote or even better yet have her husband do it for her. In her fantasy she could visualize her husband pleading for her to live and begging her forgiveness for not having treated her properly. She felt that her husband's knocking the pills out of her mouth was sufficient indication to her that she was valuable to him, a feeling which restored her self-esteem; but most of all she felt that she had now conditioned her husband into being more attentive to her for fear that she might attempt suicide again. Thus, her narcissistic supplies would keep coming and she would never again have to feel the panic related to the unconscious doubting of her own existence because her husband was now constantly on guard to react to her and acknowledge her.

On the one hand the suicidal attempt is an appeal to other people for love, protection, esteem and so forth, but at the same time it is also a *threat*. It says, in effect, "Love me or else. . . ." It is a kind of blackmail. It is meant to subtly communicate to the other, something to the effect, "I will punish you and embarrass you to the entire community. I will kill myself and everyone will know you drove me to it. You will never again have a moment's peace of mind. You have always wanted to be free of me, now I will always be in your thoughts and you will never be free of me."

There are, however, some of these patients who truly intend to go through with an actual suicide. Some of these patients feel, "I'll give him the chance to let me die if he wants me to. If he wants me to die there is no sense to living anyway. I'm too frightened to live without a close tie to someone. I just can't live with this uncertainty of not knowing whether he wants me dead or alive and with this insecurity of not feeling protected and loved. I am committed to die unless he loves me enough to save me." These persons then will never attempt suicide unless the love object is present or nearby and is in a position to save them should the desire to do so be there. This will be discussed in more detail in the section dealing with the rescue fantasy.

It should be clear that for the kind of narcissistic person discussed here, the goal of the suicide *attempt* is different from the *act* of suicide in which death is truly sought. The suicide attempt represents, as indicated above, both an appeal and a threat. But the suicide itself in some way is seen by the patient as a way of achieving a final victory over some object(s) or aspect of the patient's world. In life, the patient felt constantly defeated by an inability to totally control his world, but unconsciously the patient feels that in death a final victory will be achieved over the rejecting object. The victory lies, in part, in hurting the other without giving the other a chance to hurt back, but also involved, ironically, is the feeling on the part of the patient that via the trauma of the suicide, his "life" will endure, for his memory will always be indelibly impressed upon the mind of his love object for the duration of her life, thereby insuring for him the nonseparative and enduring union with her for which he has always yearned.

Suicide and the Rescue Fantasy

Those who have worked closely with patients who have attempted suicide have come to recognize a phenomenon termed by Jensen and Petty[3] the "rescue fantasy." It is now well recognized that most persons before attempting suicide will, either consciously or unconsciously, alert someone, whom they have chosen to be their rescuer, as to their intentions. In the preparations for and in the execution of the suicidal act are expressed not only the wish to die but also the wish to live and to be saved by this rescuer. A savior is chosen and an opportunity for rescue is provided. If the behavior of the one chosen for the rescue is not what the suicidal person hopes or needs it to be, death is probable or inevitable. When they choose a rescuer it is usually someone who has a strong ego, strong enough to serve the both of them, and also someone who is loving enough to supply him with his needs for affection and protection. It is for these reasons that the therapist is frequently chosen as the rescuer.

The prototype for the relationship that the suicidal person seeks with the rescuer is probably that relationship early in infancy when the infant and mother shared a common ego and each responded directly to the unconscious of the other as though it were his own; apparently this state is temporarily reinstated by regression in the patient contemplating suicide. In attempting to affirm the existence of this state, which to the suicidal person suggests the ultimate in protection and security, the suicidal person drops subtle clues to the person chosen as rescuer; and if the rescuer picks these up and comes to the rescue, then the patient achieves a sense of security, again through the belief that it could only have been via the union of unconsciouses that the other came to the rescue. It is only the conviction that such union exists that enables the fearfully regressed patient to continue to face life without being overwhelmed with fears of vulnerability and helplessness. If, however, the person chosen as the rescuer does not read the signs adequately enough to come in time to rescue the patient, then the suicidal person permits himself to die because to him, the failure to rescue is proof of abandonment which is so terrifying to him that death is seen as preferable to continuing to live in such terror.

Jensen and Petty[3] indicate that it often happens that a potential rescuer recognizes the role assigned to him yet refuses that role or attempts to transfer it to someone else. Interference in communication between the suicidal person and the potential rescuer frequently seems to result from the latter's unconscious wish to be rid of the patient. The rescuer's own unconscious hostility may have been so aroused by the demands, the unpleasantness, the attempt to exercise extreme control and the antagonism of the suicidal person that his predominant unconscious attitude is, "Do it and be done with it. Good riddance."

Sterba[4] elaborated upon the aggression expressed in the fantasy of rescue. The fantasy to be rescued in suicide expresses the passive wish to be saved by someone upon whom the suicidal person has projected a share of his own aggression and whom he unconsciously holds responsible for his impending death. The aggression against the potential rescuer is expressed passively through the threat of making a murderer of the potential rescuer if the fantasy to be rescued is not fulfilled in reality.

While the fantasy expresses the passive wish to be rescued, the role of the rescuer is an active one and he *cannot equivocate* if he is to function in his designated capacity; equivocation will change his function from rescuer to "murderer." This fact has special importance for psychotherapists and others who by reason of transference are likely to be chosen as rescuers. Resorting to therapeutic anonymity or passivity by the therapist to avoid the responsibilities of the rescuer is a rationalization at best and will probably end disastrously for the suicidal person and sometimes for the potential rescuer as well.

I should also point out another potential problem at the other extreme. The therapist must be clear in regard to his own need for omnipotence in that he needs to recognize that he cannot be responsible for the life of another human being. If he were to feel responsible for the life of his patients, he would suffer terribly if they should commit suicide. He then places himself in a position very vulnerable to being "blackmailed" by the patients into giving narcissistic supplies and taking the responsibility for their life. Many patients are seeking a kind of parasitic existence with another as their way of feeling safe and secure, and they will surely take advantage of the therapist in this way, to the detriment not only of the therapist but of the progress of the therapy as well. If the therapist is controllable in this way, he is not always free to act in a way which might be most therapeutic for the patient.

The following case illustrates the rescue fantasy of a 17-year-old girl, Nina. Nina was born out of wedlock and lived with her real mother, sister and stepfather, who never formally adopted Nina. She had never met her real father, but only knew that he lived in a far off city in the same state in which she lived. Her mother had told her that she had heard that he was married and had a family of his own. Nina was referred to me because she was having great difficulty in getting along with her peers and parents. Also she suffered from various phobias; the most serious and disturbing to her was one of lights hanging from a ceiling. She indicated that they reminded her of eyes that were peering at her and coming to get her. On her last visit to me prior to her suicidal attempt she brought me a poem which she asked me to read only after our session was over and she was gone. It was called "The Tree" and read as follows:

> A tree in the distance
> Is all that I can see
> But you can't convince me
> It's only a tree
>
> It stands very tall
> Very straight, very high
> Its branches reach out
> Touching clouds going by
>
> It stands in the rain
> And the sleet, and the snow
> It keeps right on standing
> When icy winds blow
>
> It reminds me of man
> Who is much like a tree
> He suffers through hardships
> And waits to be free
>
> Way off in the distance
> You ask what I see
> But I'll never tell you
> It's only a tree

On numerous occasions she had told me of a special tree that she could see from her bench in a small mall-type park, and when she felt hurt or particularly upset she would spend time in the presence of that tree. She had apparently made some kind of identification with it. The next day a letter arrived from her which read:

Right now, Dr. Hammer, I wouldn't care if the whole world exploded. I feel very sad and confused. I don't feel as if I am a part of society or anything else for that matter. Why it is that I can't seem to grasp that true self of mine which is floating in the air so close by me? Why are there so many lonely sensitive feelings blocking out the better, happier ones? Who am I? Why did God create such a thing? What was it that happened to me as a child that makes me feel this way? Where are the answers to my ever-haunting questions? I honestly feel like a dead-being roaming the earth. I have no cares for anyone. Do you think it phases me to read about someone dying? Of course not. There are no feelings whatsoever in my soul for anyone. I'm a self-centered person. I guess I could say that I feel sorry for myself. I don't know why I should but I do. Why are there times when I would think of committing suicide? I really don't know but there are. I can't sleep nights, I'm irritable, I don't want people watching me, I like to be alone, I worry a lot. I hate those who ask questions concerning my personal affairs and I hate those who nag. I honestly believe I'll always have these feelings. I'll never rid myself of them. I can't go on living in a world such as this being the person that I am. I put in a terrible night last night. I told God I wanted to die and I really do. I thought of how wonderful it would be to lie there with no more loneliness, heartache, sadness, tears or anything any more. It would be like a long sleep and for once in my life I could be left alone. Death to me is far better than this so-called life. I think it's torture to live here where people do nothing but fight and hate each other. I went to a dance the other night and no one asked me to dance. Don't ask me why. I looked as good as anyone else did. Well, maybe I didn't to those boys. I guess no one likes a sentimental person like myself when everyone else is so fun-loving. I can't understand why I feel like this and why I'm here. I dread the nights. The days aren't too bad, but at night I cry until my face is all swollen. I'm making myself sick. I don't know what to do. I don't see how I've lasted this long. The other night I suddenly became a little girl again. I wasn't even talking sensible. I found myself crying to my father. Then I could see him sitting beside my bed and he took a hold of my hand and told me he loved me and that I didn't have to be afraid any more. Then another night I was lying there and suddenly I couldn't feel anything. I couldn't do anything at all. It was like I was mentally retarded, too. Then I could see Mom in the kitchen. She was yelling at me. I wanted to cook something and she told me I didn't know how. I felt ignorant. Everything I touched I dropped. Then I cried real hard. Dr. Hammer, please help me. You're the only person I can turn to. You're the only one that understands me. Nobody knows just how terrible these feelings are. If it lasts much longer, I don't know what I'll do.

Nina

The next evening I received a long-distance telephone call from the mother who was frantic. Nina had not returned from school yet, and now it was several hours past her suppertime. The mother had called the few friends that Nina had, but none had seen her. It was an extremely cold winter's night. The mother could not imagine where the girl could be and hoped that perhaps I might have some idea. I told her to call the police immediately and have them start looking for her. Then I remembered her poem and letter and our past conversations regarding her going to visit the tree at times when she felt most unhappy. I suggested that the mother herself go to the park and search for her there near one of the large trees. I felt that it was very important that the mother be the one to find her. The mother called me back later to tell me that they had found her there and had taken her to the hospital. They found her lying nude in some bushes near the tree. She was suffering from shock and overexposure to the cold but the doctor felt that she would recover. He indicated that greater delay could possibly have been fatal. As I learned afterward, it was her goal to freeze to death, which she had learned was a very painless way to die. "You just fall asleep and it's all over." It also was apparent that in some way she was trying to achieve a kind of mystical union with the tree by dying in its presence.

She had apparently arranged the "suicide" to use both me and her mother as the rescuer because, as she had unconsciously arranged it, it would have been impossible for either one of us alone to have known enough about her at the time to save her. It was also clear that she was committed to die if we both did not come to the rescue. She apparently placed me in the role of the long lost father whom she had never met, fantasizing two loving parents expressing their love for her by coming to her rescue.

This case typically reflects many of the ingredients that one so often finds in suicide attempts: the feelings of loneliness and isolation, the confusion and uncertainty, the extreme hostility toward self and others, the feelings of numbness as though one were already dead, the equating of death with peaceful sleep and rest and escape from pain, the uncontrollable obsessive, negative thoughts which make one feel helpless and worthless, the feeling of avoiding all people because they are seen as being too hurting and the recognition that the fear of life is greater than the fear of death (which will be discussed in more detail in a later section). However, most importantly, one sees in suicidal reactions despair rather than just depression. Those extreme feelings of hopelessness suggest to the patient that not only is life painful and miserable now, but they see no possible way it can ever change in the future. Despair involves depression plus pessimism. The prospect of having to endure endless pain and feelings of vulnerability and panic is intolerable to them. At this point, suicide is considered as a serious solution to what they feel are their otherwise insoluble problems. Without the element of hopelessness, depression would very seldom lead to real suicide intent.

In the case of Nina cited above, the clues to her suicidal intent were relatively open and direct, but they are not always so apparent. In some instances, patients will reveal their suicidal intent with subtle questioning such as "Do you know how many stories the Empire State Building has?" or "I wonder what it would feel like to jump from an airplane without a parachute?" or "What would happen if a person swallowed a whole bottle of aspirins?" or even more subtly given as in the underlying theme of a poem where, for example, as one patient wrote, one hears a call from the depths of the sea with a yearning to heed the call.

Suicide as Inverted Homicide

It is true for many who kill themselves that they really did not wish to die but rather wished to kill someone else. At times this someone else is a real person such as a parent, husband or child, but the impulse to destroy is turned inward instead of outward because of intense superego development or because for years they have been conditioned by the parents never to express negative feelings. For their own security they have built up such an intense defense against the expression of negative feelings that when the rage becomes too great to bear they are forced to turn it inward against the self. At other times the someone else may not be a real person but rather a representative within the self of a particular person. Thus they may attempt to kill the voice of conscience which will not permit them a moment's rest or the goal may be to destroy the hated parent who has been introjected and operates within as superego or ego.

Sometimes they may turn their rage against the persistent and uncontrollably morbid obsessive thoughts which run through their mind and blow out their brains, which they hold responsible for their mental suffering. At other times the patient takes his stand as his idealized image and seeks to destroy what he feels to be his inadequate actual self, as Horney[2] has described. In other instances the destructiveness turned inward serves as supreme masochistic gratification or masochistic defense against the more frightened expression of sadistic impulses.

It is helpful if a patient who has repressed his rage against a parent has an opportunity to express his negative feelings toward that person before the parent dies. Once the parent has died, then the rage gets directed against the introjected parent now operating as superego or ego. When the patient considers committing suicide by killing the hated parent within himself, at the same time he preserves the magical feeling that he will somehow keep on living. If thwarted in his suicide attempt, such a person will typically remark afterward that it never occurred to him that he too would also cease to exist once the rage was discharged against the introjected parent serving now as conscience or as specific attitudes or traits within the self. He had identified himself only with the initiator of the rage but not its recipient.

Most suicidal persons do not want to die, they only want to indulge the rage to destroy. It is quite common to hear from those who attempt suicide that soon after they indulged the impulse they were sorry that they had done so and had changed their mind about wanting to die. The therapist needs to recognize that the patient has a wish to live in addition to the impulse to destroy himself, although there are times when the latter impulse grossly overshadows the former. Once the rage has been expressed they are quite satisfied and now are ready to live although at times this change of heart is too late, such as when one comes to this recognition after having mortally wounded himself.

I point this out especially for those who take the philosophical stand that the therapist has no right to interfere with a patient's decision to take his own life if the patient is not psychotic. This argument fails to recognize the ambivalent nature of the suicidal impulse. I also point out this ambivalence to the suicidal patient and try to help him recognize that he also has a great wish to live, in addition to having a strong wish to die, but he cannot feel it because his wish to destroy himself is so intense and overshadowing. Helping the patient to recognize that he does not really want to die but only wishes to indulge his rage to destroy opens the way to suggestions for sublimating this rage and may improve the patient's receptivity to these suggestions and thus to be in a position to help himself should the impulse to self-destruction return again in the future.

Suicide and Loss of Self

Typically the college student has come to identify himself with his intellect. His entire self is built around his intellect. If the intellect gains victories he is euphoric, but if the intellect meets defeats he is distraught. However, if the defeat is too severe it may lead to a feeling of loss of self. In one instance a student confided to me his fantasy of committing suicide. Fortunately he came in to talk to me about it before acting on his impulse. Since early childhood he had come to feel that the only valuable thing about him was his intellect. He did quite well until he came to graduate school where he failed an important examination which made it impossible for him to continue his graduate career. "If I am not my intelligence who am I then? Now I'm a nobody and a nothing. There is no need to continue living because there is no self left to do the living," he felt. He continued, "I'll make that professor suffer who made me a nobody. He killed me. He took away my ability to ever enjoy life. I'll do the same to him. I will write a note and leave it in my pocket. It will be addressed to my professor and I will tell him that it was his unfairness that drove me to kill myself. I will make it clear to him that he killed me. All of his friends and colleagues will also know about it. My death will be so indelibly impressed upon his conscience that he will never again be able to enjoy life. Oh, that will be sweet revenge."

Suicide as Atonement

Some persons attempt suicide in an attempt to atone for guilt, real or imagined. Especially for deeply religious persons there is sometimes the conviction that the only relief from guilt associated with a taboo act is to make the supreme sacrifice of self. They become convinced, in their logic, that God demands it. They have become identified with their religious convictions and rather than lose these, which have given their life meaning, they prefer at least to salvage something by placing themselves in the good graces of God by making the supreme sacrifice. They feel that their only hope is to make it appear as though they were giving up their life as a sacrifice in order to please God so that they might gain His forgiveness and thereby still gain entrance into Heaven.

Suicide as Martyrdom

Somewhat related to the self-sacrificing individual discussed above is the person who dies in the service of her ultimate ideal of martyrdom. Typical of this kind of suicide is the wife who discovers that her husband is in love with another woman, usually a younger or much more attractive woman whose competition seems more than the patient can deal with. In the background of such a patient is an Oedipal situation in which she felt extremely humiliated and angry in having lost out in competion with her mother for father. As a result, she vows never to compete and lose again to another woman over a man that she loves and wants.

She commits suicide and leaves a note to the husband to the effect that it is because she loves him and wants him to be happy that she is removing herself from the picture. She really commits suicide because she feels that it is inevitable that she will lose out in the competition with this woman, which will leave her so lonely and humiliated in the community that she would not be able to face anyone again. She feels that her life is over anyway. What she wants to achieve via the suicide is some victory over the other woman and some punishment of her husband. By behaving as a martyr, she tries to make her husband feel guilty for having wronged her and to make it impossible for him to ever let himself love the other woman. In this way she feels that she will be converting a defeat into a victory.

When the wife commits suicide, the husband, feeling very guilty, tends to project his guilt on to the other woman and blames her for the entire affair. In this way the suicidal wife has in a way "killed" the other woman and gained a final victory over her. In addition, the wife's image in the community, which she feels will live on and in this way give her life some enduring quality, becomes elevated because everyone feels that the patient's "unselfish" deed is a sign of her extraordinary character. Thus she feels that by her suicide she will have reversed a humiliating defeat and turned it into a total victory.

Suicide as Retaliatory Abandonment

Similar in many ways to the previous example but psychodynamically quite different is the suicide as retaliatory abandonment. Hendin[1] discusses this type of suicide in which the patient feels that she is about to be abandoned and says in essence, "If there is to be any rejecting or abandoning to be done, I'm the one who will do it." I find that these persons equate being abandoned with being treated as though they are worthless and do not exist. They still have the child's conception of death. For children death is understood basically as a separation or abandonment. It is not unusual for these persons to have dreams which portray death in this way such as taking a long sea voyage or saying goodbye at the train station or an airplane taking them higher and higher into the clouds, and the like.

Suicide, in these persons, seems to provide an illusory feeling of mastery over a situation through the control that one has over whether one lives or dies. It alleviates the feeling of helplessness by restoring the fantasy that one's omnipotence is still intact. The feeling is "If I have control over life and death then I truly am omnipotent."

Typical of this type of suicide is the young man who stands on a ledge of a tall building threatening to jump because his girl friend left him for another man or just does not love him any more. He is determined to maintain his control over her or die. He usually does not jump until he is assured that his girl friend has come and he tries to threaten her into returning to him by his threat to jump. If she does not return to him then he jumps with the satisfaction that because she is there begging for his life he is really abandoning her by taking his own life and in addition punishing her with the guilt of having to witness his suicide and his condemnation of her as he jumps.

This need to control and to maintain a sense of omnipotence or the inability to live without such assurance, I feel is one of the most basic dynamics underlying all suicides. Most of those who want to commit suicide, due to extreme insecurity, have regressed to that stage of infancy in which one feels totally helpless and needs to affirm one's omnipotence in order to feel a sense of security. The loss of control over their environment gives them no assurance that they will be protected should they require it, and so they attempt every means of manipulation to restore that sense of control over significant others and they are willing to die in the attempt should they fail to achieve it.

Suicide as Reunion

This type of suicide operates in those who are in mourning over the loss of a loved one with whom they have been extremely close over the years. They cannot tolerate the separation from their loved one usually because their dependency upon them has been so great over the years that the mate remaining feels totally helpless to care for herself. One such woman said to me, "It's like trying to live without your heart. Can a person live without a heart?" The existence of such people over the years has been affirmed only by the presence and recognition on the part of the mate and without the mate they feel lost, as though they did not exist. They cannot tolerate the separation from the loved one and they fantasize an eternal fusion with him in death. This fulfills the childlike fantasy of having love forever after. Most frequently the emphasis is not put on the dying but on the gratification to follow. Prior to the suicide attempt they frequently will report dreams to the therapist in which their mate is calling them to come and join them and they feel blissfully happy at the prospect of being reunited with the mate.

The search for an eternal fusion in death is frequently the motivating factor when young lovers commit dual suicide in what is frequently referred to as a death-pact for lovers. The Norwegian movie "Elvira Madigan," which gained great popularity in this country, also reflects the basic theme that some lovers feel that their existence is only one-half of a total whole and that once the union of the two parts is achieved, the whole cannot be destroyed without both parts also being destroyed. They equate life with love and union. Thus when this love or union is lost then life is also felt to be lost and so they consequently attempt to reestablish this union in death.

The Masochist

Masochistic tendencies are involved in various kinds of suicidal attempts, some of which have already been discussed in earlier sections. In this section, suicide as a direct result of masochism will be discussed.

Essentially, the masochist is one who turns the full vent of his destructive impulses upon himself. The masochistic person is basically one who struggles to drain an enormous amount of tension within himself only to meet with repeated failure and frustration. Much of his tension is the result of the bound-up energy of repressed sexuality. He is unable to achieve a release of this energy due to what may be called orgasm anxiety. He is fully capable of becoming sexually aroused but at the peak of his sexual excitement and just prior to orgastic release he develops an anxiety reaction which serves to inhibit the release function. The letting-go or loss of control involved in orgasm is very threatening to him for one reason or another. Frequently it is unconsciously equated with a state of helpless vulnerability or with loss of self and death. As a result of this unconscious interpretation, an anxiety reaction occurs just at the point of discharge and release.

His inability to release his blocked energy through sexual orgasm results in the attempt to channelize and discharge it through other avenues such as destructive aggression. The masochist's continuous frustration and failure to reduce his own tension usually leads to a fantasy in which he sees himself as totally bursting inside and thereby achieving a total release from tension. In essence, the tension within him is perceived as the cause of his enormous frustration and so it becomes the object of his destructive impulses. When this fantasy is acted out, it can result in suicide. To the masochist, death is the unconscious equivalent of the "big orgasm" or release of tension for which he has always sought but been denied, and the little hurts which he imposes upon himself represent the prefatory exciting foreplay. Thus, he is always burdened by the conflict of both desiring and fearing his own death and is in a constant struggle to resist yielding to the temptation to completely give up his controls and destroy himself. At some point in his life he may yield to that temptation.

Suicide as a Demonstration of Courage

On the college campus I have noticed a few cases in which some young boys are teased for their lack of masculine appearance or for their general submissiveness and they feel compelled to demonstrate to their peers that they are a man by demonstrating a lack of fear where others tend to be most fearful—that is, in regard to death. One such young man revealed to me, after his stomach was pumped for having taken a large amount of aspirins, that since the event took place, his standing with his peers has risen astronomically. One of his peers, after having heard of the young man's suicide attempt said to him, "Gee, I never knew you had that much courage in you." As he had anticipated, his suicide attempt had gained him a new respect from his peers.

Suicide and Rebirth

Many of us are tempted to go to sleep early whenever we have had a particularly bad day. The goal is not only to put an end to a day that has been bad but the belief is that the new day will bring a new beginning. "Tomorrow will bring a better day" is a phrase that is often heard. What is true for one day can also be generalized for a lifetime. For some persons, life itself is seen as a bad day or a bad dream from which one has to awaken. They also feel like going to sleep and "waking up tomorrow" to a new beginning. Waking up to a new day is unconsciously equated with a rebirth, and of course going to sleep is equated with death. This attitude of rebirth is frequently taught by parents who have difficulty getting their children to go to sleep. In essence they will tell their children that sleep will undo all the hurts of the day, and at times they tell the child that if he goes to sleep now that when he wakes up in the morning he will find a nice surprise gift near his bed. This tends to overly reward going to sleep and looking forward to tomorrow and also overly encourages the tendency to avoid the hurts of the day by going to sleep. When this kind of child grows up and experiences life as a hard day, then the unconscious yearning for a better tomorrow through a death and a rebirth becomes very attractive.

Suicide and the Patient Who Sees Himself As Already Dead

I have found this kind of suicide attempt particularly in young girls in my work at a woman's reformatory. As a result of feeling badly hurt in love relationships with their parents they make a vow never to love again because to love again and not to have that love returned is an extremely painful and humiliating experience. In order to guarantee for themselves that they will not be hurt again they have to repress all of their tender, loving feelings. In addition, they will usually repress their capacity to cry because tears permit them to feel their hurt feelings. As a result of feeling unable to love or cry they come to see themselves as an empty shell, devoid of feelings. Because we tend to equate feelings with life, these girls believe that in a sense, they are already dead. Many tell me that they feel as though they were numb. They may report dreams in which they see themselves with their eyes open, lying in a coffin, unable to move. The dream clearly reflects their unconscious attitude toward themselves.

Other persons equate sexual desire or sexual potency with life force and if they feel that they have lost their sexual desire or ability, then they may also feel that they are already dead and there is no reason in life to keep on living.

Generally, the feeling of being already dead goes along with strong feelings of detachment, repressed aggression and a fear of loving for fear of getting hurt. The case of Nina discussed earlier in this chapter is a good example of this type of person. Many of these persons see suicide as a release from the constant torture of needing to repress and avoid feelings and the people who might trigger such feelings. They feel that the actual death is merely a carrying out of an event that has already taken place. As one girl said, "I'm already dead, I just don't know enough to fall down."

THERAPEUTIC CONSIDERATIONS

The Interview

A comprehensive interview, especially with the patient under severe stress, is essential for the determination of possible suicidal intentions which may be either conscious or unconscious. To determine the likelihood of possible suicidal acting-out in a patient, the therapist needs to clearly assess the patient's capacity for tolerating psychological pain and discomfort. The patient who habitually and immediately runs from pain and tension without ever given himself an opportunity to directly experience it or effectively master it is much more likely, under intense and unusual stress, to follow the same pattern and seek an immediate and final escape and is therefore much more likely to impulsively attempt suicide than is the patient who demonstrates in his life clear indications of the capacity to tolerate and endure pain without the immediately impulsive need to escape from it. Thus, such indices in the patient as the compulsive use of alcohol, drugs, sexuality, sleep, manicky activity, etcetera for the purpose of immediate tension reduction are indicators of greater suicide potential; whereas evidence to the effect that the patient has been able in the past to endure and resolve psychological pain such as that which stems from anxiety, depression, long and intense frustrations, deprivations, disappointments and so forth, would, in most cases, be less suggestive of the likelihood of true suicidal acting-out.

If there have been past suicide attempts, the therapist needs to establish what the pattern or triggering events have been in order to recognize what basic needs or fantasies the suicide attempts are seeking to fulfill. If the patient has considered suicide in thought only, the therapist needs to obtain information as to the circumstances under which these thoughts arose and the details of how and when the patient might act out the suicidal intent. The details of his suicide fantasy need to be thoroughly explored. The device the patient would use to end his life and the persons he would require present during the act are especially crucial in providing clues as to the meaning of suicide to the particular patient. Thus, for example, patients who reveal that they would prefer to attempt suicide by bringing pain upon themselves such as by cutting a wrist or walking in front of a speeding car are probably reflecting the existence of intense masochistic tension within themselves, whereas those that would prefer to attempt suicide by means such as taking an overdose of sleeping pills or drowning are probably reflecting more of a passive-dependent personality for whom achieving a sense of merging or fusion is essential.

The therapist also needs to try to ascertain what clues the patient is likely to use for the rescue fantasy so that he and the patient's family may be alert to these clues when and if they should become apparent. The therapist also needs to determine what kinds of people the patient is likely to choose to play the role of the rescuer by determining from the patient the kinds of persons that provide him with the most security and feelings of worth. It is also important to ask the patient as well as his family how he tends to handle destructive impulses or how he reacts when he has been badly emotionally hurt or frustrated. It is important to try to establish whether the patient's pattern of handling destructive impulses is to turn them in, out, or to totally repress and deny the existence of such feelings.

Sometimes projective personality tests and inspection of recent dreams may be essential in establishing the likelihood of suicidal acting-out. It is also of value to explore for possible phobias which may reflect a defense against possible unconscious suicidal intent, such as fear of high places or of driving a car, and the like.

Still another important consideration is to ask the patient about his philosophy of life and death and whether he has a concept of an afterlife. This information can be vital for determining the likelihood of potential suicide and the circumstances around which it may most likely occur. Other vital questions that need to be asked in the interview should deal with helping the therapist decide whether or not the patient is treatable on an outpatient basis or whether hospitalization may be required.

Consideration of Hospitalization

Hospitalization needs to be considered if the therapist feels that the patient is in poor contact with reality or if the patient feels helpless in regard to defending himself against his own destructive impulses. Some patients make it very clear that they are begging for protection and no longer feel safe with themselves. Sometimes this is reflected in the fact that the patient becomes panicked whenever he has to be alone, for this is the time when he fears that he may act out his destructive impulses against himself. As long as other persons are with him he feels fairly comfortable. It becomes readily clear that this kind of patient is not considering suicide as an attempt to force narcissistic supplies from his environment but rather is struggling to contain a destructive impulse that is basically ego-dystonic.

Not infrequently the patient will externalize his self-destructive feelings and report a need to break something in order to drain the tension of his destructive impulse. Others may report having a destructive impulse to hurt or kill one of their children even though this kind of patient knows that he really loves the child dearly. The tendency to produce sadistic ideation clearly reflects its use as a defense against the more frightening masochistic or self-destructive impulses. If the patient should report a sudden increase in loss of control such as increased physical beatings of his wife or children, then this may be an indication that hospitalization is required.

If the suicidal intent is unconscious rather than conscious, then this may be another indicator that hospitalization may be required. For if the suicidal impulse is under the influence of conscious ego functioning then there is likely to be much more control over it. If the patient is to resist the destructive impulse by himself, he must have a "reality peg on which to hang his big unconscious load" and so the therapist should always attempt to make the impulse, and all its attendant aspects, conscious as soon as possible.

If the patient is struggling with suicidal preoccupations then it is obvious that once-a-week therapy will usually not be sufficient. If it becomes obvious that the patient cannot handle the problem on a once-a-week basis and the therapist does not feel that he has the time or the inclination to provide more time to the patient, then this would be another circumstance in which he would be better off considering hospitalization for his patient. I believe that the most important ingredient in this decision is how frightened the therapist is in dealing with such a problem. If the therapist is very frightened, then it is likely that he will not be able to provide the patient with the protection and help that the patient needs when the time comes, and on this basis he should consider hospitalization for the patient. Another important factor is whether there are others in the patient's family or community that are available to assist the therapist in helping the patient feel a sense of protection. If the patient manifesting suicidal intentions lives all alone and is not really close to anyone in his community, then he should be considered for hospital treatment.

I am not one of those therapists, although I do recognize that there are many who insist that hospitalization is called for under all circumstances when suicidal intent becomes apparent. The therapist also needs to recognize that although there are some patients who would welcome hospitalization as a source of protection, there are other patients to whom hospitalization would be experienced as an extreme trauma and could actually precipitate a suicidal acting-out. I am especially referring to the kind of patient whose greatest fears are of separation and abandonment. To remove them from their families or from the secure relationship with the therapist could be an overwhelming trauma. Some of the patients in trusting the therapist have come to trust someone for the first time in their lives and if the therapist recommends that they be hospitalized, these patients may find it impossible ever to trust anyone again, especially another therapist. This would make it extremely difficult, if not impossible, for them to ever work out their problems.

It is clear that no hard-and-fast rule can be applied for all patients in regard to hospitalization. However, as a general rule, I would suggest that if in doubt do the safer thing and have the patient hospitalized. It is much better to err in the direction of overcaution than undercaution.

Some General Therapeutic Considerations

The therapist needs to be cautious in assuming that because a patient's depression has lifted that therefore the threat of suicide is eliminated. On the contrary, suicide attempts in severely depressed patients often occur as the patient is emerging from the depths of psychomotor retardation. This cannot be easily explained unless perhaps one views psychomotor retardation as a depressive equivalent of catatonia which, in the depressed patient, serves as a defense against the carrying out of the suicidal impulse. Thus the therapist needs to be extremely alert to a possible suicidal reaction at those times when the patient seems to be making a spontaneous recovery from his depression.

Stone and Shein[5] provide a number of suggestions in working therapeutically with the suicidal patient. Essentially they suggest that if the therapist is convinced that suicide is in the picture, it is important that he not avoid this area but rather express his concerns frankly and discuss them explicitly with the patient. The therapist should then make it clear to the patient that suicide is a maladaptive action and basically contrary to the patient's best interests, regardless of the patient's rationalizations for why suicide might be the best alternative to his current life situation. If the patient is unwilling or unable to discuss his suicidal thoughts, then the therapist must assume that the basic therapeutic relationship necessary to treat a suicidal condition is lacking and that perhaps hospitalization needs to be discussed as possibly the best alternative.

It is important that both the therapist and patient together communicate to the closest relatives the patient's concerns regarding suicide in order to have them participate in the total monitoring and protective process that is necessary for the patient. The therapist must not permit the patient to manipulate him by insisting on therapeutic confidentiality. Suicide is one area in which such confidentialities cannot be abided by. This must be explained thoroughly to the patient and why this is in his best interest. It is also important to obtain the cooperation of the family physician and clergyman and other such persons who are close to the family so that they may be aware of the problem and be available to the patient and his family should a crisis arise and the therapist not be immediately available. The enlistment of other professionals in the crisis protects the therapist as well as the patient since it dilutes the transference elements involved in the rescue fantasy as well as lightens the burden of responsibility, while at the same time providing the patient with others who can be available to him at the time of crisis.

It is crucial that the therapist identify what the patient's conclusions concerning his reality situation are that are driving him to consider suicide and take an *active* approach in altering these conclusions. The therapist must be active and even directive if necessary, for he cannot take the chance that the patient might interpret a neutral or nonactive approach as a sign of the therapist's lack of involvement in or concern for the patient. Without the patient clearly feeling the therapist's involvement with him, the suicidal reaction remains basically untreatable. The *relationship* between the therapist and the patient is the most crucial ingredient in any therapeutic approach with suicidals.

It is also important that the initial stages of therapy focus not on the past object relationships but on current human relationships and essentially what it is about these current relationships that is making life intolerable for the patient. More intensive psychotherapeutic goals in terms of personality change ought not to be considered until both the therapist and patient feel that the patient's original convictions concerning the hopelessness and helplessness of his life situation have been significantly altered and that the suicidal impulse is no longer an imminent menace. It is only after this initial therapeutic goal has been clearly achieved that the therapist should consider eliminating the focus on current life circumstances and concentrate more on the goal of bringing about some more basic personality changes.

This can be achieved best by helping the patient come to recognize the inappropriate ways in which he deals with his own angry feelings and by encouraging the externalization of such angry feelings. The therapist must make it clear to the patient that the expression of angry feelings is a human necessity and that such expression is important not only for the reduction of tension but also to enable honesty and trust to exist in a relationship. The patient must come to recognize what his conclusions have been that have made it so difficult for him to externalize his angry feelings, and here for the first time, the therapy can begin to focus on the past and the patient can be helped to recognize that, for example, it has always been his great need to be loved and his fear of losing such love that has made it impossible for him to express any negative feelings. At this point the therapy can then proceed in the orthodox manner.

Some Specific Approaches When Suicide Seems Imminent

Upon occasion the therapist is confronted with a situation in which the patient has made it abundantly clear that as soon as he leaves the therapist's office he intends to commit suicide. He has already decided to commit suicide and essentially is coming to your office one more time to see if you can give him some reason for living. You have only this one crack at him and you must reach him in this one session in some way so as to provide some obstacle to the impulse toward self-destruction.

I have found it helpful under these circumstances to keep in mind the simple ratio:

$$\text{Tendency toward suicide} = \frac{\text{fear of life}}{\text{fear of death}}$$

It is clear that for most of us the fear of death is greater than the fear of life and so the ratio is low and there is little tendency toward suicide. However, for the suicidal person the fear of life has become greater than the fear of death, either because life has become extremely painful or because their conception or philosophy of death is such as to make it appear extremely comforting and attractive as an alternative. Thus the therapist has two avenues of approach open to him in his attempt in this one session to keep his foot in the door of life, thereby keeping it from closing. He can first attempt to lighten the patient's fear of life by attempting to lessen the reality of the fear or by contributing toward the greater gratification and enjoyment that life can offer. I find these approaches in this kind of circumstance usually less effective than the other alternative which is to contribute toward the increase of his fear of death. I feel that this is an approach which has been very little considered by therapists. I will offer some examples.

For the narcissistic patient who is pleasure principle oriented and frightened of pain, I attempt to convince him that the act of dying itself is extremely painful in contrast to what they may have heard or believed. I tell him most directly that if he cannot endure the pain of life that he will certainly find the pain of dying much more excruciating. I go into detail in regard to how each organ involved in the death process contributes toward the total pain. I point out to him that if he has the courage to face the terrible pain of dying he can certainly endure the pain of living. I tell him that he has demonstrated great courage in enduring all the pain he has had to so far, for he needs to know that his suffering has been appreciated by another. The patient has too comfortable and unrealistic an approach to death and I want him to reality-test his notions in the face of the information that I am providing. My goal is not necessarily to convince him that I am correct. All I want to do is to raise some doubt in his mind which is usually sufficient to prevent the destructive impulse from expressing itself immediately. Once it subsides I can then concentrate on decreasing the fear-of-life side of the ratio.

If the patient is relatively intelligent I attempt to demonstrate to him that his concept of death as a peaceful and restful sleep is not correct and is challenged by as eminent an authority as William Shakespeare. I find most suicidal persons to be basically romantics at heart and they feel an affinity with poets and poetry. I read to him the soliloquy from *Hamlet* (Act III, scene i) (which I always keep close at hand because if I first have to look for it the mood is shattered), and I read it slowly and particularly emphasize the words I have underlined when I come to them:

> To be, or not to be: that is the question:
> Whether 'tis nobler in the mind to suffer
> The slings and arrows of outrageous fortune,
> Or to take arms against a sea of troubles,
> And by opposing end them? To die: to sleep:

No more; and by a sleep to say we end
The heartache and the thousand natural shocks
That flesh is heir to, 'tis a consummation
Devoutly to be wish'd. To die, to sleep;
To sleep: perchance to dream: ay, there's the rub:
For in that sleep of death *what dreams may come,*
When we have shuffled off this mortal coil,
Must give us pause. There's the respect
That makes calamity of so long life;
For who could bear the whips and scorns of time,

. . . .

When he himself might his quietus make

. . . .

But that the *dread of something after death,*
The undiscover'd country from whose bourn
No traveller returns, puzzles the will
And makes us rather *bear those ills* we have
Than fly to others that *we know not of?*

I then interpret the soliloquy to him in the following manner: Shakespeare seems to be telling us that at one time or another everyone has asked himself the question of whether we ought to endure all the hurts and sufferings that life must inevitably offer us or perhaps end our life by committing suicide. We usually decide to keep on living, not so much because life is always so beautiful but rather because we do not know for certain what lies on the other shore. We cannot be sure that death is truly a peaceful sleep. As Shakespeare tells us, it is quite likely that death is not a finality but that perhaps the nightmare of mental anguish persists after death. In fact, it may be a worse torture than we have ever anticipated. This is another example of how the fear-of-death side of the ratio can be increased which lowers the likelihood of immediate suicidal acting-out.

On rare occasions I have even subtly encouraged some of these patients in whom I felt that suicide was imminent and who I felt were basically masochistic persons to use me as the object for their need to hurt. I may even needle them into some kind of angry discharge in the hope of draining the tension level associated with the destructive impulse. They try to hurt me and I show them that I feel hurt. Then, for the moment at least, their tension level is diminished and they do not need to hurt themselves. I do not advocate this approach because it is fraught with all kinds of therapeutic problems, but under what I feel to be dire circumstances I have resorted to this approach and have found it successful in the goal of preventing the imminent death of the patient.

After I am convinced that some kind of wedge against suicidal acting-out has been built or the destructive impulse has been drained, I then revert back to the other side of the ratio and attempt to decrease the fear of life and increase its gratifications. Invariably I find that in all suicides what is missing is love. Even more than their not being loved I find existing their lack of ability to love. I try to point out to them that beauty exists in the world only when one is loving, for when we are loving we are the recipient of the beauty of these feelings, but when others are loving us then only they are the happy beneficiaries of the beauty of these feelings.

I try to have these patients recognize that they have destroyed the beauty in their own lives because they have inhibited their capacity for loving due to their fear of getting hurt. Because they are committed to the fact that they will never let themselves love again, of course it is then natural to think in terms of suicide because life without love is bereft of beauty and joy. I try to explain to them why love cannot have any guarantees in terms of it being returned by the other but that when one truly loves, it is its own reward. I point out to them that it is not their loving that has hurt them but their need for a sense of possessiveness of the other and that when one truly loves the other, the fact of possession of the other adds relatively little to the beauty of the experience within. This can be made a reality to the patient only through the therapist's warm feelings toward him. It is essentially through the caring relationship between therapist and patient that the patient gains the feelings of protection and worth which are the essential ingredients in his coming to fear life less. This is usually sufficient to eliminate the suicidal intent. When this has been achieved, then the therapist can focus more on helping the patient gain greater insight into himself thereby solidifying the patient's sense of security. I feel that for one who works regularly with depressed individuals who are potentially suicidal, it is essential that the therapist have for himself a clear and meaningful philosophy of life and death, for without this the patient will surely catch him unaware with his usually well-thought-out logic of why it is necessary that he die. It is usually not sufficient for the therapist to just assert that the patient's attitudes are irrational, for the patient needs something more than just this negative approach but rather craves something positive by which he can consider a new reorientation toward life. This something positive can only come from a therapist who has first deeply explored himself and has discovered real beauty in man and in life.

REFERENCES

1. Hendin, Herbert: The psychodynamics of suicide. *J Nerv Ment Dis, 136,* 1963.
2. Horney, Karen: *Neurosis and Human Growth.* New York, W. W. Norton Co., 1956.
3. Jensen, Viggo, and Petty, Thomas: The fantasy of being rescued in suicide. *Psychoanal Q, 27,* 1958.
4. Sterba, Richard: Aggression in the rescue fantasy. *Psychoanal Q, 9,* 1940.
5. Stone, Alan, and Shein, Harvey: Psychotherapy of the hospitalized suicidal patient. *Am J Psychother, 22, (No. 1),* January 1968.

Chapter 8

Psychotherapy with Patients with Psychosomatic Disorders

GEORGE C. CURTIS

IN APPROACHING the treatment of psychosomatic disorders it is first necessary to consider what a psychosomatic disorder is. This is by no means simple. The expression "psychosomatic" does not refer to a discipline, a field of study nor a medical subspecialty, but to a point of view—a way of thinking about any process which involves the total human organism. This way of thinking is synthetic and tries to apply all available information and methods which might be useful, whether from psychodynamics, sociology, anthropology, pathology, pharmacology, genetics, physiology, immunology, medicine, surgery or related fields. In practice however, the elements for synthesis vary not only with the problem under consideration but also with the capacities and experience of the synthesizer. The term "psychosomatic" has been criticized on the grounds that it implies a mind-body dichotomy rather than unity of mind and body. In the present writer's opinion, the term and the viewpoint to which it refers are forerunners of a general systems approach to health and disease.

One of the cardinal principles both in psychosomatics and in general systems theory is that events within a system or level of description—psychological, social, anatomical, physiological and so forth—must be studied by methods appropriate to that level and described in the language of that level. Only after this has been done may events from two or more levels be correlated. Thus if we wish to study physiological changes in anxiety we cannot use physiological data to infer the presence of anxiety; if we do, our reasoning will be circular. If we wish to study psy-

---

Note: Superior letters in this chapter refer to special explanatory notes at the end of the chapter.

chodynamic patterns in thyroid disease, we cannot use psychodynamic data to infer the presence of thyroid disease nor medical
data to infer the presence of psychodynamic patterns. These
statements may seem truisms, but their principles are ignored
with surprising frequency.

The term "psychosomatic" is also used in a more limited sense
to refer to a causal sequence "from above downward"—that is,
in which events at the psychological-psychodynamic level appear
to influence events at some lower order of complexity, such as
gastric motility or cardiovascular dynamics. This usage is in contrast with the term "somatopsychic" which implies the opposite
causal sequence, such as the effect of brain damage on mental
function or psychological reactions to physical disease. Psychosomatic events have somatopsychic feedback and vice versa, so
that in a strict sense there are no purely psychosomatic or somatopsychic sequences. Nevertheless the distinction is convenient
and necessary for ordering certain types of observations.

When the term "disorder" is added to the term "psychosomatic,"
one ordinarily means clinical conditions in which "psychosomatic"
causal sequences are inferred. Some idea of the diversity of these
conditions may be conveyed by the following classification, which
should be considered as illustrative rather than definitive.

TYPES OF PSYCHOSOMATIC DISORDERS

Somatic Complaints of a Purely Ideational Nature

These are symptoms which express ideas and do not depend on
physical changes in the areas complained of. Needless to say,
the ideas may be, and often are, unconscious.

Somatic Delusions and Hallucinations

Although the idea expressed by these symptoms is conscious,
it can and usually does stand in the place of other ideas and feelings which are not conscious. A patient may complain that he has
pain and heaviness in his chest because his heart has turned to
stone or he has nausea and indigestion because he is rotten inside.
If the patient is grossly psychotic, the nature of the complaint

is quickly recognized. If his cognitive functions are relatively intact and he has only an isolated somatic delusion, then its true nature is easily missed. Being aware that people may think him crazy, he consults a general physician complaining only of chest pain or indigestion. On finding nothing wrong, the physician reassures him that his complaint is due to nerves, and the patient seeks elsewhere for someone to soften his heart of stone or to remove the rottenness inside. The examples chosen happen to be ones which convey feelings of self-accusation, but this type of "body language" may be used as well to express ideas related to other impulses and feelings. This type of complaint must, of course, be distinguished from delusional explanations erected on organically based symptoms, as for example pains of angina pectoris[a] interpreted as messages from heaven.

Obsessions About the Body

Somatic obsessions also express in body language ideas related to unconscious wishes. However, the patient recognizes them as irrational, even if this recognition does not bring relief of anxiety. As in the case of delusions, the consciously expressed idea stands instead of unconscious ones.

Hypochondriasis

This term is used loosely to refer to multiple bodily complaints which do not depend on physically based sensations. They are usually obsessional, delusional or a mixture of the two.

Conversion Reactions (Hysteria)

Like somatic delusions and obsessions, conversion reactions also express in body language ideas related to unconscious wishes. Instead of appearing in conscious thought they appear involuntarily in charade or pantomime in which the players are organ systems. In the early days of psychoanalysis all psychosomatic disorders were assumed to be conversion reactions, even those with marked tissue damage; one's blood pressure, ulcers, bleeding from the bowel, etcetera, were all assumed to be symbolic expressions of unconscious ideas. Following World War II, there was a widespread reaction against this view. Many students of psychosomatics then felt that unconscious ideas could be expressed only by the sensory and voluntary motor symptoms and that the diagnosis of conversion reaction or hysteria should be confined to symptoms in these systems. Despite explicit statements of this sort, a number of symptoms involving involuntary systems continued to be recognized as hysterical, such as vomiting and false pregnancy (including cessation of menstruation). The earlier view was never completely supplanted, and Sperling,[30] for example, continued to regard ulcerative colitis as a pregenital conversion in which bleeding from the bowel symbolizes a traumatic separation in the form of an abortion.

More recently, Engel[10] and Engel and Schmale[11] have marshalled substantial evidence that the conversion mechanism may underlie a wide variety of involuntary symptoms. They further maintain that tissue damage may occur as a complication of conversion reactions, although the damage itself is not the conversion reaction and does not have primary psychological meaning. Through the process of secondary symbolization the damage may, of course, still acquire psychological meaning after it has developed.

Medical Consequences of the Patient's Behavior

This is a heterogenious group of disorders, some of which excite the interest of psychosomatic workers and some of which do not. As a rule interest in the damage caused by suicide attempts, hepatic cirrhosis[(b)] following alcoholism or illnesses aggravated by heavy smoking is not regarded as psychosomatic interest. Interest in obesity, on the other hand, is regarded as psychosomatic interest. Most cases of obesity are caused by eating more calories than are consumed by bodily activity. The mystery lies in the reason for the dissociation between physiological need for food and eating.[24, 31, 32] It is generally recognized that neurotic and psychotic conflicts may contribute to any of these behaviors, but there is no agreement as to whether similar psychodynamic constellations underlie similar external behaviors. Behavior which is not necessarily neurotic may also have medical consequences, as for example, the eating of diets high in cholesterol which seem to contribute to the development of coronary artery disease.

Psychophysiological Symptoms

In this category belong symptoms such as perspiration and pounding of the heart in anxiety attacks, constipation and anorexia in depression, aching muscles and joints resulting from chronic muscular tension, spastic colon, emotional diarrhea, upset stomach due to emotional tension and so forth. The complaints involve physical processes at the site of the symptoms. The heart does usually beat more forcefully and rapidly during anxiety attacks. The various digestive disturbances are related to changes in the function of the gastrointestinal tract, and chronic muscular tension can be demonstrated by electrical measurements. Though inappropriate to the situation, the symptoms do not exceed the limits of normal physiological function, do not involve structural damage to the tissues and usually subside with the emotional state of which they are a part. It has not so far been possible to make rigid connections between specific symptoms and specific types of emotion, though some loose correlations, such as those mentioned above, do seem to exist. One or more symptoms may appear in the absence of, or instead of, more overt emotional displays. Such symptoms are often called "affect equivalents." It may be difficult to know whether one is dealing with a normal but inappropriate affect equivalent or with a conversion in an involuntary system, and there may indeed be no sharp separation. Physicians other than psychiatrists often refer to symptoms in this category as "functional symptoms," indicating that they are generated by physiological functions and that there is no identifiable disease.

Psychophysiological symptoms are produced by autonomic nervous system discharges to heart, lungs, digestive glands, the adrenal medulla and the digestive tract or by motor nerve discharges into skeletal muscles. Physiological discharges in emotional states are not limited to the autonomic and voluntary muscle systems but include the endocrine glands as well. The biological effects of neuroendocrine secretions are so profound as to affect the function of virtually every cell and tissue in the body. However, it is doubtful whether the secretion of hormones during emotional discharges gives rise to consciously perceived symptoms.

Psychic fatigue is a more complex symptom. Apparently it may be due in part to the added work imposed on cardiovascular and muscular systems by nervous discharge. Another contributing factor may be sleep loss. On the other hand the sensation of fatigue may disappear suddenly with a change of mood, suggesting that it also involves central perception and interpretation.

Psychic Aggravation of Existing Chronic Disease

It is sometimes unclear whether a particular disorder belongs in this category or the following one—"Psychosomatic Diseases"— which have psychic components in their etiology. Where psychic factors are involved in initial causation, they are usually also involved in subsequent aggravation. However, the reverse need not be true. Psychic aggravation may be striking and obvious in cases where psychic involvement in initial causation is more difficult to establish.

Cardiovascular diseases are among those in which psychic aggravation is clearest. Congestive heart failure or cardiac decompensation is an excellent example. Persons whose hearts have been damaged in such a way as to diminish permanently the working capacity of the heart are said to have diminished cardiac reserve. By various combinations of medication, diet and limitation of physical exertion, it is usually possible to keep the demands upon the heart within its capacity to meet them. So long as this is the case, the heart disease is said to be "compensated." A compensated system decompensates when the heart's work capacity is reduced further or when fresh demands are placed upon and exceed its capacity. One of the most common types of fresh demand is an emotional upset, the physiological effects of which are similar to those of physical exertion. The symptoms of cardiac decompensation are similar regardless of the cause and include breathlessness, accumulation of fluid in the lungs and tissues, and a shortage of oxygen in the tissues. Hospitalization, oxygen and additional medication are often necessary in order to reestablish a state of compensation. In a study of twenty-five consecutive hospital admissions for congestive heart failure (cardiac decompensation) Chambers and Reiser[4] found that emotional stress was a major precipitating factor in 76 percent.

Another type of mismatch between supply and demand can occur when the coronary arteries, which carry the blood supply to heart muscles, are diseased. In the absence of physical or emotional stress, the diseased vessels are often able to meet the heart muscle's demands for the delivery of blood, yet fail to meet the increased demands imposed by added emotional stress. In this way emotional stress may precipitate attacks of angina pectoris[a] or even full-blown myocardial infarctions.[c]

In patients so disposed, emotional stress may also precipitate attacks of irregular heartbeat, apparently mediated by emotional effects on the autonomic nervous system. The heart is less efficient when beating irregularly and this in turn may precipitate an attack of congestive heart failure if cardiac reserve is already reduced by disease. The writer once had the opportunity to observe a dramatic example of this in which a woman suffered from obesity and severe rheumatic heart disease.[d] Her disease was adequately compensated until a rejection by her family precipitated an attack of auricular fibrillation, one type of irregular heartbeat and congestive heart failure. A successful physician-patient relationship was never established. The auricular fibrillation and congestive heart failure proved refractory to medical treatment and the patient eventually died. She did not reveal the emotional rejection to her physicians, who learned of it through other sources shortly before her death.

The emotional state can and frequently does alter the insulin requirements of diabetics to such an extent that a previously well-regulated patient is precipitated into an episode of diabetic[e] acidosis[f] or coma. The other common precipitants of acidosis are infections, failure to take insulin and departures from the diet.

Psychosomatic Diseases

In this category belong a number of physical disease entities, usually with pathological tissue changes and always with functioning in some organ system which is not only inappropriate but abnormal. In addition to the impact of emotional factors upon the course of the illness once it is established, there are further reasons to believe that emotional factors also play a significant role in producing the illness. It would seem reasonable to suppose that a period of "functional" disorder in an organ or system might precede the onset of a psychosomatic disease. This has been shown to be true of ulcerative colitis[g] in which the onset of structural bowel changes is usually preceded by years of "functional" bowel disturbances.[7] As another example, peptic ulcer[h] is often preceded by "acid indigestion." It is frequently difficult to establish clinically the point at which one becomes the other. The onset of essential hypertension[i] is frequently preceded by labile blood pressure. However, psychophysiological symptoms do not necessarily lead to psychosomatic disease.

There is no rigorously established list of diseases which are and are not psychosomatic. In several, however, psychic etiological factors have been noted as especially prominent and are traditionally regarded as psychosomatic. These include peptic ulcer,[h] ulcerative colitis,[g] essential hypertension,[i] thyrotoxicosis,[j] migraine headaches,[k] rheumatoid arthritis[l] and various allergic manifestations such as bronchial asthma, hay fever, urticaria (hives) and eczema. There are also some grounds for considering diabetes mellitus,[2, (e)] pernicious anemia,[34,(m)] coronary artery disease[15] and malignant lymphomas[14, (n)] as partly psychogenic in etiology. The appropriateness of dividing diseases into psychosomatic and nonpsychosomatic categories has been challenged[6] and evidence introduced that psychic factors may play a role in the development of any illness.[26] It should be understood, however, that at the present time only a very small minority of workers consider any illness with pathological tissue changes to be purely psychogenic. The majority hold that psychic and physical factors interact to produce the disease.

PSYCHOSOMATIC ETIOLOGY

It is paradoxical that almost no one has serious doubts that psychophysiological complaints and psychosomatic diseases exist, yet there is very little agreement as to how they are brought about. Of the various theories of psychosomatic etiology, none has had sufficiently rigorous and extensive validation to warrant final acceptance or rejection. The obstacles to accomplishing these tasks are the familiar ones in psychiatric research: complexity of the psychological data, confusion as to which psychic trait or traits should be related to which illness or biological process, insufficient precision and resolving power of the psychological methodology and difficulty of obtaining adequate sampling of patients or adequate control of contaminating variables.

One of the common themes running through all psychosomatic theory is the issue of specificity versus nonspecificity. Specificity implies that a specific type of psychic event or process is related to a specific type of somatic event. It has been suggested, for example, that compulsive personality goes with ulcerative colitis[7,(g)]; that the emotion of anger is related to the secretion of the noradrenalin, and fear or anxiety to the secretion of adrenaline[13]; that intense oral needs are related to the secretion of pepsinogen[22, 34]; that depressive illness is related to depletion of brain catecholamines[25]; and so forth. Nonspecificity implies that the quantity of psychic stress is related to the quantity of physiological disturbance, but that the type or quality of one is unrelated to the type or quality of the other. Most theories of nonspecificity are not stated in such extreme terms but tend in this direction. The following theories to be discussed, and a number of others not considered here, combine specificity and nonspecificity in a variety of ways.

Pavlov

Pavlov[23] was highly critical of psychological concepts, which he regarded as unscientific. Nevertheless his work provided one of the first demonstrations, in the modern scientific sense, that psychosomatic processes are possible. In the course of research on the physiology of digestion he discovered the conditioned reflex, demonstrating that a stimulus which became a signal of food could produce physiological effects similar to those of food itself. The secretion of saliva and gastric juices which he studied were end results of parasympathetic nervous activity. Pavlov was mainly interested in these responses as a method for studying the "physiology of the cerebral cortex," of the making and breaking of temporary connections between stimuli, and of their facilitation and inhibition. He left to others the main tasks of studying the peripheral effects of conditioned responses. The specificity of his theory was high—a specific stimulus, related to a specific response, in an individual with a specific set of previous experiences.

Cannon

Cannon's work was crucial in providing a comprehensive view of the autonomic or involuntary nervous system with its two divisions, the sympathetic and the parasympathetic. He suggested that the activity levels in all branches of the sympathetic system rise and fall together, while the activities of the different parasympathetic branches vary independently of each other.[3] This was expressed by the analogy of a piano in which the keys represented different branches of the parasympathetic system and the loud-soft pedal represented the sympathetic system. The parasympathetic system promoted functions of reparation and reproduction such as digestion, defecation, urination and copulation; it also inhibited functions promoted by the sympathetic system. The sympathetic system discharged en masse during fear and rage, making preparation for and supporting the metabolic requirements of muscular exertion, fight and flight; these included accleration of the heart rate, shifting of blood from viscera to muscles, mobilizing sugar into the bloodstream, accelerating the clotting of blood and inhibiting most of the functions which are enhanced by the parasympathetic system. Subsequent developments have supported most of his views but with important exceptions. The sympathetic system has proved much more plastic and flexible than he imagined, thus allowing it to participate with the parasympathetic and endocrine systems in producing a great variety of centrally programmed arrangements of cardiovascular, digestive and metabolic function, both in preparation for anticipated events and in response to current requirements. Consequently, the physiological changes in fear and rage are much less stereotyped than he suggested.

One of the most striking departures from Cannon's all-or-none view of sympathetic function is Miller's finding[21] that autonomically mediated functions may be modified by instrumental learning. By appropriate contingencies of reward and punishment, rats whose skeletal muscle responses had been paralyzed by curare were trained to raise or lower their blood pressure, to increase or decrease intestinal motility or to modify blood vessel tone unilaterally in one or the other ear. While the role of these mechanisms in pyschosomatic etiology is unclear, their discovery opens many possibilities which were previously unsuspected and which may be of very high importance.

Cannon's influence on psychosomatic theory was enormous, especially since the autonomic nervous system was in his time the only known pathway by which the brain might influence involuntary body functions. For many years it was known that the endocrine glands regulated important metabolic and reproductive functions and that the pituitary gland regulated the other endocrine glands. Only relatively recently was it recognized that the brain is an important regulator of the pituitary.

Cannon's theories were nonspecific psychologically. Fear, rage, resentment, tension, pain or anxiety, or almost any emotional disequilibrium might provoke a fight-flight physiological pattern. Physiologically they were highly specific.

Selye

Selye proposed the concepts of "stress" and the "general adaptation syndrome,"[29] after Cannon had made major contributions but before the role of the brain in pituitary regulation was recognized. His concepts were based on the finding that a wide variety of injurious stimuli—including but not limited to toxins, burns, severe cold and mechanical injury—provoked the release of ACTH from the pituitary which in turn stimulated the release of corticoid hormones from the adrenal cortex. Adrenal hormones influence a wide variety of metabolic functions as well as biological defense reactions such as inflammation and antibody production; without adrenal hormones it is impossible to adapt to environmental changes and shifts in metabolic demands. Any stimulus which provoked ACTH release was defined as a stressor. Emotional distress was also found to provoke ACTH release and thereby emotional stimuli were placed in a class with biologically injurious ones. Selye recognized the psychosomatic implications of this concept and proposed that a number of the traditionally termed psychosomatic illnesses be called "diseases of adaptation." He further suggested that they might be caused by a disordered stress response in which there was an inbalance between adrenal cortical hormones and somatatropic hormone.

Selye's theory, like Cannon's, was psychologically nonspecific but highly specific physiologically. Later work has confirmed and extended his finding that emotional stimuli can provoke ACTH release. However, the stereotyped regularity of ACTH release by emotional stimuli predicted by Selye's theory has yet to be demonstrated. The suggestion that mild endocrine influences due to psychic factors might contribute to physical illness remains plausible but unproved. The element of preparation for anticipated events, which figured so highly in Pavlov's and Cannon's ideas, was absent from Selye's. However, it has since become clear that the pituitary-adrenal axis does make anticipatory responses.

Alexander

As mentioned previously, Alexander was instrumental in deemphasizing the role of conversion reactions in systems which are normally involuntary and hence in the production of organic disease. From experiences of his own and his followers in psychoanalyzing patients with "psychosomatic" diseases, he concluded that a specific nuclear unconscious conflict is characteristic of patients with each disease, that the conflict originated in early childhood and, in most cases, long antedated the onset of the disease.[2] The physiological "by-products" of unconscious strivings associated with the conflict caused chronic hyperactivity in the appropriate organ system and eventually led to a breakdown of normal structure and function in it. For example, peptic ulcer[h] patients were thought to have especially intense but repressed passive oral and oral aggressive strivings which were defended against by reaction formations resulting in overt behavior of ambition, hard work, self-reliance and superindependence. Because discharge of the repressed oral longings was blocked, they set up chronic substitute discharges in the parasympathetic innervations of the stomach similar to the preparations for feeding which Pavlov had demonstrated. Essential hypertension[i] was thought to be associated with anxiety over repressed hostile competitive striving. The inhibited hostility resulted in a substitution of chronic sympathetic nervous discharge along the lines of the fight-flight reaction of Cannon. This in turn produced generalized vasoconstriction, the release of adrenaline and elevation of the blood pressure. Other formulations were proposed for migraine,[k] hyperthyroidism,[j] asthma, rheumatoid arthritis[1] and ulcerative colitis.[g] In most of the formulations, pregenital and especially dependent and oral conflicts were prominent. It was recognized that not every patient with the appropriate conflict had the corresponding disease. Consequently, Alexander postulated a "somatic X factor" which was also specific for each disease. Both the conflict and the X factor were necessary to produce the disease, but neither alone was sufficient. These hypotheses entailed high specificity at both psychological and biological levels.

The pyschoanalytic observations of Alexander and his followers have proved hard to replicate and generalize. One difficulty is the sheer labor involved in psychoanalyzing enough patients with each disease and systematizing the material to provide an adequate and representative sample. Another is the fact that those patients who can and will undergo psychoanalysis already constitute a skewed sample. Yet another is that the conflicts may not be so discreet and separable as they seem. For example, persons who inhibit their oral strivings in one sphere of life may express them in another, and many persons can be shown to have more than one of the postulated conflicts. Smaller scale clinical studies have not uniformly supported the findings. In one, for example, ulcer patients were found to express their oral and dependent strivings quite freely and openly.[17]

On the other hand, the gastric hypersecretion of hydrochloric acid and gastric hypermotility due to nervous factors are characteristic of peptic ulcer patients. Hypersalivation has also been reported,[33] and it has been possible to induce gastrointestinal ulcerations by chronic stimulation of the hypothalamus in animals.[12]

Hypersecretion of pepsinogen is also characteristic of ulcer patients before, during and after the development of the disease. Pepsinogen is secreted by the cells of the gastric mucosa and then enters the blood. Hypersecretion of pepsinogen, therefore, has several features suggestive of a "somatic X factor" for peptic ulcer and provided the basis for one of the few successful predictive studies of psychosomatic illnesses.[34] Serum pepsinogen was measured in 2073 Army inductees, and a sample of those with the highest levels were selected as a group with high probability of developing ulcers during the stress of basic training. A sample with low values were selected as low probability subjects. The two groups of subjects were then given a battery of psychological tests, a medical questionnaire and a complete radiologic examination of the upper gastrointestinal tract. At the initial examination, a significantly greater number of ulcers was found in the high pepsinogen group, and this group also developed a significantly greater number of ulcers during the course of basic training. On the basis of a prediction that evidences of orality, depression, dependence, anxiety over expressing hostility and needs to please and placate in the psychological test protocols would be characteristic of the high pepsinogen group, it was possible to identify correctly 71 percent of the highs and 51 percent of the lows. Especially strong psychological characteristics of the high pepsinogen group were found in those who had or would develop ulcers. Other evidence indicating that one may be a hypersecreter from birth led Mirsky[22] to suggest that hypersecretion of pepsinogen may reflect a biological trait which contributes to the development of strong oral needs and predisposes to the development of peptic ulcers in situations of stress. Engel suggested that the other psychosomatic illness may have analogous psychobiological predisposing constellations and proposed the term "somatopsychic-psychosomatic disorder."[9]

Schur

Schur finds all the claims of psychological specificity unconvincing and argues that psychosomatic disorders tend to develop when defensive equilibria breakdown and regression occurs.[28] The particular kind of regression producing psychosomatic disorders is regression to primitive modes of ego functioning with resomatization of the channels for expression of primitive affect.

Wolff

Wolff[35] pointed out that biological threats provoke various automatic biological protective patterns. Among these were the "protective pattern of offense involving eating," which is one of the infant's earliest aggressive patterns. This pattern included gastric hyperfunction, increased blood flow and salivation. Another pattern was the "ejection-riddance reaction involving the large bowel, the stomach and duodenum." This included vomiting and diarrhea, which are nonspecific reactions of the infant to noxious agents even when the gastrointestinal tract is not invoked. Another was the "holding fast" reaction of skeletal muscles and large bowel. This was characterized by constipation with tense, aching muscles and joints. Another was the "protective reaction of nose and airways" with vasodilation, hypersecretion, contraction of smooth muscle and occlusion of airways.

According to Wolff these patterns tend to be evoked in predisposed individuals by nonspecific threats and to persist into adulthood in fragmented form. Prolonged and persistent use of a pattern tends to irritate the systems involved and predispose them to disease. The predisposition to a particular pattern when threatened was considered to be genetic—due to "stock factors"—and to be analogous to the running pattern in the horse, the hoarding pattern of the squirrel or the retriever pattern of the dog.

Engel

On the basis of an extensive study of ulcerative colitis[g] patients Engel[7] concluded that the disease tends to have its onset in the setting of a real, fantasied or threatened disruption of a key object relationship, but only if the subject reacts with feelings of helplessness and hopelessness. Later work by Engel and various of his colleagues led to similar conclusions with respect to malignant lymphomas,[n],[14] medical disease in general[26] and psychiatric illness.[1] These findings also formed the basis for another of the few successful psychosomatic predictive studies.[27] Women entering the hospital for biopsies of the uterine cervix were interviewed for evidence of object loss, helplessness and hopelessness. The prediction was borne out that this state would tend to identify those women whose cervical lesions would prove to be malignant. The state has been termed the "giving up—given up complex" and is regarded as neither necessary nor sufficient for the development of disease but as contributory.

As noted previously, Engel's more recent theoretical interests have turned to a more specific mechanism—the role of conversion in the production of disease.[10, 11] Case material has been presented[10] showing that a sensory conversion may evoke appropriate biological protective patterns similar to those described by Wolff.[35] Engel[10] describes a female patient who as a child had been struck along with her mother by a hit-and-run driver on a deserted street in the dead of winter. The child had been thrown into a snow pile and not discovered for some time. As an adult, the resurgence of ambivalent feelings toward her mother was associated with conversion attacks in which she not only experienced a sensation of cold but had shaking chills, chattering teeth and blanching of her hands and feet, which became cold to the touch.

A conversion may also produce complications, as when a sensation of breathlessness leads to overbreathing, which then results in respiratory alkalosis.[o] The associated tetany[p] and sensations of tingling about the mouth are due to alkalosis and not part of the conversion.[10] Engel[10] describes other cases in which fantasies of punishment for sexual transgression had determined the site of skin eruptions. A soldier developed an urticarial eruption ("hives") with a linear distribution which might have been produced by a whipping on the back of his legs, thighs and buttocks. As a boy in a very strict orphanage, he had been whipped for peeking in the windows of the girls' dormitory. The urticarial eruption developed about an hour after he had been apprehended loitering on the grounds of the nurses' dormitory on the military post. An enlisted man, he had hoped to see one of the nurses whom he wanted to date. The officer who apprehended him reprimanded him severely and ordered him to his barracks.

Another patient,[10] a young woman, developed an eczematoid skin eruption around her neck where it was touched by the chain of a metal crucifix which was given her at the time of her confirmation. She was apprehensive about her confession, unsure whether she had sinned and felt ashamed and unclean when the crucifix was placed around her neck. Later eruptions occurred at the site of other metals contacting her skin if associations of sexual guilt were aroused.

To account for the development of these lesions, Engel depends heavily on experiments by Chapman, Goodell and Wolff.[5] It had been known that the pain, tenderness and inflammation following injury to the skin is enhanced and sustained by antidromic (reverse direction) feedback activity along the same nerve fibers which carry the nociceptive impulses. Chemical substances (neurokinin, substance p) are released at the nerve terminals in the skin which facilitate the local inflammatory response, lower the threshhold for pain and influence clotting mechanisms. The demonstration by Chapman *et al.*[5] that the same feedback system can be activated by hypnotic suggestion of injury to the skin suggested to Engel that a similar mechanism might have operated in the cases where conversion had determined the site of skin eruptions. In these cases, skin eruptions would be complications of the conversion and not the conversion itself, just as tetany[(p)] is not a conversion but a complication of hyperventillation. Engel suggests that similar processes might also produce pathological lesions in other systems.

In applying this line of thinking, it is necessary to distinguish between primary and secondary symbolization. Primary symbolization is the type described by Engel, in which a fantasy is elaborated about a body part or system before a pathological process develops in the tissue. Secondary symbolization means the erection of fantasies about a pathological process after it develops.

Comment

The view of the present writer is that claims of similar conflicts, similar instinctual makeup, similar ego structure or similar personality makeup in patients with similar symptoms are unconvincing. The common emphasis on oral, dependent and pregenital mechanisms have developed in an era when psychoanalysts are becoming increasingly aware of these impulses in all areas of psychic development and in all symptom complexes including classical hysterical, phobic and obsessive-compulsive neuroses. While their role is being so extensively reevaluated, it seems premature to assign them some special role in psychosomatics. The position of Schur[28] would seem the soundest—namely, that there is nothing psychologically specific about psychosomatic illness, that it simply tends to be precipitated by psychological regression and the breakdown of defenses. Furthermore, Engel[10, 11] would seem to be entirely correct in observing that regression, disruption of defenses and the "giving up—given up complex" are most likely to occur when key object relationships are threatened. The physiological pathways have yet to be clarified in detail but almost certainly must involve combinations of autonomic and neuroendocrine reactions together with local biological defense reactions as outlined by Wolff[35] and Engel.[10, 11]

THERAPEUTIC CONSIDERATIONS

With such a diverse group of disorders, there can hardly be a unitary therapeutic approach determined by the fact that a psychosomatic disorder exists. On the contrary, psychosomatic disorders present the entire gamut of therapeutic problems—from grossly psychotic patients to "healthy neurotics." Hence they call for the entire repertoire of psychotherapeutic approaches—from supportive through classical psychoanalysis. The use of behavior, group and family therapies has not been reported extensively in these cases but undoubtedly each will eventually find its place in the treatment of psychosomatic patients. Miller's demonstration of operant conditioning of discreet autonomic reactions is especially suggestive that conditioning therapies might be effective in the treatment of some psychosomatic symptoms.

Despite the diversity of psychosomatic disorders and of the psychotherapeutic approaches to them, there are two central ideas of high importance, around which any type of therapeutic approach can be organized. They are (a) that the onset and exacerbations of both somatic[7, 9, 10, 14, 26, 27] and psychiatric illnesses[1] tend to occur in the setting of a real, fantasied or threatened disruption of a key object relationship, which is accompanied by disruption of defensive and adaptive patterns, psychological regression and feelings of helplessness and hopelessness and (b) that physical illness per se tends to induce psychological regression[18]; this tendency sums with any other regressive trends which the patient may bring with him to his illness.

The utility of the concept of the key relationship lies in its nonspecificity, its simplicity and its central importance in all psychic function. None of the more complicated specificity hypotheses have been so well documented and none are so readily verifiable in one's everyday clinical work. Needless to say, this concept does not substitute for a full formulation of the psychodynamics of an individual patient; it does, however, provide a nodal point around which a more complete formulation may be organized. Furthermore this concept does not preclude any of the more specific formulations which might eventually be validated as characteristic of certain disorders. In fact if any such formulation should be valid, the key relationship concept provides a path for arriving at it. The fact that a threat to such a relationship disrupts defenses, induces regression and precipitates illness is already evidence that the relationship is invested with neurotic or psychotic intensity derived from an object of early childhood, usually the mother. In fact the current relationship involved in precipitating the illness is not infrequently with the mother herself. In young adults the threat to the key relationship is also likely to be rejection by a spouse or lover. In later life the death or illness of a spouse is frequently the key precipitant of illnesses; in this age range the maturation, separation or rebellion of offspring is also often important.

It is not unusual to observe an acute rupture of a relationship, emotional collapse and the first attack of a chronic medical illness all occurring within hours. More frequent, however, is the onset of illness in a setting of gradual deterioration of a relationship and gradual failure of coping mechanisms.

The psychological forces activated by physical illness have been simply and profoundly described by Lederer.[18] During the process of falling ill—the transition from health to illness—the central experiences are pain, discomfort, loss of strength and abilities, and anxiety. In addition to the realistic fears about one's comfort and well-being, there are unconscious anxieties, including fear of regression and passivity, fantasies that illness is a punishment for transgressions and shame that one's weaknesses may be exposed. At this stage one of the most potent provokers of anxiety is facing the unknown. The nature of the illness and its implications are likely to be unknown. Diagnostic equipment and procedures are often unintelligible and mysterious. The language spoken by physicians, nurses and technicians is strange. Particularly devastating at this time are signs of apprehension, uncertainty or vacillation on the part of the physician. The lack of knowledge is well designed to draw out fantasies from the patient's unconscious. The particular patient's ways of dealing with anxiety and regressive urges are likely to be activated. These may range from denial of illness, delay in seeking treatment, aggressiveness and provocativeness to passivity, clinging and compliance.

Those who can tolerate the necessary degree of regression and dependence enter a stage of accepted illness. This is characterized by egocentricity, preoccupation with body functions, constriction of interests and a regressed dependent relationship with doctors and nurses which bears the stamp of whatever the patient's particular relationship had been with his parental objects in early childhood. The same caretaking persons are likely to be seen as omnipotent and idealized by one patient and as callous and malevolent by another. Jealousy of a nurse's or doctor's attention may extend to lengths entirely out of keeping with the patient's personality when well. Romantic heterosexual fantasies are fairly frequent. If defenses against the necessary degree of regression and dependence are too elaborate, there may be no stage of accepted illness and no secure emotional relationships with the medical team. This interferes with the treatment regimen and with the effectiveness of any treatment which he does receive. Such was undoubtedly the case with the patient, cited earlier, in whom powerful medication was ineffective against her auricular fibrillation and congestive heart failure.

Convalescence, the transition from accepted illness into relative health and responsibility, is analogous to adolescence and often runs a similar course. Doctors and nurses begin to lose their idealized qualities and may appear somewhat depreciated, like the parents of an adolescent. Patients who clung to the dependency on their parents may exhibit reluctance to give up the role of sick person and the dependence to which it entitles them. This can manifest itself in many ways such as reluctance to stop taking medicine, reluctance to resume activity appropriate to the improved state of health or actual recurrence of symptoms in the setting of discharge from the hospital.[8, 16] The "hanging on" reaction tends to be intensified by long periods of hospitalization. Thomas Mann's novel *The Magic Mountain*[19] deals with such a reaction in a patient hospitalized for tuberculosis. On the other hand, patients who broke away from their families abruptly and prematurely during adolescence are likely to follow the same pattern with their physicians during convalescence. Patients who separated from their parents gradually but smoothly and progressively during adolescence are likely to have a smooth and uneventful convalescence. The more "psychosomatic" the disorder, the more likely are complications in the progression of the psychological stages of the illness and the more likely are these complications to feed back upon the medical course of the illness.

During the stage of acute illness one faces a patient whose outbreak of symptoms was probably precipitated by the loss of an important source of dependent gratification, whether recognized or not, followed by disruption of defenses, regression, help-lessness and hopelessness. The illness itself will have induced further regression. The situation is ripe for the development of rapid and intense transference relationships. Many perceptive nonpsychiatric physicians are very aware of these matters and handle them skillfully. Others are totally oblivious and hence unaware of the enormous effect of their behavior upon the course of the illness. During the acute phase of the illness, the psycho-logical task is to effect some temporary restitution of the threat-ened object relationship, partially by replacing it with the natural-ly developing transference relationship to the physician and, if practical, by facilitating repair of the rupture with the key person. Uncovering psychotherapy during this phase is often impractical, but proper attention to developing good patient-physician rapport will usually facilitate the outpouring of a great deal of material which otherwise would be heavily defended. This readiness, even eagerness, of acutely ill patients to share heavily charged material has been noted repeatedly.[4, 8, 18] Listening to this material and gently encouraging its revelation helps to cement the therapeutic relationship necessary for recovery. Several years ago, Margolin[20] advocated a very exaggerated form of inducing this early attach-ment by means of "anaclitic therapy." In this approach the physi-cian assumed a totally giving and totally omnipotent role toward the patient, remaining available to him at any and all times, feed-ing him, stroking and massaging painful areas and attending to all minor details of physical care. This procedure was often life-saving but is very taxing for medical personnel to keep up for any length of time. Equally good results can usually be obtained less dramatically by merely being aware of the patient's likes, dislikes, dependent needs and conveying this awareness to him along with a sense of personal interest. It cannot be emphasized strongly enough that the success or failure of this relationship can and does spell the difference between effectiveness and ineffective-ness of very powerful drugs or even surgical operations. If the psy-chotherapist enters the case at this point, one of his major services may be to help restore a deteriorating relationship between pa-tient, ward personnel and physician-in-charge.

Beyond the acute phase of illness the problems to be considered are whether psychotherapy offers the hope of sufficient emotional maturation to free the patient from the more neurotic aspects of his dependence on key objects and his vulnerability to the threat of separation. In arriving at this decision, his ego strengths, capacity for relationships and capacity for insight will be weighed in the usual manner. Also to be considered are the questions whether the vulnerability of his ego and his diseased organ systems can withstand the moderate but unavoidable degrees of frustration inherent in insight giving techniques. The alternative is to establish and maintain a supportive relationship either with the general physician or the psychotherapist which may have to be maintained almost indefinitely, though with dilution during times of well-being and intensification during times of difficulty. The effectiveness of ostensibly medical visits scheduled mainly for psychological reasons is incomprehensible to many general physicians until they see it for themselves.

Whatever techniques are chosen, care must be taken that the general physician keep up his contact with the patient at a sufficient level to minimize feelings of rejection and abandonment by him during the transition period when the psychotherapeutic relationship is being built. Once the patient is established in psychotherapy, the problems of transference, countertransference, resistance, hostility and dependency differ in no characteristic way from the therapeutic problems with other patients. However, the vulnerability of the organ systems to separation and threats of separation must be borne in mind. During vacations and other interruptions one must anticipate the possibility not only of anxiety, depression and hostility but also of gastrointestinal bleeding, asthmatic attacks or whatever the particular somatic vulnerability happens to be. Even though the therapy seems to have gone well, additional exacerbations may occur around the time of termination. A gradual stepwise termination with a gradually decreasing frequency of visits is probably desirable. It is often best not to terminate officially at all but to act as though one assumes that the patient will call periodically for appointments.

Our prognostic abilities for psychosomatic patients are even less than for neurotic and psychotic patients. In general the presence of schizophrenia, serious ego impairment, secondary gain from illness and intense strivings toward passivity and helplessness tend to signal a poor prognosis in psychosomatic disorders as well as in psychiatric ones. Other traits which may be characterized generally as maturity and ego strength tend to indicate a favorable prognosis in both the psychic and somatic spheres. With successful psychotherapy and substantial maturation of the personality, even fairly severely diseased organ systems may return to normal structure and function, provided there had been no irreversible tissue damage prior to therapy. The psychotherapist, however, should not entertain the illusion that the vulnerability of the organ system has been removed. His contribution has been to reduce the impact of emotional stress on this vulnerability. Unfortunately, life provides no security against object loss or further psychological stress. Hence the therapist must be prepared for exacerbations and should work to prevent unrealistic illusions either in himself or in his patient. This is not to deny that the gains through psychotherapy may spell the difference between a productive life and invalidism, but the removal of the organ vulnerability is probably a remaining task for biological research.

NOTES

(a) Pain, usually in the midchest or left arm, occurring when diseased but still functioning coronary arteries are temporarily unable to supply enough blood to the heart muscle to meet its requirements. Pain is usually precipitated by exertion, emotion, a heavy meal or exposure to cold or rarefied air and relieved by eliminating the precipitating factor or by drugs which enlarge the lumen of the coronary artery.

(b) Gradual progressive destruction of liver tissue in severe chronic alcoholism. Death eventually results if the process is not arrested.

(c) Irreversible blocking of a coronary artery so that a portion of the heart muscle is permanently deprived of its blood supply. Symptoms of pain and breathlessness resemble the symptoms of angina pectoris but are usually more severe and are not reversed by drugs or by removing a precipitating factor. The affected area of heart muscle dies and is replaced by scar tissue. During the acute stage of the illness the patient's survival may be in doubt.

(d) Damage to heart valves which is sometimes an aftermath of rheumatic fever. If the damage is severe enough, diminished cardiac reserve results, and the patient becomes subject to episodes of cardiac decompensation or congestive heart failure.

(e) In diabetes mellitus a deficiency of insulin secretion by the pancreas is the central feature of the disease, but many other factors are involved. The naturally occurring disease is often much more severe than that caused by total removal of the pancreas. There may possibly be several types of diabetes mellitus. Diabetes insipidus is an entirely different disorder.

(f) An abnormally acid condition of the blood resulting from the accumulation of improperly metabolized materials. This occurs when insulin requirements exceed the insulin dose by too much for too long. Coma results when the condition is severe, and death will then follow if treatment is not prompt and vigorous.

(g) A generalized disease of unknown cause. Some of the outstanding symptoms are fever and bloody diarrhea or sometimes constipation. Ulcers form in the inner lining and muscular walls of the large intestine (colon) and may become secondarily infected by bacteria which inhabit the bowel. The disease is usually chronic and episodic, often leading to extensive scar formation in the large intestine. Occasionally the course is rapid and progressive, resulting in death.

(h) A disease of unknown cause involving the lower stomach or upper duodenum. Outstanding symptoms in uncomplicated cases include burning and cramping in the mid or upper abdominal area, usually when the stomach is empty. Some relief is often afforded by the intake of milk or mild anti-acids. In the affected area a single craterlike ulcer erodes the inner lining of the stomach or duodenum and into the muscular wall. Motility and acid secretion by the stomach and duodenum are usually increased.

(i) Abnormally elevated blood pressure (hypertension) in the absence of any known cause, such as impaired kidney function or hormone-secreting tumors. If prolonged and severe, the complications may include overworking of the heart or damage to the blood vessels of brain, heart or kidney.

(j) Also called Graves' disease, Basedow's disease and hyperthyroidism. Its cause is unknown. The central feature of the disorder is overproduction of thyroid hormones which are responsible for many of the symptoms, which include enlargement of the thyroid gland (goiter), general acceleration of the metabolic rate, intolerance to warm temperatures, restlessness, rapid heart beat, perspiration and sometimes protrusion of the eyeballs. Rather similar symptoms may be produced by hormone secreting tumors of the thyroid, but the mechanism of these disorders is different.

(k) Episodic headaches, usually severe, throbbing and confined to one side of the head. They are often preceded by various visual phenomena and followed by nausea and vomiting. The pre-headache phenomena are associated with constriction and the headache with dilation of cranial arteries. During the headache, the tissues surrounding cranial arteries on the involved side are swollen and tender.

(l) A disease of unknown cause which is usually chronic and recurring. Its outstanding feature is inflammation of the lining membranes of various joints which causes pain, swelling and redness over the area. In the advanced stages there may be destruction of joint cartilage, scar tissue formation and fusion of joints.

(m) Anemia due to deficiency of vitamin B_{12}. It results from failure of the stomach to secrete enough of a material which enables the intestine to absorb dietary vitamin B_{12}.

(n) A collective term referring to various malignant disorders involving spleen, lymph nodes and other lymphatic and related tissues. These disorders include Hodgkin's disease, lymphatic leukemia and lymphosarcomas.

(o) Alkalosis (the opposite of acidosis) refers to any state in which the blood is abnormally alkaline. In respiratory alkalosis the primary cause is overbreathing, which drives the carbon dioxide level in the blood (and thereby the carbonic acid level also) to abnormally low levels. In alkaline blood the solubility of calcium compounds (and hence the serum calcium concentration) is reduced. This causes a condition known as tetany.

(p) A syndrome which includes extension of the extremities with a characteristic flexion of the ankles and wrists known as carpopedal spasm. There is also twitching of the extremities and sensations of tingling about the mouth. The cause is low serum calcium concentration.

REFERENCES

1. Adamson, J. D., and Schmale, A. H., Jr.: Object loss, giving up, and the onset of psychiatric disease. *Psychosom Med*, 27:557-576, 1965.
2. Alexander, F.: *Psychosomatic Medicine—Its Principles and Applications.* New York, W. W. Norton & Company, Inc., 1950.
3. Cannon, W. B.: *Bodily Changes in Pain, Hunger, Fear and Rage.* Boston, Charles T. Branford Company, 1953.
4. Chambers, W. N., and Reiser, M. F.: Emotional stress in the precipitation of congestive heart failure. *Psychosom Med*, 25:38-60, 1953.
5. Chapman, L. F., Goodell, Helen, and Wolff, H. G.: Augmentation of the inflammatory reaction by activity of the CNS. *Arch Neurol*, 1:557-572, 1959.

6. Engel, G. L.: Selection of clinical material in psychosomatic medicine: The need for a new physiology. *Psychosom Med, 16:*368-373, 1954.
7. Engel, G. L.: Studies of ulcerative colitis: III. The nature of the psychologic processes. *Am J Med, 19:*231-256, 1955.
8. Engel, G. L.: Studies of ulcerative colitis: V. Psychological aspects and their implications for treatment. *Am J Dig Dis, 3:*315-337, 1958.
9. Engel, G. L.: *Psychological Development in Health and Disease.* Philadelphia, W. B. Saunders Company, 1962.
10. Engel, G. L.: The psychoanalytic approach to psychosomatic medicine. In *Modern Psychoanalysis,* edited by J. Marmor. New York, Basic Books, 1968.
11. Engel, G. L., and Schmale, A. J. Jr.: Psychoanalytic theory of somatic disorder: Conversion, specificity, and the disease onset situation. *J Am Psychoanal Assoc, 15:*344-365, 1967.
12. French, J. D., Porter, R. W., Cavanaugh, E. B., and Longmire, R. L.: Experimental gastroduodenal lesions by stimulation of the brain. *Psychosom Med, 19:*209-220, 1957.
13. Funkenstein, D. H., King, S. H., and Drolette, M. E.: *Mastery of Stress.* Cambridge, Harvard University Press, 1957.
14. Greene, W. A., Young, L. E., and Swisher, S. N.: Psychological factors and reticulo-endothelial disease: II. Observations on a group of women with lymphomas and leukemias. *Psychosom Med, 18:*284-303, 1956.
15. Jenkins, C. D. (with cooperation of Rosenman, R. H., and Friedman, M.): Components of the coronary-prone behavior pattern: Their relation to silent myocardial infarction and blood lipids. *J Chronic Dis, 19:* 599-609, 1966.
16. Kaplan, S. M., and Curtis, G. C.: Reactions of medical patients to discharge or threat of discharge from a psychosomatic unit of a general hospital. In *Mental Patients in Transition,* edited by M. Greenblatt, D. J. Levinson, and G. L. Klerman. Springfield, Charles C Thomas, 1961.
17. Kapp, F. T., Rosenbaum, M., and Romano, J.: Psychological factors in men with peptic ulcers. *Am J Psychiatry, 103:*700-704, 1947.
18. Lederer, H. D.: How the sick view their world. *J Soc Issues, 8:*4-15, 1952.
19. Mann, T.: *The Magic Mountain.* New York, Knopf, 1945.
20. Margolin, S.: Round table. *Bull Am Psychoanal Assoc, 8:*170-180, 1952.
21. Miller, N. E.: Learning of visceral and glandular responses. *Science, 163:*434-445, 1969.
22. Mirsky, I. A.: Physiologic, psychologic, and social determinants in the etiology of duodenal ulcer. *Am J Dig Dis, 3:*285-314, 1958.
23. Pavlov, I. P.: *Lectures on Conditioned Reflexes.* New York, International Publishers, 1928.
24. Schachter, S.: Obesity and eating. *Science, 161:*751-756, 1968.

25. Schildkraut, J. J., and Kety, S. S.: Biogenic amines and emotion. *Science, 156*:21-30, 1967.
26. Schmale, A. H. Jr.: Relationship of separation and depression to disease. *Psychosom Med, 20*:259-277, 1958.
27. Schmale, A. H. Jr., and Iker, H. P.: The affect of hopelessness and the development of cancer: I. Identification of uterine cervical cancer in women with atypical cytology. *Psychosom Med, 28*:714-721, 1968.
28. Schur, M.: Comments on the metapsychology of somatization. *The Psychoanalytic Study of the Child, 10*:119-164. New York, International Universities Press, 1955.
29. Selye, H.: *The Stress of Life.* New York, McGraw-Hill, 1956.
30. Sperling, M.: Symposium on disturbances of the digestive tract: II. Unconscious fantasy life and object relationships in ulcerative colitis. *Int J Psychoanal, 41*:450-455, 1960.
31. Stunkard, A.: Obesity and the denial of hunger. *Psychosom Med, 21:* 281-289, 1959.
32. Stunkard, A., and Koch, C.: The interpretation of gastric motility: I. Apparent bias in the reports of hunger by obese persons. *Arch Gen Psychiatry, 11*:74-82, 1964.
33. Szasz, T. S.: Psychosomatic aspects of salivary activity: I. Hypersalivation in patients with peptic ulcer. *Res Nerv Ment Dis Proc, 29*:647-655, 1950.
34. Weiner, H., Thaler, Margaret, Reiser, M. F., and Mirksy, I. A.: Etiology of duodenal ulcer: I. Relation of specific psychological characteristics to rate of gastric secretion (serum pepsinogen). *Psychosom Med, 19*:1-10, 1957.
35. Wolff, H. G.: Life stress and bodily disease—a formulation. *Res Nerv Ment Dis Proc, 29*:1059-1093, 1950.

Chapter 9

Psychotherapy with Patients with Acting-out Disorders

ROSLYN SCHWARTZ AND LEONARD J. SCHWARTZ

A CTING-OUT IS the behavioral manifestation of those impulses, desires and needs that an individual cannot accept or reconcile with his conscience. When the characteristic style of acting-out is socially or personally maladaptive such behavior is termed an "acting-out disorder." Acting-out disorders are common amongst character neurotics, impulse disorders, psychopaths, homosexuals, perverts, drug addicts and many neurotic and psychotic patients.

Not all acting-out behavior is maladaptive. Everyone acts out. All of us have life styles and characteristic ways of living. Imbedded in these stylized expressions are impulses that normally are abhorrent to the individual. The smoker, for example, would become infuriated if you told him that his smoking is a manifestation of his deep-seated wish to suck his mother's breast. The good natured, affable executive would find it repugnant to hear that he is controlling and manipulating his staff through the use of his personality. A therapist would be termed vulgar and insulting if he pointed out the seductive and sexual wishes inherent in the miniskirted, perfumed young lady's attire and toilet. National characteristics such as the German efficiency, the Irish happy-go-lucky attitude and the Latin sensuality are examples of culturally stylized ways of living which harbor sadistic, dependent and sexual urges. Indeed, in order for anyone to adapt to his environment he must incorporate those cultural traits which allow him to act out those very impulses which his society strongly condemns.

When psychotherapists speak of acting-out disorders, they generally refer to those patients whose particular behavior manifestations get them into trouble. The typical referral of such an individual for treatment comes from a law enforcement agency or some other authority. Seldom are such individuals motivated to become self-referrals.

There are patients with acting-out difficulties whose behavior is personally maladaptive rather than antisocial. These patients come into therapy as self-referrals for reasons other than their character problems. For example, homosexuals often enter treatment because of the anxiety engendered by the acquisition or loss of an intimate relationship. Their motivation is not to curb their acting-out behavior but rather to alleviate anxiety and become free to pursue their previous style of living. Sometimes middle-aged women who are sexually promiscuous initiate therapy because of a vague sense of unfulfillment and an inability to form close emotional ties. They display neither guilt nor anxiety about their sexual acting-out; instead they focus on their unfulfilled dependency needs.

Traditional psychotherapy has long seen acting-out as the main deterrent to successful treatment. The repetition compulsion to give vent to those unacceptable forces behind acting-out behavior denies the patient a conscious awareness of his motives and thus responsibility for his actions. Besides depriving the individual of gratification and satisfaction in the expression of his urges, acting-out can work against personal growth, preventing the individual from participating in a viable struggle between his impulses and his conscience. A chief factor behind this is the role the unconscious plays in acting-out behavior. Few individuals have any awareness of the motives affecting their characteristic behavior or acting-out patterns. They function in accordance with the rules and procedures they were raised with without questioning the nature of their needs or whether their conduct succeeds in bringing them the rewards their actions appear to aim at. This almost total repression serves to placate those moral and ethical standards which would normally not tolerate the manifest expression of certain needs. Yet, the unconscious manages to expedite such behavior in a fashion consistent with the ego's self-image. The key factor here is the persistence of the individual's life style, even in the face of overwhelming reality evidence of its destructive nature. In this fashion, such a person can remain emotionally fixated on an early developmental level without feeling shame or anxiety.

The chronic alcoholic typically is reared in an environment that stresses self-sufficiency but rewards passivity and dependence. Both messages are received and incorporated as a special kind of ambivalence. When the alcoholic drinks he is achieving his superego standard of individualism, independent self-fulfillment and manliness. At the same time he is living up to the ego ideal of lying passively on his back and letting the world take care of him. The force of satisfying both sides of this standard along with the habituation of his drinking becomes too great for his ego to challenge. No amount of rational or judgmental persuasion can effectively intervene against this combination of forces. The acting-out is unconscious, ego fulfilling and in consonance with the early standards of idealized behavior. The drinking is incorporated into the alcoholic's life style, hiding the destructive nature of his emotional fixation on an infantile dependency level. Effecting a behavioral change under these circumstances becomes a herculean task.

To add to the difficulty of both patients and therapists is the subjective and personal nature of standards for appropriate behavior. What is considered aggressive, controlling and manipulating conduct to one individual may be seen as assertive, ambitious and responsible behavior to another. Employing the yardstick of reality testing as a measure of adaptiveness only confuses the picture further. The industrial tycoon or general who employs psychopathic tactics to run a business or win a battle is praised and honored while the con artist who is caught is sent to jail. The overeater, compulsive gambler and accident-prone person are pitied and given sympathy while the drug addict, embezzler and pervert face legal prosecution.

The psychotherapist must ultimately rely on arousing the patient's conscience as well as his ego before he can successfully treat an individual with an acting-out disorder. In order to do this he must help the patient become aware of the motives behind his behavior. Since such patients have ego-syntonic life styles and character traits that are deeply embedded in the fabric of their personalities, helping them to become aware of the motivations inherent in their conduct is no easy task.

TRADITIONAL TREATMENT METHODS

Until twenty years ago acting-out patients were generally considered untreatable. The earliest references to this form of behavior were heavily laden with moralistic and judgmental criticism of such individuals. Prichard,[24] who coined the term "psychopath," viewed such patients as "indecent and lacking in propriety," referring to them as morally insane. Henderson[17] placed such behavior on the level of primitive savages. Cleckley[4] felt that such actions reflect constitutional inferiority. These authors held little hope for a therapeutic cure, recommending incarceration and custodial care.

Sigmund Freud introduced the term "acting-out" in his paper, "Remembering, Repeating and Working Through," published in 1914. He used the term to describe compulsive repetitive behavior as a defense against remembering past traumas. The psychoanalytic method, based on recalling early history, could not be effective while the patient's behavior expressed the very conflicts from which he was seeking relief.

The concept of acting-out became widespread and was used more loosely and vaguely. Generally, however, the literature deals with this type of pathology as a form of character defect.

The character of a healthy child, with an adequate environment, evolves gradually with the successful fulfillment of his basic needs. The style of ego expression coincides with his stages of development. As each stage of development is successfully completed the young child's experience in attempting novel ways and means of gaining satisfaction increases. The well-adjusted youngster increases his self-confidence and eventually develops a characteristic style of fulfillment that is reality oriented, flexible, anxiety free and expressive of the integrity of his needs in consonance with the demands of his environment. When there are fundamental conflicts between his urges and the standards of society, he learns to successfully sublimate.

Potentially acting-out youngsters, on the other hand, do not find adequate sublimation for their basic needs and become fixated at one or more stages of their development. The character of such children similarly becomes stunted and does not acquire the flexibility associated with mature behavior. If his oral needs are not gratified, for example, his character formation develops a fixation at this point in his history. All further growth is hampered and colored by this limitation. Whether or not neurotic symptoms and their respective defenses evolve from this fixation, the character of the child is already defective and will be observed clearly regardless of the future course of his development. He does not have the integrity to find a satisfactory outlet for his needs while remaining in harmony with his environment. It is therefore well to consider and deal with the character defects of all neurotic patients even if the form of their pathology is not that of an acting-out disorder proper.

Hartmann[15] sees the acting-out patient as having a defective ego structure. Such individuals cannot adequately regulate their reactions to environmental demands. Minor slights or rebuffs, easily tolerated by others, exceed this patient's threshold for adaptation. Spitz[29] and Erikson[8] emphasize the loss of trust in the mother-child relationship as leading to unstable ego development and maladaptive behavior. Henderson[18] cites studies indicating the high incidence of illegitimacy and the absence of a father figure as leading to psychopathic states. The inability to resolve the Oedipus complex is described by Reich[26] as operating to insulate the individual from external stimuli and render him less susceptible to adapting his behavior.

The denial of fulfillment along with punishing the child for making demands is cited by Eissler[6] as leading to delinquent behavior. Such children learn to act as though they are self-sufficient and appear submissive when confronted by authority. However, they develop covert ways of attempting gratification which neither fulfills nor brings them acceptance by the environment. Deep-seated hostility and rejection of parental standards is described by Redl and Wineman[25] as leading to acting-out behavior. Adult insincerity and exploitation of the child is pointed out by Greenwald[13] as a factor in antisocial conduct.

With a shift in outlook to the environment's effect on the acting-out patient, rather than *his* social destructiveness, the etiology of such symptoms was studied. The most common factors cited are the rejection of the child's spontaneity coupled with parental failure to establish alternative standards of conduct. Some investigators report an early history of indulgence, encouraging overt dependence. When in later life the indulgence stops, the individual tends to continue seeking gratification through acting-out. It has been shown that many parents of such patients usually fail to integrate their own forbidden impulses and seek these satisfactions vicariously through their children. Parental narcissistic investment in the child is most frequent when there is serious marital discord. Marital dissatisfactions centering around emotional and behavioral constrictions can readily influence a child to act out a parent's hostility towards those social standards that bind him to his unhappy marriage. Paradoxically, it is often the child's acting-out behavior and the family's rallying to help that keeps such a marriage from disintegrating.[1, 3, 12, 19]

Attempts to influence the acting-out patient primarily through traditional psychotherapy are met with a host of problems. Poor motivation, particularly a lack of guilt and anxiety, lack of affective identifications or transferences, poor ego controls, difficulty in postponing gratifications, infantile dependency needs and the associated hostility when denied are but a few of the obstacles cited. It is impossible for the acting-out patient to adopt the value system and controls of the therapist if he is not involved in the therapeutic relationship. The passivity of the therapist as well as his emphasis on the interpretation of unconscious material are cited as deterring a therapeutic tie.[1, 14, 16, 20, 28]

Of equal importance in the limitations of traditional psychotherapy for the acting-out patient is his lack of confidence in the ability to alter his behavior. Even with an ample understanding of the causes of his actions, he feels impotent to stop his self-defeating patterns. His poor self-image all but eliminates his active attempts to control himself. Without the support and positive participation of the patient's ego, traditional treatment methods are ineffective. The recognition of these circumstances led psychotherapists to devise novel and creative ways of intervening in the pathology of such patients.

NEW METHODS

Some clinicians, recognizing the difficulties in establishing transferences, worked instead towards the development of a narcissistic relationship. The therapist demonstrated that he was more clever and cunning and had better methods of outwitting law enforcement agencies than the patient. He would discuss a patient's plan to commit robbery, point out the flaws in the scheme and suggest a far superior alternative. One therapist attempted to get his psychopathic patients to view him as omnipotent. Often the therapist would be entertaining in order to hold the patient's interest. Some intervened in the individual's family in order to help the patient out of difficulty. Utilizing such methods, therapists were able to treat more socially maladaptive acting-out disorders successfully.[1, 6, 10, 14]

These techniques demonstrate that when an empathic bond is formed between the therapist and patient, based on the latter's needs, a close therapeutic relationship can be formed with such individuals. However, these authors stress only the patient's eventual incorporation of the therapist's social standards. It is the writers' contention that along with the evolvement of a narcissistic relationship, the patient requires a systematic approach to strengthen his self-discipline on matters related to his own value system. If he can be helped to postpone immediate gratification for purposes of achieving his goals, then he is in a position to utilize increased ego strength to understand his self-defeating style of living.

Besides the innovation of new techniques to engage the acting-out patient in treatment, psychotherapists also created and modified therapeutic structures to deal with this problem. Topic House and Synanon evolved to cope with the drug addict. Here the pressure of peer group acceptance served to establish the necessary commitment for the patient's active participation in treatment. The encounter group further helped reluctant patients to respond and relate to the immediacy of a here-and-now interaction. Lowering the defensive armor was helped through the introduction of the marathon. Therapists became more actively involved with such patients and tended to stress the experiential and existential aspects of the doctor-patient relationship. Some practitioners made house calls and occasionally invited the patient to live in his home. Combinations of traditional and newer therapies were used with the advent of the behavior modification techniques. Therapists of the latter persuasion are symptom focused rather than disease oriented and tend to concern themselves with whatever seems appropriate to aid the patient in overcoming his symptoms.

Since acting-out problems stem from character defects, successful therapeutic intervention begins with enabling the patient to view his behavior as an unsuccessful attempt to solve an internal struggle. Once the patient is aware of the self-defeating nature of his behavior, he is both motivated and prepared to take steps to undergo changes. Enlisting the patient's motivation to change is an important part of the process of Ellis' rational-emotive therapy. Not only must the patient accept the construct that he has been living with an irrational philosophy of life, but he must also be prepared to substitute a rational view of himself. To use Ellis' example, a client was initially made aware of his belief that he had to succeed in order to be a worthwhile human being. The irrationality of this concept was pointed out to him and he was encouraged to ask himself, Why must I be great in order to accept myself as a person? Homework assignments are an integral part of Ellis' therapy. They are designed to help patients depropagandize themselves from their self-defeating attitudes and values. Homework is also used by Bergin as an adjunct to his self-regulation technique for impulse control. In this treatment procedure clients are trained in a method of conscious self-control which they rehearse during the therapy hour and exercise between sessions. The Bergin method is an outgrowth of behavior modification techniques and is used in conjunction with them.[2, 7]

The concurrent use of behavior modification techniques and psychotherapy is reported by D'Alessio.[5] Both therapies are used either in alternate sessions or in specific time allotments in each session. Behavior modification techniques are used to extinguish undesirable behavior as well as to teach alternate ways of functioning while psychotherapy is employed to deal with the anxiety and resistance attendant upon subsequent progress or failure.

Farley's[9] initial treatment approach with hospitalized psychopaths involves the use of an assaultive technique. He verbally criticizes, scolds and berates the psychopath for his irresponsibility and dependency on others. He attacks their pride and self-image, invariably arousing a strong defensive response as well as a counterattack. The typically unemotional and "cool" psychopath is instantly thrust into a struggle with an authority figure upon whom he is dependent. Farley employs this ignited affect to help patients experience a new and often more rewarding relationship. Manipulations, game playing and the "put on" are minimized while authentic interaction is pronounced. Usually trust is established and a working therapeutic union is formed.

Perls[23] wastes little time in getting his character neurotic patients to relate their immediate feelings and experiences to him. Attempts at intellectualizing are termed "mindfucking" and dismissed forthright. Expressions of helplessness are challenged directly, with the internal area of blockage and discomfort identified and dealt with as a polar aspect of the patient's gestalt. The individual is guided into a dialogue between these seemingly opposite facets of his makeup. As the patient responds in his own fashion to the complaints and inadequacies of his internalized resistance to change, he begins to display a mastery over his previously impotent state.

The paradigmatic approach also employs the technique of getting the patient to find a solution to his own resistances to change. The therapist, using the patient's own expressions of helplessness as a model, expresses an extreme version of this incompetence as a statement describing him. The patient typically defends against this image and frequently paves the way for therapeutic intervention by showing the therapist how to deal with the resistance.[22]

Drug addicts are often given a no-nonsense set of rules to follow before they are permitted to enter a residential treatment center. Fellow addicts immediately engage the newcomer in his set of rationalizations, denials and projections, pointing out that they too employed such defenses against facing their true motives for acting-out. This group encounter technique, employing the experience of patients with similar conditions, affords the addict a sense of belonging and security with people who understand his problem. A somewhat similar procedure, in a nonresidential setting, is used by some alcoholic annonymous and weight watcher groups.

All of these therapies have in common the threefold goal of enlisting the patient's active involvement in therapy, bringing into awareness the motives behind his behavior and strengthening self-discipline in order to master and overcome the acting-out disorder.

TREATMENT

An initial procedure in treating socially maladaptive individuals revolves around the therapist's acceptance of the patient's needs and the formation of an alliance to fulfill them. The fact that the acting-out patient feels isolated and alien to the social mainstream and usually lacks close interpersonal ties is employed to strengthen the working relationship. Recognizing that the self-image of such individuals is concomitant with their ability to gratify basic urges the therapist strives to optimize the secondary pleasures that the patient typically seeks through this acting-out behavior. The therapist's effectiveness in helping him find ways to achieve such gratifications helps gain the patient's confidence and respect. The therapist must participate actively in the patient's immediate needs in living as opposed to the passive posture in rendering abstract interpretations typical of conventional psychotherapy. A low threshold of anxiety, coupled with a history of failure in interpersonal intimacy, leaves the patient with little tolerance for attempts to induce self-questions, self-doubts and self-awareness. The only relationship he is amenable to is one whereby he can experience himself with some success on his own terms. The therapist initially accepts the patient's view of him as an object to be used and manipulated before attempting a more intimate and trusting relationship. In order to establish this initial union authentically the therapist must unearth and appreciate those acting-out traits and tendencies in himself. Since all socially adaptive individuals, including therapists, have learned to sublimate the immediate fulfillment of their needs in favor of social acceptance, remnants of acting- out behavior remain in each of us.

The following is an example of an initial treatment procedure employed by one of the authors in his work with a psychopath.

Bette is an 18-year-old high school senior, referred for private psychotherapy by school authorities because of her sexual promiscuity, truancy, forging of her parents' names, stealing a car and attempted suicide. Despite her high IQ she is barely getting by in her schoolwork. She is seldom overtly insolent or rebellious to authority. Instead, she appears to be the epitome of innocence when confronted with her recalcitrant behavior. When caught red-handed she is quick and brilliant in providing reasons for her actions which absolve her of responsibility.

Despite her slight obesity, Bette is pretty and well groomed. She appears passively cooperative during the initial interview, indicating neither concern nor curiosity about the psychotherapeutic procedure. She readily reveals that she is the youngest of two children, her brother two years her senior. Her father is a successful self-made businessman, while her mother comes from a highly respected family in the community. Her formative years were marked by a host of family quarrels, emotional turmoils and separations. Her mother was hospitalized for two years and received private psychotherapy over a six-year period for severe depressions and many physical complaints. An alternately restricting and overprotecting maternal grandmother played an important part in her upbringing. Her father was seldom at home, appearing preoccupied and distant while in the household.

Bette thinks of her parents and most of her teachers as "dumb" and easily manipulated. She considers schoolwork, home chores and any disciplined activity as a "waste" and prefers to "route." The latter consists of riding around town, stopping at various bars, meeting different boys and staying out half the night. While she has no friends, she considers herself part of an "in-group" that is full of "action." She readily admits to a series of sexual experiences with different boys. She displays no concern, remorse or fear over her actions but does consider the restrictions placed on her at home as "criminal." She believes it is funny that she is seeing a "shrink" since it is clear to her that it is her parents who really require help. She agrees to treatment to quiet her parents and school officials.

After obtaining a detailed account of Bette's pleasure-seeking activities, I wondered why she allowed herself to be restricted at home so often. She expressed surprise at this question, exclaiming that this was obviously due to her "square" parents. I pointed out that if, according to her account, her parents watched television every night and went to bed early, it might be smarter if she waited until they were asleep and then walked to the corner where she could meet her friends. I noted further that if caught, she could truthfully say she could not sleep and went out for a walk. Bette thought this was "neat" and planned to try it. The next session she laughed uproariously as she described her "breakout" and her parent's remark the following morning on how well she looked after a good night's sleep. She quickly challenged me to help her get the use of the family car more often. I questioned her minutely regarding her parents' attitudes and habits concerning this vehicle and finally advised that she arrange to have a series of dental appointments just before dinnertime. When this too worked out well, Bette began to show a real interest in psychotherapy.

For the next several weeks I helped Bette to play truant by suggesting that she report to her homeroom at the beginning and end of the school day, turn in book reports and term papers prepared two years earlier by her brother, obtain more spending money by returning to local stores purchases that were charged to her parents' account and deceive her parents about her drinking by advising that she switch to vodka. Once, when she "just had to" get out at night to see a friend, I suggested that she tell her parents that she had a late appointment with me.

Throughout this early phase of treatment, the therapeutic relationship is focused on the patient's external reality. The therapist and patient enter into a variety of discussions, calculations, predictions and assumptions regarding this reality in order to more fully help the psychopath achieve satisfaction.

As the patient's needs become more complex and require an increased time interval before gratification can be obtained, greater emphasis is placed on postponing immediate fulfillment in order to obtain information, test reality and deliberate the execution of one or more premeditated plans.

In the course of inquiring about the environment, the therapist increasingly displays his ignorance of the facts necessary in making a decision to satisfy a need. He therefore turns to the patient and urges him to obtain this information, supporting his efforts to function independently. When the delinquent succeeds in this function, he is praised and rewarded.

In the case of Bette, the successful fulfillment of her immediate needs led to an increase in the complexity of her wants and a more demanding challenge to the therapeutic relationship. My questions concerning the nature of her needs and the reality of her environment grew more numerous and complex. We once spent a whole week trying to figure out how she could obtain her own telephone. After a series of inquiries regarding the comparative cost of an extension phone, an intercom system and a portable two-way radio, we outlined a plan that required three stages before a solution could be effected. First, Bette was to have someone call her up early in the morning and she was to allow the telephone to ring a few times before answering it. The next day the phone was to ring early again and she was not to answer it nor "awake" when her parents called her from downstairs. They would have to walk upstairs or shout loudly enough to awaken her brother. Thirdly, she was to keep the telephone occupied when her father usually expected business calls to be coming in.

By the end of the week, Bette's parents suggested to her that she get her own private telephone which they would gladly pay for.

When Bette returned to a session with information necessary to solve one of her problems, I praised her and immediately placed a great deal of importance on these facts. In one instance, she was especially clever in learning that one of her midterm examinations was marked by a school clerk. I was genuinely impressed with her detective work and she knew it. With Bette expending most of the effort, we figured out how she could achieve a perfect score on this test even before she took it. It then seemed that she tried to find ways to obtain information cleverly so as to please me. I never failed to express my approval of these efforts and results.

While the socially maladaptive patient often requires an unorthodox initial therapeutic procedure to engage him in therapy, he too must sometime deal with and become aware of the motives behind his acting-out behavior. Unlike those patients with ego-alien symptoms of phobia, anxiety or depression, his motivation to scrutinize his inner dynamics is quite poor. He, therefore, usually needs a particularly strong dependency transference on the therapist before he will examine the causes of his socially unacceptable conduct.

Such patients are typically reared in an environment that denies fulfillment and criticizes the expression of his needs. His real nature is rejected and a premium placed on his acting as though he were self-sufficient. If he decides to inhibit or suppress a wish because he has been promised some later fulfillment, invariably he is disappointed. Furthermore, his hostility towards the rejecting environment is too intense for him to contain. Nor can he be gratified by identifying with the values of the socially acceptable adults around him. He is too aware of the insincerity and exploitative nature of these values as they apply to him. The resultant stress on getting his own way, through the most expedient and rapid means, is a logical consequence of this type of upbringing. The therapist, however, knows that the emphasis on immediate gratification is a display of deep-seated dependency needs. He can employ this knowledge to help establish a dependency transference and subsequently expose the motives behind the socially maladaptive functioning in order to help the patient arrive at better ego controls.

In the case of Bette, as she identified with the therapist more and more her interests shifted to helping other people. She encouraged several friends to remain in school, helped to arrange an abortion for one of them, directed several people into psychotherapy and turned her room into a veritable way station for youngsters leaving home. She was affectionately referred to as "Dr. Bette Brothers." As her "practice" increased she sought my advice in handling her "clients." After a few successful interchanges, I told her, "You are a lousy analyst." When she recovered from this first direct criticism, she wanted to know why. I told her that she was sending out two opposing messages to her friends. In addition to the overt encouragement to act responsible she was pointing out that her own behavior was immature. She was breaking appointments with her friends, her job and me. Her lack of adequate sleep caused her to "poop out" when she could benefit by being alert. She was not eating properly. She smoked too much.

With a wry smile, Bette began to defend her own behavior. She tried rationalizing that because of her "heavy caseload," she could not realistically take proper care of her own needs. I countered with, "Do you think your 'patients' will buy that?" She shifted with, "I'm really in much better condition than most of them so that the same standards do not apply." I said, "Bullshit." She accused me of being unfair, of demanding too much from her, indicating that while I was paid for my services, she acted gratuitously. I told her that was precisely my point. How could she expect others to respect and follow her advice if she could not act in her own self-interest? She finally agreed that this was true but added that because of old habits she really did not think that she could discipline herself. She tried to diet and stop smoking, for example, but always failed. I taunted her with, "That's right, Bette, be a good girl and act just like your parents say you are. Support their view of you by being lazy, irresponsible, weakwilled and a failure. If you prove that they were right about you all along, maybe then they will love you." This got to her and she became determined to show those "bastards" that she really is adequate and independent. She soon began to stop smoking in the office, to cut down on her eating and to sleep eight hours the night before a session.

For those patients whose acting-out behavior is personally maladaptive rather than specifically antisocial, other techniques are employed. When an acting-out patient seeks help because of some vague dissatisfaction, anxiety or somatic complaint, the initial therapeutic intervention is designed to promote the patient's awareness of his behavior and enlist his cooperation to modify or change it. One possible first step in this direction involves getting the patient to act out his "acting-out" expressions in an exaggerated form, thereby forcing him to defend against the unacceptability of his typical behavior.

An extremely hostile patient who constantly ingratiates himself with others through his cooperative, friendly, helpful manner was given the task of putting down each member of a group by being overly sweet and complimentary. He started the task by saying to another group participant, "you sound intelligent." When he was asked to exaggerate this it became, "you act like you know everything." As he spoke to each member of the group his task of exaggerating the positive was performed more and more spontaneously. This exercise enabled him to experience the hidden meaning behind his characteristic behavior. When he no longer defended himself through his typical sweetness and friendliness he was able to accept and express his hostility more directly.

The potency of this approach was demonstrated by this patient in a subsequent group session. At this meeting he reported awakening early one morning feeling very angry with his wife who was lying next to him. He had two impulses almost simultaneously; one to hug her and the other to kick her out of bed. He recognized both impulses as expressions of his hostility and knew that his wife would reject him regardless of which course he took. He finally decided that hugging her would be the more hostile act because she would feel guilty when she rejected him and he, accordingly, pursued that tactic. When he recounted the story it was with both a sense of pride in his increased awareness of himself and a sense of horror at his sadism. He saw clearly for the first time that it is kinder to directly express a given feeling of anger toward a loved one than to mask it behind a pseudo-loving act.

Helping the patient become aware of, and take responsibility for, the unconscious impulses inherent in his acting-out behavior is basic to the psychotherapeutic procedure. One way to deal with this resistance is to urge the personally maladaptive patient to interact, employing his typical life style. He is given the task of relating to others with his usual self-defeating behavior. Exaggerated and pronounced forms of his actions are constructed so that he can readily become aware of the true meaning of his relationships. This method of making manifest a previously unconscious motive through a reenactment of the patient's typical acting-out behavior, the authors have termed "therapeutic acting-out."

THERAPEUTIC ACTING-OUT

The authors employ a combination of traditional and more recent psychotherapeutic structures to implement the therapeutic acting-out method. Because the aim of the unacceptable impulses of such patients is commonly directed towards the most significant people in their lives, we frequently use the vehicle of couples group therapy to utilize this technique. In couples therapy, we often discover that either one or both partners manifestly express the unconscious wishes of the other. This expression of forbidden impulses through the marital partner sometimes becomes so pronounced as to make the marriage itself appear to be the means of acting-out by both husband and wife. By keeping our focus on the process and structure of the interaction between the couple, we uncover the behavioral outlet for those urges that neither partner is aware. We devise exercises and homework assignments geared to help the couple act out that which their deeds secretly express.

We also utilize the therapeutic acting-out method along with encounter techniques. Encounter techniques in group therapy were devised to clarify and make explicit the nature of interpersonal ties. Patients are encouraged to deal directly with areas of their relationship that remain unresolved. The methods employed by Schutz[27] and Malamud and Machover[21] are designed to create an interaction that concretely depicts a problem in interpersonal living. Thus, a "one downmanship" outcome is realized by having the individuals place their hands on each others' shoulders and literally try to put one another down on the floor. Or a couple that argues repetitiously (going around in circles) are placed in the middle of the room and asked to circle one another without verbalizing. Competitive behavior designed to avoid closeness is manifestly depicted by arm or leg wrestling. The physical experience offers the participants a new perspective in which to view their conflict. The novelty of the exchange induces authentic responses rather than stereotyped behavior. The gamelike nature of the exercises creates an atmosphere of levity and friendship vital to the supportive function of the group. Encouragement and social rewards usually are spontaneously offered by other members of the group.

Another recent psychotherapeutic structure employed as a vehicle for the therapeutic acting-out method is the marathon. Marathon therapy is a time extended group session usually running for twenty-seven consecutive hours. The unique therapeutic dimension offered by a marathon evolves from the extended period of group interaction. Four factors are operative which seldom obtain in any other therapeutic structure. First, the intensity of participation mounts as one individual after another begins to unfold his story, breaks through a previously cherished defense and has a fresh insight into his condition. Each succeeding experience tends to carry over and add to the collective emotionality. Tolerance for anxiety increases as the group is exposed, without let up, to these life dramas. This additional capacity to cope with anxiety permits the release of deep feelings such as profound grief, utter despair and overwhelming love. Secondly, the continuity of the group does not allow for the typical reestablishment of defenses observed in shorter forms of therapy. Participants are deprived of their usual environments wherein they maintain life styles and roles. Those character traits and patterns of behavior dependent on such external support and reinforcement thus become more accessible to change. Thirdly, the fatigue factor is important in helping to break down defenses and resistances, leading to a more authentic, spontaneous expression of interpersonal relations. After so many hours of heightened experiences it is rare to find an individual who is unaffected. Fourthly, as the hour for termination approaches, the pressure to expose conflicts and problems increases. Knowing that the group will cease to exist shortly, each participant is struck with his personal responsibility to get from the marathon what he came for. This urgency may become desperate; in fact, during the final hours of a marathon there is a release of emotion seldom seen in any other setting.

The following case history of a couple in treatment illustrates how the above techniques and structures are employed.

Ruth and Herb sought treatment jointly and were accepted into one of the couples therapy groups led by the authors. The symptoms, as presented by Ruth, were her severe headaches, Herb's sexual impotence and his compulsive gambling. Both of them accepted her description of Herb as the irresponsible acting-out partner and Ruth as the responsible one. Before they left the first session Herb managed to inform each of the therapists privately that he had had an affair which Ruth did not know about. He said he could not tell her about this because it would "hurt her too much." He was pessimistic about being helped by the group as long as his wife was in it, because he probably "would not be able to open up." He was urged to attend for a few months to learn if his fears were justified.

Ruth was the principal complainer of the couple and initially the primary target of the group. She sat smugly judging and giving advice to every participant. Under the guise of being the practical, responsible partner in the marriage she was able to act out her deep-seated belief that unless she controlled every situation in her family something dreadful would happen. The authors used this attitude, asking her to role play "therapist" and tell each group member how he could improve his life. She started to go around the room saying,

"Sylvia—you should go on a diet and get thinner."

"Harold—you shouldn't be so quiet. You should speak up more." She began to falter and claimed the task was more difficult than she thought it would be. She was encouraged to continue and finally completed the exercise with a great deal of prodding. When asked how she felt about the experience Ruth replied, "I really don't want to tell anyone what to do and how to live. I want to be taken care of myself." Using this overt statement we worked to change the nature of her contract with Herb. She was urged to become more irresponsible and was given specific tasks to promote this kind of behavior. She had to report the results to the group each week.

Several weeks after they joined the group Herb was still a fairly silent participant and seemed to be keeping his promise to "not open up." At this time he was asked to attend a marathon without Ruth. Despite the fact that his participation in the marathon group was minimal, the experience was very meaningful to him. One lasting effect of this involvement was that he was subsequently less intimidated by his wife and the group. Under these circumstances, and motivated by a discussion of the sexual problems of another couple in the group, Herb initiated a discussion of the sexual inactivity in his marriage. When he was pushed to verbalize what he saw as the problem he reported, "When Ruth makes sexual advances to me I get turned off and if I feel warmly towards her I'm afraid to put my arms around her because I think she'll expect me to fuck her."

Both Ruth and Herb were asked to play out their bedroom scene in the group (on the floor and fully clothed). In the midst of the first tentative, amorous gestures from both of them Herb froze. When asked to sort out his feelings he expressed anxiety with respect to Ruth's expectations and anger toward her for making demands on him. He was then given his first assignment since initiating treatment. During the coming week he was to physically express his warmth for Ruth whenever he felt it, particularly when they were in bed, but under no circumstances was he to have intercourse with her. How they handled this exercise was typical of their interaction. The first time Herb expressed his warmth to Ruth he obviously became aroused. Ruth said, "You know we don't have to listen to them just because they said not to." Herb immediately was turned off and did not attempt the assignment again for the rest of the week. Ruth was furious with the therapists for giving the task and with Herb for not disobeying. Apparently, Herb's act of self-assertion was threatening enough for Ruth to regress to the point where she again had to reassure herself that she was still in control.

To help Ruth disengage from Herb, to promote some loosening and, hopefully, to enable her to experience some gratification, we had her attend a marathon without Herb. At the marathon she was urged to be as irresponsible as she could and encouraged to act out a sexual fantasy that she verbalized of having two men at once. The men entered the game enthusiastically with Ruth resisting initially. Ultimately, she abandoned herself to the simulated fantasy experience.

After the marathon Ruth was more spontaneous than she had ever been, her headaches were gone and some sexual activity ensued between her and Herb. When Ruth became more demanding, Herb's passive-resistive mode of responding again set in and she became quite bitter. When she brought this complaint to the group, some members responded by encouraging her to have an affair. She indicated that she was going to consider it, that her fifteen years of marriage had apparently been a waste. At that, Herb exploded. He claimed that was the end, he was leaving the group and the marriage—he was finished. He was persuaded to stay for a while and give Ruth more of his anger. He let out fifteen years of hostility, recounting incidents that occurred in the first year of their marriage. He claimed she had him brainwashed into believing she was always right and he was always wrong. He was particularly angry at always having to feel guilty. This reminded him of what he felt guilty about and he ended with, "so I fucked a broad; so what—I don't have to feel guilty about that forever—and I don't."

Both of them were a bit shocked by this revelation and his rage abated enough for them to begin to talk about what had happened. Ruth was completely intimidated by him and Herb was beginning to appreciate the notion, "she doesn't have to be right, she could be wrong."

For three days after that session Ruth walked around hurt and shattered. Herb stood his ground and did not act guilty. On the fourth day they began to talk and both of them were able to be open and share their feelings. When they returned for the next group session they were obviously together in a new way.

Over the next several months it became apparent that two of the presenting symptoms, the headaches and the impotency, had disappeared. The gambling had lessened considerably but still had Ruth concerned. However, Herb was able to handle her attacks on his gambling. He did not become guilty or unduly defensive and managed to suggest that she might have a problem in making an issue of it.

The key factors to be noted in this case are the use of the technique of therapeutic acting-out, consideration of the marital contract between Ruth and Herb, as another manifestation of their mutual acting-out and the use of structural innovations to enhance the ongoing therapy.

Ruth was initially encouraged to act out her typical role of being the responsible, nurturing marital partner when she was directed to give advice to the whole group. This exercise enabled her to become aware of her controlling behavior and the hidden impulse behind it; which was to demand that she be cared for. When Herb was directed to act out his usual role of withholding by being told to fondle his wife but not to have sex with her, Ruth sabotaged this assignment and clarified her part in Herb's acting-out behavior. The encounter techniques, homework assignments, marathons and role playing exercises were used to uncover the impulses behind the acting-out and enabled the patients to find a more satisfying way of expressing these urges. They also helped to make explicit the implicit contract inherent in their interpersonal behavior.

SUMMARY AND CONCLUSIONS

Acting-out has long been seen by traditional psychotherapists as a deterrent to successful treatment. Few individuals are aware of the forces affecting their acting-out patterns. The motives are imbedded in ego syntonic life styles and character traits. Because of this, patients with acting-out disorders have little or no guilt about their behavior and are not motivated to change. At best, they come into treatment either because they were coerced or to alleviate the anxiety due to circumstances other than their character problems.

Attempts to influence the acting-out patient through traditional psychotherapy have been relatively unsuccessful. In addition to poor motivation and a lack of guilt, obstacles to treatment are a lack of affective identification, poor ego controls, difficulty in postponing gratification and infantile dependency needs, and the associated hostility when these are denied.

The successful treatment of acting-out disorders centers on the establishment of an initial working relationship, bringing into awareness those unconscious needs reflected in the patient's behavior and providing positive experiences to achieve genuine gratification. Because these individuals suffer from a character defect, the therapist must reeducate them to acknowledge and respect the integrity of their insights and their related attempts at fulfillment while remaining in harmony with the demands of society. The therapist must be more involved, active and concretely focused on the patient's immediate problems in living. Traditional techniques and structures must not interfere with the practitioner's ability to demonstrate his commitment to the patient rather than to theory or a particular format of working. Acting-out patients challenge the therapist's ability to employ, innovate and create therapeutic interventions of a highly flexible and imaginative nature leveled at the specific needs of such individuals. If the therapist is not prepared for the type of intensive involvement where his own schedule, style of living and value system will likely be shaken, he should refer such patients elsewhere.

The initial therapeutic relationship with socially maladaptive persons of this type often calls for the complete acceptance of the individual's wants and needs, value system and style of attempting self-fulfillment. A low tolerance for anxiety and failure requires that such patients quickly experience the therapist as an ally in helping them achieve satisfaction. A strong dependency transference, based on trust and authentic involvement, must be built up quickly. Aiding the patient to become more effective, on his own terms, is usually necessary before such a transference can be established.

Personally maladaptive acting-out patients, on the other hand, enter therapy motivated to overcome their discomfort. The early therapeutic problems with these individuals is similar to the traditional psychotherapeutic methods with typical neurotics. While a dependency transference is established with these patients also, it is rarely as deep nor on as infantile a level as with antisocial acting-out patients.

Once the dependency transference is clearly observed through the patient's greater emphasis on pleasing the therapist than on direct self-fulfillment, it becomes possible to reveal the hidden motives behind his acting-out behavior. The precarious nature of the ego controls and positive self-image of the patient requires a heightened sensitivity to the content and timing of such interpretations. The general rule to follow is to find those areas of behavior where the unconscious meaning is closest to the patient's awareness before making an interpretation. The use of the therapeutic acting-out method is employed to this end. Given the task to exaggerate typical acting-out conduct, the patient experiences his motives in a concrete interpersonal fashion. He is often able to discern, accept, take responsibility for and articulate his real needs through this technique. Encounter, role playing and gestalt methods, as well as other techniques, are similarly employed to help uncover those unconscious factors inherent in the patient's stylized conduct. Group, encounter and marathon psychotherapeutic structures are designed to serve as a vehicle for the application of these methodologies.

After the patient displays insight into his behavior, he requires a systematic procedure to gain confidence and the skills to learn more rewarding patterns of living. The effectiveness of personal integrity is demonstrated through an emphasis on the integration of the patient's needs, his attempts at fulfillment and the reality demands of his environment. Pronouncements of helplessness, impotence and habituation as factors precluding effective change are interpreted as resistance to mature growth embedded in the unconscious dynamics of the acting-out behavior. Behavioral modification, rational-emotive, impulse control and parts of other therapeutic techniques, alone and in combination, are used to provide the patient with an increased confidence in his ability to act fruitfully. The gradual increase in the patient's repertoire of responses adds to his flexibility and appropriateness in living.

REFERENCES

1. Aichhorn, A.: *Wayward Youth*. New York, Viking Press, 1935.
2. Bergin, A.: A self-regulation technique for impulse control disorders. *Psychotherapy, 6 (2)*, 1969.
3. Chrzanowsky, G.: The psychotherapeutic management of sociopathy. *Am J Psychother, 29*, 1965.
4. Cleckley, H.: *The Mask of Sanity*. St. Louis, C. V. Mosby, 1941.
5. D'Alessio, G. R.: The concurrent use of behavior modification and psychotherapy. *Psychotherapy, 5 (3)*, 1968.
6. Eissler, K. R.: Ego psychological implication of the psychoanalytic treatment of delinquents. *The Psychoanalytic Study of the Child*, 1950, Vol. V.
7. Ellis, A.: Rational-emotive therapy. *J Contemp Psychother, 1 (2)*, 1969.
8. Erikson, E. H.: Identity and the life cycle. *Psychological Issues*. New York, International Universities Press, 1959.
9. Farley, F.: Assaultive therapy. *American Academy of Psychotherapists Workshop*. Madison, Wisconsin, 1965.
10. Freud, A.: *The Ego and the Mechanisms of Defense*. London, Hogarth Press, 1937.
11. Freud, S.: *Remembering, Repeating and Working Through*. 1914.
12. Greenacre, P.: Conscience in the psychopath. *Am J Orthopsychiatry, 15*, 1945.
13. Greenwald, H.: *The Call Girl: A Social and Psychoanalytic Study*. New York, Ballantine Books, 1958.
14. Greenwald, H.: Treatment of the psychopath. *Voices: The Art and Science of Psychotherapy, 3 (1)*, 1966.

15. Hartman, H.: The mutual influences in the development of ego and id. *The Psychoanalytic Study of the Child.* New York, International Universities Press, 1952.
16. Healy, N., and Brunner, A. F.: *New Light on Delinquency and its Treatment.* New Haven, Yale University Press, 1936.
17. Henderson, D.: *Psychopathic States.* New York, W. W. Norton & Co., 1939.
18. Henderson, D. H., and Batchelor, I. C.: *Textbook of Psychiatry.* London, Oxford University Press, 1962.
19. Johnson, A., and Szurck, S. A.: The genesis of anti-social acting out in children and adults. *Psychoanal Q, 21,* 1952.
20. Lippman, H. S.: *Treatment of the Child in Emotional Conflict.* New York, McGraw-Hill, 1956.
21. Malamud, D. Y., and Machover, S.: *Toward Self-Understanding: Grays Techniques in Self Confrontation.* Springfield, Charles C Thomas, 1965.
22. Nelson, M.: Effect of paradigmatic techniques on the psychic economy of borderline patients. *Psychiatry, 25 (2),* 1962.
23. Perls, F.: Acting out vs. acting through: an interview. *Voices: The Art and Science of Psychotherapy, 4 (4),* 1968.
24. Prichard, J. C.: *Treatise on Insanity.* London, 1835.
25. Redl, F., and Wiseman, D.: *Children Who Hate.* Glencoe, Free Press, 1951.
26. Reich, W.: *Character-analysis.* New York, Orzone Institute Press, 1945.
27. Schutz, W. C.: *Joy: Expanding Human Awareness.* New York, Grove Press, 1967.
28. Schwartz, L. J.: Treatment of the adolescent psychopath—theory and case report. *Psychotherapy, 4 (3),* 1967.
29. Spitz, R. A.: *A Genetic Field Theory of Ego Formation.* New York, International Universities Press, 1959.

Chapter 10

Psychotherapy with Patients with Sexual Disorders

LEON SALZMAN

THE THERAPY of the sexual disorders neither requires a distinctive approach nor a separate set of therapeutic tools or techniques. The same principles and technical procedures which are utilized in the psychotherapy of the neurotic disorders are applicable. The process of change may be complicated by the realistic limitations of the culture as well as the individual, but any valid therapeutic modality must clearly distinguish between adjustment and adaptation as well as between insight and alteration of behavior. We must not therefore attempt to make any artificial distinction between deep or superficial therapy or psychotherapy versus psychoanalytic therapy, as if some diagnostic categories or therapeutic modalities are outside the range of deep (meaning profound or basic) exploration because of lesser skills. There is no hierarchy of more intensive or more basic therapeutic modalities with psychoanalysis at the peak and psychotherapy at the bottom. It is beyond the scope of this chapter to examine this piece of mythological presumption. However there are variations in the methodology which includes the amount of time spent with the patient as well as the extent of utilization of such tools as transference or countertransference phenomena. Because our task is to comprehend the sexual disorder and attempt constructive changes, we should apply the best therapeutic techniques from all theoretical sources and technical modalities in order to adequately comprehend the underlying personality distortions which have produced the deviant sex behavior.

The approach one uses, however, is inevitably related to one's theoretical conceptions of the development of the sexual function in man. Prior to Freud, sex behavior was almost entirely the concern of the theologian, philosopher and moralist. Sexual deviations were sinful, immoral or inhuman and therefore the province of the priest or the law. Therapy was either punishment or absolution. Classifications of sexual abnormalities such as described in *Psychopathia Sexualis* were merely descriptive; either anatomical or according to earlier legal categories. Since they had no etiological value they supplied no guidelines for therapy. Freud, while making tremendous contributions to the understanding of sex, was nevertheless limited by his own background and the cultural emphasis on biology and instinct theory.

Following the lead of earlier sexologists like Krafft-Ebbing[1] and Magnus Hirschfield,[2] Freud[3] tried to establish a separate causative factor for the large numbers of distortions and perversions in sex behavior based on his libido theory. Thus he considered each descriptive category as a separate disorder due to fixation, regression or faulty resolution of the Oedipus complex. There was another category of sexual deviations which was attributed mainly to castration fear. These ranged from fetishism to exhibitionism and impotence. However, while he catalogued many diseases, ultimately they appeared to be due to a single cause, and the treatment was always psychoanalytic therapy without delineating any special areas of psychodynamic significance or isolating specific thwarts in that individual. In the past seventy years little has been added to his nosological scheme and the classical psychoanalytic treatment has been almost unaltered except perhaps in the major sexual aberrations like homosexuality.

In recent years there has been a tendency in some psychoanalytic circles to view the sexual deviations not as separate diseases but as symptoms of larger personality disorders.[4] The sexual difficulties are therefore not treated as separate or distinctive issues but are dealt with under the greater therapeutic burden of resolving the individual's characterological problem. In other words, they are symptoms, not diseases, and the therapeutic task is to focus on the underlying defect and not on the sexual aberrations. However, because of the social and legal implications of these symptoms, it is difficult and at times impossible to institute ideal programs of therapy based on these formulations. Therapy in the sexual disorders must therefore not only take into account medical and psychiatric issues, but social and political issues as well.

To develop a rational and valid therapeutic program we need to comprehend the role which sex plays in human functioning. Sex plays a primary role in human affairs by virtue of its unusual capacity to fulfill major psychological needs while performing its biological function. Any attempt to clarify the role of sex must take into account this significant and ubiquitous role in human behavior. What distinguishes sex activity from other physiological functions in the human? Sex activity is the only biological activity that requires "another person" for its complete biological fulfillment. As a result, it is most intimately associated with all the aspects of interrelatedness, both constructive and destructive, pleasurable and painful. It encompasses all the elements of interpersonal relationship, such as struggle, conflict, the satisfactions of tenderness and human closeness, and every maneuver, technique and dynamism of human behavior.

There is an hierarchy of our biological functions extending from the sympathetic functions which are entirely intrapersonal, to those which require increasing amounts of human cooperation. This is related to the development of man from his animal origins and involves those functions which operate independently of outside sources of stimulation (the autonomic functions) and those functions such as feeding, excretion, and sex, which, as man became socialized, impinged upon "others." Sex activity is in the extreme position in that it not only prefers cooperation but requires "another person" for its complete fulfillment. To complicate its performance still further is the fact that it begins at a period in the individual's development when his attitudes, patterns, anxieties and concerns about people of the opposite sex are already highly developed.

An aspect of its *major* role in interpersonal activity is involved in its capacity to dissipate anxiety and it is frequently called into action to deal with anxiety arising out of difficult interpersonal relationships. It is frequently used in this way, rather than to fulfill any lustful needs. Consequently the motivation for sex activity may be anxiety rather than lust or love. This fact helps us understand why it can be so easily given up as well as its widespread use under circumstances where intimacy is absent. This factor enters into the production of a great deal of deviant sex behavior.

DUAL ROLE OF SEX

The role of sex in the human being is twofold: First it relates to the problem of species preservation and can be called the procreative function. This aspect of the sexual function is most intimately related to the biological, physiological or organic functioning of the sexual apparatus. Its proper functioning is dependent upon adequate hormonal activity as well as other physiological factors. However, cultural issues, prejudices, customs and mores might dictate the modes of courting and mating. The other aspect of sex relates to man's other needs which are not essentially biological in nature but which result from his development from prehuman to human existence. This involves special needs such as the avoidance of loneliness, the need for love and intimacy.

Although large numbers of mammals and possibly other animals maintain close relationships in family units, the arrangement appears based largely on biological considerations rather than on the basis of tender regard for the opposite sex. In the human, however, the association of male and female serves other than procreative purposes so that heterosexual intimacy as well as homosexual intimacy may occur with or without sexual contact or procreation. On the other hand, it is often very difficult to determine in a particular relationship whether the sexual activity serves the purpose of procreation, to alleviate loneliness, to alleviate anxiety, to prove one's manliness or to enforce some demand on one's partner. It is this varied and diverse use of sex that makes it so complicated and significant an issue in human behavior. Because so much of the human drama can be enacted in our sexual performances, they can illuminate the total personality structure of an individual most dramatically as it unfolds in an interpersonal context.

SEXUAL DEVIATIONS

Many sexual deviations not only involve major distortions in the sphere of sex but involve profound alterations of the individual affectional capacities and relationships. While Freud and others assumed that love and the tender emotions were derived from sexuality through a process of sublimation, sexual biological maturity has no direct relationship to love, since it is a purely physiological development which occurs uniformly in all of us who have no biological or hormonal impediments. However, the presence of love which is a human development arising out of our "sociological" or post-animal needs is intimately involved in our sexual performances. The capacity to enjoy the sex act to the fullest is determined by the amount of intimate, tender regard one has for the partner. Maturity in a biological sense is not synonymous with competence or total capacity for utilization of the matured functions. This is particularly noticeable in the neuroses and psychoses, where there are striking limitations and impediments in performing physiological and psychological functions in spite of the presence of matured organic capacities for doing so. The presence of a physiologically matured sexual apparatus is no guarantee of a wholesome sexual existence. It is a necessary but not a sufficient precondition. The potentialities for pleasure and "happiness" (totality of satisfaction) in sexual activity are dependent upon the capacity to love and to be loved by another person. This is the reverse of the formula—sexual maturity implies love, since love or a tender regard for another human develops prior to maturation of the sexual function. There is some reason to believe that these affectional reactions derive from other sources, like the quality of the maternal relationship with the infant, and participate in the sex function to the degree that they are already present in the individual. The presence of love in a human relationship permits the maximum satisfaction in sexual performances. Whatever else is involved it is abundantly clear that every type, variety and category of sexual deviation evidences a failure, deficiency or alteration in the individual capacity for tender, loving involvement with another human of the same or opposite sex or both. This is a constant and ubiquitous accompaniment of all distortions, perversions and deviations of the sexual life of man.

Concepts of normality and deviation would be simple if sex behavior in man were merely an instinctual performance with only a minimal of learned refinements. We could then proceed to label all sexual behavior not directly involved in the biological procreative function as abnormal, and we would be spared a multitude of disagreements and criticisms from legal, theological, sociological and psychological sources. However, an overview of the advances in the understanding of sexual behavior, both normal and abnormal, bears out the severe limitations of the original psychoanalytic conceptions of sex and its role in human behavior. Its deficiencies are particularly apparent in the area of sexual behavior involving the so-called perversions, deviations or abnormalities—or less pejoratively, the variations of sexual behavior.[5]

What is normal and what is abnormal in sex behavior? This apparently simple yet complex question requires the combined efforts of sociologists, psychiatrists and public administrators to clarify. Normality is not simply a psychological or physiological determination. It involves definitions which evolve from the history, religious orientation and sophistication of a culture, both in aesthetic and scientific matters. Normality in one sense is established by the prevailing theological and scientific attitudes toward sex behavior. Legal formulations of normality and deviance can and often do change with advances or changes in theological doctrine or scientific evidence regarding human physiology.

Thus the definition of normal sex behavior cannot be established in absolute terms. A workable formulation that can serve for many years to come asserts that normal sex behavior is largely a subjective determination and consists of sexual activity which is acceptable to both partners and which produces satisfaction and pleasure without damage, either psychologically or physiologically, to either partner or the community and broader culture in which they live. This formulation, however, requires the additional dimension that such behavior should not be contrary to public interest either because of the immaturity or incapacity of one of the partners to decide or resist the invitation or because public displays of such behavior tend to be offensive to others. This is analogous to concepts of normality with regard to other biological activities such as eating, urinating or defecating where peculiar, idiosyncratic or statistically unpopular practices are not considered abnormal or illegal unless they impinge on others. Social value judgments have no place in regard to variations in sex activity between freely consenting adult partners under circumstances of privacy. In view of the individual preferences and prejudices among people of various cultures, psychiatric intervention or labels of deviancy arise only if anxiety accompanies the activity. We are referring here to variational behavior such as the positioning in the sex act or the orifices which may be used as well as the sex of the partners. These variations are qualitatively and quantitatively different from major deviations in the sex act which constitute serious social and psychiatric problems and have been minutely catalogued and described in the classic volumes such as Krafft-Ebing's[1] *Psychopathia Sexualis*. It is these activities which will be dealt with in this chapter. The tendency, as I indicated earlier, however, to view such deviations as separate disease entities is neither theoretically nor therapeutically sound. Such classifications are holdovers of a nosology which predated present knowledge of sex.

Almost all of the sexual deviations are largely involved in processes which are not related to biological defects or faults but rather to interpersonal deficiencies. Where hormonal, constitutional or genetic factors are involved, the manifestations are not usually called perversions or deviations.

Most often sex serves no procreative purpose, whether in childless couples (through no design on their part), for whom sex can be the most intimate expression of their companionship and love, or when conception is not the goal. At these times it serves as a source of pleasure and expression of intimacy, but it can also be used to fulfill the neurotic needs of both partners. By this I mean that sex activity does not necessarily arise as a result of lust promoted by tender feelings towards one's partner. It may frequently be precipitated by a need to overcome tension and restore amicable relationships during periods of stress, disagreements or following heated exchanges in basically friendly relationships. At other times it may express or convey feelings of strength, potency or hostility designed to reassure or overwhelm one's partner. It may be part of a competitive struggle in which one may perform or refuse to perform in order to fulfill some neurotic goal or else it may be a pseudomanifestation of one's generosity devoid of true tenderness. There are endless possibilities in which sex activity attempts to deal with anxiety of one sort or another rather than as an expression of sexual need or tender regard. The sexual deviations are prime examples of sex activity where the motives for the behavior are rarely lustful needs but are expressions or manifestations of neurotic tendencies or attempts to appease or resolve some anxiety. In sex deviants of all sorts we find that except in the rare endocrine disorders, they are capable of functioning biologically. However, they avoid the sexual apparatus of the opposite sex for a variety of reasons, other than physiological.

Deviates always have problems in interpersonal functioning which involve aspects such as intimacy, closeness or the capacity to love and trust. Although they prefer sexual outlets other than genital intercouse, rarely is this outlet permanently interfered with. Their procreative functions are intact even though their preference reduces such a possibility. It is very common to find deviates of all kinds being married and having children. The problems which are expressed or involved in the sexual deviation are almost always a part of their total personality structure and manifested in all areas of their living. For example, the exhibitionist who achieves sexual satisfaction through exposure of his genitals thus avoids an active and aggressive involvement with the opposite sex. In other areas of his living he is overtly shy, passive and timid as well. No two deviates are ever precisely alike either in their personality makeup or in the method of expressing the deviation. The deviation is specific to the individual personality makeup even though it can be categorized under broad headings.

ETIOLOGY

The issue of a biological versus interpersonal basis for the sexual deviations can be illuminated by the understanding of a common sexual difficulty. Premature ejaculation is a widespread phenomenon which has been variously interpreted as being due to biological deficits in the urethral stage of libidinal development or as the result of faulty interpersonal relationships. Since it is a condition which highlights the elements of participation in the sex act, it can illuminate the role culture plays in human sexual activity.[6] Except for rare instances, there must be a maximum of mutual participation for the sex act to proceed to climax, and each participant must perform the role dictated by his sexual organs. Consequently, both male and female are indispensable for a fully satisfactory sex experience and neither has any special or preferred status in the performance. In recent years, and closely related to the emancipation of the female, sexually and otherwise, the responsibility for the pleasure and orgasm in the female has been assigned to the male. It is his responsibility for orgasm to take place in the female. This requires that a sufficient duration of time transpire in intercourse. The anxieties and issues about an earlier ejaculation has brought the phenomenon of premature ejaculation to considerable prominence in recent years.*

Premature ejaculation is a sexual disorder that has no counterpart in the female, although frigidity is often considered to be the female counterpart. Operationally, impotence is the masculine counterpart of frigidity in the female. Frigidity involves the inability to achieve a sexual climax, while premature ejaculation implies an exaggerated readiness to climax. Thus early orgasm in the female is never considered premature, since whenever it occurs it does not necessarily terminate intercourse. It is not

---

*Krafft-Ebing in his classic work *Psychopathia Sexualis* does not even mention premature ejaculation, while Forel, the author of a very popular and widely disseminated book *The Sexual Question* published in 1922 does not include it either. I have had no success in finding any reference to this disorder in any publications prior to 1900. In pursuing the matter I wrote to Dr. Ernest Jones who replied in a personal communication in 1962 that "My impression is that hardly anything was written on that subject prior to Freud."

equivalent to premature ejaculation and is often highly valued by the female and is flattering to the male. It is regarded as a desirable feminine trait in contrast to premature ejaculation, which is viewed as evidence of inadequate masculinity. Thus the sexual syndrome, premature ejaculation, cannot be understood without an elaborate analysis of gender roles and sexual expectations, as well as the social attitudes towards female rights and privileges.

The sexual deviations can be classified in a variety of ways. Freud's classification was biological and was based on his libido theory. This classification was based on motivational concepts and involved a structural examination of the sex instinct into its partial components. Sandor Rado,[7] in his adaptational view of sex behavior, classified sex behavior as being either standard or modified. The modifications were divided into three groups: (a) reparative, (b) situational and (c) variational. While the situational and variational modifications are sometimes called deviant, most deviations fall into the class of the reparative patterns. In this framework, Rado classified the patterns as either (a) replacement of sexual organs by other organs for example, anus, mouth, armpit; (b) sexual pain-dependence or masochistic or sadistic sexual patterns, (c) contact avoidance of partners for example, voyeurism, exhibitionism, etcetera; (d) patterns of solitary gratification for example, fetishism, compulsive masturbation; and (e) homosexuality. This classification had the advantage over earlier classifications in that the therapeutic goals were illuminated by a recognition of the dynamics of the behavior and its adaptive purpose. Another type of classification is phenomenological and is based on the elements of the sex act as an interpersonal phenomenon. This orientation includes the existentialist view of sex behavior which sees sex not as a collection of partial instincts or separate elements but rather as a total performance in which the individual expresses his involvement, participation and commitment to another person. The sexual deviations are therefore manifestations of failures in commitment and involvement.

We can also view the sex act in terms of (a) preliminary behavior and (b) the act of sexual intercourse. Thus voyeurism, fetishism, exhibitionism and so forth can be viewed as deviations preliminary to intercourse, while sadism or other organ contact or intercourse with animals could be viewed as deviations involving intercourse.

There is a miscellaneous group of perversions and deviations that do not fit into categories and are merely descriptive. They include coprolalia (use of obscene language during sex), mixoscopia (pleasure from witnessing sex acts)and osphresiophilia (love of odors as a sex stimulant). Others involve extremes of behavior such as paedophilia (sex with children), necrophilia (sex with dead bodies) and troilism (sex involving three people). The broad categories of sexual excesses which can become disruptive and therefore pathological include (a) nymphomania and promiscuity, (b) Don Juanism and satyriasis; (c) pederasty (sodomy); (d) fellatio and cunnilingus; (e) prostitution, pandering, prudery, rape and sexual apathy.

The genesis of a sexual deviation can be derived from the following:

1. Primary genital phobias. Such genital avoidances result from the early conditioning in which the genital is viewed as a dangerous, dirty and disgusting organ to be shunned and avoided. They may produce a wide variety of sexual difficulties in later life involving the avoidance of the individual's own genitals, thereby eliminating sexual contact. The existence of the genital may be denied or its presence an embarrassment thereby shortening the sexual contact resulting in premature ejaculation. It may also produce frigidity and the whole range of deviations in which genital contact is avoided such as voyeurism, exhibitionism or fetishism. Such phobias may involve avoidance of the genitals of the opposite sex due to persistent fears of the genital as dangerous as in the notion of a dentata vagina. When the genitals are viewed as unclean, diseased, etcetera, they will also be avoided in oneself and the opposite or same sex.

2. Fixating experiences in which sexual pleasure becomes associated with traumatic or other pain-induced stimuli. Fixating experiences may also involve nonpainful stimuli in connection with other organs such as repeated enemas or fetishes involving clothing or any other symbolic object. This may be the explanation of

many fetishistic practices where pleasure is intimately connected or conditioned with either accidental or coincidental occurrences. Silk clothing, pleasant or unpleasant odors, or pain produced by whipping or physical contact which produces or is associated with an unexpected genital discharge may produce a lifetime pattern of sexual deviant behavior.

3. Early activities tied directly to the genitals producing pleasurable or exciting experiences. This may be due to deliberate stimulation or accidental stimulation of irritating clothes or bed sheets. This usually produces deviations involving the patterns of intercourse rather than foreplay. This may often be the early experience of the homosexual where direct contact began as exploratory or nonsexual, playful behavior. It could also account for some deviations involving animals, compulsive masturbation or other solo sex outlets.

4. Character structure in which sex is implicated—self-effacing or aggressive character manifesting these traits in the sexual behavior, as with Don Juanism or a display of strength played out in sex, but having no necessary relation to sexuality.

THERAPY

Since the variations in sex behavior are derived from multiple sources and are the outgrowths of the interactions of the biological gender substrates with the culture both immediate and more distant, the therapy of such variations or deviations must take these factors into account. Only rarely will operative procedure, hormones, gonadal influencing drugs or other manipulative procedures prove to be effective. A broadly based therapeutic approach based on the recognition of the influence of psychological forces on physiological functioning will be required. Therefore, we cannot simply trace the libidinal development of the individual in the traditional zonal or epochal framework and discover where the fixation or regression occurred. Instead, we must use the techniques that have been derived from an analysis of character structure in which a flexible approach to the traditional concepts of free association and the revival of early experiencing is emphasized.

In order to comprehend the character structure of an individual, it is necessary to know how he functions and adapts in the present. This calls for a detailed presentation of his current experiencing in order to identify areas of anxiety and the way he deals with these anxieties. Consequently, the therapy proceeds in a more directed fashion with immediate goals that are clear to the patient. The therapist is generally more active and may direct the patient to areas which he feels may be illuminating. Such activity is manifested by more frequent questions and interpretations and a variety of techniques both verbal and nonverbal designed to encourage the patient to see how his present patterns of behavior are contributing to his difficulties in living. For example, it is most important in the treatment of the exhibitionist to demonstrate his prevailing patterns of immaturity and passivity in all areas of his living. We would, however, need to explore this issue in some detail with regard to the opposite sex involving his mother, early and later girl friends and particularly in a detailed exploration of the actual exhibitionistic acts. His fear of contact coupled with need for some recognition without challenge to his fantasies of a powerful, successfully aggressive male must be clearly exposed in therapy. This same situation may be present in the case of the voyeur with some additional elements of early fixating experiences as well as the safety and security of being physically uninvolved with the partner. For example, a 24-year-old exhibitionist lived with his mother and was an ideal son. He brought home flowers, was always on time for dinner and was a "good boy" in every regard. On his dates he rarely tried to kiss his girl friends or go any further than holding their hands. He was a good boy, respected by all his girl friends, even while he was having sex relations with prostitutes. Even though his girl friends would have been interested in intercourse, he was very reluctant to suggest it. His greatest sexual satisfaction came in exhibiting himself to young girls when he could proudly display his penis and prowess without fear of humiliation or rejection. In therapy he came to recognize the purpose of his compulsive need to exhibit himself. This involved profound doubts about his acceptability as a man. He felt certain of himself only as a little boy who was always good and who never disturbed mother. As puberty approached, he was intensely afraid of being rejected if he made any sexual gestures at all towards the girls he liked or admired. He could only have sex with prostitutes, which proved nothing to him, or else expose himself to strangers where it was safe in the sense that he could sustain his grandiose fantasies about his competence. If the observer was frightened away, it proved how successfully potent he was. If he stayed to look, it proved how fascinating he must be. This became clear only when we explored in detail those occasions on which he exhibited himself. A minute scrutiny of his feelings and associations in connection with such events enabled us to elucidate the dynamics of his behavior. The same issue, in which the total personality of the individual was revealed in the deviation, was manifested in a severe obsessional girl who would achieve orgasm only when she fantasized an extensive whipping while being subdued by bandits who had intercourse with her from the front and behind at the same time. Her inability to allow herself to enjoy sex by her own choice since it was dirty and indecent made it necessary for her to be overwhelmed and forced beyond her control to submit. This is a very common picture in the pain-dependent deviations. This patient could become aware of the significance of this fantasy only as she became aware of her overall obsessional need to be in control at all times including during the sex act. Since orgasm in the female requires that the female "let go" and give up control, she required a fantasy of being overwhelmed and out of control before she could let go. As her personality structure unfolded and she no longer needed to be in absolute control all the time, sex activity became more of a game and less of an exercise in control. She became increasingly able to have orgasm without her typical fantasy. In other deviations such as sadism or masochism we will discover similar patterns of response in which the necessity to inflict or endure pain is associated with the broader personality structure in which receiving or producing pain is the requisite price for pleasure of any sort. Calvinist doctrine was very influential in this regard and often this philosophy participated in the sex function either by some accidental or coincidental fixating experience in early puberty.

Thus in most of the deviations once we discover the adaptive or symbolic meaning of the act we attempt to relate it to the total personality picture and try to demonstrate how its beginnings may have set up a pattern of behavior that is no longer necessary. If we can help the patient see that there is no danger of being physically hurt or emotionally humiliated or that his or his partner's genitals are not dirty or diseased and that the pressures of sexual needs can be satisfied directly with equal if not greater pleasure, then we have opened up the way for some alteration of the deviated sex pattern.

The therapist's role becomes more than a mere facilitant to reliving the past; it becomes that of a collaborating partner in examining the neurotic structure and the particular symptom complex and recognizing the defenses which serve to produce or encourage failures in the patient's present-day interpersonal relations, sexually and otherwise. Through such maneuvers the patient is assisted in recognizing the sexual distortions and how they relate to his transference attitudes. This means that we try to establish the relationship and similarity of his emotional attitudes towards sex and other persons and his attitudes towards nonsexual relationships and his therapist in particular. This matter was strikingly illuminated in a 37-year-old patient who came to therapy because of his phobias of open spaces. As therapy regarding his phobia unfolded, he related his obsessive fear of molesting little girls. He had great difficulty in maintaining an erection in his sex activity with women his own age and invariably ejaculated prematurely when he managed to sustain an erection. Our relationship was characterized by his putting me into the role of the idealized father who was perfect and whom he had to overwhelm and defeat. His need always to be right and never less than perfect led to a number of grandiose expectations of himself. His pride and fear of being humiliated if he were less than a superman led to many transference "tugs of war." During one such engagement he revealed that his preference for little girls came from the necessity of not looking inadequate or less informed than others. He was then involved with proving how he knew more than I. Through associating the need to know everything and perform perfectly in sex, he could see that his present sexual patterns were incongruent with these demands. However, with little girls he could clearly dominate the relationship and be their teacher and master. This was a most illuminating insight which served to remove most of his horror and his intense anxiety about the possibility of attacking young girls. In the course of therapy this problem was entirely resolved and he could finally attempt a continuous sexual relationship which culminated in marriage. He has managed not only to sustain an erection with his wife but also to prolong the sex act not infrequently. While he still feels uncertain about whether his wife is comparing him unfavorably with her first husband, his security is sufficiently adequate that no longer has he any fears or doubts about molesting young girls. Used in this way, transference becomes more than a mere revival of infant-parent relationship; it is viewed as a collection of distortions or a set of characteristic attitudes toward a variety of people who have played meaningful and determining roles in the patient's life. Irrational attitudes are examined in terms of their historical development as well as an understanding of their current adaptive value.

Transference is a major tool of therapy since it allows for the most direct observation of the distorted attitudes developed in the course of maturing. The exhibitionist tends to develop a relationship of extensive passivity with a parent figure transference, while the homosexual may become involved in a typical seductive relationship with a therapist of the same sex. At the same time the sexual masochist or sadist will tend to relate to the therapist in a way which clearly conveys their need to be hurt or to be cruel and hurtful. Thus the transference attitudes will reveal details about the individual's sexual behavior which will help elucidate the origins and present adaptive values of such behavior.

In the relationship of the "here and now," the patient is forced to acknowledge that some of his attitudes toward the therapist do not arise out of a response to the therapist as he is, but to the therapist that the patient personifies. This opens up a broad avenue for exploration of the function and history of this distortion. This view of transference goes much further than the classical view which limits the distortion to that of a parental figure. A patient's irrational hatred of his therapist arises not only from a hatred of his father, for example, but also because of a series of relationships in which the patient has been abused and mistreated by authority figures which leads him to expect malevolence also from the therapist. This will certainly include fixating experiences or a prevailing atmosphere of pain-related incidents if the individual has some sadistic deviation or variety of a masochistic sexual perversion from the minor needs of being pinched, bitten or merely roughly treated to the severe beating that some masochists require for sexual satisfaction. This data will unfold as the transference relationship is examined in detail. On such occasions the patient will find malevolence in the multitude of opportunities offered in any close relationship like therapy. The clarification of the transference can reveal the background for a variety of sexual disturbances ranging from impotence and frigidity to coital infrequency and sexual avoidance.

A young lady whose father was a severe alcoholic during her early years came to know him as a dangerous and disgusting man whom she had to put to bed and care for during his hangovers. She sought therapy because of concerns about being homosexual and her intense anxiety about sexual activity. She had had a few boy friends, some intercourse, but no homosexual activities whatsoever. She avoided intimate relationships because she expected that they would produce mutual dependencies which she feared but wanted. Her expectations of total dependency, which she visualized as exceedingly dangerous, clashed with her demands to be completely independent and in this way she was prevented from establishing any deep involvements with her boy friends. These issues became clearly manifested in her transference attitudes with me and her fears and expectations of being overwhelmed and taken advantage of if she became too trusting and devoted. Her hatred for her father was largely an expression of her resentment and disappointment in not having established a loving relationship with him. The exploration of this attitude towards men enabled her to acknowledge her femininity without shame or fear of being taken advantage of. She began to experience and enjoy her sexual activities and ultimately married a man many years older than herself. What began as almost total frigidity and fear of homosexuality was resolved into a satisfactory marriage with extremely enjoyable sexual contacts.

Transference becomes more than a mere repetition and transferring of feeling; it becomes a dynamic process which represents and reproduces the effect of early experiencing on present behavior as a current, active functioning issue in a patient's life. The activity and lack of anonymity which characterizes such a therapeutic approach arises out of the theoretical conception that transference attitudes are more meaningful and revealing when they are produced through contact and experiencing than in a vacuum of pure fantasizing. The therapist should not limit his activity or avoid revealing facets of his own personality. Face-to-face encounters with the patient sitting up rather than on the couch is frequently more productive than the traditional procedures. In addition, since we now know a great deal about mental operations we can be more energetic in using shortcuts and not always be cautious about our interpretations. All these innovations tend to produce stronger transference relationship which permits a sharper and more convincing awareness of the personality factors which have led to the sexual distortions.

Because of our growing conviction of the validity of our concepts of mental functioning, we should not be too wary about actively intervening and encouraging productive areas of inquiry while discouraging endless and fruitless meanderings and distractions of patients. Thus the free association technique, while undoubtedly useful, can be abused and therefore should be limited at times. This is particularly relevant in the treatment of the sexual deviations, since we can go far afield unless we are aware of the constant necessity to tie our observations and associations to the issues involved in the sexual deviation. This notion has been supported by most ego analysts who use the free association technique with caution and judgment.

When the therapist becomes more active it becomes more apparent that not all the patient's attitudes toward the therapist could be viewed as irrational responses. Some of the patient's attitudes represent realistic and rational attitudes in response to the kind of person the therapist really is. While this is considered an artifact in orthodox analytic therapy, it is apparent that the most stringent efforts of the analyst to remain incognito are largely impossible to achieve. In spite of all the safeguards the patient can discover many important pieces of data about the analyst through his verbalizations as well as information about his public life, which is available if one is interested. The office habits and practices of the therapist can stir up responses which are related realistic issues. Thus we must distinguish between the true transference responses and the realistic responses. This can serve the important function of increasing the patient's convictions regarding the significance of his transference reaction. Indirectly, this distinction can lessen the authoritative atmosphere of the analytic situation and permits a realistic appraisal of the analyst, which is a vital need for the neurotic, who is already overburdened with distorted conceptions about others.[8]

This is particularly apt in dealing with the sexual deviations, since these individuals are already overwhelmed and overburdened by the cultural taboos and restraints and the authoritative family situations in which they grow up. The deviations generally arise in an authoritative, restricted and inhibited family structure where restraints and prohibitions led to all sorts of distorted ideas about the sexual apparatus. Whether primary phobias or fixating experiences have occurred, a continuation of the authoritative situation in the therapeutic atmosphere will only complicate or prevent the resolution of the patient's distortions. The authoritative atmosphere of the therapeutic situation is also lessened by the use of chairs instead of having the patient lie on a couch, which encourages the child-parent interaction.

Since our current view of the origins of the sexual deviations does not require a genetic reconstruction of the past as essential to the elucidation of a patient's character structure, the use of the couch cannot always be justified in theory. It can even become an obstacle and encourage regression and dependency as in the exhibitionist or sexual masochist where it may strongly reinforce current character trends and serve as a resistance to therapy.

A most significant outgrowth of the increase in activity by the therapist is to encourage the exploration of the role of countertransference in the therapeutic process. Early in his therapeutic work Freud[9] recognized the potential influence of the therapist's own personality on the therapeutic process. This led to the requirement that every therapist be analyzed himself in order to become aware of his own distortions and neurotic difficulties. However, the personality of the therapist can never be entirely eliminated from the process. While being attentive to this matter, the therapist's moralistic responses to some of the more extreme responses such as rape, sexual sadism or his horror at necrophilia or the like must be taken into account. He must also be aware of the subtle and at times successful activities of the homosexual to attempt to seduce and the therapist's covert encouragements. Likewise he must be particularly cautious about fulfilling the masochist's need for some critical denunciation or the exhibitionist's effort to be taken care of as a child. All the reactions cannot be avoided nor is it entirely useful that they should be. It has become most apparent that countertransference elements in the therapeutic process can be utilized to great advantage in the process of therapy.

The therapist's attitude toward the patient can be a very powerful tool in elucidating the character structure of the patient. When the therapist is free, flexible and willing to become involved in the therapy his reactions can be most useful in learning about the subtleties of his patient's performances. This is particularly true in the behavior of many exhibitionists, fetishists and voyeurs who expose their immaturity in the therapeutic relationship. The therapist must be free to convey his reactions to these manifestations in order to bring them into the open and thereby get them into the therapeutic work at the earliest possible time. It can open up major lines of inquiry, since the patient's effect on others can be examined in the "here and now" as it affects the therapist. Such reactions on the part of the therapist can infuse new meanings to the therapeutic process and are often invaluable in overcoming resistances and stalemates. It is obvious that the therapist cannot like all his patients equally, or at all. With some he recognizes stronger interest and attachments than with others. Such a variety of attitudes does not necessarily offer any clues to the possibilities of successful therapy. It does, however, offer many opportunities to the keen and competent therapist to make rapid and fruitful formulations about his patient's patterns of operation. The utilization of countertransference feelings can be equally detrimental to the therapeutic process if used in ill-advised ways or as poorly timed interpretations. For example, the inclination to tell a patient how irritating he might be or how seductive her behavior is, must be tempered by the strength of the relationship and the readiness of the patient to accept unflattering or uncomplimentary statements. This is particularly apt in the treatment of homosexuals or other seductive heterosexual problems such as nymphomania, satyriasis, etcetera. The time must come if the therapeutic work is proceeding well, when the patient will make sexual demands on the therapist, which must be met with a firm, definitive and clear-cut refusal without increasing the patient's feelings of being rejected or chastised. The distinction must be clearly made between rejecting the request and rejecting the person. This is a crucial distinction in the disease process and the ability to convey this difference to the patient will be an essential ingredient in his ultimate care.

Not only is the manner, tone and attitude of the therapist crucial to this maneuver, but the timing is equally important. One must select the proper time to inform the exhibitionist that he is passively aggressive and that his behavior represents a childish attempt to achieve his desires without assuming any responsibility for his activities. At one point it could open up profitable lines of inquiry while at another time it can produce resentful criticism of the therapist's envy.

The responses of the therapist to the subtle clues of the patient's behavior are generally difficult for the patient to acknowledge because he is genuinely unable to recognize them himself. It probably has not been brought to his attention before and therefore to really make an impact on him requires not only the proper timing but an example which will be clear and indisputable rather than one which is too shrouded in confusing ambivalences. It takes considerable skill to decide when it is safe to make an observation which might produce a significant response from the patient. When used wisely it can accelerate therapy and inaugurate a contact with the patient which becomes invaluable for the further progress of therapy. The utilization of countertransference reactions is becoming more widespread and an essential part of current psychotherapeutic practice.

It is essential in the therapy of the sexual distortions to get a complete and detailed account of these difficulties at the outset. In view of the widespread confusion of definitions, it is necessary to identify the patient's label of his behavior with some more meaningful or causal conceptions of the disorder. For example, the patient may complain of being impotent because he occasionally fails to perform sexually or because he cannot meet his wife's demands. However, in these cases we may not be dealing with impotency, but with a variation of the extreme expectations of the partner. Similarly, the frequent complaints of unsatisfactory sexual adjustment, whether it is a failure to achieve orgasm, frigidity in the female or premature ejaculation or inadequate potency in the male, often has more reference to unawareness of the physiological spectrum of sexual potentialities and the excessive expectations of the partners than a valid sexual difficulty. This problem is particularly important in the looseness with which the terms "homosexuality," "sexual masochism," "nymphomania" and others are used. Often the patient applies this label to himself out of ignorance, guilt or moral condemnation and it does not really apply to him.

A patient considered her husband to be sexually inadequate because he was unable to have intercourse every time she desired it. She took no account of the necessity for sufficient rest periods for the male or the difference between the availability of the male and female for sexual activity. The failure to understand this simple physiological fact produced exaggerated expectations which could not be fulfilled. The resulting anger, frustration and disappointment produced a vicious circle which then truly incapacitated her husband for adequate sexual performances. He began to feel impotent and incompetent and each attempt at intercourse was accompanied by great anxiety producing either premature ejaculation or failure to maintain an erection. His wife's anger increased his anxiety and stirred up great anger towards her. Thus the vicious circle grew larger and more destructive until the wife came for some assistance.

Another patient considered himself to be homosexual in spite of his never having had a homosexual experience. He did have numerous heterosexual contacts but never felt that they came off adequately or that he had produced an orgasm in the women. This, coupled with his prior analyst's interpretation that his passive attitudes were evidence of his latent homosexual trends, focused his obsessive preoccupations on his masculinity. He began to scrutinize his behavior for evidences of homosexuality and if he stopped for a hitchhiker, he wondered if it was for homosexual purposes. The fact that he had many male friends, that he liked dancing and so forth, all became "evidence" of his homosexuality. This preoccupation, produced largely by the theoretical preconception of his earlier therapist, took the focus away from his real difficulties which revolved about his pervasive needs for magical control of every element in his living as well as his phobic avoidances of every situation in which he could not see himself immediately as the "master." He was not homosexual at all but a perfectionistic, grandiose person who had to excel at everything. Since he did not excel at lechery he began, with the assistance of psychological theorizing, to attribute homosexual tendencies to his already overburdened compulsive neurosis. In this example, the failure to distinguish homosexuality as an actual distortion of sexual object choice from homosexuality used as an obsessional distraction and a pejorative label would put the therapeutic focus in the wrong place. Unfortunately, this is a very common occurrence in the treatment of obsessive patients with homosexual doubts.

Thus the definition of prematurity in ejaculation, homosexuality, frigidity, etcetera, must be clear and delimited if any useful therapeutic benefits are to take place. For example, we cannot leave the definition of homosexuality so wide open that it includes any behavior that is discrepant from conventional gender behavior. It should be called homosexuality only when the person foregoes and avoids any interest or attempt to integrate on a heterosexual level and establishes his life in exclusive, compulsively preferred relationships with the same sex. The label should not include those people whose living is integrated with people of the opposite sex, whatever the degree of deficiency or distortion of this relationship there may be, and it should certainly not include those sexual experimenters who dabble in every deviation or who remain celibate for reasons other than true homosexuality.

Many sexual deviates come to the therapist, either directed by the courts, one's mate or one's own guilt or need to improve one's living. While the symptoms must be explored, the investigation of the total personality and the role the symptom plays in the total character structure must be completely understood. There are particular problems in the treatment of the specific deviations. For example, the passivity of the exhibitionist or the anger of the rapist and sadist create technical problems that cannot be anticipated entirely. However there is no special dynamic constellation that characterizes one deviation as opposed to another, even though we can make general statements about some of them. For example, the avoidance deviations like voyeurism, exhibitionism or fetishism all involve some feeling of danger in genital contact that would be called castration fear. Impotence could be viewed as total avoidance of any sexual involvement, while satyriasis, nymphomania or Don Juanism are all efforts to overcome doubts of one's masculinity or femininity. Aside from these general statements, however, every deviate must be studied and understood in terms of his own past and personality development. His avoidance of adult sexual contacts can only be understood in terms of his own idiosyncratic life history. Therefore, it is misleading to describe the therapeutic handling of each of the labeled deviations. Since they do not have a separate etiology, there is no specific therapy that applies to them. Therefore I will close the chapter by showing in some detail how the understanding of the total personality is the method of choice in treating all the deviations. It also demonstrates how the distorted sexual behavior is only a symptom of a broader personality disorder rather than a disease in itself.

PREMATURE EJACULATION

Premature ejaculation is an extremely common symptom and seems to be intimately related to the obsessive-compulsive dynamism and to subserve the operation of power.

The symptom occurs only in relation to a specific person and in specific situations. Unlike other mental phenomena, it cannot occur in the absence of the sexual object. This is the reason why premature ejaculators masturbate without ejaculating prematurely. It occurs only with real people as opposed to fantasized partners. It probably occurs on some occasions in all people, since it is essentially a response to anxiety. Although premature ejaculation can occur in fatigue states, hyperactive drug states, prolonged abstention or excessive excitement, it is primarily an anxiety-provoked phenomenon which occurs in relation to a conflict situation in which the individual is involved. The symptom results from this conflict but does not solve it. It produces instead further anxiety since the sexual performance does not improve while the conflict continues. The brief case history which follows will illustrate some of the points discussed above.

Patient A had an active and successful sex life during the first year of his marriage. During the second year some difficulties arose, and although the relationship appeared to be working out, he began to notice that he was ejaculating prematurely. The ejaculation would occur after a few strokes and under very special circumstances. It occurred only when intercourse was stimulated and precipitated by his wife, who was an aggressive, domineering individual. During the first year of marriage the patient was active and energetic in his marital affairs. As he slowly relinquished this role to his wife, quarrels became more frequent and the patient always felt subdued by his wife. Premature ejaculation invariably occurred when he was angry with her. In this way he punished her and indicated his indispensable role in the marriage. Although there was some guilt about his supposed inadequacy, there was at the same time a secret satisfaction and a lack of real impetus to eliminate the difficulty. He did not recognize any problem, and it was his wife who had pushed him into treatment. The symptom was a relatively minor problem in a severe obsessional character structure. The occasions for premature ejaculation became less frequent as the tug of war and power struggles lessened in the patient's living.

What transpires in the man who suffers the discomforts of premature ejaculation? The situation is approximately the following: from the outset of his sex life or during the course of it, he has the distressing experience of either ejaculating before penetration or after a few strokes. He is left anxious and ashamed and behaves as though he were a disgraced male. Consequently, at the next attempt, he is very anxious lest he again ejaculate prematurely. He senses the woman's anxiety and concern, and in his earnest desire to perform well, he tends to exaggerate the effect he is producing on the female. At this point, he becomes caught in the sociological and cultural attitudes towards the male, such as the equation of prolonged intercourse with potency, and conceives of his partner in the sex act as being dissatisfied, distraught, tense and angry. He must eliminate the prematurity, and in this tense atmosphere, it either gets worse or continues unabated. With increasing concern and anxiety, it becomes less and less possible to overcome it. After a short while, his partner complains, threatens and possibly denies him any contact. He is miserable, and thinks of himself as a failure, unmanly, impotent, weak.

What goes on covertly is quite different. As the wife becomes more angry, she also begins to recognize the importance of her husband in his potential capacity to afford her some gratification. He has become more essential to her existence and through his inadequate performance has managed to control her pleasure and affect her living. If she becomes more tender, concerned and interested and the husband temporarily feels victorious, his anxiety diminishes and premature ejaculation may disappear. However if it continues, his partner may become more vitally concerned and encourage him to see a psychiatrist. If it is only temporary, we may see recurring episodes, for as his orgasm improves, his partner demonstrates less interest, concern and tolerance for him. Premature ejaculation returns and the cycle begins over again.

This is perhaps an oversimplified version of the involved and complicated interchange that occurs, but it does demonstrate some aspects of the power struggle involved in this symptom. The problem is often initiated in marriages where the partners are prudish, uninformed and uncommunicative in sexual matters. They may have secret expectations with regard to their sexual activity and hesitate to voice their disappointments. Although they appear resigned to unsatisfactory sexual relationships, they covertly resent and demand more from it. This often produces premature ejaculation in the male and increases the tension in the relationship. In these instances, the problem, which may originally have been due somewhat to ignorance or prudery, now becomes a matter of demand, control and manipulation of the partners.

In this symptom we can notice most clearly the element of power as utilized by the sexual function. The very presence of the symptom serves to put the male in the role of the generous, giving person who in his generosity may or may not give pleasure to the female. The variations and fluctuations in the appearance of the symptom coincide most clearly with this element in the relationship between man and woman. It provides a most sensitive weapon for vindictively punishing or graciously satisfying the woman. The patient's problems may involve fear of feminine aggressiveness, unconscious jealousy, injured feelings, expressions of contempt, fear of women's genitals, concern over conception, etcetera, but operationally it is used as an instrument of power and manipulation in interpersonal relations.

This helps us understand those instances where premature ejaculation may occur with one's wife but not with other women or with prostitutes. The power struggle which may be producing it in the wife is absent with the prostitute or the other woman.

There is no dependent relationship with the prostitute, and one's ability to dominate, control and manipulate the situation is amply satisfied. The seduction and winning of the girl other than one's wife often satisfies the power element, and since there are few ties and tensions, the struggles are minimal and prolonged intercourse can occur. Although the individual may have many obvious problems with regard to women, the prostitute or paramour does not stir them up, and so there is no premature ejaculation, although other sexual deviations may be present, reflecting these other problems.

This symptom is often seen in homosexuals who are capable of some heterosexual contact. In these cases one can clearly see the role power, control and manipulation play in the symptom. It does not represent the feminine component in the personality—quite the contrary. It represents the attempts at more masculine expression of the aggressive need. The homosexual who is capable of heterosexual contact frequently suffers from delayed ejaculation (ejaculatio tarda as contrasted with ejaculatio praecox). It has been noted also that in heterosexual marriages, the homosexual partner has had premature ejaculation, which serves the purpose of shortening the contact, disappointing his wife and "showing her who's boss!"

Premature ejaculation is probably present much of the time in the obsessional dynamism, where there are elements of obscure power operations directed at maintenance of control over everything that happens.

Some sexual deviations run afoul of the law and the therapy is complicated by the intervention of the courts and the public attitudes toward such disorders. It must be recognized that the public attitude towards some deviations does not alter our theoretical understanding, even though it might greatly influence the practical limitations imposed on the technique for dealing with them. Neither should this fact distort the emphasis of the psychological significance of the deviations. Thus, while voyeurism, fetishism, masochism, sadism and other forms of sexual deviation may result in legal action, they have no other significance as neurotic symptoms than any other distortions of human activity which is private and outside of legal sanctions. The particular symptoms must be understood in their own right as part of the total personality structure. Consequently, the general techniques that apply to the therapy of the neurosis can be applied to the sexual disorders. A search for separate etiology with a distinctive therapy for each category is not only misleading but probably invalid.

REFERENCES

1. Krafft-Ebing, R. Von: *Psychopathia Sexualis,* 12th ed. New York, Phys. and Surf., 1922.
2. Hirshfield, M.: *Sexual Anomalies and Perversions,* London, Encyclopaedic Press, 1944.
3. Freud, S.: Three essays on the theory of sexuality. *The Standard Edition of the Complete Psychological Works of Freud.* London, Hogarth Press, vol. 7.
4. Salzman, L.: *Developments in Psychoanalysis.* New York, Grune & Stratton, 1962.
5. Money, J. (Ed.): *Sex Research.* New York, Holt & Rinehart & Winston, 1965.
6. Salzman, L.: Premature ejaculation. *Int J Sexology,* 3, 1954.
7. Rado, S.: *Psychoanalysis of Behavior Collected Papers.* New York, Grune & Stratton, 1956, vol. 1.
8. Salzman, L. *Obsessive Personality.* New York, Science House, 1968.
9. Freud, S.: New introductory lectures on psychoanalysis. *The Standard Edition of the Complete Psychological Works of Freud.* London, Hogarth Press, vol. 22.

Chapter 11

Psychotherapy with Schizophrenic Patients

BENJAMIN B. WOLMAN

THE TREATMENT OF schizophrenics belongs to the category of unpredictables. The same method of treatment may fail in one case and succeed in another. An experienced therapist may fail with a patient with whom a beginner may succeed. Diametrically opposed philosophies claim good results. Some authors even believe in recovery without treatment.

Classic psychoanalysis is not the choice treatment of schizophrenia. The reclining position and the psychoanalyst's spare comments are likely to increase anxiety in the patient and facilitate regression. Even Freudians, such as Bychowski,[9] Brody,[7] Eissler,[12, 13] Federn,[15] Knight,[28] Rosen[40, 42] and Wolman[52] deviate from Freud's techniques when they treat schizophrenics. Thus the gulf between Freudians and non-Freudians such as Sullivan,[43] Fromm-Reichmann,[22-24] and Arieti[2] has been reduced. Today both groups emphasize face-to-face relations as essential for a successful treatment.

Encouraging psychotic patients to associate freely is strictly contraindicated, since "free association induces and increases disintegrated thinking."[22] Melanie Klein and her school interpret unconscious processes in treating schizophrenics.[38, 42, 47] But Eissler in discussing Rosen's direct interpretation says, "another set of interpretations might have achieved a similar result."[13] An evaluation of Rosen's methods did not prove that his interpretations were specifically helpful.[14]

It seems that successful therapists proceed in a similar way notwithstanding semantic differences in their reports. Federn[15] was most successful with patients he took into his home. J. N. Rosen[41] writes

> In order to treat the schizophrenic, the physician must have such
> a degree of inner security that he is able to function independently,

whether he is loved by the patient or not. . . . . He must make up for
the tremendous deficit of love experienced in the patient's life. Some
people have this capacity for loving as a divine gift.

Arieti stressed the necessity to give the patient the feeling "that he
has been given something" without demands.[2] Redlich finds that
all the methods being reviewed reflect the "eternal common sense
methods of love and patience." This common element in the various therapeutic techniques, despite their theoretical differences,
has inspired the developments of the method of interactional psychotherapy with schizophrenics.[49, 51, 52]

I start from a brief description of schizophrenic dynamics and
etiology. Since there is no agreement on what schizophrenia is,
I can only say what I believe its true nature to be. I believe
schizophrenia is a sociopsychosomatic disorder[57] caused by disturbed interactional patterns. The noxious interactional patterns
affect behavior and personality structure and, in turn, cause organic disorders; thus, the sociopsychosomatic chain.

An individual becomes schizophrenic through morbid involvement with other individuals, usually parents or parental substitutes, and the disorder severely affects his interaction with others.
A schizophrenic may be more schizophrenic with some people
than with others.

My theoretical frame of reference is a modified Freudian model.
While Sullivan's emphasis on interpersonal relations has been
invaluable, I see no reason to abandon Freud's personality model.
The need to include interindividual relations dictates some modifications in Freud's theory. A new theoretical construct, "interindividual cathexis," revises Freud's pleasure and pain theory,
and a new interpretation of the role of hate and destructive impulses in mental disorders is offered.[52]

Interaction patterns are divided into instrumental (take), mutual (give and take) and vectorial (give) types of interaction.[48, 50, 53]
In normal families, parent versus parent relationship is mutual;
parent versus child, vectorial; and child versus parent, instrumental.

In families with schizophrenic offspring, parent-parent relationship is hostile-instrumental; mother-child attitude is pseudovectorial, but actually exploitative-instrumental; father-child relationship is frankly instrumental in a seductive or competitive fashion.

The preschizophrenic starts his life as any other newborn child in a state of primary narcissism with all his libido invested in himself and all his destrudo (aggressive energy) ready to be directed against threatening objects. In a normal development, the loving and protecting (vectorial) parental attitude enables the child to grow and develop normal instrumental, mutual and vectorial attitudes. The preschizophrenic child, however, realizes that his parents are not protective and that, therefore, unless he protects them, he may lose them. The schizophrenic paradox reads as follows: "I want to live, but I must sacrifice my own life to protect those upon whom my survival depends." This attitude leads to an abundant, hypervectorial cathexis of the child's libido in his parents and extreme efforts on his part to inhibit his self-protective outbursts of destrudo directed against those whom he must protect at his own expense. The schizophrenic fears that his inadequate love of parents and loss of control over his own hostility may kill them and then he will be lost forever.

Schizophrenia can be viewed as an *irrational struggle for survival.* The fear of losing the love object forces the individual to care more for the object than he does for himself. This hypervectorial object cathexis reduces the individual's own resources and prevents adequate self-cathexis.[15] When the shrinking amount of libido left for self-cathexis is unable to protect the individual, the destrudo takes over.

The toilet training stage is the one during which the normal child develops a sense of mutuality. Feces are the first indisputable possession of the child, and toilet training introduces the first gift-giving relationship and the first sacrifice. The child learns to postpone immediate satisfaction for a future gratification derived from delayed elimination and maternal approval.[61]

The preschizophrenic, however, never receives whole-hearted approval, for no matter what he gives, it is not enough. His efforts do not satisfy his mother, and his true or alleged imperfections are held responsible for the mother's true or imaginary ailments. Thus, he continually feels that he must strive harder in his efforts to love and protect her.

The preschizophrenic learns early to sacrifice his *pleasure principle* without obtaining an adequate *reality principle*. Normally, the infant learns to postpone immediate gratification and pleasure for a future, a better and a less threatening one. This is the reality principle. But the *preschizophrenic is forced to renounce his pleasure principle without any further compensation*. He is forced to sacrifice his own needs for those of others and pushed into a hypervectorial position.

This self-hypocathexis is often disastrous for the individual, and one of the impending signs of this disaster is the breaking through of destrudo. It is here assumed that libido and destrudo are two types of the same mental energy and are mutually transferable. Libido is the higher, destrudo the lower energy, and when libido fails in serving survival, destrudo takes over.

In brief, there are three main causes precipitating outbursts of hostility. When the individual supply of *libido is exhausted,* he becomes hostile in an effort to protect himself. Hostility is also provoked when the individual's *hypervectorial libidinal cathexes are turned down* by his love object. Finally, in an effort to protect himself from the devastating effect of his self-directed hostility in the form of guilt and self-recrimination, the individual may *project* his hostility against others. Yet outbursts of hostility represent a threat to the individual's parental pseudoprotectors, and thus the fear of his own destructive power forms an important theme of the schizophrenic's preoccupations and, in some cases, hallucinations.

These abnormal interactional patterns represent a dysbalance in interindividual cathexes. A child, normally "a taker" (instrumental), is forced into precocious giving (hypervectorial). Hence *vectoriasis praecox* is the proposed name for schizophrenia.

Several workers describe "schizogenic" mothers as narcissistic, cold and demanding, but there is no real agreement on the pathology of mothers or fathers of schizophrenics. Alanen[1] found 10 percent of the mothers and 5 percent of the fathers to be schizophrenic. I have found[49, 55, 59] about 40 percent of fathers and 50 percent of mothers displaying a great variety of pathological conditions, but not any one particular type of disorder.

Lidz and associates[32-34] discovered peculiar interaction between the parents of schizophrenics. "We realized soon, that the intrapsychic disturbances of the mothers were not nearly as relevant . . . as was the fact that these women were paired with husbands who would either acquiesce to their many irrational and bizarre notions of how the family should be run, or would constantly battle and undermine an already anxious and insecure mother."[17] Similar findings have been reported by Wolman,[49, 55, 61] Lu[35, 36] and others: "The etiology of schizophrenia requires the failure of the father to assume his masculine controlling function. . . . To produce schizophrenia, it appears necessary for the mother to assume the father's role."[46] "The mother, the overadequate one in relation to the inadequate child, is in charge of the child. . . . The father is then in the functioning position of a substitute mother."[6]

It is not the "weak father and strong mother" that produce schizophrenia in their offspring. Were this so, *all* siblings of a schizophrenic would be schizophrenic also. Also observations of families of manic-depressives point to several cases of domineering mothers and submissive fathers. It is *the frustrated instrumentalism in interparental relationship that causes schizophrenia.* A woman who married hoping for an ideal father hates her husband and uses the child as an emotional substitute. The man who married a woman hoping she would become his mother is frustrated and tries to compete with or seduce his own child. These mothers cannot tolerate the child's growth toward independence. They demand an unlimited love, appreciation and never-ending gratitude.

The normal reaction of a child to this emotional extortion should be hatred, but the avenues of hate are blocked. Mother convinces the child that she protects him, and the child begins to hate himself for having hostile feelings toward his self-sacrificing mother.

As suggested earlier, schizophrenia develops as a paradoxical action of an organism that abandons its own protection to protect those who should protect it. The dysbalance in interindividual cathexes leads to a severe dysbalance in intraindividual cathexes of libido and destrudo. These psychological changes affect the nervous system, endocrine and other organic processes. Most somatic symptoms in schizophrenia are psychosomatic;[2] however, schizophrenics, as all other people, may develop physical diseases. Their inadequate self-cathexis may make them more prone to succumb to physical disease and most schizophrenics suffer from a variety of physical illnesses.

PROGNOSIS

Kraepelin[30] believed that only 4 percent of schizophrenics completely recover. The fact that about half of all inmates of mental hospitals are schizophrenics while only one-fourth of admissions are schizophrenics speaks for a poor prognosis.

It is my conviction that *schizophrenia is incurable only when there is no one willing and capable of curing the schizophrenic.* Each schizophrenic requires a great deal of consideration, patience, understanding and prolonged vectorial relationship. The amount of individual care, emotional investment and therapeutic skill necessary for the cure of one schizophrenic is tremendous. Small wonder most schizophrenics are neglected.

The alleged "spontaneous recovery" cases are probably patients who evoked interest and sympathy in the staff and have received a scientific or intuitive, planned or unplanned, psychotherapy given to them by a vectorially minded individual.

The therapeutic interaction with schizophrenics is full of hazards. A schizophrenic may fear to ask for love or be frightened whenever it is offered. If he is still capable of accepting affection, he may clutch to the giver and become possessive and overdemanding. The schizophrenic's vehement love and violent hatred represent a serious challenge even to an experienced psychotherapist. Schizophrenics often put exaggerated demands on the time and work of their therapist. One patient used to telephone the therapist several times a day and at odd hours of the night. Another patient refused to eat unless "her doctor" would feed her.

Another patient insisted on seeing his doctor any time he felt the need to see him, irrespective of the doctor's obligations toward other patients. Thus, many psychotherapists become impatient and disappointed in their work.

Thus, only a *field-theoretical* approach which includes the patient, the therapist and other environmental factors permits prognostic judgment. The attitude of the therapist to the patient and the patient to the therapist is not the only prognostic factor but certainly the most important one.

THE THERAPEUTIC GOAL

The main aim of the interactional psychotherapy is the reversal of libido cathexes with a resultant reorganization of personality structure.

Many psychotherapists who otherwise differed from each other have *a vectorial, unconditionally giving attitude. It is a helping, giving attitude irrespective of the friendly or hostile reactions of the one who receives (just as good parents love good and bad children alike).*

Even untrained individuals have been successful in treating schizophrenics. When a friendly person shows interest and a desire to help, this vectorial attitude helps the schizophrenic patient to improve the balance of libido cathexes. A visit of an old friend who comes to the hospital and shows affection may produce miracles and cause remission.[5] Freudian, Adlerian, Jungian, Sullivanian and Horneyan psychotherapists can be successful in the treatment of schizophrenics; apparently the differences between all these theories are not significant for the treatment. What is significant is *common* to all successful therapists regardless of their philosophies.

But this is more than "common sense, love and patience." A successful psychotherapy is a distinct interactional pattern aiming at the restoration of intraindividual balance of cathexes and realistic perception of life. A detailed description of the interactional rules follows.

Rules of Therapeutic Interaction

1. The first rule is *unconditional support,* protecting the patient's self-esteem by siding with him, by accepting him as an individual, by treating him in a dignified and respectful manner. A genuinely friendly attitude and atmosphere are a *conditio sine qua non.* The therapist must encourage adult (never regressive) pleasure-procuring activities. An unreserved yet rational support is necessary to counteract the process of regression and downward adjustment.

2. The second rule is *ego therapy.* The main aim of interactional psychotherapy is to strengthen the patient's ego. In neurosis the ego is struggling against undue pressures from within; the *ego-protective,* neurotic symptoms bear witness to the struggle. In psychosis the ego has lost the battle and psychotic, *ego-deficiency* symptoms develop, such as loss of reality testing (delusions and hallucinations), loss of control over unconscious impulses, deterioration of motor coordination and so forth.

Ego therapy means the strengthening and reestablishment of the defeated ego. Thus, the therapist must never become part of the irrational transactions of the psychotic mind, be it delusions, hallucinations or anything else. He must never offer support to erroneous perceptions of reality. The therapist must not interpret unconscious motivation processes if this interpretation may weaken the patient's ego.

For example, the aggressive and obstinate Mrs. Hart was not treated (as she was at home) as the crazy Betsy but as Mrs. Hart who happened to be presently disturbed and therefore hospitalized. The psychotherapist, the nurses and the attendants must not make her regress further and perceive herself as the nasty little Betsy, the "black sheep" as she was in her childhood. Presently, Mrs. Hart is Mrs. Hart; she is a mental patient, but an *adult* patient, and enhancement of her self-esteem is a necessary part of treatment.

Physical appearance and bodily cleanliness are important factors in one's self-image. Uncombed hair, untidy clothing, unshaved face and dirty hands foster the patient's feeling that he is what he deserves to be. Scratching of one's own face or banging one's own head against the wall are clear indications of an inadequate self-cathexis and lack of self-esteem. Vectorial attitude of the therapist will increase self-love of the patient and will reduce self-depreciation. For love and respect from without enhance love and respect from within.

Vectorial attitude implies our unconditional willingness to help. Schizophrenics learned that parental love was given to them on a Shylock rate of interest. Whenever the mother did a favor to the child, she expected ten times as many favors in return. Whenever she showed affection, she expected in return unlimited gratitude.

Schizophrenic patients tend to test the therapist. Will the therapist demand unlimited obedience, unswerving loyalty and never-ending gratitude? Will he react with disappointment, anger and punitiveness when the patient will not comply and obey, as the patient's mother reacted?

The therapist must never play a parental role. He does neither love nor hate, neither show affection nor anger. His job is to help, irrespective of whether the patient is friendly or hostile. The therapist must never get entangled in the web of the patient's emotions and must retain his unconditionally helping attitude. A responsible surgeon or a dentist does not get angry at a patient who fights treatment; a psychotherapist is expected to be even more rational, balanced and calm.

The patient must be treated in a respectful and dignified manner, notwithstanding his regressive behavior. When an adult patient uses baby-talk, the therapist must never join him in regression; when an adult patient throws a temper tantrum, the therapist must avoid the pitfalls of talking to the patient as if he were a child. Even the most disturbed schizophrenic knows what he is, and the therapist's friendly attitude combined with respect helps the patient to regain self-confidence. Many cured patients recalled that my treating them as if they were normal adults made them feel that they were not completely crazy and there was a hope for improvement.

Control of instinctual impulses is one of the most severe issues in schizophrenia; a catatonic patient in remission describes this inner struggle: "I want to be strong to be able to control myself and here I am again doing terrible things." A gifted latent schizophrenic woman said once: "I can't do what I want to do. I feel like expressing my feelings with quick motions of the brush over the canvas, but something holds me back and I paint silly little houses that I detest. I would like to let myself go in nonobjective art, but something tells me it must be a composition, a plan. Maybe I am afraid to let myself go, for I may do something wrong. So I sit for hours, as if paralyzed, afraid to move. . . ."

Inability to make decisions and restraint of motor freedom are typical for the schizophrenic type. This conflict between the desire to "let go" and the fear of one's own impulses may, in some cases, lead to catatonic mutism and stupor. One could not, therefore, encourage the young painter to follow her need for a free expression that would have inevitably led to a panic state and perhaps even to a catatonic episode. Nor would it be wise to enhance self-restraint that would produce an unbearable tension. Thus, the best method was to foster self-esteem; with the increasing self-confidence, the painter was less afraid to express her feelings on the canvas. She began to believe in herself, despite her past experiences.

3. *"One step up"* is the third rule. It implies support of less dangerous symptoms against more dangerous ones, never forgetting that the ultimate goal is to strengthen the patient's ego. When the patient seems to be giving up life, even simple pleasures should be used as a lure.

Pleasure encourages, pain discourages. Especially in the case of the simple-deterioration syndrome, when the patients are profoundly discouraged and suicidal, every bit of joy counts. Thus, the therapist must seek out areas of work or entertainment in which the patient may partake without risking further damage to his catastrophically low self-esteem. Artistic activities—clay work, drawing, playing an instrument, easy handicraft—in short, whatever the patient can do and derive some satisfaction from should be encouraged.

Schizophrenia is a regression for survival. The psychotherapeutic vectorial interaction makes it unnecessary to lose the mind in order to survive. It calls the patient back to life, to growth, to joy, to normal self-protection and self-esteem.

Treatment of an adult schizophrenic as if he were an infant does not serve this purpose; it may foster unnecessary regression. Therefore, I see no reason in giving milk bottles to adult schizophrenics.

4. *The fourth rule is pragmatic flexibility of interaction.* Should the therapist be protective or demanding? Should he interpret unconscious or avoid interpretation? Should he be directive or nondirective, permissive or nonpermissive, frank or diplomatic?

Each of these points of view finds supporters and critics. The correct reply is determined by the state of the patient's mind and the ability of the therapist to handle it. When the failing ego is unable to control outbursts of unconscious impulses, the patient's moralistic superego must be supported instead. In hebephrenia, the ego has lost the battle to the id; thus, it may be advisable to strengthen the superego in order to prevent further deterioration. The therapist may, therefore, take a stern and demanding attitude and support whatever moral or religious convictions the patient may have. When the failing ego cannot control incestuous, homosexual or destructive impulses, the therapist might decide that he must, so to speak, "take over" and check the flood. This decision varies from case to case. In some cases, when the lesser risk is to give direct guidance, such guidance must be given, even if it violates all principles of classic psychoanalytic theory. It is, however, a temporary device, for the supremacy of the ego and not of the superego is the therapeutic objective.

In some severely deteriorated and suicidal cases, the therapist may even side with the id. When in simple deterioration, a patient renounces all enjoyment, pleasure and desire to live, the therapist may become very permissive and encourage pleasure-producing activities. However, any behavior that impairs the patient's reality testing, control of emotions and control of motility and reduces his self-esteem must be prevented at any cost, for it is ego-damaging.

5. The fifth rule is *individualization.* I have supervised psychotherapists for many years. Quite often a young therapist would

ask me: "And what would *you* have done in this case?" My answer is always the same:

> Psychotherapy is interaction and depends upon the two interacting individuals. There are rules, but each therapist applies them differently depending upon who is the *therapist* and who is the *patient*. Your job is to understand *your* patient. He is not the same, even if he seems to be, as any of the "cases" described by the masters. In fact, he is not a "case" at all. He is a definite individual, an unhappy and disturbed human being. Try to understand him and at the same time try to understand yourself. Your patient is a withdrawn, or an irritable, or an hallucinating, or a hostile individual. Can you take that? Can you face that much of an emotional demand? Please don't try to be what you are not. You cannot treat him the way Sullivan, or Fromm-Reichmann, or Schwing or Rosen did. But if you understand *your* patient, and are aware of *your* limitations and resources, and are genuinely interested in the patient, the chances are that you will be a successful psychotherapist.

6. The sixth rule is *reality testing*. The problem of interpretation and insight cannot be answered by a flat "yes" or "no."

> For example, a 30-year-old paranoid patient told me once that his beloved girl who lived 1,000 miles away disguised herself and came to a restaurant as a waitress. He blamed himself for not chasing her; he felt she must be angry at him for he had deserted her. But in the evening she returned to the restaurant; this time her hair was dyed so he could not recognize her. The patient wanted to approach her, but she disappeared.
>
> The patient said he expected the therapist to "side with him" or he would be "through" with treatment. It was obvious that disagreement would have been perceived by the patient as rejection and would have caused further deterioration and possibly an outburst of violence. Yet an acceptance of the patient's delusions could have served no therapeutic purpose.
>
> I started to *test reality* with the help of the patient. I asked him about his girl friend. He told me she had married two years ago and lived in the South, about 1,000 miles away from New York. His sister wrote him that the young lady had recently had a baby. Gradually the patient himself began to doubt whether the two waitresses were one person. The patient himself remarked, "How could she work in a restaurant if she has a baby? But it was a striking similarity, wasn't it, doc?" At this point, I felt that there

was a good opportunity to strengthen his reality testing. I admitted that some people strikingly resemble others and all of us may err. My comment was welcome and the patient smiled with obvious relief. He said, "So, after all, I am not completely crazy. This girl looked exactly like my girl-friend. It was just a little mistake."

In the past the patient has had visual and auditory hallucinations. He was often ridiculed, ostracized, and insulted. His parents have never missed the opportunity to call him crazy or lunatic.

An overt disapproval of delusions and hallucinations, and even efforts to undermine them by rational reasoning was doomed to failure. A too early interpretation might have caused, in this case, deeper regression and withdrawal.

When one hospitalized patient told me how she discovered God and spoke to him, I did not comment; my attentive listening to her was apparently very reassuring. I began to talk to her about her daily life and chores and she replied in a realistic way. Instead of challenging her hallucinatory omnipotence, I brought her closer to reality. When we talked about occupational therapy, her real achievements in work pushed aside the hallucinatory daydreams of omnipotence.

Even the most disturbed patient is, at least partially, aware of what is going on. He knows who is the patient and who is the therapist; he knows when the therapeutic session comes to an end and when he leaves your office to go back to the ward.

It is not advisable to deny flatly or to contradict the content of delusions and hallucinations, but it is never advisable to join the patient and to share or support the delusions. The therapist may not interpret the content of delusions and hallucinations until he is reasonably sure that the interpretation will help the patient restore his reality testing.

A realistic attitude on the part of the therapist helps the patient to keep contact with reality. One patient insisted on his "right" to call my home whenever he pleased, at any time of day and night, whenever he felt upset. I told him that if he would do that, I would discontinue my work with him. He accused me of being selfish and inconsiderate. I calmly replied that I needed rest and sleep, otherwise I would not be able to help anyone. If someone asks more than I can do, I must refuse.

7. The seventh rule is *parsimony of interpretation.* Fromm-Reichmann believed that "unqualified thriftness in content interpretation is indicated even more than with other patients, because, unlike neurotic, he is many times aware himself of the content meaning of his communications."[23]

The question is not whether to interpret but *when, how* and *how much.* I give priority to certain types of unconscious material—namely, to those that threaten to disrupt the functioning of the ego. A profound guilt feeling is often the most urgent issue and must be interpreted. If such an intepretation alleviates guilt feelings and reduces suicidal tendencies, it is a sound therapeutic step.

Some cases must go on without any interpretation whatsoever or with only as much interpretation as is given by the patient himself. The main goal of psychotherapy with schizophrenics is redistribution of cathexes and restoration of ego controls; therapeutic interpretation, no matter how correct and penetrating it is, does not mean much unless it helps to redistribute the mental energies and strengthen the ego.

I have, as a rule, avoided interpretations unless firmly convinced of their therapeutic usefulness at a given moment. In some cases, the last phase of psychotherapy was conducted on more or less psychoanalytic lines, bringing deep insights through interpretation of unconscious phenomena. In most cases, interpretations were given by the patients themselves.

8. The eighth rule is *realistic management of transference.* In his deep transference, the schizophrenic expects love, forgiveness and care from the therapist. Many schizophrenic patients wish to be fed, dressed, supported and taken care of by the therapist who represents the dream-parent. Some patients develop an infantile, symbiotic attachment and call the therapist at any time of day or night, just as a baby would call his mother. Most patients develop powerful heterosexual or homosexual desires reflecting the incestuous involvement with parents and try to enact them here and now. To accept the patient on his terms means to share his psychosis, but to reject him may cause further aggravation and regression.

Schizophrenics are exceedingly sensitive and empathic. A self-centered, aloof, disinterested and emotionally cold therapist could not establish rapport with the patient and, as a result, would not be able to help him. The patient must feel that the therapist is genuinely and profoundly interested in helping him.

At the same time, the emotionally starved schizophrenic may provoke such a trying situation that unless the therapist is genuinely interested in the patient's case and is ready to go out of his way to help him, the therapeutic relationship may become unbearable to the therapist. *The vectorial attitude of the therapist who is involved with the sufferings of the patient and not with the patient per se,* enables him to be interested in the patient because the patient needs help and not because the treated individual is young and good looking or intelligent.

The maintaining of this *vectorial professional attitude* is a *conditio sine qua non* for a successful treatment. The eventual emotional maturity of the patient will make future protection and guidance superfluous. Psychotherapy is an interaction that aims at being terminated. Once a satisfactory level of cure is attained, the doctor-patient relationship must be dissolved.

There is no one way of how transference should be handled. In most cases, a truthful, honest and simple explanation of the transient nature of the therapist-patient relationship is the best method. When a male therapist quietly turned down the love advances of his female patient, he pointed to his professional duties. The patient took the explanation calmly; it was not meant as a rejection of her as a female nor as a person. She understood the *reality* of the therapeutic relationship and accepted it. Although she felt frustrated, she understood that this was the right (superego) and realistic (ego) thing to do. The frank and open manner in which transference was handled helped a great deal in psychotherapeutic interaction.

The therapist may at times not tell the entire truth to an agitated patient, but he must never forget it. Nor should the therapist ever lie or make false promises. He must use judgment in timing of explanations. The therapist must not be carried away by anger, annoyance or impatience in the face of the patient's exaggerated demands, but he must treat them in a realistic and professional manner, respecting not only the present feelings of the patient but also his future reactions. A friendly but firm, considerate but realistic, frank but tactful attitude is usually the best way of handling transference. When a patient keeps calling the therapist asking to see him more and more, neither impatience nor yielding to the patient's whims is the proper therapeutic reaction. Impatience is an unfair reaction to somebody's pain but yielding to irrationality encourages irrationality.

A thorough cure is impossible without a resolution of the Oedipal entanglements, but this must be postponed until the patient's ego has gained adequate strength. In some cases, this ideal solution may be unattainable and it may not be advisable to analyze the incestuous impulses but rather repress them. In many cases, it may not be advisable to analyze transference at all. The strength of the patient's ego is the chief determinant as to how far one may go in interpretation. Not all schizophrenics are schizophrenic all the time and in the same degree. In treating schizophrenics, one must have an estimate of how much their ego is in control of their thought processes. The apearance of primary processes, such as condensation, symbolization, etcetera, should counterindicate interpretation and especially the interpretation of the transference.

9. The ninth rule requires a firm *control of countertransference.* "What should I do," asked a young psychotherapist whom I supervised, "when L. R. (a beautiful schizophrenic patient) throws her arms around me telling how much she loves me? She is exceedingly attractive and I become sexually aroused. Should I quit psychotherapy as Joseph Breuer did? Or should I 'give love,' hug her, kiss her, comfort her? Would this be unfair, unethical and professionally wrong? Wouldn't it be more harming for the patient to feel rejected? Frankly, I am attracted to her. She is attractive."

There can be no hesitation in such a case. The patient came to receive help, psychotherapeutic treatment. Her desire to go to bed with someone who was kind to her was just one of the symptoms. It was an attempt to prove that she was at least sexually accepted, while she could not believe she was accepted in any other way. To do so is just as unethical as to receive monetary gifts from a patient. In both cases, accepting the patient's offer would be taking advantage of the state of the patient. She tries to give sex or money because she doubts her own value as a human being. It is a bribe that must be turned down and explained when the patient is ready to accept the explanation.

Any transgression of the vectorial attitude on the part of the therapist is a violation of professional ethics. The therapist must like the patient but this libido cathexis must be vectorial and aim-inhibited. The therapist's love for the patient must be desexualized and never ask anything in return except the agreed upon fee.

Any intimacy between the doctor and patient is a severe violation of professional ethics and of the psychotherapeutic interaction. It may confuse the patient and bring back memories of incestuous parents who, instead of caring for the child, demanded the child's love.

10. *Rational handling of hostility.* A patient's acting-out hostile impulses may be catastrophic to his environment, as well as damaging to his weak ego. Thus, violence must be banned, repressed and kept under iron control. When patients describe their fights, I do not condemn them, for this would increase their guilt feeling and weaken their ego. But permissiveness on my part would be even more harmful. Whenever the superego has lost control, permissiveness would mean an invitation to license, freedom to the id and further deterioration of the ego.

Thus, I try to explain that even when they are right, violence is not the right behavior. My comments sometimes bypass the report of the fight as an insignificant event. Once a 25-year-old girl reported that she threw a bottle at her mother, but she did not intend to hit her mother and intentionally missed. I felt that the best policy was not to comment, thus expressing a silent approval for whatever self-restraint the patient has exercised. A male patient reported that he hit his sister; since he might have repeated it, I told him that I did not approve and would not allow any use of force even when he was provoked. I told him that I understood his feelings; obviously he was provoked and momentarily carried away, but I absolutely forbade any violence whatsoever.

Do patients listen? If a good relationship has been established and the therapist is respectful toward the patient, patients accept the therapist as a sort of externalized superego and conform.

> Once a hospitalized schizophrenic told me he had hit a nurse: he waited for my reaction. I felt that a lenient attitude would be perceived as siding with the unrestricted id and, implicitly, an approval of insanity. On the other hand, my condemnation of violence would have increased his already unbearable guilt feeling. I therefore made no comment and kept silent for a minute or two. I believe the patient understood my silence and felt grateful. He spoke aloud as if talking to himself: "You don't like it, do you? But you don't say I am a pig. You don't want to hurt my feelings. I guess I am a pig. I am ashamed of myself. I was just carried away. I am sorry. Don't be mad at me, doc. I shall not do it again. It was silly."

Schiozphrenic patients often display hostile feelings toward the therapist. Sometimes it is a part of their emotional growth.

> A 25-year-old schizophrenic explained it as follows: "Doc, I knew I had to fight against you. My mother forced me to be what she wanted me to be. I had to rebel against her to become myself. I had to assert myself to be me. I had to say what I wanted to say— so she blamed me for her misery.
>
> My father was even worse. Any time I was in trouble, he was making himself sick to avoid responsibility. When I was very sick, he pretended to be sick, too, so he wouldn't have to help me. Or he would just run away.
>
> I had to fight against you. I love you so much and I did not want to hurt your feelings, but I had to crush your shell. I had to test you and see how much you could take. Would my hostility make you weak and sick? Would you quit me, reject me? My father got sick. My father quit. I had to see your reaction. I had to test you."
>
> A friendly and understanding attitude on part of the therapist helped the patient to pass the stormy period. The patient was, for a while, highly critical of whatever the therapist did or said. When the therapist remarked, "You are just testing me," the patient reacted in the above-quoted explanation.

A 40-year-old ambulatory female patient screamed and yelled for fifteen minutes threatening to kill me. I offered her a cigarette and asked about her job. She calmed down and said, "Of course, I yell because my boss yelled at me today. I thought you would yell back, and I would be justified to feel that everybody hates me. But you are calm, friendly, smiling, as if nothing happened. To hell with you! I provoked my boss, but I could not provoke you."

Fear or hate in face of a threatening schizophrenic may increase the danger of a physical assault. A fearful therapist leads the patient to think that even the therapist believes that the patient is a hostile and dangerous individual. The best way is to preserve the friendly and understanding attitude of the therapist in face of the patient's irrational anger. The calm, self-assured and friendly attitude of the therapist disarms the patient and brings him back to reality.

Sometimes the choice is to *strengthen the patient's superego*. When the therapist, supporting the superego, sternly says, "It is not right," he helps the patient to control hostile impulses. The therapist may say, "I know you would not hurt anyone." Most often it is advisable to continue the friendly conversation and ignore the patient's threats. The therapist must imply or say it directly that he believes the patient is a good and friendly individual, capable of controlling the momentary outbursts of destrudo. At a later stage, when the patient has calmed down, the best policy is to treat the incident as an insignificant loss of self-control that need never occur again. Reproaches will hurt the patient's self-esteem. Should past hostility be recalled by the patient, the therapist must state clearly his disapproval of hostile actions and violence.

In case of physical violence, the therapist must be well protected and absolutely sure that the patient's violence be immediately restrained. Masochists and self-styled martyrs do not make good therapists. Too often the schizophrenic is forced to feel sorry for the "poor" daddy and mommy. Those who want to help the schizophrenic must be perceived as strong and friendly and capable of a truly vectorial, therapeutic attitude. Hostility and depression are interlocked, for the more hostility is expressed, the more guilt is felt.

To analyze acute hostility is tantamount to inviting an unnecessary challenge. The patient's hatred towards the therapist is irrational and a discussion of this hostility at this very moment means participation in irrationality. It is almost a *folie a deux* when the patient says that the therapist has stolen his ideas and the therapist desperately tries to deny it or when the patient says, "You hate me" and the irritated therapist repeats, "I do not."

One should draw a line between physical violence, verbal abuse ("you are a liar") and expression of hostility ("I hate my brother, but I wouldn't tell him"). Physical violence must be unconditionally restrained, but verbal abuse indicates that at least some delay and symbolization took place. Hostility is not always transference; when the therapist broke an appointment, the patient's anger, though exaggerated, is a legitimate expression of defensive hostility. Whether verbal hostility is a realistic or a transference phenomenon, whatever was rational in it should be accepted and explained. Schizophrenics tend to be self-righteous; thus the expression of hostile feelings should be encouraged, analyzed and worked through.

GROUP PSYCHOTHERAPY WITH SCHIZOPHRENICS

Ten years ago, I began to experiment in private practice with admitting schizophrenics to psychotherapeutic groups with other types of patients. However, I insisted on combined individual and group treatment. There were times when the patient could not open up to the group; there were moments when he needed privacy to confide; and ultimately, every schizophrenic needed a close person-to-person relationship with his therapist.

But, if this is so, why have groups?

One of the main reasons for groups is precisely the vehement transference schizophrenics develop. Freud erroneously assumed that schizophrenia is a narcissistic disorder. Federn and Sullivan, who worked with schizophrenics face to face, witnessed the intense transference phenomena. A schizophrenic easily goes from one extreme to another: from a cold, shallow lack of affect to stormy feelings, from rigid sexual abstention to compulsive promiscuity and from fear of expressing disappointment to malicious destructiveness.

There is nothing more healing for an unrealistic emotionality than a group setting where people are frank and express their feelings in an uninhibited way. For instance, Rose, a charming, 27-year-old woman believed that I was the greatest thing that ever walked on earth and boldly said, "I want you." She had incestuous experiences with her psychopathic daddy. I faced her offer head on. "O. K.," I said to her, "That would be fine, but from now on who will pay whom, and how much? Is this going to be a pure physical relationship or perhaps a more refined affair, or maybe a marriage? And who will be your therapist from now on while we develop such a nice love relationship?"

The group was waiting for her reaction. She was usually very outspoken and vociferous. My frankness took her aback. She did not want to lose me as her doctor, she said meekly. But she was very much in love with me and several group members expressed words of understanding for her feelings. One by one they came out with confessions. A female group member, 32-year-old, married, admitted that she too had a crush on the therapist. Fred, the homosexual college professor, stammered out his homosexual fantasies revolving around the therapist.

Participation in a psychotherapeutic group and awareness that most patients develop similar infatuations had a refreshingly therapeutic effect on patients. There is nothing more healing than reality, especially in regard to schizophrenics who regress into infantile and often preverbal levels of experience to escape the too painful reality.

The psychotherapeutic group mollifies transference in many other ways. It helps the schizophrenic to see the therapist outside the intense one-to-one human relationship and enables him to assess him in interacting with other individuals. The therapist certainly serves as a parental figure, but not as the seductive, exploitative father nor as the suffering and self-sacrificing mother. The therapist is rational all of the time, come what may. He is friendly and has the patient's well-being on his mind, thus he is truly vectorial as a parent should be. He does not become a partner of the homosexual group member, Fred, nor is he angry at Fred's sexual aberrations. He does not fall apart when the manic-depressive Tom raises his voice (and the chair), nor does he seek revenge.

The incident with Tom is an interesting case in point. Tom was gloomy and irritable, as usual. When he interrupted Jerry, the shy and withdrawn schizophrenic, two other group members protested. Tom yelled, "You bunch of neurotics, what do you know! Doc, tell them to shut up!"

I advised Tom to shut up and wait for his turn. Tom, red in the face, raised the chair threatening me. Jerry was shocked. I turned calmly to Tom saying, "Let that thing stand on the floor."

Jerry burst out in tears. He was afraid that Tom would hurt me. Fights are a daily occurrence in the schizogenic family, and all schizophrenics, even those who practice violence, are horrified by violence including their own. My calm was reassuring to Jerry and other latent and manifest schizophrenics in the group.

Rationality is no less contagious than irrationality, and the multiple irrational transferences can be dealt with better in a group setting than in individual sessions. Seeing one's own irrational behavior projected against the irrationality of others is a much more powerful medicine than just talking about it. A patient often feels better after seeing how silly other people could be. The interaction in groups contains both the regressive elements of transference, and the here-and-now relationship; but the prevalence of the last one opens the road toward rationality.

NEGATIVE TRANSFERENCE AND AGGRESSION

The group setting offers opportunities for checking and analyzing away the negative transferences and hostile acting out.[54] Often it requires a good deal of tact on the part of the therapist to soften the blows and protect those who are so hurt that they cannot take additional offense.

Latent schizophrenics are usually afraid to express their hostility and may bend over backwards to please the most arrogant and aggressive members of the group. For reasons that I shall explain later, I always put two or three manic-depressive patients in with schizophrenics and at least one colorful and nasty psychopathic patient. At the beginning, latent schizophrenics are shocked and terribly scared of the hostility freely expressed by the manic-depressive patients (I include them in the category of dysmutuals who swing from love to hate, from elation to depression) and even more so by the psychopaths (I call them hyper-instrumentals, pointing to their unlimited selfishness).

As a rule, hostility is directed against the therapist. Latent schizophrenics reexperience severe fears; they are afraid that the therapist will either lash out back at them or fall apart as their parents did. However when the therapist reacts calmly to hostility, analyzing its sources and explaining its components, the hostile assaults end, as a rule, by disarming the assailants. This offers an unusually valuable therapeutic experience. Latent schizophrenics learn to accept hostility as a normal human reaction, whether it originates from themselves or is expressed by other group members.

Paranoid schizophrenics may express their accusations verbally. Those who act out physically must not be admitted to a psychotherapeutic group. While the expression of hostility should be encouraged, the underlying rationality or irrationality must be scrutinized.

One patient maintains that the therapist calls him frequently at his home, saying nothing and hanging up on him. Another patient resents the therapist's refusal to give her additional sessions, while she believes that he gives them willingly to all the other patients. In both cases, similar complaints by the other group members and their criticism by the group have a healing effect. These patients themselves begin to question the accuracy of their stories, notice the displacement of their aggression and become more amenable to admitting their true grievances.

Another patient was constantly critical of others while blaming them for being unfriendly. She was domineering, bossy and provoked fights. The group acted in her case as sort of an ego, helping her in checking reality and becoming aware of her anxious belligerence.

I do not admit hebephrenics to my groups, because hebephrenic behavior may be too disruptive for the functioning of the group. I do occasionally admit catatonics in remission. When they sometimes report their past hostile acts, the group usually takes a tolerant attitude that alleviates their guilt feelings.

The simple deteriorated schizophrenics usually benefit by group interaction. Being withdrawn, shy and suffering from a severe feeling of inferiority, they usually require some time to get adjusted to the group.

The interactional process in the group is a two level process. George, thirty-three, was afraid of everyone on his job and in his neighborhood, but terrorized his frightened parents. He was exceedingly friendly and nice to strangers and selfish and exploitative to his own family. He acted out this tendency in the group; he was afraid of and tried to please the other group members but was arrogant in regard to the therapist, whom he expected to be permissive no matter how he behaved.

I was not permissive. I strongly disapprove of giving baby bottles to adult schizophrenics and making them regress. Schizophrenia is a regressing process to begin with and whoever intends to help a schizophrenic must help him to grow *up* and not to grow down. I did not interpret George's transference; interpretations, while usually useful, would have been meaningless in this case. I was George's third therapist, and he knew by heart all the stories about Oedipus the King. What George needed and received at this point was firm interaction with someone who would not take any nonsense. The interpretation came from the group members who noticed how nice he was to the loud Laura and how rude to the therapist.

Once a patient pulled a knife on me. Needless to say, I had no time for interpretation. I had to use the same techniques as with George—namely, to take over his superego. I gave firm orders and the knife landed safely on my desk.

INTERPRETATION AND INSIGHT

Hegel's famous dictum "Minerva's owl arrives at sunset" applies to the treatment of schizophrenics. The owl of insight should come toward the end of treatment, and in some cases, its presence is altogether superfluous. One can talk himself blue to schizophrenics without doing them one bit of good. For example, one brilliant latent schizophrenic young woman led a senselessly promiscuous life, often getting herself pregnant. She knew that she was self-destructive; she read Sullivan, Menninger and Fromm. But as soon as the transference was deep enough, she gave up promiscuity.

As mentioned before, interaction is a split-level process. It goes on in the realistic field of the here-and-now relationship, but also in the unrealistic field of transference buried in the unconscious memories of infantile experiences. A mere unraveling of the past does not produce a cure. In fact, most schizophrenics have an uncanny access to the unconscious, and they are the first ones in the correct interpretation of dreams brought by other group members. They are often morbidly aware of their unconscious impulses.

The interpretation of unconscious processes in latent schizophrenics should be avoided or at least postponed until the patient's ego is strong enough. A premature interpretation may destroy the defenses and precipitate a psychotic collapse. Interpretation of unconscious material must be highly individualized.

This caution does not apply to the here-and-now realistic interactional processes. The rule of interpretation in schizophrenia reads: Start from the surface and proceed cautiously. Go as deeply as necessary but avoid tampering with a weak ego structure. But do not be afraid to tell the truth concerning overt behavior, for truthful and realistic statements strengthen the ego. Sometimes I wonder whether there is any other place outside of the psychotherapeutic groups where truth is not only preached but practiced. In real life, full of vested, invested and hidden interests, people rarely tell each other the truth. I do not favor alternate group sessions, nor do I allow socialization outside group sessions. Thus, in a group session, love does not lead to a marital union and hate does not lead to destruction and murder. People tell each other the entire truth, because the fear of consequences which paralyzes people in an open society is removed in the group setting.

Tom told the unfaithful Marianne, "You are whoring away your marriage." Marianne cried and asked for my protection. I commented, "It is important for you to know that some people view your behavior in this way."

REMARKS ON GROUP STRUCTURE

I would never treat a group composed of schizophrenics only. Maybe it is because I am not strong or brave enough to do so, but I believe there are also objective reasons to consider.

I believe all mental disorders can be divided into five *levels of severity* of the disorder (neurosis, character neurosis, latent psychosis, psychosis and dementive stage) and three *types* representing the main trends of the overt behavior.[58]

CLASSIFICATION OF SOCIOGENIC MENTAL DISORDERS

	Hyperinstrumental Type (I)	*Dysmutual Type (M)*	*Hypervectorial Type (V)*
Neurotic Level	**Hyperinstrumental Neurosis** (Certain anxiety and depressive neuroses)	**Dysmutual Neurosis** (Dissociative and conversion neuroses)	**Hypervectorial Neurosis** (Obsessional, phobic and neurasthenic neuroses)
Character Neurotic Level	**Hyperinstrumental Character Neurosis** (Sociopathic or psychopathic character)	**Dysmutual Character Neurosis** (Cyclothymic and hysteric character)	**Hypervectorial Character Neurosis** (Schizoid and compulsive character)
Latent Psychotic Level	**Latent Hyperinstrumental Psychosis** (Psychopathic reactions bordering on psychosis)	**Latent Dysmutual Psychosis** (Borderline manic-depressive psychosis)	**Latent Vectoriasis Praecox** (Borderline and latent schizophrenia)
Manifest Psychotic Level	**Hyperinstrumental Psychosis** (Psychotic psychopathy and moral insanity)	**Dysmutual Psychosis** (Manifest manic-depressive psychosis)	**Vectoriasis Praecox** (Manifest schizophrenia)
Dementive Level	Collapse of Personality Structure		

Obsessive compulsive, schizoid and schizophrenic patients are included in the hypervectorial type. As explained before, these people are forced in their childhood to make costly object ca-thexes of their libido which inevitably lead to an impoverishment of self-cathexes. The hypervectorial patients fear their own hostil-ity and overrepress it. In the overt psychotic stage, destrudo breaks through, causing their overgrown superego to increase its self-destructive assaults.

The hysteric and manic-depressive patients swing from one extreme to the other—from love to hate, from self-directed to object-directed love or hate. In this dysmutual type, the super-ego is inconsistent, shifting from merciless self-hate and depres-sion to an euphoric self-love of elation.

I believe a group is balanced *horizontally* when it comprises all three types of mental disorder, and it is balanced *vertically* when it is not spread too much in the levels of severity. The horizontal balance permits a good deal of therapeutic interaction, for each of the three clinical types offers an emotional challenge to the other two. The vertical balance facilitates intragroup com-munication; for instance, a neurotic can understand a character neurotic (one level before) and perhaps a latent psychotic, but could not communicate too well with a too severe case.

REMARKS ON THE THERAPIST

I am in favor of a flexible approach bordering on inconsistency. With some patients, one must be supportive, with some not. I suggest certain basic rules related mainly to the three clinical types with variations necessitated by the level of regression. But even this is not enough. One has to allow a large margin for the personality of the therapist. I could not act the way Schwing, Fromm-Reichmann, Federn, Sullivan or Rosen acted. There are general principles, but each therapist applies them differently in a way appropriate to his own potentialities and to the needs of a particular patient.

REFERENCES

1. Alanen, Y. O.: The mothers of schizophrenic patients. *Acta Psychiat Scand 33*, suppl. 124, 1958.
2. Arieti, S.: *Interpretation of Schizophrenia.* New York, Bruner, 1955.
3. Bateson, G., Jackson, D. D., Haley, J., and Weakland, J.: Toward a theory of schizophrenia. *Behav Sci, 1*:251-264, 1956.
4. Bellak, L. (Ed.): *Schizophrenia: A Review of the Syndrome.* New York, Logos, 1958.
5. Bleuler, E.: *Das autistisch-undisziplinierte Denken in der Medizin und seine Uberwindung.* Berlin, Springer, 1919.
6. Bowen, M.: A family concept in schizophrenia. In *The Etiology of Schizophrenia,* edited by D. D. Jackson. New York, Basic Books, 1960.
7. Brody, E. B., and Redlich, F. C. (Eds.): *Psychotherapy with Schizophrenics: A Symposium.* New York, International University Press, 1952.
8. Bychowski, G.: Psychoanalytisches aus der psychiatrischen Abteilung. *Int Z Psychoanal, 11*:350-352, 1925.
9. Bychowski, G.: *Psychotherapy of Psychosis.* New York, Grune & Stratton, 1952.
10. Davis, D. R.: The family triangle in schizophrenia. *Br J Med Psychol, 34*:53-63, 1961.
11. Dawson, J. G., Stone, H. K., and Dellis, N. T. (Eds.): *Psychotherapy with Schizophrenics.* Baton Rouge, Louisiana State University, 1961.
12. Eissler, K. R.: Dementia praecox therapy—psychiatric ward management of the acute schizophrenic patient. *J Nerv Ment Dis, 105*:397-402, 1947.
13. Eissler, K. R.: Remarks on the psychoanalysis of schizophrenia. In *Psychotherapy with Schizophrenics,* edited by E. B. Brody and F. C. Redlich. New York, International University Press, 1952.
14. English, O. S., Hanupe, W. W., Bacon, C. L., and Settlage, C. F.: *Direct Analysis and Schizophrenia.* New York, Grune & Stratton, 1961.
15. Federn, P.: *Ego Psychology and the Psychoses.* New York, Basic Books, 1952.
16. Ferenczi, S.: *Further Contributions to the Theory and Technique of Psychoanalysis.* London, Hogarth Press, 1926.
17. Fleck, S.: Family dynamics and origin of schizophrenia. *Psychosom Med, 2*:333-344, 1960.
18. Foudraine, J.: Schizophrenia and the family: A survey of the literature 1956-1960 on the etiology of schizophrenia. *Acta Psychother, 9*:82-110, 1961.
19. Freeman, T., Cameron, J. L., and McGhie, A.: *Chronic Schizophrenia.* New York, International University Press, 1958.
20. Freud, S.: *Collected Papers.* London, Hogarth Press, 1924.

21. Freyhan, F. A.: Course and outcome of schizophrenia. *Am J Psychiatry*, 112:161-169, 1955.
22. Fromm-Reichmann, F.: *Principles of Intensive Psychotherapy*. Chicago, University Chicago Press, 1950.
23. Fromm-Reichmann, F.: Some aspects of psychoanalytic psychotherapy with schizophrenics. In *Psychotherapy with Schizophrenics*, edited by E. B. Brody and F. C. Redlich. New York, International University Press, 1952.
24. Fromm-Reichmann, F.: *Psychoanalysis and Psychotherapy*. Chicago, Chicago University Press, 1959.
25. Hill, L. B.: *Psychotherapeutic Intervention in Schizophrenia*. Chicago, Chicago University Press, 1955.
26. Hollingshead, A. B., and Redlich, F. C.: Schizophrenia and social structure. *Am J Psychiatry*, 110:695-701, 1954.
27. Kanner, L., and Eisenberg, L.: Notes on the follow-up studies of autistic children. In *Psychopathology of Childhood*, edited by P. H. Hoch and J. Zubin. New York, Grune & Stratton, 1955.
28. Knight, R. P.: Psychotherapy of an adolescent catatonic schizophrenic with mutism. *Psychiatry*, 9:323, 1946.
29. Knight, R. P.: Management and psychotherapy of the borderline schizophrenic patient. *Bull Menninger Clin*, 17:139, 1953.
30. Kraepelin, E.: *Dementia Praecox and Paraphrenia*. Chicago, Chicago Medical Book, 1919.
31. Kramer, M., Goldstein, H., Israel, R. H., and Johnson, N. A.: Application of life table methodology to the study of mental hospital populations. *Psychiatr Res Rep Am Psychiatr Assoc*, 1956, vol. 5.
32. Lidz, T. *et al.*: The intrafamilial environment of schizophrenic patients: II. Marital schism and marital skew. *Am J. Psychiatry*, 114:241-248, 1957.
33. Lidz, T. *et al.*: The intrafamilial environment of the schizophrenic patient: IV. Parental personalities and family interaction. *Am J Orthopsychiatry*, 28:764-776, 1958.
34. Lidz, T., and Fleck, S.: Schizophrenia, human integration, and the role of the family. In *The Etiology of Schizophrenia*, edited by D. D. Jackson. New York, Basic Books, 1960.
35. Lu, Y. C.: Mother-child role relations in schizophrenia. *Psychiatry*, 24:133-142, 1961.
36. Lu, Y. C.: Contradictory parental expectations in schizophrenia. *Arch Gen Psychiatry*, 6:219-234, 1962.
37. Philipps, L.: Case history data and progress in schizophrenia. *J Nerv Ment Dis*, 117:515-535, 1953.
38. Pichon-Riviere, de E.: Quelques observations sur le transfere de patients psychotiques. *Rev Francaise Psychoanal*, 16:254-262, 1952.

39. Rifkin, A. H.: *Schizophrenia in Psychoanalytic Office Practice.* New York, Grune & Stratton, 1957.
40. Rosen, J. N.: The treatment of schizophrenic psychosis by direct analytic therapy. *Psychiatry Q, 21:*117-119, 1947.
41. Rosen, J. N.: *Direct Analysis.* New York, Grune & Stratton, 1953.
42. Rosenfeld, H.: Considerations regarding the psychoanalytic approach to acute and chronic schizophrenia. *Int J Psychoanal, 35:*153, 1953.
43. Schofield, W., Hathaway, S. R., Hastings, D. W., and Bell, D. M.: Prognostic factors in schizophrenia. *J Consult Clin Psychol, 18:*155-166, 1954.
44. Sullivan, H. S.: *Conceptions of Modern Psychiatry.* Washington, D.C., William Alanson White Foundation, 1947.
45. Weakland, J. H.: The double-bind hypothesis of schizophrenia and three party interaction. In *The Etiology of Schizophrenia,* edited by D. D. Jackson. New York, Basic Books, 1960.
46. Whitaker, C. A. (Ed.): *Psychotherapy of Chronic Schizophrenic Patients.* Boston, Little, Brown & Co., 1958.
47. Winnicot, D. W.: Regression et repli. *Rev Francaise Psychoanal, 19:* 323-330, 1955.
48. Wolman, B. B.: Leadership and group dynamics. *J Soc Psychol, 13:*11-25, 1956.
49. Wolman, B. B.: Explorations in latent schizophrenia. *Am J Psychother, 11:*560-588, 1957.
50. Wolman, B. B.: Instrumental, mutual acceptance, and vectorial groups. *Acta Sociol, 3:*19-28, 1958.
51. Wolman, B. B.: Psychotherapy with latent schizophrenics. *Am J Psychother, 13:*343-359, 1959.
52. Wolman, B. B.: *Contemporary Theories and Systems in Psychology.* New York, Harper & Row, 1960.
53. Wolman, B. B.: Impact of failure on group cohesiveness. *J Soc Psychol, 51:*409-418, 1960.
54. Wolman, B. B.: Group psychotherapy with latent schizophrenics. *Int J Group Psychother, 10:*301-312, 1960.
55. Wolman, B. B.: Fathers of schizophrenic patients. *Acta Psychother, 9:* 193-210, 1961.
56. Wolman, B. B.: Hostility experiences in group psychotherapy. *Int J Soc Psychiatry, 10:*56-61, 1964.
57. Wolman, B. B. (Ed.): The socio-psycho-somatic theory of schizophrenia. In *Handbook of Clinical Psychology.* New York, McGraw-Hill, 1965.
58. Wolman, B. B. (Ed.): Mental health and mental disorders. In *Handbook of Clinical Psychology.* New York, McGraw-Hill, 1965.
59. Wolman, B. B.: *Vectoriasis Praecox or the Group of Schizophrenias.* Springfield, Charles C Thomas, 1965.

60. Wolman, B. B.: Interactional psychoanalysis. In *Psychoanalytic Techniques: A Handbook for the Practicing Psychoanalyst,* edited by B. B. Wolman. New York, Basic Books, 1967.
61. Wolman, B. B.: *Children Without Childhood: A Study of Childhood Schizophrenia.* New York, Grune & Stratton, 1970.
62. Wynne, L. C., Rychoff, I., Day, J., and Hersh, S. H.: Pseudo-mutuality in the family relations in schizophrenics. *Psychiatry, 21:*205-220, 1958.

Chapter 12

Therapeutic Procedures with Schizophrenic Patients

EUGENE T. GENDLIN

THE NATURE OF SCHIZOPHRENIA

WHAT IS THE NATURE of that "illness"? First of all, "schizophrenia" is the catch-all category in hospitals, a label attached to anyone who is not clearly manic-depressive, alcoholic, epileptic or something else one can define. This means it includes about half the hospital's population and consists of just anyone. Some of these people are no different from anyone else, except that things recently happened to them which made life impossible and pushed them out of the world, so to speak. If someone can help them back into the world, they are not fundamentally different from other people.

Another group in that mixed population were perhaps pushed out of the world very early; they may never have been quite fully into the human interpersonal world. These people may be much more difficult to help. However, I use the same words about them. I think schizophrenics suffer from being disconnected from the world. Being in a hospital, particularly a state hospital, is a late, visible, physical dramatization of their being disconnected from the world—and this is the disease we try to treat in the hospital! At first, these people were abandoned and isolated as persons and often lived in situations which seemed externally all right. Other people could have existed interpersonally in such a situation, but this person could not. His inward isolation explains why finally he could not last.[20] Being isolated in a hospital in physical space is at least the second sense in which he has been abandoned. First he was abandoned many, many times in interpersonal space.

The point I want to make is that human beings are not machines who have loose wires in them or burnt-out tubes. There is not

333

in us the kind of broken machinery that an ideal surgeon can reach and fix, or readjust, or take out the thing that is wrong or reconnect something inside this machine. We are interactive, experiential organisms.[1, 9-15, 21] *When* I respond to what goes on in a person, *then* something goes on *in him.* Of course, something goes on in him also before I respond. He is in pain, anxious or dulled; he has lost his sense of himself; he does not have any feelings; everything is flat. When I respond (or let us say, when I succeed in responding, because I often try and fail for weeks and months), then something more is suddenly going on, he does feel something, there is a surprising sense of self and he feels "Gee, maybe I'm not lost." He does not say that. On the contrary, only then does he first say he feels lost. That is when he first says, "There is no place for me in the world." A person can *feel* and express anything only as he *is in an ongoing process.* Without *any* place or world he feels nothing, only weird and selfless. With me there is enough of a place and world so that he feels interactively ongoing. Then he feels lost. It is not the inside that is sick. The "illness" is not internal pieces we have to eradicate. The "illness" is not "in" the human being as if he were a separated, boxed, packaged machine. We live as interactive processes.

How we live toward the world and others, how we sense ourselves in situations and referred to by others, that is us. If there is nobody there to refer to me personally and if I have not somehow learned in other relationships to respond to myself personally, or cannot now do so, then I am not there, and everything gets very flat, very strange and very weird. If you have ever spent five or six days by yourself without talking to anyone else, then you know something of the quality of feeling it is. But many people can live well toward nature or with their own responses to themselves. Others find only stoppage and weirdness when intolerable events and feelings have been ground into dullness and inner isolation has long been permanent.

What kind of an illness is that? We talk of *"resolving the symptoms* and not reaching *the basic illness."* This would be the case when there are no more hallucinations but the person is still miserable, cut off, alone. It is then said that "the basic personality trouble" has not changed. Thus, "schizophrenia" is not really the "crazy" symptoms as such. Then again, other people talk of just the opposite: "I know many schizophrenics who are out there in the streets, who are working, and they are all right, but they still have the same crazy experiences," says one well-known therapist. Here the personality difficulty seems ameliorated, but *that* is not what schizophrenia is either. Despite solutions in personality difficulty, these people still have "schizophrenic" experiences. It is the symptom-mode which is "crazy." But, we say that the symptoms also are not quite what schizophrenia is. These symptoms can go on or off within minutes. When we cure the symptom we are not content. The overt psychotic manifestations do not really define schizophrenia.

A third factor is indicated in the evidence that schizophrenia is really a relationship.[1, 12] It is a sick way of being married or a sick family, it is an untenable way of being with another person. One is "isolated" from the world by reacting always within a given single intolerable relationship.

Within this relationship one's experiential feeling processes cannot be interactively ongoing—yet one is stuck within that relationship and not in the world.[9] Not the bad relationship as such, but the stoppage of experiential process in it is the "illness."

The policy of many hospitals (in Wisconsin, for example) is to send patients back to the same relatives that signed the patient in. This policy sends him back exactly to the relationship in which he can be no more than his sickness. We are tending in two directions with that problem. One is to treat the whole family, which gives some recognition to this interactive nature of the illness.[1] The other direction is to try and make a new life possible for the patient (protected workshops, halfway houses, new lodgings and work). But, the possibility of a new life for the patient should be held out to him right at the beginning, when he is sitting there silent, has no hope and nothing to say.[8] I can say to him "I think I can help you get out of the hospital, and if you want to, you can live in the city instead of going home. I suppose you don't believe that you could get out of here, but I do. First you work upstairs, and then we will help you find a job outside, and then

I'll help you find another job and a room in town, if you want one. I'll stick with you and get you out of here. I know you don't think that's possible now." If that is held out to patients when it still makes little sense, then the fundamental cut-offness can yield to a beginning interaction process into the world. We must *begin* by overcoming the break that has happened between the patient and the world, his sense that he is not in the world and cannot be. Inside himself he is not feelingly alive to think about this, or feel and express himself about it, hence we must begin by restoring the possibility for such feelings and thoughts.

My conception of the illness: *It is not so much what is there as what is not there.* The interactive experiential process is lacking, stuck, deadened in old hurt stoppages and in disconnection from the world. It cannot be ongoing, except in and toward someone and in the world. If a toaster is unplugged, would you take it apart to find out what is wrong inside of it?

The concrete reality of humans is the experiential process, and this is no purely internal thing, but a feeling-toward others in situations. If it is not ongoing, then it cannot be made ongoing, except as we respond empathically to make interaction happen, as well as reconnect the person at least to a promised and imagined outside situation in which he might be able to live. Only if he can later actually try such situations long before he is objectively well enough to do so can he usually become well enough to do so. Later, we really must help him with job and room, be available for calls at night and meetings in odd places. It was through what some released patients taught me in this respect that I came to promise such things to other patients at the start.

Of course, we do not yet really understand what schizophrenia is. We cannot claim to know. In addition to symptoms, personality difficulty and experiential interactive stoppage, there may be physiologic conditions both etiologic and accumulated results of long isolation. If pharmologic help is found, it may greatly speed the recovery. But, someone must respond. Only in being responded to does the patient then seem to *have* ongoing feelings and therefore the ability to "be aware" of them. It seems likely that the absence of this experiential interaction process is schizophrenia.

PSYCHOTHERAPEUTIC CONSIDERATIONS

Client-centered therapy was first defined in terms of the discovery that a deep, self-propelled therapeutic process arises when the therapist "reflects feelings." In this type of therapist response, discovered by Rogers,[16] the therapist freshly phrases his sense of the client's implied affective message or felt personal meaning.[17] For a time this was hard to distinguish from mere repetition by the therapist of what the client *says.* Seeman[19] moved further toward an experiential formulation by clarifying this question. The therapist does not repeat what the client says or clearly feels. Rather, he "reflects the *unformed* emotional experience" (my italics) of the client. The therapist aims at the client's directly felt, not yet formulated, experiential meanings.[3-5, 7]

On the therapist's side, the same experiential development meant that he would no longer hide his own person behind a screen. Rather than mechanically "reflecting," the therapist was becoming more "spontaneous,"[2] tending to voice his "immediate" feelings and responses to the client. Finally, Rogers[18] redefined psychotherapy entirely in terms of therapist "attitudes" ("necessary and sufficient" for psychotherapy, regardless of the technique and orientation). Among these attitudes, the most important was genuineness or "congruence" of the therapist, eschewing any false front, screen, artificial maneuvers or techniques as such. The therapist was to be "himself," as he really is and reacts within this relationship.

Thus during this period client-centered therapy, like other orientations, moved toward emphasis on experiential concreteness in client, therapist and their interaction.

Similar developments have been occurring in the other therapeutic orientations. In the last two decades the emphasis has shifted from the different verbal contents and techniques toward a common experiential focus.[4]

Psychotherapy has become less technique oriented, less mechanical, less cognitive, less limited to the best adjusted and most verbal patients, and less divided along the old lines. Therapists of many orientations sense a common movement which transcends the divisions between "reflection of feeling" and "interpretation," between "analytic" ("exploratory") and "supportive," between emphasis on sex and emphasis on self-concepts, power strivings, will struggles, interpersonal feelings or other favorite *contents*. Very gentle and receptive therapists and very active and interventive therapists agree that when they are successful a similar experiential process transcends differences of words and techniques.

The roles of patient, therapist and relationship are coming to be viewed in terms of concrete experience. In the patient, psychotherapy no longer aims exclusively at one kind of content (Oedipal conflicts, self-concepts, etcetera). Although various orientations still favor one or another of these kinds of content ("vocabularies," I would call them), a basic experiential feeling process is widely held to be what really constitutes psychotherapy. Without this feeling process there is mere intellectualization or rationalization. With this feeling process, patients change concretely, whatever vocabulary is employed. The therapist can aim his responses at the patient's concretely felt meanings: the preverbal, preconceptual experiencing. Of course, the therapist will conceive and phrase whatever he senses and will employ words and concepts that make sense to him. However, the object of the words and concepts will be the concrete, felt experience in the patient. The therapist's chief aim will not be to devise objectively correct sentences to describe the patient but rather to get the patient to attend directly to the concretely felt experience he has there in the immediate moment. In psychoanalytic terms, this is called the "preconscious," what one *can* feel and verbalize if attention is drawn to it. As the concretely felt "preconscious" is carried forward and responded to, more and more facets *become* preconscious—that is, they become directly felt and thereby capable of being verbalized. If the patient will attend to and work through what he directly and feelingly has there (to which the response points), then therapy will move and succeed, whatever the vocabulary of the response. With this emphasis on this concretely felt "working through" process, therapists have come to agree that how one points one's response matters more than the terms in which the response is phrased. Therefore, we commonly say today that a different therapist with a different conceptual vocabulary may do psychotherapy as well as those who share our own vocabulary. What matters is whether he can engender the experiential concretely felt "working through" process in the patient.

Within the therapist too conceptual, professional machinery and technique have yielded to an emphasis on the therapist's real person in the interaction. Mere techniques are seen as self-defeating. By their very formality, inhumanness, mechanical or abstract character, they will fail to point at and carry forward the patient's unformed personal meanings. The therapist must use his actual personal responses and actual felt impression of what is happening. The therapist uses his own felt experiencing of the moment, much as he aims his responses at the patient's felt experiencing of the moment.

Finally, the interaction between patient and therapist is seen as an ongoing experiential process in which both persons change and are alive in new ways. Only a concretely felt new interaction can bring about newly emergent facets of feeling in the patient so that he is alive in new ways and actually *changes*, rather than merely finding out how he *is* and *has been*.

Characteristics of Schizophrenic Individuals in Regard to Psychotherapy

Work with the hospitalized schizophrenic patient greatly accelerated the experiential trend in client-centered therapy. This was partly because of the way we selected these individuals for therapy. We did not consider their desire or suitability for therapy or the hospital staff's recommendations. Individuals selected on the basis of such considerations are those likely to succeed because of their desire for help, because of "suitable" (that is good) prognosis for therapy or because they have been able to attract staff interest. Instead we chose clients by strict research criteria (age, sex, social class, length of hospitalization) and so obtained much more typical (and much less hopeful) individuals. Here are a few of the characteristics we frequently found in our patients:

Silence

Over and over again we met hours of solid silence. This was not the kind of silence we value in psychotherapy when the individual deeply explores himself inwardly. Rather, it was a silence of emptiness, resistance, of not knowing what to do. Another type of "silence" was nonstop talk about trivial and external matters.

The Set for an Exploration Process Missing

Whether silent or talking, the patient would not share the therapist's "set" of searching for what is wrong, of exploring or helping with what is wrong. The patient had no such "exploration set." He might be totally silent or speak incessantly, but if he spoke, it would be about the bad hospital food, the troubles of his ward, his desire to go home or that nothing was wrong with him. The therapist's attempts to reflect or interpret troublesome feelings would be rejected by the patient or would puzzle the patient. He would see no point in focusing on such feelings. The patient was not asking himself questions, was not embarked on an endeavor to explore himself or to understand or change himself. What seemed missing was not just a specific feeling. The patient did not see the *relevance* of a therapist's *sort* of concern, for exploration was missing.

No Self-propelled Process

Perhaps because of the lack of explorative set, perhaps for other reasons, the usual self-propelled therapeutic experiential process did not take place. (With more usual clients, such a process usually moves of its own accord after an initial period of therapy. At first, the therapist must pull the process along, must always refer anew to the experiential, felt aspect of what the client says; but soon more and more personal felt meanings emerge of their own accord, and both client and therapist are pulled along by "it," the concrete felt meaning which next emerges.) With these hospitalized patients, a therapy-like process might occur on a rare day, yet the next time it would be as though that had never happened. No continuous, self-propelled process developed.

Rejecting the Therapist

With great regularity both silent and verbal patients would reject therapy and the therapist. Such rejection was not part of the give-and-take of interview encounter as we are used to it. Rather, it was a total refusal to meet with the therapist. The message, often said explicitly, was—"Go away and leave me alone. I do talk to some people but not to you. Don't you have other patients you can go to see? I am not coming anymore. Don't come to see me." This might be the patient's consistent attitude over a number of months. Had it not been for research, we would not have continued with these patients and would not have learned how to continue without violating their personal rights.

The Challenge to the Therapist

These patient characteristics greatly accelerated the already developing experiential method. For example, a therapist accustomed to "reflecting" feelings is confronted by ten or twenty hours of absolute silence—what feelings shall he "reflect"? Or if the therapist usually "interprets," what will he do after he has variously "interpreted" the continuing silence? Whatever the therapist's techniques, he sees himself failing to reach the patient's feeling life. He does not know much about it specifically (it is probably deadened, or sore, highly chaotic, and unknowable even to the patient), yet he must somehow reach it, point at it, relate himself to it, ask about it, *respond to it even without specifically knowing what it is.* Thus, these patients force therapists to point themselves at the directly felt, concrete, preverbal experiencing in the patient.

Let us say the therapist decides that exploratory techniques are not indicated and employs supportive therapy instead. The distinction may mean that the therapist ceases even to try to respond to implicit meanings. But then, silence. Nothing happens. Or let us say the patient speaks in a highly autistic way with personal meanings and events compressed into hardly interpretable masses. The supportive therapist just "lets him talk." Not only is this not supportive, it is positively harmful: The patient's rather desperate efforts to communicate continue to fail with a therapist who "lets him talk" or gives only broad suggestions. The therapist is forced to give up both abstract exploration and mere support. Instead, he must respond in such a way that the patient can bear it, can concretely feel and know what is meant, can attend better to his own immediately available feelings and can experience himself as perceived by and understandable to another person. There is no way to do that by simply using or simply avoiding interpretive insight. There must be explorative response, but of a different kind. The therapist must try to sense the patient's presently available felt referents and must show the patient that this is what the therapist values and responds to. With long-hospitalized schizophrenic individuals, experiential referents are often deadened, painful, chaotic and frightening masses of feelings and meanings. These are preverbal and felt, but only capable of being carried forward gently in terms of (any) verbal vocabulary.

Thus, the characteristics of these patients lead therapists to transcend the old techniques. From whatever point the therapist starts, he moves toward responding to the patient's directly experienceable, felt referents, even when these have to be verbalized in very tentative and concrete words.

Similarly, these clients lead the therapist to employ his own concretely felt experiencing as a source of his response behavior. At first, the therapist may notice only that many difficult and unaccustomed feelings occur in him with these clients. But soon he comes to use these feelings to create interaction. In another place I described this development in these words:

> The client is silent or talks of trivia. Attempts to verbalize his implicit communications make him angry, fearful or withdrawing; or, as we try to respond to a deeper level of feeling, we find that the client simply has not meant to look at himself more deeply—and

misunderstands us. We have all sorts of impressions and images of what the client feels. Perhaps we only imagine these, or perhaps subverbally the patient does communicate. We wonder what to do with all this richness of events which occurs in our own moment-to-moment experiencing, as we sit quietly or converse superficially. We feel much empathy but can show little. As we go along on a casual level or in silence, we wonder if we aren't allowing ourselves to be just as helpless as this fearful person. We are in conflict, not knowing whether to push harder or to attempt being even safer. We blame ourselves for too much helpless waiting, then minutes later, for too much interruption, pressure and demand. We wonder whether the client is doing anything significant with us, whether we are failing him. We become impatient and angry at giving so much inward receptivity while so little of it seems communicated. We value deeply what little or trivial communication he gives us, and we do not want to push that away. Yet we feel dishonest when we seemingly assent to silence or to this trivial level of communication.[6]

We then become able to *use* these many feelings, images and impressions. They are our impressions of the patient and our incipient *moves toward the patient*. In suppressing them, we suppress our incipient interaction with the patient. Each minute we suppress five or ten such potential moves. Since the patient is unable to initiate a meaningful interaction, it is left to us to do so. Genuine starts for such interaction occur within us constantly. So we learn to use our own experiencing as therapists, but our feelings and images do not always come to us already shaped and verbalized in usable form. Therefore, we must focus on our own directly felt meanings and go through "a few steps of self-attention"[5] to fashion a usable response to the patient.

Finally, we also learn from these patients that new, concrete interaction can precede new feelings and new words. When the patient cannot yet verbalize or hear much verbalization, therapeutic movement depends on positive relationship events. The many difficulties which arise in relating to a hospitalized patient offer the therapist opportunities to relate to his patient as to a valuable and sensible person. For no matter how objectively wrong and obnoxious a patient's behavior may be, it can be met and opposed in a person-to-person encounter, and (while the behavior itself is stopped) the therapist can search for, find and respond to a positive thrust and integrity implicit in the patient's behavior.

Thus, just the difficult characteristics of these patients most highlight the role of experiential concreteness in patient, therapist and interaction.

THERAPEUTIC PROCEDURES

Different therapists' styles vary greatly. Each therapist finds different behavior to convey *himself* directly and spontaneously. My descriptions present the *scope* and the *kind* of therapeutic procedures we learned in working with these schizophrenic individuals.

I am going to describe in detail the processes that occurred in me as I worked with these patients, my attitudes, steps of thought and private procedures. I believe that in this way you can best evaluate what I do, take from it anything useful or be stimulated by it toward something different.

We must develop *a vocabulary—a science—about the therapist's personal procedures;* we cannot leave these private and unnamed. Without detailed vocabulary about what we do inwardly, we cannot talk to each other or train new therapists. We need a science of doing psychotherapy, and the first step is to develop a vocabulary that names some of the procedures we employ both within ourselves and externally. That is what this chapter attempts to do with a series of descriptions of situations and methods of handling them, which grew out of my work with schizophrenic patients.

Three Categories of Patient In-therapy Behavior

Not everything I describe here would be appropriate for every patient. Much of it has the following form: "If the patient at the moment does so and so, then I find it helpful to do so and so." Such formulae create categories, classifications of patient in-therapy behavior. These are different from the usual categories of psychopathology.

Few terms from psychopathology tell us what to do in psychotherapy. For example, if the patient is "schizophrenic—undifferentiated tendencies," what does that tell me about how to approach him? Little can be said about what to do which would be applicable to all who are given this label and not applicable to many patients with other labels. Compare this diagnostic label with the category: "If the patient is quite verbal, but speaks only about externals and daily events . . ." This category requires certain kinds of therapist procedures and allows us to discuss what we do. Notice that this is not a category of psychopathology! Some schizophrenic individuals, some neurotics and some normals will present a therapist with this problem. Nor is it a class of patients. The same individual who presents one type of in-therapy behavior now may present a different sort later. Why settle on any one patient-class for an individual? After all, we hope he will change! I group my various descriptions under three categories of in-therapy behavior, not of patients:

I. The patient is totally *silent and unresponsive,* giving me no feedback at all, either verbal or gestural or postural. He sits or stands silently, unchanging and unmoved throughout.

II. The patient is *silent but responsive;* his face, gestures and rare words respond in continual, subverbal interaction.

III. The patient is *verbal but externalized;* he never speaks about feelings or personal meanings, only about others, situations, events without their affective aspects.

Interview Behavior I: Silent and Unresponsive

Throughout this section picture the patient sitting somewhat bent over, looking down at the floor between his feet, never stirring, never looking up or giving any sound or body indication that he hears. Imagine him in this position when we begin and throughout the interview. (This may be in my office, in the hallway or where he sits in the day room.) When I leave he is still sitting in the very same position. He has made no sound and has not moved.

No FEEDBACK DEMAND. I used to depend on what the patient said to lead me to the next thing I would say or do. I needed the patient's response to let me know whether what I did was good or effective. I now think therapists should have *many* patients so that their sense of effectiveness does not depend on any one given patient at a given time. I can continue to work, speak and act without the patient's showing me that he hears me, that he agrees, denies or commits himself in any way.

THE "SENSIBLE PERSON" ASSUMPTION. I always assume that I am speaking to a sensible person, there inside the patient. This assumption has never failed of later confirmation, but in the face of *this* person's total unresponsiveness it is an assumption requiring imagination! I imagine I know I am talking to the person in there, somewhere—a fully human, almost certainly suffering, person—half lost and weird, perhaps—unable and unwilling to send up any sign—but there. I think of it as throwing something over a wall to someone. I cannot hear it land there, and I cannot tell if it is any good to him. I throw it over the wall without expecting to hear anything for some time.

My ways of being expressive as a therapist seem rather radical to me and have seemed so to some other therapists. I seem to be "out on a limb," not knowing if I imagine the patient or if he is really there. But much later the patient will say, "Why were you so silent? Why did you take so long? Why didn't you say much more of that kind of thing? Seemed like you knew I couldn't talk, and still you often didn't do much."

From such statements I know that my assumption is not really very doubtful at all.

THE THERAPIST IS SELF-GROUNDED. I make clear that I speak and act on my own responsibility, because I want to say it or do it. Since the patient gives no response or commitment of wanting to meet with me, I tell him that I will continue to meet with him because I have decided to. Since he does not respond to what I say, it will stand simply as what I want to say. Since he says nothing when I tell him what feelings I imagine he feels, I make it clear that these are my imaginings. ("I don't know how *you* feel about it. You haven't said. This is just what *I* think of it.")

OWNERSHIP OF FEELINGS IS SPECIFIED. When I intend to refer to *his* feelings, I make that clear. When I speak about *my* feelings, I make that equally clear. I specify who is the owner of the feeling.

This distinction lets the patient know that I point at whatever *he actually* feels. On the other hand, when it is something *I* feel or want to say and do, I make that clear. It leaves him uncommitted. It does not require that his feelings be already clear to him or bearable enough to look at. The patient is rarely disturbed by whatever I am, think, feel or want to do if I can keep it clear that this is me and leave him uncommitted.

THE CONCRETE SILENCE. I talk about silent sitting together as something concrete. In ordinary social intercourse we must fill time with words. In a living room with others, even thirty seconds without talk brings strong discomfort. We *must* say something.

We usually think we are doing nothing (at least, nothing useful) if we just sit in silence next to someone. Sitting down next to a silent patient, one feels one's own implicit demand: "Say something!" Especially if the therapist has spoken, the eventuating silence builds a tension. The patient knows he should say something, but he won't. The time is a bad time, much like the rest of hospital time, wherein the patient refuses and resists while staff loudly or silently demand and criticize. Therefore, there is relief for the patient (I believe) when I say, as I usually do, "It's all right to be quiet. I'll just sit with you a while."

Perhaps after some time, I may say, "Now I'll sit with you a little longer, then I'll go. I'll be back on Tuesday."

When I sit with someone, I know that *is something*, even if I have nothing valuable to say. I no longer need constant evidence that I am being effective and helpful. I can just sit and give my company. I have been in situations where my pain could not be understood, and I have taken comfort just being with someone willing to *be* with me, someone who required nothing, could not grasp my torn-up feelings but was human company—like a place to go when you are down and out, a human presence, civilization after wilderness. It is a lot when I just sit with someone. But I believe it helps to *say* that I mean to sit in silence. It helps to make it something.

MANIFESTING PRESENCE PERIODICALLY. I speak every few minutes when I sit in such a silence. I let myself be heard from. I feel the the patient needs to hear me often, to find himself in touch with me even while he cannot yet reach out for me or establish interaction. I do not want to be forgotten, so that he returns to isolated aloneness even while I am with him. What I say usually demands no answer. If I do demand an answer (and get none), I indicate it is all right. ("I wish you'd tell me, but it's all right for you not to.") My statements, every few minutes, are often about myself, about what is going on in me, what I think, feel, imagine, wish or do inside myself as I sit there.

Usually in therapy with neurotics, the transcripts of the tape-recorded interview show what therapist and client say alternately: T. C. T. C., etcetera. The sort of transcripts which come from the above, when it is tape-recorded, run—T. T. T. T. T. T. T. T. T.—throughout a whole interview! The patient may say something once, or twice, or not at all. The therapist says something every few minutes.

ACTUAL RESPONSE PROCESSES. My actual trains of thought and feeling are the source of my responses. I think many things of all kinds in these minutes of silence. A minute of silence is a very long time! I could never possibly say all I think and feel—even if thoughts and feelings came in little verbal units, ready to be spoken. Actually they come in felt masses, only little of it in words. I put *some of* what I feelingly think into words for myself, as I sit there. After a time, one or another of these thoughts seems fitting to tell the patient. Perhaps I still mull about it, ponder it, see other sides of it, find a simpler way of phrasing something. But I do not stick at this or that phrasing. I let it run on in my mind. When I decide to say it (whatever "it" is, "this" thought or feeling), I won't have all the words prearranged for it. It will come out of my mouth spontaneously.

I will now describe several sources for such responses.

WHAT THE THERAPIST MIGHT EXPRESS. Some of my responses come from a chain of thought that is well known to every therapist, though few use it as a source of responses. This is my thinking about what I just said or did and why I should perhaps have done otherwise.

Especially with silent and unresponsive patients, if the therapist says something and gets no response he can think of ten reasons why it might have been a stupid, wrong or threatening thing to say. These feelings used to burden us as therapists, but they have become a source of responses instead. In the following I will describe my intervening thoughts to show how such a sequence of thoughts leads me to something further which I can tell the patient.

Suppose I had said (as I just described), "I'll just sit with you a while. It's all right to keep quiet."

Now I might find myself thinking: Silence is very well for me but he needs help. What if my saying that silence is "all right" means to him that I don't care to help, don't even know something is wrong, that I don't realize the silence is really terrible, awful, horrible, and not a bit "all right." Maybe he wishes he *could* say something, but he can't. Now I have quite a lot I want to tell him. There's no hurry. It is only a few seconds later. I mull it a while. Somehow I am going to tell him that I know he is suffering and that I want to help, although I do not need speech from him right away. I know from his sitting there like that, head down, looking at his feet, that he is suffering, discouraged, hopeless, something like that. But I do not *know* about him, and I do not want him to think I know all about him, have read his record, or am connected with one of the people in his life. I will have to tell him also that I do not really know anything about him. Now I feel I know what I want to tell him, something like: I think he is suffering; I don't really know that; I'd like to help; I need nothing special right now. After a while of mulling, I might simply say, "Most people in here are really suffering pretty badly. I'd like to help you. Sometime maybe I can."

But he does not know I mean help via his talking to me. Perhaps he thinks I could "help" him "sometime"; I'm not doing it now because I don't feel like doing it yet. I'll have to tell him I want to hear from him what is wrong, what to help with. After a while, I might say, "Sometime I hope you'll tell me something about how you came to be in this hospital." Then I wonder what if he thinks I want an explanation or a defense? After all, I want to hear about his feelings, not the events as such, objectively. I might say, after a while, "I bet you went through a really tough time. I don't know anything about you, that's just my guess."

Then I might think perhaps he'll take that as curiosity, my trying to find out about him, wanting to hear dirty stories or embarrassing facts. So I might say after a while, "Whatever hurts inside you and makes you feel bad, that's what I would care to hear about, whatever has you so silent and sad."

Then I might think what if he isn't sad at all, just lost or sullen, or what not? So I might say after a while, "To me you seem sad, sitting there so silently with your head down. Of course, I don't know how you really feel."

Words like "sad" or "angry" or "rough time" turn an individual's thoughts to his own feelings rather than to other people's views of him and condemnations of him. Many patients expect to talk in the frame of reference of what they should have done or not done, or what they have been condemned for or are innocent of. "To me you seem sad" indicates my wish to talk and think about him, his feelings, not about outward events, condemnations and excuses. Inside himself he might find for a moment what he *does* feel, not sad but———, and this will help. For an instant, he might feel like stirring and answering me, to correct me: "Not sad, just flat, empty, hopeless" or perhaps, "I wish I did feel sad, it would be something." My patient here says nothing, does not stir, but I feel it helps to talk to him about his feelings and to indicate that I am thinking about his feelings, even if I have to call them by misnomers. I make it plain: "I realize I don't know what your feelings really are."

Perhaps he does not know himself. I might tell him that too after a while: "Often people's feelings are all mixed up, they don't know just what they feel, except maybe just bad. It might be that way with you, or anyway that's what I was just thinking." It lets him know I was thinking about him, about how he feels.

But now I think further: Maybe he knows exactly what he feels, just can't *say* anything. What if he is quite ready to say it, except that it's the sort of thing you *never* say to anyone? Perhaps he doesn't know that the kind of thing he *would* say is appropriate to say to me. I wish he would say it! I want him to know that. I want him to know I am a therapist, a feeling doctor. I want him to know what I am doing here and that the sort of thing he feels is the right kind of thing to say to me. How can he know that? I have to tell him.

Then I might say, "I'm the kind of doctor that understands about people's feelings. Of course, I don't know yours, but I know a lot about this kind of trouble. That's the kind of doctor I am. Sometime I hope you'll tell me what you feel that bothers you. I might help with it."

Then perhaps I think: What if he is ready to talk *now*, why do I keep saying *sometime*? So I might say after a while: "Anything at all, whatever it is, that you would care to tell me, I'd care to hear it." Then, as the silence continues, I might think what if he wants to and can't? Then I might say: "If it's too hard to talk now, that's O.K." Then I might think that I'm just encouraging his flabby, heavy, discouraged tendency to do nothing and so I'll say, after a while, "I sure wish I'd hear more from you."

From these descriptions you can see the thought sequence which leads me to responses. It is that familiar sequence in which the therapist has his doubts about whether what he just said was fitting and wonders if it was perhaps stupid, hurtful, wrong or misunderstood. We all have these thoughts, and they include the reasons *why* we doubt the worth of what we have just said. These need not be left as uncomfortable feelings. With silent and unresponsive patient behavior, we can use such sequences as a source of responses.

The "Imagined Patient" Sequence. Another sequence of thoughts which gives rise to responses concerns the patient. Later in therapy (perhaps the patient is still silent and totally unresponsive), I am active in many more ways. Among other things, I say more about him. So far I have used examples only from the first few meetings with patients who are silent and unresponsive. Here are some examples of what I might say a week or two later: "My God, you're sitting in the same place I left you last Friday! It seems awful that you would just sit and sit like that!" or "I don't know, of course, but it seems to me you look *so* sad. I wonder if you're just feeling like you're hopeless, like it's no use."

Saying such things gives rise in me to a whole sequence of thoughts about someone who feels hopeless and no use. Of course I do not know if he feels that way (and I will tell him that, too), but *the kind of interaction* we have as I talk is helpful, even if the *content* of my words may not fit him. I might say after a while: "Sometimes a person can feel so no-use and no-good, he just tries to give up on himself."

I might ponder that a while and then say, "But, you know, it doesn't really work to give up on yourself. Maybe you try and try to give up, but it only hurts."

Then, after a while, "Maybe it's hard to even think of picking things up again. Sometimes a person feels that to try again is like telling people it's all right that they hurt you."

After I ponder that, I might say, "If they did hurt you, that's *never* all right."

That will lead me after a while to another thing, perhaps: "Sometimes the ones that hurt you are just the people you most wish loved you. That's the hardest to take, I think."

Some of these sequences will fit anyone, but just as often the sequence will not fit the patient. These are responses to a person I imagine—a sad person, silent, broken, given up, hurt by those he cared about, in a state hospital, not cared for enough or not understood. As I respond to such a person, all the while phrasing clearly that I do not know how the patient really feels, he experiences me reacting to him, much as he would if he were verbal. He experiences (he need not understand) my intention, which is to focus on his feelings, his hurts as they were to him, since that is the frame of reference of the things I say. His feelings may stir, become a little more alive and perhaps a shade less unbearable and disorganizing than they were when he last could stand to look at them, which he did alone.

Then perhaps I shift. It strikes me that being hurt by those you care for and therefore not wanting to try again is too specific, probably wrong. Perhaps he is just out cold, too confused to feel anything, hearing my words as mere distant music or noise from someone too frightened to hear. I begin to respond to his possibly global confusion. I might say, "Maybe what happened to you and what you feel is all one big mess that just hurts. Maybe you don't know *what* it all is." So I begin another sequence, perhaps without specifically thinking of it as another sequence. It occurs to me that this global confusion might be full of crazy stuff too. I say, "When a person gets *too* hurt, sometimes a lot of strange stuff goes on in him. I don't know about you but I know about *that kind* of thing."

Even a Few Minutes Help. Unless we *arrange* fifty-minute hours with a patient, he does not expect that. In a hospital, I leave myself free. I come when I can. Only if I really know that I certainly will be there on Tuesdays, do I tell the patient that. Often I do not say how long I am coming to stay. I do not leave abruptly. When I want to leave, I usually say I will go, and then I stay a little longer.

But this may be after ten minutes. Especially if I am tense or the patient has been very violently rejecting of me (sometimes patients are totally silent *except* to say quite verbally, "Go away, don't come anymore, can't you understand that?"), I might impose myself on him only briefly, both for his sake and for mine. I might say, "I know you said you don't want me to come anymore. I won't stay long." Then I might stay only a few minutes.

Other more verbal patients may stop me in the hallway. I speak with them intensely for a few minutes. They may know that I cannot stay long. They accept my moving on quite soon, but I listen intently and respond to what is going on deeply within me in the time I do spend. In this way I can carry a somewhat larger number of relationships than I otherwise could.

It is a mistake to think we should not respond therapeutically to patients if we cannot commit ourselves to them totally for many whole hours. This view comes from concern not for patients but for therapists and clinical agencies and out of tradition. It is true that if you help someone open up his feelings he may then be more trouble than if he had not been responded to. (But he may also be less trouble as a result.) We are protecting *ourselves*, not the patient, when we say, "If you can't commit hours and months, don't respond at all." For the patient, a few minutes can be of crucial help. The experience of making sense to another person and living less autistically, even for a few minutes, may provide something the patient can keep and work with for weeks. I mention this here because one of the ways in which a few minutes can help involves the following principle that is important in working with the silent and unresponsive patient.

The Continuing Interaction. The patient can live in interaction with me even when I am not there. Let us say I have spent a few minutes—fifty, twenty or five—with my silent and unresponsive patient. Now I leave. He is more alive and upset, perhaps more of a "self" inside than before. He hates me (for example) because I make him hope and he cannot stand the pain that comes the moment he hopes. So he fights it down. He is again totally still, empty inside. He goes to lunch, waits in line, silently, thinking to himself, "Maybe, next time he comes, I'll hit him." He visualizes all that, sees and feels it, decides not to hit me. "Maybe I'll tell him I'm going to hit him." He experiences all this, imagines it, decides he won't say anything to me, ever. He eats lunch. He thinks maybe he will tell me he isn't any of the things I say; he is just angry at what "they" did to him (perhaps to himself he calls them "the jury" or "the machine" or what not); he decides not to tell me because it will sound crazy. He decides never to say anything. He finds himself "talking to me," saying this and that to me, justifying himself, explaining, wishing, demanding, carrying on; catches himself, decides to say nothing to me, ever. He returns to the day room and sits in his corner, as usual, looking at the floor. That reminds him of my having sat next to him. He kicks the chair hard, away from him. His heart pounds, he is live anger. The attendants come over. He subsides, thinks of nothing or tries to think of nothing. Visitors are announced on the loudspeaker for another patient. His tears seem to want to come. He chokes them down, finds himself mentally telling me how busy his own folks are, why they can't come to visit him. He imagines that he finds himself crying with me, gets furious, decides to tell me nothing, ever, thinks perhaps he will tell me that nobody has any use for him. It is only one hour since I left.

Naturally enough, when I come the next Tuesday he is totally silent again, as if nothing had intervened. But a lot has happened, some of it in the context of talking to me, feeling with and at me.

For this reason, the *kind* of interaction I have with a patient seems to me much more important than exactly what I talk about. Even if he says nothing and even if everything I say is foolishness and fits him not at all, I believe that this kind of interaction and pointing at feelings gives him a context to live in, imagine in and relate in during the many, many hours when I am not there, as well as when I am.

Making Contact. Apart from these examples of what I might *say,* there are also things I *do* to make contact with my patient. I might get down on the floor in front of him and look up into his face for a moment. I might explain it as: "Sometimes I get to wishing you'd look up at me." I would not do it for long, but if our eyes met once, I would be glad, and say so.

I might put my hand on his shoulder, or I might grasp his hand. I might do this in some context or in my effort to reach him somehow. (Perhaps I first said, "I sure want to hear *something* from you.")

Isolated people need physical touch, especially children, whom one can pick up and hug. I think children are not different for being my patients from any other children. We deprive them of what we would easily give normal children (and these need more) when we refuse to hug them because they are patients.

Similarly, with an adult, physical touch is often the only way to make contact. I make my touching a mode that won't be confusing, sexual-like, or frightening. It is a message, a contact, a firm holding of hand. Or I hold shoulders, keeping my arms extended and stiff. It is a way of saying, "You. I am looking for you." It is important, then and later, that the patient is not threatened by, or forced to speculate about, the possibility of a sexual pass or overture. These are frequent in hospitals and even more prevalent in patients' minds. However, other forms of physical contact, like being pushed about by aides, are just as prevalent. A firm grasp of a shoulder confuses few patients. In many contexts it is the only clear, fast and impactful way of saying, "I am here, and I know you are here."

Interview Behavior II: Silent But Responsive

In this section please picture a patient who says very little. He may offer barely understandable, highly compressed, summary statements like "Must be somebody has a use for a person" or "I'd like to take them and shake them." For the most part, he is silent. However, he is highly responsive. He looks at the therapist at times, can look quickly away or down, and back again. He may stand, sit, walk away quickly, come back. He may jump backward three paces if what I say disturbs him. He may get angry and seem to walk at me as if to walk through me. His face tells every moment that something new is happening, though the therapist may have only a vague sense of what it is.

The "silent but responsive" patient today may be the same individual who was silent and totally unresponsive at first. Or the patient may be "silent but responsive" from the start. When he is quite silent for long periods, much of what I said in category I will apply. "Silent But Responsive" is a category of in-therapy behavior, not a category of patient. I will again present procedures applicable at the beginning and then mention procedures appropriate later in therapy.

ACCEPTING REJECTION. It is all right with me—though I surely do not like it—when the patient rejects me. Suppose as I sit down, intending to keep the patient a few minutes of silent company, he gets up and sits down elsewhere. As I join him, he angrily moves away again. I call that "responsive," compared to no reaction at all. Now it is not the case that I have nothing to work with except what I bring. The patient is doing and expressing a lot. He gives me a lot to work with if I can tolerate it.

If he continues to leave wherever I go, then I stay where I am, and let him stay there. This is an interaction. He is there but he knows I am here, waiting. He won't join me, but he knows I am here. Much is happening. The whole day room may be tense with it. Or this may occur in an office: he walks out into the hall. Now he is out there and knows I am here. Or I may go out and stand next to him. If he leaves again, I may walk within sight of him and then stop and stay there. The ongoing interaction is a tensed rubber band between us.

My assumption is that I can be rejected. It is not a bad thing for him, if I can take it. How often has he repeatedly rejected someone who nevertheless continued to want to know him? Almost certainly never.

A few minutes of this can be very important. After a while I can go. Before I go I want *some* contact with him. I might say loudly, "I'll see you Friday," and go. Or if he stays within closer hearing distance long enough, I might say, "I know you don't want me to, but I think I can help and I'll be back."

If he will stay where we can talk, I might say, "Why be so scared?" or "I wish you'd stay put for a minute." or (if I see it on his face) "I guess you're mad at me for not leaving you alone," to which his face might say, "Damn right!" and I might then join in a harder-sounding way of talking: "Yeah, but what good is it if I leave you alone, you'd just stay in here. You've been here—how long? Whatever it is, it's probably long enough. What good am I to you if I leave you alone? That doesn't help anybody." Or his face might say, "You're strange; I don't get you at all; what are you doing?" to which I would say, perhaps, hard and briefly: "I'm a doctor and I sometimes can help people in here. Quit running away from me—I'm not gonna do anything to you." Or I'll just say, "It's all right. I'll be back Friday." Only a few minutes do I impose myself this way, but before I go I want a moment to indicate I have not been overly hurt. Perhaps I just wave good-bye from a distance and go.

Often the patient will refuse to come to a therapy office, yet he will be quite willing to meet the therapist in the day room or hallway. He knows he is free to walk away. Therefore, when he continues to stand next to me, I know I am not imposing upon his freedom if I stay. We stand in the hall. He says nothing. I say the same type of things I already have outlined, but his face and posture respond. Then I respond to that. "I don't know for sure, but maybe you feel . . ." whatever I get from his gesture or motions. I end many such responses with, "But, of course, I don't really know what you feel, that's just what I imagine" or "That's just what *I* was thinking maybe you felt, then, when you jumped away from me."

Many instances of rejecting the therapist require such an interim period of uncommitted hall meetings, in which the patient is free to walk away, but does not.

I must now mention a series of procedures that involve my actions, before I can deal more fully with this largely subverbal therapeutic interaction.

BEING ACTIVE. If little therapy is happening, the broadest scope of action is desirable. I find it helps me to shift, move, get up, sit down, go for a drink, tell about how my day has been (briefly), smoke, offer cigarettes (as I would do with anyone who is with me when I take out a cigarette), offer to buy him a soda (as I would with anyone when I buy myself a soda), and generally widen what I might do to include whatever occurs to me.

OFFERING HEALTH-APPROACHING ACTIVITY. Any patient activities closer to what healthy people do is probably a good thing. If the patient just sits, then looking up is probably a good thing. If he is always in the hospital, then going out on the grounds and to the canteen is probably toward health. If he will come to the nearby store with me (off the grounds) that is probably toward health. One can see the patient getting his land legs back. "Gee," he thinks, "I still know how to go to a store! I can still get around." Perhaps at first he is frightened, goes up to the counter, stands, lets others go ahead, backs off again, no cigarettes bought.

Perhaps we walk into the store together and immediately he wants to leave ("It's too crowded."). But whatever move he can make toward ordinary health is probably a good thing.

Long before he is willing, I invite him to come outside on the grounds with me to the canteen. He does not even answer perhaps, but then I say that I think he might later want to, and *I'd like that. I thought he might, some time.* This process moves from the candy or soda machines, downstairs to the canteen, to the store outside the hospital, to going downtown to a drug store, bar or store.

HELPING THE PATIENT RECONNECT. Long before he is really ready, the patient needs to be invited and helped to reconnect himself to the outside world. We professionals have cut up the field so that one profession, "psychotherapy," is supposed to move the patient from the sick stage (occurring in the office) to the nearly well stage. At that point another profession (social work) is supposed to help the patient with the world he returns to. Still another profession (vocational rehabilitation) works with his possible job, and so on. These other professions often refuse to help until the patient is "well enough," but the patient is not cut up into such slices. He is all one piece and often falls into the gaps between our professions. I have (rather painfully) learned that if I want my patient to move toward getting well, I have to be willing to do these things *before* he is "well enough." I will say, "Later on we will help you find a job in the city; you might want that then." I say this at a time when the patient cannot even talk. I also say, "I know you can't do that now, but you might be able to, later." Getting reconnected to the world (and perhaps in a situation different from that in which he became sick) is an essential part of the process of getting well. It must not be left "until the patient is ready," or he won't become so.

One of our very good therapists saw his patient for more than two years once or twice weekly. She was often silent and very quiet. Finally he became impatient and urged her to think about getting out of the hospital, perhaps with the aid of vocational rehabilitation set up by the therapist. She responded by saying, "I've been wondering if you'd ever want to *help* me." It seems she had much appreciated this nice man's coming to see her and had silently hoped that sometime he might wish to help her. To her that meant help with her whole situation, not just some truncated separate part (her feelings or "illness").

"Schizophrenia" is being disconnected from the world, rather than in interaction with it. One cannot get well from it first and then become reconnected and interact in the world.

I must invite the patient long before he is ready. After a time, we go to the soft drink machine, the canteen, the store, the city, a job. (Of course, I have time for this only with some. I try to arrange for someone else who will do this with other patients.)

OPPORTUNITIES FOR INTERACTION. When activities no longer serve as therapeutic vehicles, they can be stopped. Such stopping gives opportunities for therapeutic work. Patients get used to having soft drinks and taking walks, and therein lie two pitfalls: (a) that I shall have trouble bringing to an end for the patient a particularly desirable pattern—a convenient way of getting soft drinks, cigarettes, time out of the hospital—when it ceases to be producing therapeutic movement. Making this break used to be difficult for me, but now I use my feelings of this difficulty just as I use my other feelings. For example, "I don't want to buy you soda anymore—it makes me think now that I'm just keeping things the same, when really you could go out and work and buy your own sodas. So it doesn't seem right anymore. But I worry that I'm letting you down now, when I say this. After all, I was the one who first invited you to accept sodas. In those days you didn't want to take anything from anyone. I kind of forced it on you and I know that." (b) that the patient will not begin therapy at all but will take me for a Gray Lady whose purpose is to make his life slightly better with the soft drinks and canteen. To these patients I say often, "You know, what I am here for is to help you with what keeps you in the hospital," or "And now it's time you tell me something of how you feel, if you can and want to." "Whatever hurts you and has you stuck, so you aren't getting out of here, that's what I'm supposed to help you with. I know you might not think you can get out of here, or maybe you don't want to, or you aren't sure what you want, but I guess you know, *I* want you out of here. I am looking forward to meeting you in town, in my office. I really can't stand for you to be in here."

Aside from constituting the movement toward health, candy and soda machines and stores provide vehicles for ongoing interaction. You will see that many of my examples in the next section concern my interaction with a patient in front of the candy machine, in the drugstore or in going from the day room to the machine downstairs. For these reasons, I have mentioned these things here.

Occupational therapy was once intended to be this type of vehicle—supplying events so that therapists could respond to patients. In many hospitals it has degenerated into making belts and wallets, usually in silence. (The patient usually does not need a wallet, let alone three!) It has been largely forgotten that such activities were intended to be situational occasions to help interaction occur so that therapeutic responding might thereby be possible.

But one *need* not do all this. Even with the patient I see occasionally for a few minutes in the hall, *there is a situation:* where we should stand, how he feels about others listening, my hurrying away so soon. His and my feelings in any *situation* are a vehicle for therapeutic responding, especially if the patient is only subverbally responsive.

DOUBLING BACK. Some of my feelings about him in the situation are a good source of responses, if I tell them in a personal, detailed way. The patient we are speaking about may be silent or not, but he is responsive. Every moment something is happening with him, and he shows some of it. Perhaps I cannot be sure just what he feels, but I see he feels *something.* (Note: we are almost always wrong in guessing just what someone feels, but never in seeing visibly that he feels *some* reaction. One can talk to, refer to and accept that reaction, whatever it is, without ever knowing *what* it is!)

One whole set of feelings I have for others in situations comes to me at first simply as discomfort. As I look to see why I am uncomfortable I find content relevant to the person I am with, to what we just did or said. Often it is quite personal. I was stupid, rude, hurrying, embarrassed, avoidant, on the spot; I wish I didn't have to go since he wants me to stay. I wish I hadn't hurried him out of the store in front of all those people; I feel bad that I don't know what to say; I am embarrassed that the nurses see us looking silent and stupid; I wish I had a chair to sit down on.

As we get outside the store (after I have had to insist that we leave), I might say, "Now I'm sad that I embarrassed you in there. I am always worrying about being late and I get rattled. But I wish I hadn't rushed you in front of all those people—that bad feeling is just what I wish you didn't have to put up with."

Or, as we arrive downstairs at the candy machine, where we are alone, I might tell him, "I am never as comfortable upstairs where everybody listens to us" or "I didn't feel like saying this to you upstairs, I just didn't feel at ease with all the aides watching us."

Or "just then, when you made that face, I didn't say anything about it because I didn't know what to say, but now I wonder, are you mad at me?" or "I don't mind us standing here, but I am getting tired standing. I wish we could go to the lounge, downstairs, where I could sit down." So, a week later, he might lead me to the lounge; it is clear to both of us that this is not what *he* wants, we are doing that for *me* because I get tired standing. "I am very glad you want to do that for me. Thanks!"

Or "I guess you're mad at me because I'm leaving. I don't feel good about it either. It just never feels right to me to go away and leave you in here. I have to go, or else I'll be late for everything I have to do all day today, and I'll feel lousy about that." Silence. "In a way, I'm glad you don't want me to go. I wouldn't like it at all if you didn't care one way or the other."

These examples have in common that I express feelings of mine which are at first troublesome or difficult, the sort I would at first tend to ignore in myself. It requires a kind of *doubling back*. When I first notice it, I have *already* ignored, avoided or belied my feelings—only now do I notice what it was or is. I must double back to express it. At first, this seems a sheer impossibility! How can I express this all-tied-up, troublesome, puzzling feeling? Never! But a moment later I see that it is only another perfectly human way to feel and in fact includes much concern for the patient and empathic sensitivity to him. It is him I feel unhappy about—or what I just did to him.

A very warm and open kind of interaction is created in telling my feelings this way. I am not greatly superior, wiser or better than the other people in the patient's life. I have as many weaknesses, needs and stupidities. But the other people in his life rarely extend him this type of response.

THE INWARD SIDE OF A FEELING. What I term the "inward side" of a feeling is the safest aspect to express. We tend to express the *outer* edges of our feelings. That leaves *us* protected and makes the other person unsafe. We say, "This and this (which *you* did) hurt me." We do not say, "This and this weakness of mine *made me be* hurt when you did this and this."

To find this inward edge of me in my feelings, I need only ask myself, "Why?" When I find myself bored, angry, tense, hurt, at a loss, or worried, I ask myself, "Why?" Then, instead of "You bore me" or "This makes me mad," I find the "why" *in me* which makes it so. That is always more personal and positive and much safer to express. Instead of "You bore me," I find "I want to hear more personally from you" or "You tell me what happened, but I want to hear also what it all meant to you." Instead of saying, "When you move so slowly and go back three times, it makes me mad," I say, "I get to thinking that all our time will be gone and I'll have to go without having done a thing for you, and that will bother me all day."

It is surprising how positive are the feelings in us which first come up as anger, impatience, boredom or criticism. However, it is natural, since our needs with the patient are nearly all positive ones for him. I need to be effective in helping him. I need to be successful in helping him arrive at his truth and a way to live. I need to feel therapeutic. When my feelings are for the moment constricted, tense, bad, sad or critical, it is because in terms of some of these very positive needs I have with him, we have gone off the track. No wonder then that when I ask "why" concerning my bad feelings, the emergent answer is positive feelings. I am bored because I want to hear more personal, feeling-relevant things from him. I am angry because our time is being wasted— the time on which I count to be an effective therapist. I am critical of him because I wish something better for him.

But often there is also a peculiarity of mine involved, and this must be expressed. Do such expressions make the patient feel that the therapist is weak, in need of help or unreliable? I make sure the patient knows I can perfectly well stand what I feel. I will not say much about my unresolved personal problems or situations. I might say, "Today I feel rattled about something that happened to me. It isn't too bad, but it means I might have trouble with the people I work with downtown." Again, here my way of saying it conveys that I know what it is and I can stand it.

OPENNESS TO WHAT COMES NEXT. A response is not in itself right or wrong. One must be sensitive to the *next* moment, the patient's reaction to the response. If I can respond sensitively and well to his reaction at the *next* moment, even if I just said something foolish, hurtful or wrong, a meaningful and positive interaction will emerge.

I used to ponder whether I was about to say a right or wrong thing. Then, if it was wrong (as I could tell from the patient's reaction), I would not know what to do. Now, I spend moments letting my feelings clarify themselves, but once they feel clear, I no longer wonder so much whether it is right or wrong to express them. Rather, I have open curiosity, sensitivity and a readiness to meet whatever reaction I will get. This may tell me what I said was "wrong," but all will be well if *now* I respond sensitively to what I have stirred. I now say whatever I now sense which *makes* what I said before "wrong." (It is not my admission that I was wrong which matters here. I rarely make a point of having been wrong. That matters only to me. I am the only one who cares how often I am right or wrong. But whatever it is in him which I now sense and which *makes* what I said wrong, I now see it in his further reaction—*that* is what I have to respond to at the next moment.)

ALMOST ANYTHING IS AN OPPORTUNITY FOR FURTHER INTER-ACTION. Under these circumstances a very intense and eventful interaction occurs. Perhaps on the side of the patient it is non-verbal but visible and active. On the therapist's side, it involves both the concrete moves and facial expressions he cannot help and the verbalizing of his thought processes. Many therapists have remarked about the schizophrenic patient's "exquisite sensitivity." There is a great deal of subverbal patient response. The therapist must respond further to make *further* interaction proceed with warmth and openness.

Therefore, when I have taken a patient out to some stores and then want to discontinue it, I may actually welcome the difficulty. It is an occasion for a close interaction. I will have to tell him that I feel bad about letting him down on a promise, perhaps say that I well remember it was I who first invited him. Perhaps he feels let down, betrayed, angry, disappointed, or what? Whatever it is, we won't hide from each other. I will also tell him I feel it is not a new breakthrough thing anymore. I want to see him well soon and able to go places alone. I don't feel useful anymore doing this and I don't feel good if I think I am not useful. (Or whatever I do feel, in some form I can tell him.)

In these last sections, I have emphasized bad, troublesome or difficult therapist feelings, because they offer rich sources of personal, positive responding. Of course, I also have many "good" feelings. For these, too, I need a few moments to find a form in which to say them. It is most noteworthy, however, that just in those instances in which we feel stuck or sense that we have just fallen down or are strongly puzzled over what to do next, we have incipient therapeutic responses, if we allow what we sense to become clarified in ourselves. After all, the patient is someone who has difficulties in relating. The patient can move beyond these only if the therapist moves beyond them as he feels them in terms of himself.

IF THE PATIENT CANNOT BEAR ANY RESPONSE WHILE HE TALKS. Sometimes a patient who says a few things after a long silence is sorely oversensitive and cannot bear anything I say in response. If he winces in pain at whatever I say, I am content to be silent.

I just nod when I understand, or I ask for a repetition. I keep my responses and make them *later,* when he is no longer trying to say something to me. At that time, I make them *mine,* rather than loading them on him. I need not imply, "What *you* said meant . . ." or "means to me. . . ." Rather, I probably say, "I've been thinking—maybe you feel . . ." (as I would put it if it were all my own). Some patients can stand anything *I* think but cannot bear the same statements as implications of what *they* have said. It is as if what they said is all that can be stood and *no more.*

Compressed, Hard-To-Understand Patient Speech Can Be Responded to Bit by Bit. When an isolated, autistic person at last tries to speak with someone, twenty significant allusions may trip over each other in one sentence. I will say, "Just a minute. I want to understand. I understood when you said so-and-so, and I know, I think, that this made you feel such-and-such. Is that right? (Yes.) And then you said . . . and I didn't know what you meant by that. I got you up to there. Tell me again from there. Did I hear it right?" The patient may have said ten or twenty things before I stopped him, and I grasped only the first little thing. But the patient is soon glad to repeat and expand, as he senses that the therapist really wants to grasp each thing, and from then on I really do grasp each thing one by one.

I never let such a patient mumble on. The therapist's bit-by-bit solid grasp and response is like a pier in the patient's sea of autism and self-loss. As each bit is tied to another person who grasps it, the vast, lost, swampy weirdness goes out of things. It is not a matter of this or that content as much as the autistic, isolated manner of feeling and living. If I let him talk, I can then make only a general response which does not affect the patient's lonely autism. The therapist's bit-by-bit grasping and response is needed.

Interview Behavior III: Verbal But Externalized

The third type of interview behavior characteristic of many hospitalized individuals is free and reality-oriented verbalization, none of it "therapeutically relevant" in the usual sense. It is all about external events, about what others did or do, what happened dur-

ing the week, and so forth. This third category of interview behavior is common not only in hospitals but also in ordinary outpatient psychotherapy. Nearly every therapist has worked for a long
period with an individual who spoke almost never about his feelings and affective meanings but almost always about situations
and events. Coming to psychotherapy meetings can mean very
much to these people. It can be like a life raft for them. One
knows something of importance is happening. But it is not psychotherapy, as the repetitions over the years eventually show.
Without rejecting or destroying the desperately needed support
which such a relationship does give, how can we bring into it the
missing therapeutic process?

This "verbal but externalized" group included a number of our
hospitalized patients as well as most of our *normal* subjects. Thus
one should not assume too quickly that externalized talking indicates abject fear, "schizophrenic flattened affect" or unusually
great repression. Perhaps externalized talking also indicates that
the individual does not feel it to be appropriate to express his
feelings. Whether the individual is labeled normal, neurotic or
schizophrenic, verbal but externalized interview behavior presents the same problem and demands some of the same kinds of
response from the therapist.

THE INTERNAL FRAME OF REFERENCE REDEFINED. I respond in
such a way that what I say about the individual's feelings *can be
checked by him if he will directly refer to what he feels.* Quite
often, unfortunately, he will not try to check what I say, will not
try to pay inward attention to his felt meaning. But my responses
are intended and phrased so that he *could* directly find and feel
what I say. My response achieves its purpose if he refers directly
to his felt meaning. My responses need not be correct; it is just
as helpful if it results in "— No, it's really more like. . . ."

Rogers[17] called this type of therapist response "taking the client's
internal frame of reference." As I define it, such a response says
something which *could be* directly found and felt by the client.
It is not an explanation, generalization, external observation or
behavior definition. What is it then? It is a statement such that
if the individual will attend inwardly directly to his whole "feel"

of what he is saying or doing just then, he will find there the feeling or meaning at which my response points. Or if I am not quite right, he will find there whatever *is* there.

This type of response moves from the sharply defined units of speech (in what he *says*) to the as yet undefined (but directly felt) mass of personal meanings and feelings he has as he speaks.

For example, the client is angry (says or shows it) or, more exactly, he *might be* angry (so often my first impression is wrong). But in addition to a well-defined unit (like "anger") there is always a whole mesh of feelings and meanings. He is angry *at* me *for* doing such and such *because* it seemed to prove I did not care for him in a certain important way, and this upsets him *because* he had invested himself and now feels let down, which makes him feel desperate and makes him vow not to get "conned" again as he has so often before, when he . . . . This chain is just an example of the texture always implicit in felt meanings. Therapeutic movement in depth consists of such further steps into a felt meaning. I want to respond to the felt meaning so that he will attend to it and move such steps. I can do that by pointing my words at "this whole way you feel" without knowing much about it. (Any bit I do sense helps me phrase a more specific pointer.) I *point* there and invite the client to look there. I would like to know what he really *does* find as he looks there. I am gladly corrected if he finds something different or if other words seem to him to fit better.

For example, I say, "I guess you're scared." He checks against his feeling of it and says, "No, I'm not scared at all, I'm determined." I accept that. The word "determined" better names what he has there. Whatever he names it, I want to hear more from it. He continues, "—— determined not to let them get me, not this time, by God!" Now I am hearing more from it. Again I respond, "They've always got you before, but you've made up your mind, you won't give in now." "Right, and another thing is . . ." (I prize this "and another thing is"; another thing usually will come up when we move into felt meaning). "And another thing is . . . the way they get me is . . . I start to say, 'No, I won't go along with it' but then I get mad and I don't get mad like I should, but instead I go to pieces, I get all nutty, I carry on, and then they've got me."

Notice that if I am a stickler I can insist that of course this patient *is* scared. I was right in the first place. But we would not get into felt specifics if I stick at general words. It does not make much useful sense to say he *is* or he *is not* scared. What he has there is always a texture of much more specific felt facets. He *is* (if you insist) scared *of* that which he is "determined" to avoid. I am content with any words and any corrections of what I say, so long as we can keep *pointing* at his present mesh of felt meaning and taking concrete steps in it.

An Imagined Felt Referent. Even when I know perfectly well that the client is not working on anything, I ask myself what *might* he be working on if he *had* said this given thing as part of a therapeutic exploration? That leads me to sense or imagine an aspect of it which he might feel and which can set a therapeutic process into motion.

Creating an "It." Even when the patient does not indicate that he has any tissue felt meaning there at all, I create it. I imagine it: a felt sense of "all that" he has there, feels and *could* pay attention to if only he would! I have no sharp idea what it might be like, but I can respond deeply, even with my vague sense of it. For instance, he says, "She'll take me for every cent I've got" (meaning his wife, who is getting a divorce). I know he is not "working on" anything therapeutically now. Yet, if he were, he might what?—look at his whole texture of felt meanings concerning his marriage, his being imposed upon, his helpless feelings, his passivity, his important anger, his sense that some of his perceptions are after all realistic and trustworthy. He is not intending to look at, or work on, any of these themes, but I can invite him to just by responding, "And what's awful is, here you are, helpless to do a thing about it." Perhaps his next remark enables me again to point at a felt referent. I nearly always point at felt referents. If one in a hundred opens out, that is an adequate percentage for movement.

Referring Interpretations Back to Patient's Speech or Act. Whatever general (diagnostic or other) conclusion or impression

I have of him, I received it *from him*—from his behavior and speech. I can give it to him best if I remind myself how he gave me this impression. Then I can respond to that more specific feeling, statement or behavior rather than giving him only the general conclusion. For example, I can say, "When you said . . . it got me to thinking . . ." Another example: "The way you stand there so sadly—it looks sad to me, I don't really know—it makes me wonder whether maybe you think they won't visit you, even though you say they will . . ."

Anything Is "an Opener." I can choose to look at anything said as only an opener to a more personal communication. If the patient sees me smoking and says, "Smoking is bad for you," I take it as an opener to relate, to talk about me, touch me, discuss both his and my self-destructive behaviors, weaknesses and so forth. Similarly, if the patient says, "Can you get me a weekend pass?" (I know I can't), this can become an opener to a conversation about me, him, wishing to get out of the hospital, home, the people he would see if he went home, whether they really want to see him or not, etcetera. Of course, nine times out of ten my attempts at such a conversation fail, but the tenth time I succeed in developing it.

Retroactive Responding. If I wish I had responded some way a few minutes ago or last week, I do so now. (I used to think I had to wait until the client brought it up again.) I might say, "You know, a while back, when you said such and such, well, now I think about that, and I think . . ." or "Last week, when I drove home, I thought that maybe you . . ."

Untwisting. I will not remain what I call "twisted." If the patient has somehow gotten me to seem in a way I do not feel, then I no longer feel "straight." I feel "twisted." Perhaps I am responding socially, smiling, while actually I know we are avoiding something. Or perhaps I have promised something I do not wish. I feel "twisted" out of my own shape, and I will not stay that way. It may take me a few minutes to work my way out, but I won't silently let it pass. Soon I will say, "I think now that I don't want to do this thing, which I promised a while ago. I don't feel good about disappointing you, and maybe, if you're mad, you're right—but I won't do it." or "Well, a while ago that business about so and so seemed real fine, and we both said it was great, but now I wonder, maybe are you making it sound better than it is?" Such instances are opportunities for more direct relating between us.

No UNMENTIONABLES. Anything that seems unmentionable is really an opportunity for more direct relating. If the client implies (or I sense) some very painful, threatening thing, I respond to it. I believe the client *already* has and lives such a thing, if it is there (if, as he checks inside himself, he finds it there), and I cannot protect him from that. I have the choice only whether to leave him alone with it or keep him interactive company with it. I won't wait until the client brings it up himself. He is probably doing just that, right now, as best he is able.

Often the patient refers to something which is unmentionable because it "dare not be," can not be tolerated; for example, "that they don't care for me"; "that I am crazy"; "that the therapist doesn't care for me"; "that I am ugly" and so forth. It helps if I speak these out loud. The patient is still here. He has not been shattered. I phrase it with a "maybe" so we can back out if need be. I say almost lightly, "Maybe you're awful scared you really *are* crazy." or "Maybe I don't care for you at all" or "Maybe you're too ugly for anybody to like." The result is usually relief. I respect the patient, not the trap he is caught in.

TWO-SIDED COMPOUND. The reasons against expressing something must also be included. Whatever in my feelings holds me back from expressing something, that too I can express, and in fact, I *can* express the two-sided compound, whereas I did not feel I could express just the one feeling.

For example, to say just, "I think maybe you're very scared that you really are crazy," might scare him all the more because he might feel that *I* think he is. Actually, he often makes very good sense about many things and if I express that too, "Actually, you make very good sense about a lot of things," the first sentence becomes a safe one. This therapist expression becomes possible for me as I decide to voice also that which at first stopped me from expressing my feeling. Another example: "I don't like it when you do that, and I don't want you to do it anymore. *But I think you do it to* . . . and I like *that*."

POSITIVE RECOGNITION. That last example illustrates a special case, the case where I need to set a limit or call a halt to some behavior. I can do this more easily (and I think more therapeutically) when I find and voice the patient's positive thrust in so acting. For example, I might not let a patient touch me or grab me. I will stop the patient, but in the same words and gesture I will try to respond positively to the positive desire for closeness or physical relations. I will make personal touch with my hand as I hold the patient away from me, contact the patient's eyes and declare that I think the physical reaching out is positive and I welcome it, even though I cannot allow it. (I know at such times that I may be partly creating this positive aspect. Perhaps this reaching is more hostile right now than warm. But there is warmth and health in anyone's sexual or physical need, and I can recognize that as such.) The total effect of such stopping is therapeutic and positive, a moment of contact, because I have expressed not only the limit but I have also met the positive thrust.

We often find it difficult to set limits because we fear to hurt. I do not say, "I'm afraid to hurt your feelings," but rather I say what these feelings are in him (which one might fear to hurt). I can recognize these in him, and usually they are positive.

THERAPIST-SUPPLIED AFFECTIVE MEANING. The patient talks, perhaps gets much value from having a friendly caring listener, but nothing of therapeutic relevance is said. There is only talk about hospital food, the events of the week, the behavior of others, a little anger or sadness, no exploration.

I become the one who expresses the feelings and felt meanings. I say, "What a spot to be in!" or "Gee, and they don't even *care* what *you* think about it," or "I guess that leaves you feeling helpless, does it?" or "Boy, that would make *me* mad," or "It must be sad that he doesn't care more for you than *that*," or "I don't know, of course, but I wonder, do you wish you *could* get mad, but maybe you don't dare?" or "I guess you could cry about that, if let yourself cry."

Sometimes I must retell the events in such a way that the probable felt meaning emerges. For example, "So your mother and your husband decide even which laundry you should send your stuff to. I guess they decide everything. Not much of a home of your own? Must be a helpless feeling?" (Patient says nothing.) "Maybe kind of *insulting* to you?"

Sometimes I say such things on my own responsibility: "I wish they'd care for you more than they seem to."

At first the patient's only reaction may be a brief blank look, after which he resumes his narrative, grateful that I let him (that I do not stop us and insist on the feelings to which I pointed). I am always willing to let him ignore what I say and go on; that helps him to stand my expressing such feelings.

THERAPIST TRUTHFULNESS. I try not to do anything phoney, artificial, untrue, distracting or unreal, ever. Of course I do many phoney things before I even notice them, but that gives me a chance to double back and express the truth. We must help patients live with, in and through what *does* confront them, the world they *already do* live in. The patient can successfully live only with what *is* there. There is no way to live with what is not, with falsehoods, with artificial roles played by psychologists. One cannot learn to live with the untrue, no matter how good its untruth might be. Really, the untrue is not there in a fullness that can be lived *with*. On the other hand, saying what is true helps because it is *already* there and one can learn to live with it better and differently.

For the therapist to be committed to the truth has another advantage: truth has its own check within the patient's (or the therapist's) felt mesh of experiencing. To seek truth we need not be bright, or guess rightly, or choose wisely.

THE CLIENT-CENTERED RESPONSE. Whenever there is anything to respond *to*, when the patient says, does, conveys or acts out anything, then the best response is still the client-centered response. In such a response I attempt as plainly and purely as possible to voice my impression of what the patient means and feels at this moment. Nothing else is as helpful and powerful as that sort of response. It lets the patient know that he has been understood;

it focuses his attention on his felt referents so that he can check what is said and carry it further; it shows him that I consider his felt meanings the ultimate deciding basis for what is true and what is not; it generates the therapeutic process of experiential movement; it tends to lead him to pay attention directly to his felt meanings without distorting them by what he or I may think; it lifts erstwhile private, hardly bearable aspects into the non-autistic interpersonal world; it lets the patient experience not only what he already knows he feels, but also what he almost but not quite feels (so that he feels it clearly, after it is spoken of); it keeps my own person and feelings clearly separate from his person and feelings so that there is room for both to be clear and undistorted; and it is the only way I know in which feelings that are too chaotic, weird and painful to bear can come to be lived with and borne. Such an interaction process provides solidity, clear intention, simplicity, respect and openness. Any feelings that are concretely lived in that manner become not only known, but also take on that manner. Therefore, their implicit sense and positive life thrust can emerge and the individual can come alive in a way that lessens the desperation and alters the very quality of these feelings.

Thus the various procedures I have described in this chapter are primarily used when the patient does *not* interact with me, is *not* (over a long period) saying, expressing or acting-out anything meaningful. When, through any of these channels, he *is* communicating meaningfully, then my response is the one long associated with client-centered therapy—the effort accurately to sense the client's felt meaning at that moment and to communicate to him my understanding of that meaning as clearly as possible.

REFERENCES

1. Bowen, M.: Family participation in schizophrenia. In *The Etiology of Schizophrenia*, edited by R. D. Jackson. New York, Basic Books, 1960.
2. Butler, J. M.: Client-centered counseling and psychotherapy. In *Progress in Clinical Psychology*. Vol. III: *Changing Conceptions in Psychotherapy*, edited by C. Brower and L. E. Abt. New York, Grune & Stratton, 1958.

3. Gendlin, E. T., and Zimring, F. M.: The qualities or dimensions of experiencing and their change. *Counseling Center Discussion Papers.* (Mimeographed). Chicago, University of Chicago Library, 1955, Vol. I, No. 3.
4. Gendlin, E. T.: Experiencing: a variable in the process of therapeutic change. *Am J Psychother, 15:*233-245, 1961.
5. Gendlin, E. T.: Initiating psychotherapy with "unmotivated" patients. *Psychiat Q, 35:*134-139, 1961.
6. Gendlin, E. T.: Client-centered developments and work with schizophrenics. *J Counsel Psychol, 9:*205, 1962.
7. Gendlin, E. T.: *Experiencing and the Creation of Meaning.* New York, The Free Press of Glencoe, 1962.
8. Gendlin, E. T.: Schizophrenia: Problems and methods of psychotherapy. *Rev Exist Psychol, 4:*168, 1964.
9. Gendlin, E. T.: A theory of personality change. In *Personality Change,* edited by P. Worchel, and D. Byrne. New York, John Wiley, 1964.
10. Gendlin, E. T.: Expressive meanings. In *Invitation to Phenomenology,* edited by J. Edie. Chicago, Quadrangle Books, 1965.
11. Heidegger, M.: *Being and Time.* New York, Harper & Row, 1962.
12. Jackson, D. D.: *The Etiology of Schizophrenia.* New York, Basic Books, 1960.
13. Maslow, A. H.: *Toward a Psychology of Being.* New York, Van Nostrand, 1962.
14. Mead, G. H.: *The Philosophy of the Act.* Chicago, University of Chicago Press, 1938.
15. Merleau-Ponty, M.: *Phenomenology of Perception.* New York, Humanities Press, 1962.
16. Rogers, C. R.: *Counseling and Psychotherapy.* Boston, Houghton Mifflin, 1942.
17. Rogers, C. R.: *Client-Centered Therapy: Its Current Practice, Implications, and Theory.* Boston, Houghton Mifflin, 1951.
18. Rogers, C. R.: The necessary and sufficient conditions of therapeutic personality change. *J Consult Psychol, 21:*95-103, 1957.
19. Seeman, J.: Client-centered therapy. In *Progress in Clinical Psychology,* edited by D. Brower and L. E. Abt. New York, Grune & Stratton, 1956, Vol. II, pp. 98-113.
20. Shlien, J. M.: A client-centered approach to schizophrenia: first approximation. In *Psychotherapy of the Psychoses,* edited by A. Burton. New York, Basic Books, 1961.
21. Sullivan, H. S.: *The Interpersonal Theory of Psychiatry.* New York, W. W. Norton, 1953.

Chapter 13

Psychotherapy with the Aged

MAX HAMMER

PROBABLY NO OTHER group has been denied an opportunity for psychotherapeutic assistance as much as have the aged. The reason for this probably relates in large measure to the feeling on the part of most psychotherapists that the patient's life is almost over and professional efforts might be wasted. There are also concerns about senility and other brain dysfunctions and a general rigidity of personality which leads many therapists to expect an extremely poor prognosis. Much of the pessimism related to working with the elderly can be attributed to the influence of Freud,[3] who saw geriatric rigidity as precluding successful analysis of the elderly. It was his opinion that "near or above the fifties, the elasticity of the mental processes, on which the treatment depends, is as a rule lacking . . . the old people are no longer educable." He also felt that "the mass of material to be dealt with would prolong the duration of the treatment indefinitely."

However, I believe probably the most important reason for pessimism relates to the personal countertransference feelings of the therapist which will be discussed in some greater detail in a later section of this chapter. At this time it suffices to say that I feel that the prevalent pessimism that exists in working therapeutically with elderly persons is basically unwarranted, for on the whole, I have found working with this group extremely rewarding. It is also my impression that psychotherapy may be less wasteful than other approaches to the problems of aging because of its broadly beneficial effects on the mental and physical health of the patient as well as the emotional and economic relief derived by family, friends and community.

376

This chapter will present the basic symptoms, psychodynamics and therapeutic problems that the psychotherapist is likely to confront in working with elderly persons, as well as suggestions in regard to various approaches which can be helpful in working psychotherapeutically with these persons.

SYMPTOMS OF AGED REFERRED FOR PSYCHOLOGICAL HELP

Typically, the symptoms that lead the person in advanced years to be referred for psychotherapy are not too unlike those found in most neurotic conditions. They include depression; anxiety; extreme obsessiveness or compulsive behavior; restlessness; quarrelsomeness; complaining; negativistic, agitated, clinging, dependent and childish behavior; threats of suicide; somatic complaints of all kinds; and sexual behavior unacceptable to the community ranging from exhibitionism to what is felt to be unreasonable desires in regard to remarriage.

Essentially, elderly persons are referred because they are considered a nuisance and an embarrassment to the family or community. These patients are frequently quite resistive to therapy because they see the therapist as an extension of the rejecting community and as someone who does not understand them and who wants coercively to make them change their attitudes and behavior. They resent the referral to the therapist because of its implication that they are "crazy."

In some instances, the family may be convinced that their aged relative is psychotic because of behavior associated with cerebral arteriosclerosis, but typically they are most concerned with what they feel is paranoid type behavior. Due to a heightened state of fearfulness and feelings of vulnerability, many elderly persons feel extremely insecure and easily threatened; also, because they feel so much outside of the mainstream of family life, they may develop attitudes which sound quite paranoid. They constantly verbalize that no one likes them or they feel certain that everyone dislikes them. They may insist that the family is just waiting for them to die so that they can collect the patient's financial savings. The patient may generalize even further and assume that because the family "wants" him to die that perhaps they are deliberately depriving him of the care and assistance he requires to survive.

It is not unusual to hear elderly patients voice feelings that a conspiracy exists to get them hospitalized or into some kind of institution for the aged. They feel certain that they are being "railroaded." Many times their intense reactions are not only related to feelings of extreme vulnerability but may also be the result of guilt feelings. They may verbalize to the therapist that they see themselves as a terrible bother, embarrassment and expense to the family, which leads them to believe that the family is justified in wanting them dead or out of the way. Most times these attitudes disappear with the security that comes with the development of the therapeutic relationship.

Depression

Depression is probably the most frequent psychological difficulty encountered in the aged. Depression is most often associated with some kind of loss, and the aged have to face and deal with a wide variety of losses. There are the losses through death of close relatives and old friends and the losses that come with separation when children are grown and not only leave home but frequently also leave the community in this highly mobile age in which we live. There are also losses associated with physical potency and also the loss of sexual potency and interest. The loss of sexual potency and interest means much more to the aged than just the loss of sexual gratification. Sexual libido is frequently unconsciously associated with the life force and its loss is quite often interpreted to confirm and remind the patient that he is close to death. There are also the losses in mental and physical ability and these may also serve as harbingers of their feared impending fate which also contributes greatly to their dysphoric state.

Declines in the effectiveness of sensory functioning such as impaired vision and hearing along with the added contamination at times of other central nervous system difficulties which may affect speech and other organs of communication contributes greatly to feelings of alienation and isolation in the elderly person. This impaired sensory functioning also serves to decrease the steady stream of incoming stimuli which deprives the elderly person of the pleasurable action and opportunities to affirm the sense of self which usually result from such stimuli and thereby also contributes to feelings of depression. Depression in the aged associated with a diminution in physical and sensory adequacy, can sometimes be relieved with close medical attention. The therapist who works with an elerly patient also needs to work very closely with the family physician because the psychological well-being of his elderly patient is very closely related to their physical well-being.

There are also losses in the older person's sense of self-esteem related to not feeling wanted or needed which can contribute to depression. The grown-up children are no longer in need of the aging parent, the spouse no longer needs him in terms of sexual gratification, and in many ways, he is considered a nuisance around the house. There are very few takers in regard to the wisdom he feels that he has accumulated over the years, and he also feels less needed in terms of his vocational skills now that he has been forced to retire. These are just typical of the many losses, along with losses in financial and emotional independence, which contribute toward a diminution of self-esteem and therefore contribute toward depression.

The loss of work opportunity and income also leads to deprivations and frustrations due to the necessity of having to readjust to a new standard of living which calls for the loss of various comforts and pleasures. Many times it may even necessitate a relocation, which can be quite traumatic for the elderly person due to the loss of the familiar and the secure. The loss of work opportunity also makes them lose the opportunity to sublimate which leads to greater regression and increased hostility or depression.

The aged feel terribly helpless and vulnerable because they feel that they are progressively losing control over themselves and the world in which they live and this makes them regress in search of someone to fill their needs for protective dependency. They may use depression as a means of getting their narcissistic and dependency needs met.

Many elderly people feel angry at the fates for robbing them of their strength and abilities, but because they have nothing tangible upon which to express their hostility, they suppress it. This suppressed hostility is another cause of depression in these people. Depression may also be the result of self-hatred and guilt related to the fact that they may blame themselves for not fulfilling their lifelong goals and ambitions and now they feel that it is too late. Rather than accept the conclusion that perhaps they never had exceptional ability, they tend instead to berate themselves for opportunities lost due to insufficient motivation or insight. This preserves the illusion that had they really tried, they probably could have succeeded, so that berating themselves for lack of motivation becomes a necessity even though it results in a depression.

Probably the most serious problem associated with depression in the aged is the tendency for suicide to seem an attractive solution to their state of unhappiness. The element of despair and hopelessness is what makes suicide a serious consideration. They feel that there is no longer any hope for them ever to achieve their goals and ambitions, the lost recognition or the lost physical and mental abilities which they once treasured so highly. The fact that they are convinced that nothing can change in their life, along with their fear of living with the loss of security, independence and gratifications, makes suicide a distinct possibility. When along with this there is the element of wanting to gain revenge on family members, because of real or fantasied hurts, through the humiliation that their suicide will bring to the family, then the possibility becomes a distinct likelihood.

Anxiety

Anxiety is another very prevalent symptom in those elderly persons who are referred for psychotherapy. All the basic anxieties known to man are found in their most intensified forms in the aged. Due to the fact that the elderly person tends to regress in an attempt to achieve a sense of protection and security, many of the fears which were so prevalent in infancy and childhood such as abandonment and separation anxiety, castration anxiety and death anxiety return now in an exaggerated form and add to his already highly insecure state.

Abandonment anxiety is aroused due to the death of many close relatives and friends and the loss of others due to emotional and physical separation. This intensifies his fears of unprotectedness, vulnerability and isolation. His enormous sense of insecurity many times will lead to the development of various kinds of phobias which is the regressed and weakened ego's attempt to deal with the diffuse and threatening anxiety.

Castration anxiety is roused due to the elderly person's recognition of his progressive loss of physical, mental and sexual potency, which are unconsciously interpreted as a castration. This may either lead to overreactive compensatory behavior in terms of increased attempts at demonstrating prowess in these various areas of deficiency or it may lead to overexaggerated fears of authority figures, with the result that the elderly patient feels that it is necessary to resist and compete with the therapist, for if he did not, such nonresistance would be seen as a submission and therefore a castration.

Death anxiety becomes more intense, of course, because of the recognition that more and more people of his age are dying and also because he is aware of his progressive physical and mental deterioration, which serve as a constant reminder of his imminent fate. This anxiety tends to make the elderly person more compulsive and controlling because he is trying to regain a feeling of omnipotence in an attempt to allay his anxiety around death. The control provides the illusion of omnipotence which permits the pretense that through his omnipotent control he might be able to forestall his own death. This often accounts for his extreme compulsiveness, rigidity and controllingness which become so offensive to the members of his family and community. There is usually also an intensification of obsessiveness of some thought which, through its ability to totally absorb the mind, serves as a defense against thinking about an even more disturbing subject which is really disturbing him the most—the fear of his own death.

Dependency Problems

Dependency and regressive behavior are other very prevalent manifestations in the aged. Financial and physical dependency tends to heighten their psychological dependency. The fact that they are compelled to rely on others for various kinds of assistance intensifies their feeling of helplessness and vulnerability, which tends to make them more psychologically dependent in order to force others in the environment to provide them with a source of protection and security. As a result they may become very childish and clinging in their behavior.

Some elderly persons deliberately intensify their regressive behavior because they believe that time is growing short for them to gratify the basic infantile and childish needs which have for so long gone unmet. They can become extremely demanding of narcissistic supplies which usually engenders rejection from others and, as a result, intensifies their insecurity. There is thus a strong relationship between their state of dependency and their level of anxiety. The more dependent they are, the more crucial is it for them to feel a sense of protection and gratification and when they are rejected because of the excessiveness of their demands, it leaves them feeling like a helpless, vulnerable and abandoned child. This intensifies their demandingness even more, which leads to even greater rejection and a deteriorative vicious circle is established.

Sexual Problems

Many family members will refer their elderly relative for psychotherapeutic assistance because they have become very disturbed and frightened in regard to unacceptable sexual behavior, either within or outside the family. In addition to the prevalent problem of impotence and lack of sexual interest, one also sees a relatively large number of cases of exhibitionism and child molestation in the aged. Both of these problems usually relate to the attempt to overcompensate for the intensification of castration anxiety discussed earlier as the result of deterioration in sexual and physical potency. Aging itself is unconsciously seen by some elderly males as a castration for they feel that they are losing their potency in all areas which is a great threat to their sense of masculinity. This is especially likely to be true if this has always been an unresolved problem in their background.

For the male, the phallic exhibitionism is an attempt to shock the perceiver. This reaction of shock is confirmation to the aging male of the fact that the castration he fears is not a reality. It affirms that he is still being perceived as a sexual being. Similar factors are involved in his molesting of little girls in that young children have a greater tendency to be shocked by the phallic exhibition, plus the fact that his penis takes on an appearance of being very large when compared to the genitals of a child, which unconsciously also tends to allay castration concerns.

Another problem that one often confronts is the family's concern about what they feel is an unrealistic desire on the part of their elderly relative to marry a much younger woman. Many older men do not find older women sexually stimulating enough, and fearing impotence as a confirmation of their castration, they tend to become involved with younger women. It also helps them deny their age and feel younger just being around younger women.

Many elderly women may also manifest a problem in the sexual area because they interpret the diminution in their attractiveness and desirability as a blow to their sense of worth and value. Many women have become overly identified with their physical and sexual attractiveness, and when they feel that they have lost these, it may result in overcompensatory seductive or promiscuous behavior which may get them into difficulty with their family or community. It becomes a challenge then for the therapist to help the elderly person substitute a new definition of beauty for the one they have always held. In order to restore their feeling of worth and esteem they need to understand beauty as something which emanates from inner qualities rather than just a physical sense of beauty. The importance in therapy of setting up new models and criteria for self-assessment by the aged will be discussed in more detail in a later section of this chapter.

PROBLEMS FOR THE THERAPIST IN WORKING WITH THE AGED

Of all the difficult psychological problems that the elderly patient may manifest, the therapist himself tends to be the single greatest problem in working successfully with the aged. Working with the aged is likely to produce a wider variety and more intense countertransference reactions on the part of the therapist than with any other group of patients with whom he is likely to work.

It is a rare therapist who has completely resolved all of his anxieties around death and he is not likely to be very pleased to have reminders and provocators of this problem, which is what the elderly patient represents. He tends to, consciously or unconsciously, reject the elderly person or deny him therapeutic services in an attempt to reject and deny the aging process in himself and the fact that he too will someday have to die. The therapist may rationalize his rejection of the elderly patient by insisting that this kind of patient is too rigid to change and that "you can't teach old dogs new tricks."

It is difficult to work with any elderly person without, in some way, triggering in the therapist all the unresolved problems that the therapist may have had with his own parents. Many therapists typically find themselves unconsciously punishing their elderly patient because of past, resentful feelings toward their own parents which were never resolved. This may occur because many therapists, as children, always resented their own helpless and dependent position in regard to their parents. When in therapy, the roles are reversed and this elderly patient, as parent symbol, is helplessly dependent on them, these therapists may try to get even for past hurts by parents by attempting to hurt the elderly patient through subtle or direct punishment and rejection.

There is also a great tendency for the older patient to view the therapist as his son which is a kind of "reversed transference." This plays havoc with attempts to bring the Oedipal struggle to resolution. A therapist may also become very angry when his elderly patient treats him like a little child and does not give him all the respect which he feels he deserves for being an adult and an authority. There is frequently a very subtle but intense competition that goes on between the elderly patient and the particular kind of therapist who deliberately becomes a therapist because he essentially needs to be in the position and role of the controlling parent. This kind of therapist unconsciously delights in treating all of his patients as though they were helpless children. Some elderly patients, who also are unwilling to relinquish their parental attitudes toward all younger persons, will run into real conflict with this kind of therapist.

Some therapists cannot tolerate the elderly patient's regression and the reversal of the parent-child relationship for other reasons. They may still need to respect older persons as parent figures, or else they may have their own ungratified dependency needs which may come out into the open because of their craving for such gratification from the elderly patient. These therapists tend to very much resent the older person's helpless regression and they may attempt rather forcefully to coerce the patient into more mature and autonomous attitudes and behavior.

Some therapists tend to overreact to their own sense of guilt related to their feeling of superiority over the elderly patient. They are inwardly very glad that it is the patient and not themselves who is old, deteriorating and close to death. Consequently, they may tend to overreact to this feeling of guilt with condescending pity or else tolerate too much inappropriate anger and demandingness on the part of the patient as being justified. It is as though the therapist were inwardly saying to himself, "If I were in that old man's shoes, I would also hate people who were healthy, happy and not so close to death." Other therapists become so revolted and disturbed by the elderly person's problems or their own guilt feelings that they may overreact negatively and hostilely to the elderly patient.

Some therapists have difficulty in dealing with the sexual seductiveness which may come from the elderly patient of the opposite sex. Some of these patients have recently lost their own spouse and they are likely to see the therapist as a man whom they have to impress in order to confirm for themselves that they are still physically attractive and desirable. For some therapists, especially the younger ones, the patient's sexual seductiveness may be an even more intense problem because of the unconscious Oedipal elements that are involved. If the therapist has not resolved his own Oedipal strivings, then this kind of patient will trigger all sorts of uncomfortable feelings in the therapist and threaten him very badly.

Therapists also tend to be highly disturbed by the extreme rigidity and demandingness on the part of the elderly patient. It may readily become clear to the therapist that the elderly patient is not coming to therapy to work out his problems but only to get his dependency and narcissistic needs met and also to use the therapist for the necessary companionship to offset his intense feelings of loneliness and isolation. Some therapists feel very sensitive to being used and manipulated, and they tend to respond with great resentment and hostility. It usually reflects their own past, unresolved problems in terms of inability to trust persons, especially parent figures.

Other therapists, who have some doubts about their own worth and adequacy, need to see fast results in their patients and the aged's rigidity tends to greatly frustrate and disturb them. Many therapists are also disturbed by the fact that some elderly patients tend to use their "senility" as an excuse for their failures or lack of achievements and the therapist may become quite annoyed at the patient's unwillingness or inability to be more realistic. The therapist may also find himself annoyed at the elderly patient's use of his "senility" in order to achieve the secondary gains which accrue in terms of the gratification of nurturance and dependency needs.

What some therapists find most disturbing in working with the aged is that their own lack of meaning or philosophy in regard to death may become exposed, and this can be extremely traumatic for the therapist. Until he has to deal therapeutically with an elderly person, it is quite likely that the therapist has never been in a position where he has had to examine his own convictions in regard to the problem of death. Now that he has to deal with this problem as an imminent reality to his elderly patient, the therapist may find himself lost for words or helpful suggestions which could constructively help to reduce the patient's level of anxiety. Probably philosophical issues and psychological realities become more confused in working with the aged than with any other group. All too frequently I have observed the therapist become relatively traumatized as he comes to recognize that he, himself, is not prepared to deal with the fear of death, the meaning of life and other related issues which heretofore he considered only philosophical and not especially relevant to psychotherapeutic practice.

THERAPEUTIC APPROACHES WITH THE AGED

Abraham,[1] in contrast to Freud, sounded a note of optimism regarding the analysis of the aged when he concluded from his own studies that "the prognosis in cases even at an advanced age is favorable if the neurosis has set in in its full severity only after a long period has elapsed since puberty. . . . In other words the age of the neurosis is more important than the age of the patient." Meerloo[5] was another author who displayed a persistent optimism on the subject. He spoke (in contrast to the rigidity issue espoused by Freud) of the elderly patient as being almost too open to self-examination. "My impression is that because of the weakening defenses, there is a better and more direct contact with the unconscious. Older patients react more easily to interpretations and feel more easily relieved by relating the actual conflicts with those of the past." Jungians, such as Cutner,[2] insist that patients in the second half of life are more concerned with individuation than are younger patients because the introversion of libido is in the service of discovering and integrating the heretofore unconscious parts of the psyche. She goes on to say, "It is because the intrinsic tasks of the second half of life are so different from those of the first, that analytical psychology believes in the value of analysis and the possibility of a new start even after the chances of fulfillment on the biological plane have gone." Goldfarb,[4] Wolff,[7] Wolk *et al.*[8] and Oberleder[6] are just a few of the more current workers who have found that elderly persons are capable of change, redirection and rehabilitation through psychotherapy.

Unfortunately, treatment for the aged is not usually considered until an emergency state of mental and personality breakdown has developed. While symptoms of depression, anxiety, loneliness, irritability, sleeplessness and loss of self-esteem may justify psychotherapy for the younger patient, they are considered "par for the course" in the elderly person and are therefore not likely to attract attention. Usually the elderly person must qualify on the basis of loss of memory, disorientation or incontinence before he is considered for the same treatment, at which time, paradoxically, its feasibility may indeed be questioned.

The need for flexibility in the approach to the treatment of the aged needs to be emphasized. Appointments may be infrequent and sessions brief, but these arrangements may need to change with the advent of new crises. Environmental manipulation and the role of ancillary personnel in the treatment of the aged may even be more important than the sessions with the therapist. The psychotherapist must be a member of the treatment team, each of whom is on the alert for signs of which the others should be informed.

Thus, for example, misguided, overprotective treatment or undue neglect augments the fear and anger of the elderly person who tends to feel helpless and vulnerable to begin with. Such attitudes tend to worsen the elderly patient's psychological difficulties, increase the patient's inefficiencies and further disorganize his overt behavior. This fact makes it imperative that the family or those who act in nursing and attendant capacity be properly oriented to the patient's needs and that they have a working concept which can sustain them by providing them with a belief in their own capacity to master the problem. The family members must be helped to understand that the patient's aberrant behavior is really a call for help to which they need to respond constructively. One cannot overemphasize the importance of a cooperative social environment, when psychotherapy is attempted with the elderly patient. There needs to be frequent and open communication between the family members and the therapist. The family members need to feel comfortable in and recognize the importance of bringing all their reservations or negative feelings toward the patient out into the open with the therapist. Only then can there be erected the consistent supportive atmosphere which is so necessary for the rehabilitation of the elderly patient. Poor communication can lead to the family and therapist working at cross purposes with each other which only serves to intensify the patient's insecurity and defeat the therapeutic endeavor.

THE USE OF THE TRANSFERENCE

Due to their regression, the aged typically tend to regard the therapist as a parent figure from whom they expect will come a feeling of protection as well as suggestions and guidance. They expect a great deal of direction and if the therapist does not initially meet some of these expectations or tends to be too nondirective, it will usually cause them to drop out of treatment because it undermines their sense of security and protectedness.

What the patient needs to believe is that there is hope and help. The therapist ought not to go out of his way to disillusion the patient as to the therapist's realistic capacity to help, even though he may recognize that their perceptions of his capacities are fraught with elements of the positive transference. The patient's belief in the helping capacity of the therapist gives the patient hope and provides him with the feeling of security which is necessary for him to adjust to his confusing world.

Early in therapy elderly patients tend to interpret all the therapist's suggestions to them for greater autonomy and active mastery, as a rejection of their needs for protection and narcissistic gratification. Initially they do not come to treatment in order to grow and mature emotionally. Such maturity represents to them greater autonomy, isolation, vulnerability and insecurity.

Most of all they are searching for a parent figure. They want protection, first and foremost. They feel analogously that they are "drowning" and first need to be thrown a life raft and later they can be taught how to swim. The therapist's insistence that the elderly patient perform autonomously and maturely too early in therapy is interpreted many times by the patient as though the therapist were shouting swimming lessons to a drowning man. Once they have achieved a sense of security through the therapy relationship, they can then consider a more mature means of dealing with their world.

The elderly patient's need to find a convincingly helpful figure is a trend which is usually hidden from himself as well as from others. It is not consciously embarked upon and carried out. The manner in which the campaign is conducted and carried out can deceive the therapist. The patient is likely to put the therapist through so many devious tests that the therapist is likely to conclude that he is not at all valued by the patient. For the elderly patient to view a person as being potentially helpful, he must somehow first try to dominate, manipulate and maneuver him in a variety of ways and the therapist is likely to fail to appreciate that the patient may, by so doing, be displaying a genuine interest in and involvement with the therapist. He is basically only trying to test the therapist's emotional strength and security in order to be able to trust him and feel protected by him.

The receipt of specific advice, within acceptable ranges, is often taken as a symbol of having gained the therapist as an ally, friend or protector and simultaneously as proof of having triumphed over or controlled the therapist. In this way they come to feel that they have won the therapist's omnipotence and now own it themselves.

THE SHAME OF BEING OLD

There is obviously a great deal of shame attributed to being old. It is well recognized that once a person reaches the age of thirty both men and women become very sensitive and even may lie about their age. In our society and in many others as well there is a definite stigma attached to being old. Youth and the ways of the young tend to be highly valued and imitated. It appears that youth, vigor and life have all become equated. It is difficult for many people to feel fully alive without also feeling vigorous and young.

The shame of old age seems to be unconscious and deeply ingrained and apparently relates basically to the aged's diminution in sexual potency and ability to compete in the vocational arena. For a male to feel like a man it is apparently necessary that he still regard himself and be regarded by others as a sexual being. Sexual vigor and a sense of personal value seem to go together. Old people tend to be seen as sexually impotent or asexual which makes it difficult for the elderly male to be perceived as and feel like a man. There is shame in feeling like a eunuch.

For most females, to be a woman is to be able to bear children. When a female becomes old and is beyond her child-bearing years it is often quite difficult for her to feel like a woman, for most women tend to identify themselves as a woman with their ability to bear children. She feels embarrassed, at least at an unconscious level, to have to admit that this loss of function is a reality even though at the more conscious level she may seem to be relieved at the thought that she can no longer be pregnant. Women also tend to identify themselves and their worth with their physical attractiveness and sexual desirability. They always want to be perceived as being younger than their true age. This enhances their feeling of worth and helps them believe that they will always be able to compete with women of their own age for attention and recognition. Even if a woman cannot be competitive in regard to her beauty she can always feel competitively more desirable by being more youthful looking than others her own age.

In this society, one's sense of personal value is very much related to one's ability to compete. This is especially true for men. Striving and achievement tend to be equated with aggressiveness and masculinity. Elderly men are ashamed to admit that they have not achieved as much as they should have for someone of such advanced years. There is a sense of shame in the loss of ability to compete because we are all in the competitive arena and those who are unable to compete feel like they are the vanquished in the contest called life. In that feeling of defeat and failure is shame experienced.

Every age group, except the elderly, has particular characteristics which it accepts and values as being distinctly its own. Youth has aspects which it values as distinctly its own as does middle age but the elderly do not value and tend to reject what is distinctly their own and attempt instead to emulate the younger groups. To accept that one is old is tantamount to accepting that one has been defeated by life and is out of the mainstream of life. One can accept the fact of retirement from the competitive arena only if one has felt victorious in the game of life and has some visible signs to demonstrate that supremacy; otherwise one cannot retire without also feeling some sense of defeat and shame.

If we applaud the old at all, it is almost never for doing what is typically characteristic for their age but rather for things that younger people do. Thus, for example, we may applaud the old man who can still play three sets of tennis, run a marathon race or father a child; or the old lady for looking as young as her daughter. However they are rarely applauded for that which should be a distinctive achievement for old age such as a sense of wisdom and a nonstriving peacefulness. For this reason older persons are under even more stress than younger persons to demonstrate their competitive adequacy. Younger persons who are not too successful are not yet failures because they still have the advantage of saying that they are still young and that in the future they will be successful, whereas this excuse is not possible for the elderly. They are under great pressure to demonstrate to all that they are still in the competitive arena and still able to do battle; otherwise they will have to admit that the game of life is all over for them and thereby have to accept their worthlessness.

Old people also feel a sense of shame because they are the constant reminders to the young of the deterioration that will one day also beset them. This produces an attitude of an almost reflexive rejection of old people. The elderly also serve as reminders to the young of their eventual fate of death. There seems to exist an unwritten, unconscious agreement that we must all help each other be distracted from the reality of death. In this respect, old people feel very culpable in the breach of this unwritten contract. The French have a saying, *le temps passe, la mort approche*. Every day one moves closer and closer to death. The feeling of abhorrence toward death tends to be projected onto the elderly which makes him feel a certain disgust about himself. This also contributes toward his feeling ashamed of himself and makes him tend to deny the reality of his age, at least to others.

All these various factors contribute to the elderly person feeling ashamed of being old, which leads him to reject his own age group and accounts for why he continues to use the middle-age model as the criterion for success and adequacy.

ELIMINATION OF THE MIDDLE-AGE MODEL

Too often there has been a social, medical and psychological attitude which rigidly insists that people must learn to accept their limitations, must resign themselves to their disabilities and must stop their struggling against these realities. With some patients this kind of attitude is helpful for it facilitates reality testing. But for the elderly patient it is not always appropriate. This attitude and the treatment based upon it often encourages feelings of failure, depression, despair or apathy in the elderly patient. To encourage acceptance of limitations and disabilities is usually to foster self-recrimination and loss of self-respect. It encourages the regarding of oneself as crippled and weak. This is not to imply that the therapist needs to encourage the distortion of the realities of the patient's limitations but rather suggests that the patient needs to come to see himself as *different* than, instead of *lesser* than, other, younger persons. He needs to come to compare himself to a new model of success and adequacy in place of the one he has been using.

The middle-age model, as the criterion for success and adequacy, has to be eliminated and replaced by a more appropriate model. He is a new person living in a new phase of life and he ought not to be judged or judge himself against the accomplishments and functioning of a forty or fifty year old any more than we can judge a child's accomplishments in comparison with those of an adolescent. These are qualitatively different people and we need new models and criteria of success for these different kinds of people.

Unfortunately the aged are still being compared and are comparing themselves with middle-aged persons in terms of adequacy and success, with resulting feelings of inadequacy and impotence. The therapist has to help the elderly person recognize that similar to other ages, old age has its advantages and disadvantages. The elderly patient needs to understand that he ought to be beyond the model of striving, achieving and competition. He needs to recognize that he has graduated into a new stage of life that others that are younger than he often wish they could move into. It is now permissible for him to rest and enjoy life. He can live creatively, instead of routinely, and follow his own whims. There is no longer any pressure to be adequate or to impress others. He needs to understand how fortunate he is to be out of this race for superiority.

He needs to come to see his new state as an advantage and as an age of liberation rather than loss. He is now liberated from the many hungers, passions and strivings which kept the organism in constant turmoil. There is time now to be sensitive to and enjoy the things that one never quite had enough time to enjoy—the sunset, the grandchildren, the flowers, the birds in flight. How good it is to be free of the many past burdensome responsibilities. One is free to go places and do things that previously one could not give time to. One has the time to sit and talk with friends and really get to know people intimately rather than superficially as we have been so prone to do in the past.

A NEED TO FEEL USEFUL

The aged have collected a great deal of wisdom and experience over the years, and they need an opportunity to use it. A sense of feeling useful and unselfish is essential to developing an intrinsic sense of worth, so that one's sense of worth is no longer dependent upon competitive achievements. Aged persons need to be needed, not only because of a need to maintain a sense of personal worth and esteem but also as the means of dissolving their profound sense of loneliness. Many of these aged persons have been obliged to retire professionally, some find themselves alienated from their families and others have given up their homes to live in groups and shared loneliness, and for these reasons they need human contact and involvement desperately as the means of transcending their deep sense of isolation and loneliness. Even more than being loved and nurtured they need to love and give of themselves to others for only by establishing communion outside of the boundaries of one's own ego is the sense of isolation and loneliness really dissolved. There are probably many more disabled, older persons whom the patient can help by reading to them or serving as a companion in their loneliness. There may be homeless children in institutions who desperately need the love, affection and physical and emotional contact that he can give. He can work on his avocational interests and hobbies and perhaps give the fruit of his labors to others who might be in greater need. He has a great need to be involved, but he needs to learn that he can be involved but in different ways than he has been in the past. Helping to make life meaningful helps to make life worth living and the best way to feel life is meaningful is to feel useful and needed by someone and to give of oneself unselfishly.

Activity is therapeutic for the aged. One of the therapist's primary responsibilities is to prevent the deterioration which results from withdrawal and disuse. The need for continuing human contacts, social participation and meaningful work in order to maintain function cannot be minimized. Psychotherapy must often be reinforced with a concrete activity program and the therapist must be prepared to assume the role of social planner, family consultant, recreational or vocational advisor, or just plain good friend.

Sometimes working with the surviving family to eliminate frictions and competitions can go a long way to reducing the elderly person's tensions and anxiety. They need to be encouraged to help the elderly one feel needed. The therapist needs to help the family recognize that their elderly relative is not trying to compete or feel superior when he attempts to show them how to do something properly. Most often he is just trying to demonstrate to the family that he still has some use to them. He wants the family members to turn to him more and use him for his wisdom and experience and for what he can contribute. He is really saying, "Don't relegate me to the rubbish heap."

Much of psychotherapy with the aged involves providing them with opportunities for ventilation rather than insight. Sometimes it is therapeutic simply to siphon off immobilizing tensions by allowing expression of petty complaints. Another usually important aspect of therapy with the aged is helping them deal with any guilt feelings related to the death of past loved ones. Some tend, irrationally and omnipotently, to blame themselves or feel guilty that they never treated the lost loved one better than they did.

Part of the unique work with the aged is helping them to deal with their anxiety around death if this is a problem for them, as it usually is. They need to be able to look at and, if necessary, revise their attitudes and philosophy around death in order to be able to live without the constant preoccupation and fear of it. To help the elderly patient, who has concerns in this area, accomplish this, it is essential that the therapist first review for himself his own tenets and confront his own fears in regard to death. He must first derive for himself a personal and direct understanding of the meaning of death if he is to ever work comfortably with the aged. Such meaning and understanding can never be given from one to another. It does not lie in theory, dogma, belief or philosophy and it is not something that can be handed down by some authority. Such personal meaning can come only through self-confrontation and self-discovery of the essence of the nature of one's fear of death. It is only then that the therapist will be in a position to encourage the patient to do the same.

Although no specific philosophy of death can be offered, the reader might find it helpful, in his exploration of his own fear of death, to reflect on the statement that "the meaning of death cannot be considered as an issue apart from the meaning of life." Finding meaning in life does not imply living according to a particular philosophy of life but rather has to do with one's ability to live fully and creatively. Life is very real; it is not an abstraction and therefore it is foolish to search for a philosophical or other abstract or conceptual meaning of life. If the reader now reflects deeply on the question of "How is one to live fully and creatively?" and clearly and personally sees the truth of the statement that "for one to live fully, creatively, and without the fear of death, one must live in a state of constant renewal, which means that one must know what it means to die to continuity, to die to the old, to the past, every moment," then he will be approaching not only a personal understanding of the meaning of life and the meaning of death, but the essence of joy and beauty as well.

The following case is presented in order to help illustrate many of the characteristics of the aged presented in this chapter.

Mr. M, a 68-year-old man, was referred to me by a neighbor of his who was quite concerned about him because of a persistent depression. Mr. M had been a musician, a piano player in a small band, nearly all of his working life. Of late he had been fired from several bands because his playing had become badly affected due to a severe arthritic condition in his fingers and also because of progressively deteriorating eyesight. His inability to play well was not only affecting his ability to earn a living but he felt that it was depriving him of that which had always given him joy and meaning in life. In addition his wife had recently died and he felt terribly abandoned because he had come to depend upon her very heavily. He had almost no friends and had used his wife as the sole source of interpersonal gratification. Basically he was always very frightened of people and his wife had sheltered him like a protective mother. His feeling of loneliness and isolation was intensified by the fact that he had been unable to have any children and his life seemed to be totally empty.

Another contributing factor to his depression was the fact that he had always been very competitive with his brother who had surpassed the patient in competence in almost every area. His younger brother had learned to play the piano much more easily than the patient and was currently still enjoying good health and a successful musical career. Mr. M felt terribly defeated by his brother and by life in general and inflicted a great deal of hate upon himself.

He talked about never having fulfilled any of his ambitions in life and he felt that it was now too late. In particular he had an ambition to write a song and get it published This was something his brother had never done. However he had never been able to find the time to devote to writing a good song and now his failing eyesight made it impossible for him to read and write musical notes clearly.

As we explored the problem together it soon became clear that what troubled him the most was that his impending death seemed to him to be such a final thing. He indicated that if he had had children to carry on his name and remember him or if he had written a famous song that this would help in some way to perpetuate his memory. He felt that he had in no way left his mark upon the earth and it was as though he had never existed at all. His sense of desperation brought him great agony. He wanted some place in immortality. He was desperately afraid of losing all hold on a sense of continuity and permanence. His death seemed too final, too absolute a termination to him.

The more he confronted and talked about his yearning for a place in eternity, the more he came to realize that he was overly preoccupied with death and in a sense had already "buried" himself. Spontaneously he began to feel that there might still be a lot of life in him yet and that maybe he had given up too soon. At this point we were able to talk about other vocational possibilities, and it occurred to me that there was a particular section of town that had no music teacher and that many of the mothers had expressed a wish to have a music teacher for their children. The idea of working with young children seemed to excite him very much. It seemed to offer him an opportunity to fill many of his unmet needs. He was even able to joke about the fact that the children would be less likely to be critical of his playing ability. The opportunity to bring the love of music into the lives of young people seemed to give his life new meaning. After some five or six sessions his depression lifted and he felt that he could now carry on with courage and purpose.

REFERENCES

1. Abraham, K.: *Selected Papers of Psychoanalysis.* London, Hogarth Press, 1927, p. 316.
2. Cutner, N.: Analysis in later life. *Br J Med Psychol, 23:*75-86, 1950.
3. Freud, S.: On psychotherapy. *Collected Papers,* Vol. I. New York, Basic Books, 1959, vol. 1, p. 258.
4. Goldfarb, A.: Psychotherapy of aged persons. *Psychoanal Rev, 43:*180-187, 1955.
5. Meerloo, J.: Contribution of psychoanalysis to problems of the aged. In *Psychoanalysis and Social Work,* edited by M. Heiman. New York, International Universities Press, 1953, pp. 321-337.
6. Oberleder, M.: Psychotherapy with the aging: an art of the possible? *Psychotherapy: Theory, Research and Practice,* 1966, vol. 3, no. 3, pp. 139-142.
7. Wolff, K.: Group psychotherapy. *J Am Geriatr Soc, 10:*1077-1080, 1962.
8. Wolk, R., Reder, E., Seiden, R., and Solomon, V.: Five-year psychiatric assessment of patients in an out-patient geriatric guidance clinic. *J Am Geriatr Soc, 13:*222-229, 1965.

Chapter 14

The Essence of an Effective
Therapeutic Process

MAX HAMMER

IN THIS FINAL SECTION I would like to summarize the basic material in this book in the form of presenting my conclusions in regard to what I feel to be the essential aspects of an effective therapeutic process. This is an extremely difficult thing to do because one's definition of an effective therapeutic process very much depends upon how one defines a successful therapeutic outcome. As the reader is probably already very much aware, there is very little consensual validation or agreement in regard to a definition of successful therapeutic outcome because there is very little agreement in regard to a definition of the essence of cure, growth or psychological health. The research literature in the field of psychotherapy is full of grandiose claims in regard to a particular approach achieving a high rate of successful therapeutic outcomes but when one looks at how they defined successful outcome, cure or growth, there is quite often a rejection of that definition by the reader to whom these terms mean something entirely different. As long as value judgments exist in regard to how one defines the nature of man, and therefore also the nature of optimal psychic functioning, there will always be disagreements in regard to the essence of an effective therapeutic process.

Thus, if we had a set of clear criteria and a sense of consensual validation in regard to the nature of cure, growth and psychological health, it would then be a relatively simple matter to set up criteria for an effective therapeutic process. However, in spite of all of these inherent problems and difficulties I would like to share with the reader my most basic conclusions in regard to the essence of an effective therapeutic process. It is based upon my own understanding of the nature of cure, growth and psychological

400

health, much of which the reader will find presented in the various chapters that I have written in this book, plus what I have observed as being elements in common in the therapeutic approaches of other psychotherapists who are consistently effective.

I present these basic conclusions not with the intent of having the reader believe them and accept them as an absolute truth but rather as a challenge to the reader to reflect deeply upon them and question them as well as question others who hold similar and dissimilar conclusions. In addition, ask yourself about the essence of your own growth and that of the patients you work with in psychotherapy and see if something becomes meaningful to you about the essence of psychotherapy as a result of all this inquiry and observation. In understanding that process of inquiry itself, the reader may discover something more meaningful about the essence of therapy than the intellectual conclusions he finally settles upon.

Permit me to caution the reader not to adopt a therapeutic approach just because someone presents it to you in a very persuasive manner. The reader should not take anything written in this book or any other book as the truth, for at this point in his understanding it would only be a belief, and a belief is not a truth but a conviction without knowledge. The truth never resides in someone else's verbal communication but becomes a truth only when there is personal self-discovered knowledge. The reader should recognize that a book can give you only what the author has to tell but the learning that comes through self-discovered knowledge has no limit, because to learn through your own self-knowledge is to know how to listen, how to observe, how to hear and therefore to be in a position to learn from all of life. Therefore, as with a good poem, what is presented here is not the truth, nor is it an untruth, but only a hint of something which coaxes the reader to reach up beyond his current level of understanding and try to meet the author where his understanding is at.

CONCLUSIONS

My first conclusion is that no therapeutic process can be effective unless a therapeutic alliance is established between the therapist and the patient. No matter what it is that the therapist is offering or suggesting to the patient, if there is no openness and receptivity on the part of the patient to the therapist and the process of growth then all the therapist's efforts will be to no avail. The therapeutic alliance involves not only the patient being open and receptive to what the therapist is offering, but it also involves a commitment on the part of the patient to taking risks for growth in contrast to just utilizing the therapeutic relationship as a means of achieving the gratification of some basic dependency needs or as a means of entering into contest with the therapist as a way of gaining a feeling of power by defeating the therapist in his attempts to be therapeutic. When there is a therapeutic alliance the patient utilizes the therapist as an ally in the voyage that he has to take through the dark and unknown muddied waters of his psyche.

The existence of the therapeutic alliance seems to be dependent upon a sense of trust that exists between the therapist and patient and the development of this sense of trust necessitates that there exist a particular kind of relationship. Part of this relationship involves the patient perceiving the therapist as a model for growth. This is not to suggest that the therapist offers up his own personality for identification but rather the patient often makes a commitment to grow as a result of his recognizing the comfort, maturity, spontaneity and creativity of the therapist and he feels intuitively that he also would like to grow beyond his own sense of constriction and conflict and possess a similar sense of internal freedom. In addition, he must perceive the therapist as being internally consistent, congruent or integrated; otherwise the inconsistencies and contradictions that he perceives will limit his capacity to trust the therapist. From the therapist's point of view he must be truly affectively involved with the patient, have warm and valuing feelings toward the patient and be able to sensitively hear the patient's subjective reality, for without this involvement and hearing, there is just too great a sense of distance between the patient and the therapist and without that close bond, the necessary sense of trust will not exist and then neither will the therapeutic alliance. In essence then, by whatever means the therapeutic alliance is developed, it must exist if the patient is to really grow.

It also seems clear to me that if a therapeutic process is to really be effective it must enhance rather than discourage the patient's greater confrontation with rejected, fearful and painful inner and outer realities. If psychotherapy is selling anything at all, it is selling the truth. The highest form of psychotherapy known to man is the truth. Since the early days of the scriptures man has been told "know thyself," "see the truth for yourself and the truth will set you free," "to thine own self be true," and the like. In a sense the process of psychotherapy is like a surrounding wall of mirrors put up by the therapist by which the patient sees the truth of himself reflected whichever way he turns.

The essence of psychopathology must somehow lie in the avoidance of the truth of oneself, in one form or another, along with the pursuit of some kind of imaginal self or idealized image. In the very desire to become a certain something that one feels one ought to be, there is inherently a kind of internal contradiction and conflict as well as a distortion of reality because in the pursuit of what one ought to be there is also involved the process of attempting to deny and escape from the reality of what one really is already. On the other hand, psychological health, most basically, must involve an openness to the clear perception and acceptance of reality; an awareness and acceptance of what actually is, rather than the pursuit of what ought to be. More specifically, psychological health is that process of being totally open and fully sensitively aware and accepting of one's moment-to-moment experiential reality. The essence of psychological health lies in living in that state of communion and integration with the actual moment-to-moment experiential reality, which may be referred to as the state of "Being," whereas the essence of psychopathology lies in the rejection of what is real and the living in the imaginal state of pursuing the "What ought to be," referred to as the state of "Becoming."[2]

Psychological health is referred to as a process rather than some kind of final end state because all end states are noncreative and therefore forms of "death" because there is no continuous opportunity for renewal possible in them. Psychological health must be a condition of optimal aliveness. Life must involve continuous renewal; otherwise it ceases to be life. Therefore, psychological health can never be some kind of an end state, and any process of therapy which seeks to direct the patient toward the atttainment of some kind of ideal objective or end state must be moving away from being a truly effective therapy.

It should also be clear that there should be nothing in the process of therapy which encourages the patient to escape from painful reality such as through the use of some form of suppression, distortion, camouflaging, withdrawal or avoidance. Patients usually decide to go for psychotherapeutic assistance in the first place because they seek to escape from some kind of painful reality. This is precisely why they are pathological; therefore any process of therapy which offers the patient some form of escape from or avoidance of his problems or some other painful reality cannot really be an effective therapeutic process and is, on the contrary, really encouraging the pathological process. Psychotherapy should not involve teaching the patient new and better techniques for hiding from himself but rather must encourage a greater sense of union and integration with himself. Those approaches that encourage the continued rejection or suppression of unacceptable parts of oneself are basically involved in the heightening of conflict. Being taught to control unacceptable behavior is not the same as growth, in which there results a true liberation from the need to express such behavior. A process cannot be considered therapeutic if it heightens conflict rather than integration. Therapy should not pit one part of the self against another part. Psychic energy is a unitary system and when it is divided and turned upon itself it must, through this sense of conflict and disintegration, produce a greater sense of tension and pathology. Attempting to solve a conflict by suppressing the conscious awareness of one side of it does not eliminate tension because it does not untie the turning of energy upon itself; it only, at best, reduces the conscious awareness of the tension.

Therefore, to be effective the process of therapy must of its own nature involve the patient in a state of integration rather than keeping him constantly outside of himself by offering him an intellectual survey of his problems through the process of presenting him with a set of intellectual explanations and theories. For the patient to end up being an integrated human being the process of therapy itself must be integrative in its nature. Thus, it is only when the patient is in a state of integration with his symptom or problem—that is, when the observer is not outside of but rather is one with the observed—that the patient is in a state of integration, from which a liberating self-understanding can occur. Therefore it is clear that insight or intellectual awareness is really the *consequence* of growth and not its antecedent *cause* as many therapists erroneously believe. There must first occur in the patient the state of integration with his own rejected painful feelings, which is the essence of growth, and *only then* is that boundary, which separates conscious from unconsciousness, produced by the ego as the observer and controller of thought, dissolved which then permits the intellectual awareness of the rejected truths to take place. The particular rejected truth presented to the patient in the form of intellectual interpretations by the therapist, in his attempt to produce that necessary state of integration and growth, is not adequate to remove the ego's separation from and control of thought which is necessary for dissolving the separation and barrier between consciousness and unconsciousness and therefore there occurs, at best, only a kind of intellectual synthesis instead of the necessary integration produced through the direct experiential contacting of and communion with the rejected truth and all of its associated feelings. In fact, intellectual explanations only serve to prematurely put an end to the deeper inquiry into and the establishment of full contact with some rejected truth and in this way serves as a form of escape which makes it an accomplice of the pathological process. Intellectual interpretation or analysis is basically nothing more than theoretical speculation and this is not sufficient to produce integration and liberation; only the resolution of the duality between the observer and the observed accomplishes that liberating integration which yields true self-understanding.

Because psychological health involves the confronting and making contact with one's moment-to-moment experiential reality, it suggests that the process of psychotherapy itself must encourage the patient to confront and contact his moment-to-moment experiential reality. This means that the therapist should always take the patient where his moment-to-moment consciousness is and not where it ought to be. For example, the therapist should not predetermine to have the patient deal only with his past history or with some aspect of his future or even some aspect of what is referred to as the present time, such as his current job or marriage situation, because all of these are forms of escape from the patient's moment-to-moment experiential reality.

Therefore, to teach the patient to live in the healthy process of contact with his moment-to-moment reality, the therapist has to encourage the patient to be totally attentive *only* to that which is *currently* in his free-flowing consciousness—that is, that consciousness which is unencumbered by a directing censor and deliberate thinker that is initiating and controlling the content and movement of thought. Encouraging the patient to deal with any other subject matter than this current experiential reality is encouraging the process of avoidance of reality and is therefore enhancing the pathological process. Thus, any system of therapy that has a predetermined focus of attention for the patient encourages his escape from reality. The patient has found a new means of escape from confronting himself by using the therapy process itself for that purpose even though in theory the process of psychotherapy is supposed to enhance the patient's contact with reality.

It should be pointed out that the present, as a moment in time, is not the same as the moment-to-moment experiential reality because the former is only a relative present rather than an immediate present. The fact that the patient may have had a fight with his wife or boss may not at all relate to what is in his current moment-to-moment consciousness and is therefore really of the past and not of the present even though the event may have occurred shortly before the therapy session. Whatever thoughts or feelings invade his uncontrolled current awareness is that which has the greatest investment of psychic energy at the moment and *that* is what has to be dealt with first. That which intrudes into his awareness when the controlling thinker is absent is that which is really concerning him the most. To try to deal with anything else is bound to be fruitless because the patient will not be able to effectively concentrate on anything else. He will only be in a state of internal conflict and distraction. A state of conflict is set up when the patient's attention is pulled away from where it naturally wants to flow and made to focus on an area where little psychic energy is currently invested.

There are several systems of psychotherapy and Eastern forms of mind discipline which emphasize the therapeutic and peaceful effects of focusing the mind's attention on and the complete absorption in the here and now external reality, but they apparently do not recognize that contact with external reality is not the result of an act of the will or of deliberate effort and therefore one cannot be instructed to do it. For example, the fact that I may be in your physical presence does not necessarily mean that I am also in your psychological presence or awareness. Whether or not you attend to me is not a function so much of your conscious intention but rather is more dependent upon the degree to which psychological tension within your mind is drawing your conscious attention to its source. The mind's conscious attention is naturally drawn towards and wants to follow that path that leads to that place where psychic tension exists. Attention always naturally wants to follow tension because tension is painful and demands recognition. This process is the means by which that which is repressed tries to free itself of its dammed up energy and drain itself into conscious awareness.

Thus any attempt to forcefully make the mind consciously attend to some reality other than where it naturally wants to flow only serves to produce a greater sense of conflict and tension and is therefore a servant of the pathological process. When there is no longer any intense internal state of conflict and tension which is demanding recognition and expression then the mind's attention is free to be in communion with whatever external reality confronts it for no internal draw will exist to distract it away from that contact. Therefore it should be clear that a full and complete contact with external reality is possible only after the tensions of repressed internal realities have been drained and resolved.

This kind of conflict situation is another example of how psychotherapy can encourage the pathological process whereas encouraging the patient to be one with his moment-to-moment experiential reality enhances the process of integration as well as contact with reality and is therefore enhancing of the process of psychological health. The patient is learning, through the process of therapy, to be more open to the truth of himself which enables him to resolve more of his own problems by himself.

This leads directly into the next major conclusion which is that an effective therapeutic process should enable the patient to leave therapy with a greater ability to resolve his own problems by himself than when he first came in, otherwise psychotherapy becomes nothing more than "patchwork." In an effective psychotherapy process the patient learns the process of reintegration of himself— that is, he learns how to retrieve, "welcome home" and live compatibly with all aspects of his formerly unacceptable self, which he branded as a not-self. He learns basically to say to all of his moment-to-moment painful experiential realities, such as his anxiety, depression, anger, sexual feelings, guilt, etcetera, that "this too is me." At the conclusion of therapy his capacity to face psychological pain is greater and he knows how to maintain his new-found state of integration by "never rejecting any of his own children from home," and thus he never disintegrates himself again.

Thus, psychotherapy cannot be considered as being complete unless the patient has come to learn to value the truth of himself and learn something of the essence of being open to the truth of himself. He must personally experience the self-integrating, self-healing and liberating process of being one with his moment-to-moment experiential reality; otherwise he is sure to work himself into new and insoluble conflicts and problems and have to seek assistance again. But having learned the self-integrating process he then has received more than just the immediate profit of the resolution of the problems that he brought with him into therapy because he has also learned the process of being able to resolve his own problems for himself in the future. *Every patient should leave therapy capable of being his own therapist.*

The real essential task of psychotherapy, therefore, is not so much the retrieving of the specific contents of consciousness which are repressed but much more it lies in helping the patient learn the process of retrieving, that is to say, the process of bridging the psychological gap or distance between the existence of some painful experiential reality and the immediate awareness of that reality, which is essentially the process of psychological integration. This is accomplished basically by helping the patient to heighten his self-sensitivity through the process of communing or being one with his own moment-to-moment experiential reality. The mind seeks to integrate and heal itself by presenting to conscious awareness that which has been rejected and repressed. Once the patient learns to quiet the deliberate thinking process and learns to be open and receptive to contacting and hearing these strivings from his own unconscious then he has learned the basic self-integrating and self-healing therapeutic process.

An effective process of therapy must also help the patient become more, rather than less, real. This means that psychotherapy must involve the patient in his own subjective or experiential reality rather than work with the enhancement of various concepts or imaginal images of himself. The goal of therapy is not to help the patient achieve his idealized image but to help him transcend his identification with and pursuit of all concepts and images of self. First of all it must be clearly seen that it is not possible to ever actualize a concept of self. Any thing that you conceptualize yourself to be is an illusion because to really be a particular thing is to be that thing absolutely, for to be it only relatively is also to be its relative opposite and therefore one is not the thing at all. Thus, if I hold myself to be intelligent, strong, kind, or whatever, I spend my life trying to absolutely affirm this thing that I believe myself to be but I can never succeed in this vain pursuit and therefore my life is always full of fear, frustration and tension. For me to truly be intelligent, for example, as a fixed characteristic, I would have to be absolutely intelligent which is impossible for that would necessitate my being omnipotent. If I am not absolutely intelligent then I am only relatively intelligent which means that I am also relatively unintelligent and therefore I cannot assert that I am that thing called intelligent. Thus it should be clear that I can never be any conceptual thing for all such traits are really relative opposites and these relative opposites can never be affirmed absolutely. All I can really ever be is an unlabeled whole which is the essence of psychological integration, unity and health. Any psychotherapeutic approach which encourages the patient to actualize some concept or ideal of himself serves to put the patient in a chronic state of frustration and fear and takes him away from the reality of that which he really is experientially, from moment to moment and therefore cannot ever really be growth producing or therapeutic. Only when the patient is free of his identification with his various masks and personas is he in the position to really hear and become integrated with that which is most real in himself. Bergman's movie "Persona" is a classic visual illustration of this basic psychotherapeutic principle, and I highly recommend it to psychotherapists of all levels and disciplines and as an excellent device for the training of students in psychotherapy.

The therapies that conceptualize growth as a moving from a negative self-concept to a more positive self-concept fail to recognize that the positiveness of one's self-concept is only as high as one's last success. With the first real significant failure that comes along the concept is back to being negative again. A positive self-concept requires the living under the pressure of constant victories and makes a combat out of interpersonal relationships and all of life. It is not possible to have a high self-esteem without also being involved in the competition and comparison of esteeming others lower than yourself, for after all, the positiveness of your esteem is only relative to the degree to which you compare yourself favorably to the esteem of others.

The same is true for those systems which conceptualize therapy as a system for building confidence in their patients. Confidence, like a positive self-concept, is dependent upon a continuous feeling of mastery. Confidence is really nothing more than the anticipation or expectation of mastery in regard to a particular challenging situation and therefore it is relative to insecurity. Inherent in any feeling of confidence is the basic attempt to escape from feelings of insecurity. Absolute confidence is omnipotence and because that is not possible to achieve except through illusional fantasy, which is pathological insecurity always rides the coattails of confidence. It should be clear that if the patient did not feel insecure he would not pursue confidence any more either. Thus, a system of therapy which focuses on helping the patient feel more confident is really only encouraging the patient to escape from reality—that is, the reality of his basic feelings of insecurity—and it is that which needs to be transcended and not compensated for by seeking confidence.

When one is free of his identification with any and all concepts and images, which are really all false selves, then one is free to be with what is real in oneself, which is basically one's moment-to-moment experiential reality. One is then free of the anxiety and dread that one day that which is positive will become negative and that which is confident will become insecure. Being free of all conceptual selves, one is then also free of the internal judger. Peace of mind does not come when one's achievements finally meet with the internal judger's expectations and ideals, as some therapists seem to believe, but rather when the judger itself is transcended. If the process of therapy does not in some way deal with the transcendence of the judger itself then the patient must be left with a sense of anxiety and pressure that he will not live up to his concepts and ideals of himself. Change is not real growth or transformation but only modification, when the judger remains.

An effective therapeutic process must also enhance rather than diminish the patient's capacity to live more creatively and spontaneously, for most therapists will agree that creativity and spontaneity must be intrinsic to a person who is psychologically healthy. The transcendence of identifications with false images and concepts of self permits for more creativity and spontaneity in the patient. No real sense of spontaneity can exist if the self is fragmented into different images all competing to represent the response to a particular stimulus or challenge.

To live creatively is to live life as constant renewal, but concepts of self demand continuity and self-perpetuation which prevents any real sense of renewal. For the new to really be experienced as the new one must die to the old and the continuous. Self concepts and images predetermine that one's response must be consistent with, in order to be confirming of, that particular concept of self and so unless the identification with all images and concepts is transcended one cannot live creatively and spontaneously. Thus, in essence then, any system of therapy that through its process encourages the patient to react to himself and to life conceptually cannot be a truly effective therapeutic process. Psychotherapy should not be antithetical to life and helping patients live more fully which requires the capacity to enter into full and complete contact with the real. However, concepts are only *symbols* of the real and only operate to filter and prevent direct contact with the real. The word is not the fact or thing itself. The word and the symbol are really a turning away from the fact. Therefore, any system of therapy which is overly abstract, intellectual or philosophical in its process and approach to the patient and encourages the patient to approach himself and life conceptually is antithetical to life and therefore also antithetical to psychological health.

Many therapy approaches, through the use of controlling and manipulative techniques, also serve as another means of destroying the full development of creativity and spontaneity in their patients. Authority by the therapist in any form leads to impersonation and imitative behavior on the part of the patient and copying in any form in antithetical to creativity. Creativity and spontaneity reflect an inner state of freedom and any system of therapy which overly patterns and controls the patient's mind destroys the free flow of consciousness and thereby destroys the opportunity for creative and spontaneous expression. Therefore, it should be clear to the reader that no so-called therapeutic system or technique can ever really be effective in helping the patient become more creative and spontaneous because a system or a technique is a form of programming which is really the antithesis of creativity and spontaneity. A system or a technique necessitates a procedural commitment or attitudinal set on the part of the therapist which programs the interaction between himself and his patient and therefore destroys any opportunity for a sense of creativity and spontaneity to develop in the encounter. A programmed interaction as the means or process of therapy can never lead to a creatively functioning patient as its end result.

All techniques are basically gimmicks which are used by the therapists who lack the necessary sensitivity to hear where their patient's experiential reality really is at. Feeling lost and confused in their interaction with their patients they resort to the use of some kind of technique which they feel will provide the interaction with the necessary structure and direction to make it appear as though real movement and progress were occurring. The technique provides the procedural recipe or formula which predetermines the therapist's reactions and responses to his patient which obviates the necessity for contacting and hearing the patient and therefore also makes it unnecessary for the patient to contact and integrate his own rejected and painful experiential realities and therefore can never be therapeutic.

The reader should also recognize that a truly effective therapeutic process must maximize rather than minimize the patient's opportunity to advance in terms of emotional, social and sexual maturity. Any system of therapy whose means involves treating the patient like a child cannot hope to end up with a patient who is mature. The ends in therapy cannot be separate from the means. If the therapist sets himself up as an authority and *the* one who possesses the truth then he will make all of the patient's major decisions, offer a plenitude of advice and suggestions, give the patient "homework" and in general treat him like a child, but he cannot expect the patient to end up being mature. For the patient to end up being mature the process itself must provide for that opportunity through the patient taking more autonomous responsibility for his own functioning and self-understanding. It must encourage self-discovery and minimize instruction, explanation and dependency in all forms.

It should be clear to the reader that imitating and impersonating an adult is not the same as being one. The child who acts like an adult and the child who acts like a child are still essentially the same, because the child is still a child. Acting like an adult does not make one an adult, no matter how good the impersonating performance may be. Effective therapy is not a process that molds an "as if" but one that encourages the patient to grow and "be." It is essential that the patient be an adult and not just act as if he were an adult. "As if" never becomes "is" through the process of continuous repetition of playing the role, as some approaches seem to believe, any more than a violent person can terminate his violence by practicing acting as if he were not violent. He is still a violent person, acting nonviolently and eventually that which is real in him will express itself. The use of authority to cultivate imitation and impersonation at best can only produce a modification in behavior, but in the long run must be antithetical to real transformation and growth.

Thus it should be clear that there can be no real advance toward maturity without there first being some element of regression, and no process of psychotherapy can really be effective unless this occurs. Growth involves a process of regression not only in terms of going back into the unconscious depths of oneself but also in terms of going backward and contacting the early immature feelings and aspects of one's personality which have been repressed. It is only through the communing with and integrating of these immature aspects of the personality that they are freed to develop and mature with the rest of the personality.

The patient is, in some developmental ways, still like a child because he has rejected some aspect of the weak, helpless and vulnerable feeling child in himself and has devised for himself some compensatory and imaginal means of pretending to himself that he is invulnerable and secure. In his childhood the patient needed, but was never given the opportunity, to thoroughly be his natural weak, helpless and vulnerable feelings and still recognize that he would be loved, protected and made to feel secure by his parents even though he could not provide his own security. But not having had this occur he never let himself totally be that weak, helpless and vulnerable feeling child but rather rejected and repressed this aspect of himself into the cellar of his psyche and by so doing preserved its existence, unaltered, and so he remains fixated. As long as these immature feelings exist and are not resolved they pop out and manifest themselves whenever they are triggered by related events and so he continues to remain immature no matter what kind of adult style of behavior he superimposes on the surface of these feelings.

Thus, greater maturity does not take place unless the patient first permits himself to have contact and communion with these more regressive aspects of his personality and by so doing integrate them into the rest of his developing personality thereby transcending or outgrowing them. Therefore the patient must come to recognize that he must first be weak before he can be strong. He cannot circumvent his real feelings of weakness and hope through some kind of defensive or imaginal alteration to compensate for the concious awareness of these feelings but rather must first totally be immersed in these feelings and let himself be his weak, childish self before real maturity can occur; and then no longer feeling weak, helpless and vulnerable he will no longer need the defenses and compensatory pursuit of needing to feel strong either. However if the process of therapy encourages some form of circumvention or compensation and prevents the patient from being and integrating with that child in himself, then he continues to preserve that in himself and no real advance in maturity can really take place.

Another basic conclusion is that an effective therapeutic process should go beyond just the elimination of the negative but also ought to accentuate the positive. In other words effective psychotherapy must involve more than just symptom removal but must also involve a heightening of the patient's capacity for experiencing his most positive feelings of joy and love. Many systems of therapy are under the mistaken notion that the positive is the immediate result of the elimination of the negative but this is not true. The arousal of joy and love is not just the immediate consequence of the elimination of one's pathological symptoms. The rapid growth of what is referred to as growth centers and centers for sensitivity training attests to the fact that many persons who are not considered pathological still are interested in growing and enhancing their capacities for experiencing intimacy, joy and love.

The greatest obstacle to the enhancement of the more positive experiential states is the ego and one's identification of self with the ego. The ego has only apparent existence and is nothing real but borrows its apparent reality from the self-defined labels with which it identifies. The ego is essentially an illusion and one's devotion to the basic ego drives for self-aggrandizement, self-protection and self-affirmation only represents an intensification of that illusion which makes the arousal of negative experiential states a much greater likelihood. Threats to the ego and its labeled attributes and frustration of its basic drives are responsible for the producing of symptoms such as anxiety, tension, hostility, depression, loneliness and the like. For example, most basically, anger occurs as a reaction to the frustration of the will and represents an assertion of the self through an exaggerated response of the will, with which it is identified, in an attempt to deny the feeling of impotence or nonexistence of the will through its capacity to produce an influencing effect on the other. Anxiety represents the perception of the threat of possible disaffirmation of the self. Depression represents the reaction to the recognition that the self has already been disaffirmed and now feels diminished in esteem and moving in the direction of total worthlessness and nullity. Loneliness represents the feeling of loss of the principal object that was used for self-affirmation and the yearning for the return of such an object. Therefore, when reduced to its basics, it can be seen that the various negative psychological experiential states are really heightened forms of egoism. In these negative states, psychological threat to the self-defined ego has produced an intensification of self-awareness through interpreted feelings of vulnerability and the particular symptom that results represents some form of attempt to escape from the direct awareness of the feelings of vulnerability and the threat of extinction to the ego.

Transcendence of one's identification with the ego is therefore the elimination of all negative psychological states and the awakening to oneself as a new reality which, for want of a descriptive label, may be called love. Love is the antithesis of egoism. Love is the state of selflessness and desirelessness. In the state of love there is the total surrender of the sense of self-awareness which is absorbed totally in the awareness of the object of our love. Love comes into being within us as an experiential reality not when we are being loved or valued by another but rather when our own consciousness is making contact and is in a state of communion with the experiential reality of the other person outside the boundaries of our own ego. When conscious awareness has transcended the boundaries of one's own ego and has lost itself totally in the state of communion with another person, then love becomes our natural state of being. Love cannot be volitionally self-induced for all such efforts are acts by the ego operating as the agent of those acts, but rather love is something that one *is* when one is not ego.

It is egoism that makes man live in the state of duality which separates and alienates him from his fellow man and makes him devoted to the goals of self-enhancement, self-protection and self-affirmation. These goals are inevitably frustrated, because they strive for absoluteness, and therefore one feels psychologically threatened with extinction which then results in the various negative experiential states such as fear, tension, hostility, depression and loneliness. The fear of the extinction of the psychological self underlies all of the various negative experiential states and all of man's basic psychological problems. The only respite from these negative experiential states are the periodic moments of elation which come when the ego feels itself to have been enhanced or affirmed in some way. But these relatively infrequent moments of elation are short-lived because the ego will soon again feel threatened because it is compulsed to continuously put its self-defined identity on the line in the attempt to attain a feeling of absolute affirmation.

Most therapists have correctly come to recognize that the arousal of threat and symptoms are the result of the ego's need for affirmation and preservation and so they have therefore assumed that affirming, protecting and enhancing the patient's ego must be the essence of the therapeutic process. But that assumption is not valid because they have not correctly understood that ego affirmation only temporarily relieves threat to the ego and therefore symptoms of one type or another generally reoccur. Symptoms must continue to arise because the patient is still basically irrational. The patient's prime irrationality is that he is trying to make absolute that which can only be relative. He is trying to prove the absolute existence of a thing which has only apparent or conceptual existence. The ego can never really ever be permanently affirmed because it cannot be absolute and therefore by encouraging the affirmation and preservation of the ego, the therapist has only served to ultimately preserve the continuance of all the patient's negative experiential states rather than their transcendence. That transcendence can occur only with the transcendence of one's identification with the ego. Love is that transcendence.

From love flows all the positive experiential states. Life without love is joyless and it is also without beauty and the inspirirational feelings which flow from it, for love is the mother of all of these offspring. Love also brings with it a deep sense of peace, for love is the full release from the tension that comes from maintaining self-defense and the striving toward some ideal of self-aggrandizement. Psychological pain and tension is caused basically by frustrated desire and threats to the ego. Desire is egoism, for the ego feeling is absent when desire is absent. Love is egolessness and desirelessness and therefore love is peace, for love is freedom from psychological pain and tension. Egoism, on the other hand, has fear, loneliness, depression, tension and hostility as its constant companions. One feels chronically bitter and hostile because all desires and attempts to find a profound sense of joy, beauty and release from tension are constantly frustrated. Love is not open to the egoist as the means of attaining these positive feelings because to love another person makes him feel too threatened. To the egoist love connotes a sense of openness, penetrability and vulnerability of the self to being hurt or possibly destroyed. Love also connotes a surrendering of the self; a self to which he has devoted his psychological life to protect, affirm and enhance. Love is union, which involves the loss of the sense of self-awareness and loss of the feeling of separateness upon which the ego is dependent in order to maintain its individuality and integrity feeling. Without these feelings the ego fears that it will be dissolved. Therefore, love must be rejected and his life is consequently devoid of a real sense of joy, beauty and peace, and as a result, negative experiential states predominate. Thus, one must either love or be in psychological hell.

In essence, then, man is a twofold being. At one time or another in his relationships, he is either ego or love. When he is ego, he lives in the state of becoming in which he is ambitious and is continuously and totally devoted to the goals of self-aggrandizement, self-protection and self-affirmation. In fact, *all* psychological drives are forms of egoism and are essentially reduceable to one of the basic ego drives or goals of self-aggrandizement, self-protection or self-affirmation. Because of the illusory nature of these goals and their demand for absolute fulfillment he constantly feels threatened and frustrated and the negative experiential states of loneliness, anxiety, tension, hostility, depression and inner feelings of coldness, worthlessness and ugliness are his constant experiential realities. When he is love, then he lives in the state of being in which he is content just to be an unlabeled, indivisible whole and in that state his experiential realities are marked with warmth, joy, sensitivity, beauty, inspiration, creativity and peace, and he is free from all psychopathological states.

The greater the degree of egoism, in terms of one's preoccupation with and devotion to the goals of self-affirmation, self-aggrandizement and self-protection, the greater is the severity of one's pathology. Pathological symptoms basically represent the danger signal that one is becoming too far removed from what is most essentially real in oneself. Because of the prevalence of this condition, the state of egoism and the drive to absolutely affirm the ego may be referred to as the "universal neurosis" and by the same token, the state of love may be referred to as the "universal psychotherapy" or the state of psychological health, when the labels of pathology and health are reduced to their most basic elements.

Therefore, in essence, psychopathology, as a manifestation of the relatively exclusive living in the egoistic state, is a reflection of that person's inability to love. To eliminate the problem of the predominance of negative experiential states the patient's capacity to love is what essentially has to be enhanced. Or put in Buber's[1] terms, one has to move from the exclusive living in I-It relationships to living in the I-Thou relationship. Essentially, the I-It relationship involves defining oneself as some labeled attribute or part and bringing only that part to a dualistic relationship in which the other is also related to as a labeled part and as an object to be experienced, manipulated and influenced as the means of affirming, protecting or enhancing the ego. In contrast, in an I-Thou relationship, one comes to the other as an unlabeled, indivisible whole and also relates to the other as being an unlabeled whole resulting in a relationship of unity and communion. Only the labeled, the part, can be experienced and manipulated, the unlabeled whole can only be communed with. It is a relationship free of egoism and selfish motive. If therapy does not help the patient to achieve this, then the patient is still operating in the realm of egoism exclusively and the negative psychological states will continue to persist in one form or another.

To be free of one's identification with the ego the patient's consciousness ultimately has to come to dis-identify from all of the concepts and self-defined labels with which it has falsely come to identify itself and also from the various other objectifications with which one typically becomes identified, such as the body, intellect, emotions, senses, will, etcetera (as, for example, when one says, respectively, I am beautiful, I think, I feel, I see, I want, etcetera), of which the ego feels itself to be the hub and integrator, and just permit oneself to be the unlabeled, indivisible whole, the "silent witness," the pure "subject" that one really is, identifying with no-thing objective to that "subjective conciousness." Most patients resist relinquishing their identification with the self-defined ego because of the erroneous belief that being no-thing (that is, no labeled thing) is the same as being nothing, a void, that is to say, psychologically extinct. In truth, we are all essentially no-thing, for to be some-thing one would have to be that thing absolutely which is impossible for no one is omnipotent and therefore we are only relatively some-thing (for example, in-

thology first. Facilities for the training of psychotherapists need to take this factor into greater account than they have in the past. Once it is clearly recognized that psychotherapy is not a set of techniques to be applied or some kind of blueprint to follow but rather is related to the capacity to commune with and hear the patient at his deepest depths then it is likely that training of psychotherapists will achieve a new emphasis on the enhancement of the sensitivity and personal growth of the therapist. The primary data for study for the therapist in training are the depths of his own psyche.

This leads to the last and probably most basic conclusion which is that the essence of the effectiveness of any psychotherapy process depends most of all upon the person of the therapist and his capacity to really hear his patient and because of this fact the primary concern for the field of psychotherapy should not be to objectify the most effective therapeutic system but rather the major concern should be in regard to exploring those factors that make for an effective therapist with a sensitive and consistent ability to hear his patient. Systems, as such, cannot be effective; only people can be effective. There is not the successful or unsuccessful system; there is only the successful or unsuccessful therapist. Therefore, the basic element to study is not what the therapist *does* but essentially what the therapist *is,* because observing what he does can provide no clues in regard to how he is able to hear the patient's subjective realities with such sensitivity, precision and clarity. But if one truly understands "how" the effective therapist hears, one will then also be able to understand what he does, for one will then also be an effective therapist himself.

REFERENCES

1. Buber, Martin: *I and Thou.* New York, Scribner's Sons, 1958.
2. Hammer, M.: The hopelessness of hope. *Voices: The Art and Science of Psychotherapy.* 6, (No. 3):15-17, Winter 1970.
3. Hammer, M.: Quiet mind therapy. *Voices: The Art and Science of Psychotherapy,* 7 (1):52-56, Spring 1971.

INDEX